FINANCIAL TRAIN

CIMA
STUDY PACK

Stage 1 Paper 3

BUSINESS LAW

First published July 1989 Financial Training Courses, Parkway House, Sheen Lane, London SW14 8LS

Second edition May 1990

Copyright © 1990 The Financial Training Company Limited

ISBN 1 85179 234 1

Printed in England by Da Costa Print, 111 Salusbury Road, London NW6 6RG

0062x

Contents

0062x

0062x

Introduction

The Study Pack has been specially prepared for the examination in Business Law at Stage 1.

This is a fairly typical Law paper, with considerable emphasis being placed on the law of contract and tort, in particular the tort of negligence. The sort of questions set are a mixture of questions that simply test your ability to explain a specific area of the law and questions that present you with a particular problem. The latter are in many ways the more difficult type of question to answer because you need to know which area of law and in particular which cases are relevant to the particular problem. This Study Pack contains numerous examples of this type of problem and it is essential that you attempt these without reference to the answer or much of their value will be lost.

The Study Pack has been produced specifically for this examination. A quick comparison of the syllabus and the contents pages will show that the Pack follows the order of the syllabus very closely, covering all areas thoroughly and comprehensively.

Learning is a cumulative process, and at the end of each session there are revision exercises for you to check your recall and understanding of areas you have previously read. There are also sets of exam-style questions relating to the particular session. Answers are provided in the final session of the Study Pack, but remember to write out your answer before you look at the provided answer.

The Institute has announced that it is exploring ways in which objective testing may be used for part of the examinations. You should read *Management Accounting* magazine to keep yourself up-to-date with developments in this area and we have included a selection of objective test questions at the end of each session.

The CIMA have indicated that not only is the syllabus from Stage 1 to Stage 4 of a cumulative nature but also that they do not see the individual papers as falling into watertight compartments. The diagram of the syllabus structure reproduced overleaf shows that Business Law follows through to Company Law at Stage 3 and the four papers at Stage 4. When studying for this Business Law examination, you must therefore be aware that what you are learning now may form the foundation of questions at Stages 3 and 4. Similarly other papers at Stage 1 may require a knowledge and understanding of Business Law.

This Pack is almost certainly one of the most comprehensive and up-to-date texts available for this particular examination. If you read it conscientiously and attempt all the quiz questions and examination-style questions without prior reference to their answers then you will be amongst the most thoroughly prepared students and have an excellent chance of passing.

Syllabus structure

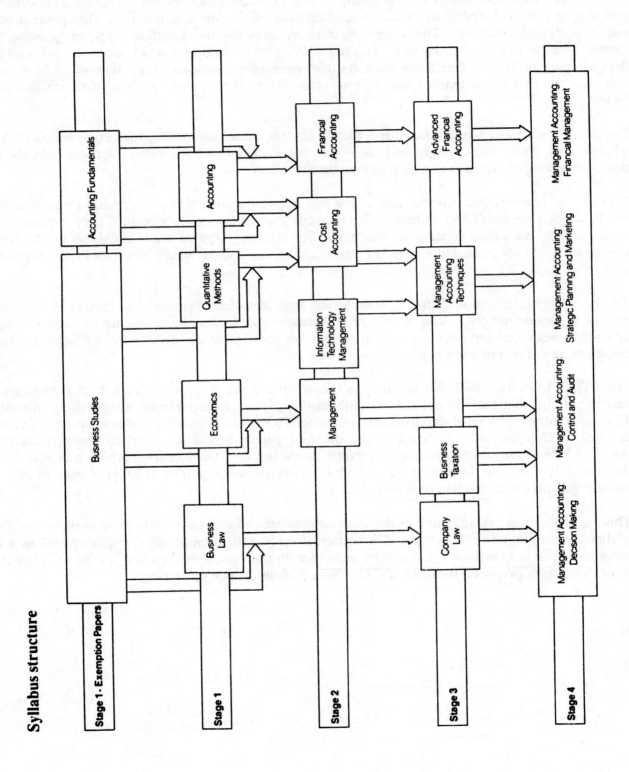

Stage 1 - Exemption Papers

- Accounting Fundamentals
- Business Studies

Stage 1

- Accounting
- Quantitative Methods
- Economics
- Business Law

Stage 2

- Financial Accounting
- Cost Accounting
- Information Technology Management
- Management

Stage 3

- Advanced Financial Accounting
- Management Accounting Techniques
- Business Taxation
- Company Law

Stage 4

- Management Accounting: Financial Management
- Management Accounting: Strategic Planning and Marketing
- Management Accounting: Control and Audit
- Management Accounting: Decision Making

0062x

Syllabus

Abilities required in the examination

In the CIMA syllabus each examination paper contains a number of topics. Each topic has been given a number to indicate the level of ability required of the candidate.

The numbers range from 1 to 4 and represent the following ability levels:

Ranking for syllabus topics

Appreciation

To understand a knowledge area at an early stage of learning, or outside the core of management accounting, at a level which enables the accountant to communicate and work with other members of the management team.

1

Knowledge

To advise on such matters as laws, standards, facts and techniques at a level of detail appropriate to a management accounting specialist.

2

Skill

To apply theoretical knowledge, concepts and techniques to the solution of problems where it is clear what technique has to be used and the information needed is clearly indicated.

3

Application

To apply knowledge and skills where candidates have to determine from a number of techniques which is the most appropriate and select the information required from a fairly wide range of data, some of which might not be relevant; to exercise professional judgement and to communicate and work with members of the management team and other recipients of financial reports.

4

Study weightings

A percentage weighting is shown against each topic in the syllabus; this is intended as a **guide** to the amount of study time each topic requires.

All topics in a syllabus must be studied, as a question may examine more than one topic or carry a higher proportion of marks than the percentage study time suggested.

The weightings **do not** specify the number of marks which will be allocated to topics in the examination.

0062x

Business Law

Aims

To test the candidate's ability to:

(a)   explain those basic principles of law which affect business relationships and transactions;

(b)   inform management on areas where legal considerations apply.

Content			Ability required
1	**The legal system**	(Weighting 10%)	
1.1	Sources of law: judical precedent, statutes, delegated legislation		1
1.2	Civil and criminal law		1
1.3	Settlement of disputes		1
1.4	Structure of the courts, tribunals, arbitration		1
2	**Law of contract**	(Weighting 25%)	
2.1	The nature of a contract; intention to create legal relations; agreement, certainty, consideration, form, capacity		2
2.2	Contractual terms, standard form contracts and exemption clauses		2
2.3	Mistake; misrepresentation; illegality and contracts contrary to public policy, including restraint of trade		2
2.4	Discharge of contract with special reference to frustration and breach		2
2.5	Remedies for breach		2
2.6	Privity		2
2.7	Limitation of actions		2
3	**Types of contract**	(Weighting 25%)	
3.1	Principles of agency with special reference to the authority of persons to act on behalf of others, particularly companies and partnerships		2

0062x

Content		Ability required
3.2	Sale of goods, hire purchase and credit sales including implied terms; transfers of property and of title, rights and duties of the buyer and seller; negotiable instruments	2
4	**Tort and negligence**	(Weighting 15%)
4.1	The nature of liability in tort	2
4.2	Negligence, with special reference to professional advice, dangerous goods, industrial accidents and dangerous premises	2
4.3	Strict liability	2
4.4	Breach of statutory duty	2
4.5	Defences in tort, particularly 'violenti non fit injuria' and contributory negligence	2
4.6	Vicarious liability	2
4.7	Remedies	2
5	**Employment**	(Weighting 25%)
5.1	Engagement, dismissal and redundancy	2
5.2	Terms of employment wages and provision of safe working conditions, including health and safety legislation	2

Exam format

The paper is divided into two sections, A and B, both with four questions. You will be required to answer five questions out of the eight, with at least two from each section.

Answers should include legislation, case law and SSAPs up to and including 31 December prior to the exam.

0062x

Publisher's note

This Study Pack is closely tailored to the needs of students studying for the exam for Paper 3 at Stage 1. Studied properly, it will help you cover all parts of the syllabus in detail. However, the CIMA examiners have repeatedly stressed the need for candidates to have a real understanding of the topics being examined, and of their relevance in real-life situations, rather than merely reproduce information from memory.

The key to this understanding is to follow the examiners' advice, and read round the subject as widely as you can; and, ideally, to work through the Study Pack in the structured context provided by a correspondence course or (even better) classroom tuition.

Financial Training Courses offer a range of correspondence, revision and link courses tailored to the individual student's needs. For full details, write or phone us at Parkway House, Sheen Lane, London SW14 8LS. Telephone: 01 876 0499. Fax: 01 878 1749.

How to study

An accountancy qualification is not something that is automatically awarded to you after a specified period of time. You must make it happen by taking the decision at the start of your studies to commit yourself 100%.

Having made the commitment you must then get the best from your study time. The following tips should help you:

- Do not leave studying to impulse - work out a feasible timetable covering, say, a two week period and then **stick** to it.

- Work in short bursts up to a maximum of 45 minutes. After this your attention falls away and study becomes less effective.

- Keep your breaks short and do not allow them to overrun.

- Try to get into a study routine, always starting work and breaking off at the same times.

- Make sure that your timetable is a mixture of different types of study - taking notes, reading, doing questions. Too much of one type gets monotonous.

- Make your **own** notes on any material that must be learnt. Notes in your own hand will be easier to revise from later.

- Your notes should consist of lots of short, sharp sentences and paragraphs, well spaced out with concise headings. Do not just copy from the Study Pack.

- Use tricks to ease the memorising process - brief notes or headings on index cards to carry with you, mnemonics to learn a list of points, test yourself regularly or get someone else to quiz you.

- Revise what you have learnt constantly. Do not leave revision to the last minute.

Each individual must develop the method of study that suits him best and we hope that the ideas given above will help you to do this. Remember - plan, work consistently and above all, be committed to success.

1.1   The nature and development of English law

1.1.1   The characteristics of English law

'English law' means the law of England. England for these purposes includes Wales. English law, as such, has certain distinguishing characteristics:

(a)   *Antiquity and continuity* - English law shows continuous growth from the earliest period of our national independence. There has been no violent or revolutionary break in its history since the Anglo-Saxon laws of Ethelbert, King of Kent in AD 560, but the Anglo-Saxon detail is so scarce that the Norman Conquest affords a good starting point.

(b)   *Uncodified* - English law is, in general, not codified and in this respect, contrasts markedly with the systems of continental countries where much of the law is codified in 'statutes'.

(c)   *Judicial character* - A corollary of the uncodified nature of our law is its judicial character. This factor is particularly significant, and the role played by the judiciary in the development of our legal system will become evident as your studies progress.

(d)   *Influence of procedure* - The influence of procedure on the development of our law is still evidenced today in the nature of our substantive law. Litigation in the royal courts had to be commenced by one of a limited number of writs or royal commands. The sum total of the law was thus to be found at any given time in the sum total of authorised writs or forms of action - a form of action being the term used to describe the entire legal process, commencing with the issue of the writ and concluding with the mode of enforcing the judgment, whereby a wrong was sought to be remedied. Where there was a writ there was a right. Conversely, no writ, no right. Although the forms of action were finally abolished by the Common Law Procedure Act 1852 (and indeed they were not entirely dead until the Judicature Acts 1873-5) our substantive law is still based on them.

(e)   *Feudal survivals* - English law and, in particular, our land law, still contains some feudal elements.

(f)   *No influence of Roman law* - There has been no reception of Roman law as such, although some areas of English law do evidence such an influence.

(g)   *Independence of the judiciary* - Based on the Act of Settlement 1701, this independence is reinforced by tradition, convention and practice. Allied to the independence of the judiciary is that of the legal profession.

(h)   *English law is common law* - English law is common law, ie, one law throughout the country.

1.1.2   Pre-Conquest law

As already mentioned above, English law is regarded as beginning with the Norman Conquest, and in the sense that there was no unified or 'English' system until after the Conquest, this is a correct view. But the Anglo-Saxon period of influence lasted for almost five hundred years and produced a continuous stream of characteristically Anglo-Saxon sources, some of which were still in evidence after the Conquest. However, during this period, English society lacked both systemisation and uniformity; the kingdom was divided and influences, though strong, could not dominate the country as a whole. Local law played a predominant part in the legal system, decisions on similar facts often varying from one district to another.

The courts of the Anglo-Saxons were essentially public meetings, rather than judicial proceedings in the modern sense. Courts were held monthly in the Hundreds and roughly quarterly in the Shires. In addition to these communal courts, there were also the seignorial courts in which the large landowners exercised private jurisdiction.

1.1.3   The Norman Conquest and the development of the common law

Having conquered a country which he believed was already his by right, William I was determined to strengthen his position by creating a strong, centralised bureaucratic system. In this he was aided by the fact that both he and his advisers had gained experience of such a system in Normandy, which was one of the best ruled states in Europe.

William was not so foolish as to make immediate radical changes in the existing legal system, for he expressly confirmed the laws of his predecessors, including all the customs of the local communities. However, he made immediate administrative reforms which were to have a far reaching effect. In particular, the practice arose of sending commissioners round the country on such royal business as gathering information for fiscal purposes (as, for example, the Domesday Book). Although, at first, these commissioners were not concerned with justice, Henry I seems to have used the commissioners for legal as well as fiscal business. By the reign of Henry II, the justices were touring the country regularly on assizes and acting under their various civil, criminal and fiscal commissions, assisting the centralisation of justice and the spread throughout the country of the same justice as obtained at Westminster, a system of common law.

Along with the unification of the law through the Itinerant Justices, went the development of the Curia Regis or King's Council. This exercised all three governmental functions - executive, legislative and judicial - without heed to the theory of separation. However, with the passage of time and the regularisation of administrative procedures, the three functions of the Council came to be exercised by virtually distinct bodies.

1.1.4   Development of the judicial function

The judicial functions of the Council came to be exercised in the common law aspect by the Courts of Exchequer, Common Pleas and King's Bench, which split off from the Council in that order.

In 1357, a court known as the Court of Exchequer Chamber was established to hear appeals from the Court of Exchequer, and another court of the same name was set up in 1585 to hear appeals from the King's Bench.

In addition to the above, other courts were established to deal with the growth of trade, both national and international. The courts of the Law Merchant, the Pie Poudre Courts and the Courts of Staple, administered instant justice at markets and fairs, but eventually the work of these courts was taken over by the Common Law Courts.

As we have seen, William did not make radical changes in the existing legal system, and initially the King's Courts were only concerned with matters of state and causes of peculiar difficulty where justice could not be done in the inferior courts, so that in those causes which came before the King's Court, it was a national corollary for the procedure to follow formulary lines. This, of course, was an advantage in many ways, of which the least was certainly not the limitation of the activities of the administration by keeping it within well-defined boundaries.

To enlarge the scope of the King's Courts, nothing more was necessary than to invent a new set of forms; once this practice was adopted, the development of jurisdiction was simple and efficient; and in theory unlimited. The jurisdiction of the Royal courts expanded in this way from their early concern with land to encompass an ever widening range of disputes. Also relevant to the extension of Royal jurisdiction was the introduction of new and improved methods of trial, such as trial by jury. Medieval law was essentially a business and the King, through the agency of his courts, provided a superior 'product' and obtained a lucrative return.

1.1.5   The growth of equity

The expansion of Royal jurisdiction and power, through the agency of the writ system, angered Parliament, which regarded the invention of new writs as a usurpation of its power as the supreme lawgiver. Further, it took much work from the local courts, diminishing the income of the local barons, who persuaded Parliament to pass a statute called the Provisions of Oxford in 1258, forbidding, in effect, the practice of creating new writs to fit new cases. The subsequent modification of this by the Statute of Westminster II 1285, authorising the clerks in Chancery to issue new writs in like cases, seems to have had little effect.

This, however, was not the only factor relevant to the premature rigidity of the common law. The separation of the judicial function from the main body of the Curia Regis and the growth of a professional judiciary, saw the common law judges abandon the discretion they had exercised in the eleventh and twelfth centuries and assume the detached mantle which is more typical of the modern judiciary.

This change in attitude was soon reflected in the narrowness of the rights and remedies available in the common law courts, and was highlighted by the increasing complexity of social and commercial life. Many people, therefore, unable to gain access or satisfaction from the common law courts, began to petition the King - 'the fountain of justice' - for specific relief on the grounds of justice. Originally dealt with by the King in Council, the petitions were later passed on to the Lord Chancellor whose Court of Chancery became distinct from the Council some time in the fifteenth century.

Already involved in legal matters, the Chancellor, who was originally a cleric and keeper of the King's conscience, judged such cases in the light of conscience and fair dealings. He acted on the conscience of the parties and against the person of the defendant, issuing writs of attendance, hearing evidence on oath and decreeing relief upon pain of fine and imprisonment.

The creative energy of a long line of able Chancellors built up a body of equitable principles to supplement the deficiencies of the common law; but this system itself became as rigid, if not more rigid, then the common law. The circumstances of its origin and growth, however, indicate that equity is not a self-sufficient system but presupposes the existence of the common law - a gloss written by later hands around an ancient and venerable text. The ancient common law represents the ancient and venerable text: equity the gloss whose province, as expressed by Bacon, was to 'supply the defects of the text'.

1.1.6 Conflict between equity and the Common Law Courts

The existence of equity, a rival to the common law with superior remedies under penalty, gave rise to conflict in the seventeenth century. The personality of Coke, the Chief Justice, was enough to render a delicate situation impossible, and in 1615, in the Earl of Oxford's Case, James I decreed on the advice of Bacon that where the rules of common law and equity conflicted, the latter should prevail, a principle formally enacted by the Judicature Acts 1873-5.

1.1.7 The Judicature Acts 1873-5

In spite of the past conflicts between common law and equity, harmonious relations existed between the two throughout the eighteenth century and beyond. There was a gradual introduction into the common law courts of some of the doctrines that had been solely the province of equity.

Finally came the Judicature Acts 1873-5. The main effect of these Acts was the establishment of a Supreme Court of Judicature, now known as the Supreme Court, administering both common law and equity, so that a plaintiff could now bring his action in the same court, whether the relief he sought was legal or equitable. The net result of this fusion of administration was not to alter the law, but to modify and simplify procedure, and apart from cases of conflict, where generally equity was to prevail, the rules of common law and equity were to continue to be applied respectively in accordance with the same principles as when they were administered in separate courts. Thus, equitable remedies are still discretionary and are awarded as and when the court thinks fit. Despite this fact, the two systems have been administered together for so long that, in recent years, both Denning MR and Viscount Simmonds have expressed the opinion that a fusion of law and equity has taken place.

1.2 Sources and types of law

1.2.1 Meaning of the term 'sources'

The expression 'source of law' has several distinct meanings:

Formal source

The term may be used to refer to that which gives the law its validity, that is to its formal source. What is taken to be the formal source of English law will depend on one's general theory of politics and law.

Legal sources

The term may be used to refer to what are known as the legal sources of law: the means by which it is made or comes into existence. The legal sources of English law are legislation, judicial precedent and custom.

Literary sources

The literary sources of law are those written materials from which knowledge of the law is obtained.

Historical or material sources

Such are the factors that have influenced the development of the law. Mercantile customs, natural justice, public policy, etc, are all sources of law in this respect.

1.2.2   Common law

Meanings of the term 'common law'

The term 'common law' has several different meanings according to its context.

(a)   The term is used to refer to that law which became common throughout the country through the agency of the Itinerants. By selecting the best customary rulings and applying these outside the country of origin, the Itinerants gradually moulded the numerous local customary laws into one uniform law 'common' to the whole Kingdom. Thus, customs originally local in origin ultimately applied throughout the whole of the realm. However, although the common law in general has a customary origin, many new rules were created and applied by the royal judges as they went on circuit, and these were added to local customary law to make one uniform body of law called 'common law'.

(b)   The term 'common law' often refers to those principles of English law evolved in the common law courts, as opposed to the principles which were applied in the Chancery, Admiralty and Ecclesiastical courts. In particular, the term is used in contrast to Equity, which evolved in the Courts of Equity as a supplement and appendix to the term 'common law'.

(c)   Sometimes the term 'common law' is used in contradistinction to the term 'statute law'. In early times, the proportion of law actually created by statute was very small, and, in a sense, the judges 'made' the law. This judge-made law was known as 'common law', the doctrine of judicial precedent showing the manner in which such judge-made law became part of the actual fabric of our legal system.

(d)   Finally, and in its widest and most generalised sense, the term is used to differentiate the so-called common law systems, having their basis in English common law, from the generally codified systems of Continental Europe, having their basis in the Roman 'jus civile' and known as the civil law systems.

1.2.3   Equity

Meanings of the term 'equity'

In its broadest and most general signification, the term 'equity' denotes the spirit and the habit of fairness, justness and right dealing which would regulate the intercourse of man with man - the rule

1.5

of doing to all others as we desire them to do to us. It is, therefore, the synonym of natural right or justice. But, in this sense, its obligation is ethical rather than jural and its discussion belongs to the sphere of morals. It is grounded in the precepts of the conscience, not in any sanction of positive law.

In a restricted sense, the word denotes equal and impartial justice as between two persons whose rights or claims are in conflict; justice, that is, as ascertained by natural reason or ethical insight, but independent of the formulated body of law. This is not a technical meaning of the term, except in so far as courts which administer equity seek to discover it by the agencies above mentioned or apply it beyond the strict lines of positive law.

In a still more restricted sense, it is a system of jurisprudence, or branch of remedial justice, administered by certain tribunals, distinct from the common law courts and empowered to decree 'equity' in the sense last given. Here it becomes a complex of well-settled and well-understood rules, principles, and precedents.

It is in this last sense that the term 'equity' is utilised technically in English law - the term being used to describe the law administered in the Courts of Chancery prior to 1875 and the enactment of the Judicature Acts 1873-5.

Equity, in this sense, was a gloss on the common law, a factor best illustrated by examining the nineteenth century classification of the jurisdiction of the Court of Chancery:

(a)   *Exclusive* - The court had an exclusive jurisdiction in certain cases where the common law gave no relief, as in the enforcement of trusts. Here, both the right and remedy were equitable. The trust, as we know it today, can only be understood by examining the 'use' of medieval times. A 'use' arose in medieval times where a person conveyed property of any sort to another - feoffee to uses - upon the understanding that the other was to hold it on behalf of himself - the donor - or on behalf of some third party - the cestui que trust. Consequently, the rights of the cestui que trust or beneficiary required protection. The common law courts, however, refused to recognise uses, for they defeated the feudal incidents attaching to the property and hence denied the King revenue, and therefore failed to afford the protection required. At an early date, the Court of Chancery, acting as a court of 'conscience', intervened to force the feoffee to uses to administer the property for the benefit of the cestui que trust according to the terms of the grant.

(b)   *Concurrent* - The concurrent jurisdiction arose where the common law recognised the right but did not grant an adequate remedy. Thus, at common law the basic remedy for breach of contract was an award of damages. This, however, might not always be the most appropriate remedy and in these cases, equity offered remedies known as 'specific performance' and 'injunction'. 'Specific performance' being a decree of the court ordering a party to carry out the contract according to its terms, and 'injunction' being a decree of the court ordering a party to refrain from committing or continuing the nuisance.

(c)   *Auxiliary* - The term auxiliary jurisdiction referred to those cases where the common law recognised the right and gave an adequate remedy but was unable, owing to defective process, to enforce it. Thus, the Chancellor could compel discovery of documents (ordering the defendant to produce for the plaintiff's inspection documents relative to the case which were in his possession).

1.2.4   Case law

The nature of judicial precedent

In examining the development of our law, reference was made to the role played by the judges in its evolution, the common law and equity being the product of judicial reasoning in that they have both evolved through the system of case law, whereby law is made for the purpose of the decision of the specific case before the court. It is natural that if a similar dispute should arise again then the previous decision should be used as a precedent, in this way the law becomes more certain and more uniform in its application. This practice of referring to previous decisions and arguing by analogy to them, the present case in order to arrive at a judgement is known as the application of judicial precedent.

Binding and persuasive precedent

Thus judicial precedents have played and continue to play a singularly important role in the administration of justice in England. But they do more than this, for not only are they regarded as authoritative pronouncements of the law, but certain precedents are regarded as binding upon courts which are subsequently called upon to try similar issues. Such precedents are not merely persuasive authorities which may be followed if they appear to be correct; they are precedents which must be followed.

However, it was not until a reliable system of law reporting was started in 1866 and the administration of the courts was re-organised by the Judicature Acts 1873-5, that judicial precedent, through the system of binding judicial precedents, became an established source of law.

As regards the re-organisation of the judicial system arising from the Judicature Acts 1873-5, its significance in relation to the system of binding judicial precedent is to be found in the fact that, if the decision concerned was of a superior court, then the lower court must follow it, whereas a superior court is not bound by the previous decisions of an inferior court, such decision being merely persuasive upon it.

Law reporting

The basis of judicial precedent is the reporting of cases. Without a reliable system of reporting, it would be impossible for case law to be a source of law.

Law reporting had its origins in the *Year Books*, a series of notes written in Anglo-Norman, covering roughly a period of two and a half centuries from the reign of Edward I to that of Henry VIII. The Books were technical and procedural in content and dealt with civil law rather than the criminal law. It is now generally believed that they were the work of enterprising students and practitioners who made notes of interesting cases which they heard in the courts and sent them to some compiler or publisher who made collection of such notes for anyone interested enough to buy them. On the rare occasions on which the *Year Books* are consulted, it is usually through the medium of the *Abridgements*, which are the brief summaries of the *Year Books* published in the sixteenth and seventeenth centuries.

Some notable sixteenth century lawyers and judges, such as Coke, prepared private publications of reports on contemporary and earlier cases. Some were copied from imperfect manuscripts and contained much trivial detail. However, by the sixteenth century, pleadings in civil cases were written down, so that it was possible, thereafter, to cite a case in support of a particular case. These reports are known as the *Private Reports*.

The first regular reports were known as *Term Reports* and were published by Dunford and East (1785-1800). Once reporting of cases became systematic and regular, the reports became authorised and were accepted by the courts as accurately representing the judgment made. Nevertheless, the system of reporting was expensive, inconsistent in standard and slow in production.

As a result, in order to ensure a satisfactory standard of reporting of cases of legal significance, the Inns of Court established in 1865 the Council of Law Reporting. In 1870 the Council was incorporated. All the old series of authorised reports were absorbed and a consolidated set of reports was established under the control of the legal profession.

The Council of Law Reporting is a quasi-official body consisting of representatives of both branches of the legal profession. It employs an editor and a staff of reporters (who are barristers) and produces a series of reports of cases in all the superior courts. Not all cases are reported; a selection is made by the editor. Where it is decided to report a case, a copy of the report made by the reporter is passed to the judge who has an opportunity of revising the wording of his judgement. The reports so produced are known as the *Law Reports*.

In 1953, the Council began publication of the *Weekly Law Reports*. These are subsequently consolidated and issued in volumes so that at the end of a year there are usually about three volumes of the reports.

The Council has no monopoly in the field of reporting and other companies and private organisations publish reports which have equal authority. The best known are the *All England Law Reports*, while reports from *The Times* are frequently cited in court.

As regards the citation of cases from the *Law Reports*, the plaintiff is cited first and the defendant second; thus *Lewis v Averay (1972) IQB198* indicates that the report of that case will be found in the first volume of Queen's Bench Division Reports for the year 1972 at page 198.

Reports of decisions of the Court of Appeal appear under the reference of the Division from which the appeal is made. AC indicates an appeal case heard in the House of Lords. On appeal, the party making the appeal is known as the appellant and the other party as the respondent, but the order of their names in the case reference is not changed unless it is a House of Lords case, when the appellant's name is placed first. Thus in the House of Lords Law Report, *Bolton v Stone (1951) AC850* is to be found on page 850 of the Appeal Cases reports for 1951. The Court of Appeal decision in the same case is reported under the entry *Stone v Bolton (1950) 1KB201* and is to be found on page 201 of the first volume of King's Bench Division Reports for 1950.

Judiciary hierarchy

Also of significance in the operation of the binding system of judicial precedent is the hierarchical structure of the court system, for whether a court is bound to follow a previous decision depends to a very large extent on which court gave the previous decision. Generally, if the decision was of a superior court then the lower court must follow it, but a superior court is not bound by the previous decisions of an inferior court. The hierarchy of the courts as regards the operation of precedent is as follows:

The House of Lords

With the exception of decisions made 'per incuriam', ie, where an important case or statute has not been brought to the attention of the House when the previous decision was made, the House of Lords was bound by its own former decisions. However, in 1966, the Lord Chancellor issued a statement that in future the House would not regard itself as bound by its own decisions, although in this connection they would bear in mind the danger of disturbing retrospectively the basis on which contracts, settlements of property and fiscal arrangements have been entered into and also of especial need for certainty as to the criminal law.

All decisions of the House of Lords are absolutely binding on all other courts.

The Court of Appeal (Civil Division)

This court is bound by its own previous decisions, as well as those of the House of Lords: *Young v Bristol Aeroplane Company (1944)*. The Court is not bound by its own previous decisions:

(a)   where it considers that a decision was made *per incuriam*, ie, in error;

(b)   where there are two previous conflicting decisions, the court may choose which decision is correct and the other decision is overruled;

(c)   where a later House of Lords decision applies, this must be followed.

Decisions of the Court of Appeal bind all other lower courts, but do not bind the Criminal Division of the Court of Appeal.

The Court of Appeal (Criminal Division)

The court follows its own decisions in favour of appellants, and its decisions probably bind Divisional Courts, but not the Court of Appeal (Civil Division).

The Divisional Courts of the High Court

These courts are bound by the decisions of the House of Lords and Courts of Appeal. The civil divisional courts are bound by their own previous decisions, but the Divisional Court of the Queen's Bench Division (which deals with criminal matters) is not so strictly held to its previous decisions.

Decisions of the Divisional Court are binding on judges of the same division of the High Court sitting alone, and on the inferior courts.

The High Court

A High Court judge is not bound by decisions of another High Court judge: *Huddersfield Police Authority v Watson (1947)*, although he would treat such decisions as of strong persuasive authority.

A decision of the Queen's Bench Divisional Court will not bind a judge of the Chancery Division.

Crown Court

A judge sitting in a Crown Court is bound by decisions made in criminal matters by the House of Lords and the Criminal division of the Court of Appeal.

The Inferior Courts

The county courts and the magistrates' courts are bound by decisions of the superior courts. The inferior courts are not bound by their own decisions as they cannot create a precedent.

It must be realised that the system of precedent is not as mechanical as would appear from the above, and a court is not always bound to follow a precedent which according to the rules outlined above ought to be binding upon it. In particular, the court may be able to **distinguish** the case before it from the previous case on the facts.

Where a higher court considers the precedent by a lower court is not the correct law, it may **overrule** that precedent when another case is argued before it on similar facts, thereby setting a new precedent to be followed in future cases. Alternatively, the superior court may consider that there is some doubt as to the standing of a previous principle and may **disapprove**, but not expressly overrule, the earlier precedent. A decision is said to be **reversed** when the party who lost the case appeals to a high court, and the appeal is allowed.

Ratio decidendi and obiter dicta

Precedents have thus far been described as 'decisions'. However, the judicial decision or judgement in the strict sense is binding only on the parties to the case - *res judicata*. Nevertheless, the case may give rise to a principle of more general application - the *ratio decidendi* - and it is this which forms the precedent.

The *ratio decidendi* of a case is the reason for the actual decision or the principle underlying the decision, and if the judge made a clear statement of the reason for his decision, or laid down a legal principle, it will not be difficult to extract the *ratio decidendi*, but this is not often the case. Many matters would have to be taken into consideration before it can be said with certainty what the true reason may have been, such as the circumstances and facts of the case, the arguments of counsel on both sides and the state of the law at the time when the decision was given. In addition, a judge may give several reasons for his decision and the court may be composed of several judges and each judge may give a different reason for the court's judgement. The true *ratio decidendi* seems to be the product of the material facts, the actual decision and the material facts as related in the judgement, though in practice other methods may be relied on for accepting the direct reason or a series of reasons, given by the judge for the decision.

The *ratio decidendi* must not be confused with *obiter dicta*. Such expressions of opinion or illustrations emanating from the Bench during the course of the judgement have no binding force, as does the ratio; they are simply statements 'by the way' but they do possess some authority which is entitled to respect varying with the reputation of the particular judge.

Case report

Set out below are extracts from the Law Reports' report of *Rother Iron Works Limited v Canterbury Precision Engineers Limited (1974) 1QBI (CA)*. It is given merely as an example of a law report to give you the 'flavour' of these reports. You do not need to learn, understand or remember the arguments contained within it. It is simply included to let you see how reliance is placed on the precedents set by past cases in order to decide a current case.

Rother Iron Works Limited v Canterbury Precision Engineers Limited (1972)

APPEAL from Judge Sumner at Canterbury County Court.

On August 11, 1971, the plaintiff company, Rother Iron Works Limited, executed a mortgage debenture in favour of the National Westminster Bank Limited. On October 21, 1971, pursuant to that debenture, the bank appointed Eric George Barrett receiver and manager of the plaintiff company. On November 3, 1971, goods to the value of £159.15 were delivered to the defendant company, Canterbury Precision Engineers Limited, in fulfilment of a contract made prior to the appointment of the receiver and at a time when the plaintiff owed the defendant £124. The defendant paid the receiver £35.15 claiming the right to set off the £124 outstanding. The receiver brought an action in the Canterbury County Court to recover a further £124. On June 8, 1972, Judge Sumner dismissed the plaintiff's claim.

The plaintiff appealed on the ground that the judge erred in law in holding that the defendant was entitled to set off against its indebtedness to the plaintiff a like sum due from the plaintiff to the defendant.

Robin Potts for the plaintiff. The chose in action, namely, the debt which the defendant owed the plaintiff, became assigned in equity to the debenture holder immediately it arose upon the delivery of goods. (Reference was made to *NW Robbie and Company Limited v Witney Warehouse Company Limited (1963) 1 WLR 1324*.) There is no authority precisely in point though *Robbie* does help on the concept of mutuality required for set off . . .

In so far as the judge relied on *Forster v Nixon's Navigation Company Limited (1906) 23 TLR 138* as applying to the facts of the present case he was mistaken, but it is accepted that that case was rightly decided. The distinction between that case and the present is that in *Forster* the two claims in question - that of the outsider and that of the receiver - arose out of one and the same contract. The receiver was attempting to take the benefit of the contract without taking any burden at all which is clearly unjust. Whereas, in the present case the two claims arose out of different contracts.

Again, in *Parsons v Sovereign Bank of Canada (1913) AC 160* the ratio turns on the fact that mutual choses in action arose out of the same contract and the receiver cannot take the benefit of a contract without also taking the burden . . .

Set off can only arise if there is a moment of time when there is an identity of interest. There is no notional time gap when the chose was free of the charge and it is a fiction to say that it could have existed as a separate entity for any notional time. Reliance is made on the words 'the debt as it arose became charged in equity to the debenture holders' in *NW Robbie and Company Limited v Witney Warehouse Company Limited (1963) 1WLR 1324*, per Sellers LJ at p 1331 and per Russel LJ at pp 1336 and 1337 . . .

John Vallat for the defendant. It is accepted that a dichotomy would be produced between the law of receivership and the law of liquidation, but it is not accepted that it would necessarily be undesirable or unjust, and there are good reasons for the fundamental distinctions which already exist between the two situations. Their purposes are different and consequently they have different effects.

A receiver carries out existing orders on behalf of the company whether appointed by the court or under a debenture: see *Kerr on Receivers*, 14th ed (1972), pp 309-310. A receiver can be justified in fulfilling a contract albeit that thereby a creditor acquires a benefit: see *Forster v Nixon's Navigation Company Limited, 23 TLR 138* and *Parsons v Sovereign Bank of Canada (1913) AC 160* . . .

The 'critical date' is the date of delivery of the goods by the company and at that time there was already an existing right of set off against the company. The passage in *Kerr on Receivers*, 14th ed, p 314 refers only to cases where the cross claim was not in existence at the date of the appointment of the receiver. (Reference was made to *Handley Page Limited v Customs and Excise Commissioners (1970) 2 Lloyd's Rep 459, 464*; and *Halsbury's Laws of England* 3rd ed, vol 4 (1953) . . .

Potts in reply. It is conceded that the assignee of a debt will take subject to equities in existence at the date of assignment, but an acceptance of that principle is in no way inconsistent with the argument that there is no right of set off on the present facts. The facts in all the authorities cited differ in fundamental respects from those of the present case . . .

Handley Page Limited v Customs and Excise Commissioners (1970) 2 Lloyd's Rep 459 both claims arose out of the same transaction; also the timetable of events was different from the present case . . .

It is not legitimate to draw the inference from *Ince Hall Rolling Mills Company Limited v Douglas Forge Company 8QBD 179* that the liquidator in that case, after the winding up had commenced, entered into a new contract, as Lindley LJ said in *Mersey Steel and Iron Company v Naylor, Benzon and Company* . . .

December 8. RUSSELL LJ read the following judgment of the court. This appeal raises a question of a right of set off . . .

The argument for the plaintiff may be shortly stated . . .

The opposing contentions are these . . .

In our judgement, the argument for the defendant is to be preferred . . .

Much dependence was put for the plaintiff on the language used in this court in *NW Robbie and Company Limited v Witney Warehouse Company Limited (1963) 1 WLR 1324* when referring to the charge attaching to the debt due to the company 'as it arose'. But of course in that case it was not necessary to consider the point here argued and the language cannot be taken as directed to that point.

Further, our attention was drawn to *Ince Hall Rolling Mills Company Limited v Douglas Forge Company (1882) 8 QBD 179* which was a matter of disallowances of set off in a liquidation, as producing (if set off is available in the present case) an illogical distinction between the case of a company in liquidation and a company under receivership. We are not satisfied that the **Ince Hall** case does necessarily show such an illogical distinction . . .

The appeal is accordingly dismissed . . .

1.3   Legislation

1.3.1   Nature and forms of legislation

In its widest sense the term 'legislation' includes all methods of making law. To legislate is to make new law in any fashion. In its narrow or strict sense, legislation is that source of law which consists in the declaration of legal rules by a competent authority. It is such an enunciation or promulgation of principles as confers upon them the force of law and it is such a declaration of principles as constitutes a legal ground for their recognition as law for the future by the tribunals of the State.

Legislation is the hallmark of a fully developed legal system and develops law by enacting new law, repealing old law or altering it; in its strict sense it means law made deliberately in statutory form by some competent authority invested with that definite function as representative of the State.

Law, having its source in legislation, is best termed enacted law, though the more familiar term is statute law.

Inherent in the nature of legislation is the fact that the words in which it is expressed - the *litera scripta* - constitutes a part of the law itself. The spirit of the law cannot be distinguished from the written expression of that spirit.

Forms of legislation

Legislation may be classified as supreme or subordinate. Supreme legislation is that which proceeds from the supreme or sovereign power in the state and which is therefore incapable of being repealed, annulled or controlled by any other legislative authority. In England, supreme and, indeed, omnipotent legislative authority is rested in Parliament, and is expressed in the form of Acts of Parliament. Such Acts cannot be questioned and obtain their authority from the fact that they have been enacted in accordance with the procedure specified by the State and recognised by the courts for that purpose.

Subordinate legislation is that which proceeds from any authority other than the sovereign power and is therefore dependent for its continued existence and validity on some superior or supreme authority. Such subordinate legislative power must be exercised within the limits and forms prescribed by the supreme legislative body. Thus, in England, Parliament, through the complexity of modern life and the pressures on Parliamentary time, has found it necessary to delegate legislative powers to Ministers, Government Departments and the like. Such delegated legislation must remain within the four corners of the power conferred by Parliament and may be questioned in the courts on the grounds that it exceeds these limits and that the subordinate authority has acted *ultra vires* or beyond its powers.

1.3.2   The legislative process

A statute is law that has been passed by the House of Commons and the House of Lords and has received the Royal Assent.

There is a set procedure which has to be followed and until this has been completed the statute or act is known as a bill. In general, the procedure involved starts in the House of Commons, though this is not invariably the case. The procedure involved as follows:

(a)   *First reading* - This is purely formal and a sheet of paper with only the title of the bill and the name of the member introducing it is read out by an official. The bill is then ordered to be printed.

(b)   *Second reading* - This involves a discussion of the general principles of the bill. If nobody opposes it, or if a vote is taken on the bill and there is a majority in favour of it, the bill will pass on to the committee stage.

(c)   *Committee stage* - At this stage the bill is examined in detail and each clause is debated and may be amended or even excluded.

(d)   *Report stage* - At the report stage the committee which has considered the bill will report back to the House on its discussion and proposed amendments.

(e)   *Third reading* - This constitutes the final debate on the general principles of the bill, and a vote is taken. Assuming the bill passes its third reading it then passes to the other House.

(f)   *The House of Lords* - The procedure followed in the Commons is repeated in the Lords.

(g)   *The Royal Assent* - After a bill has passed through both Houses of Parliament, it receives the Royal Assent and unless it provides otherwise, immediately becomes law.

Acts of Parliament are now generally cited by their short titles and the year in which they were passed. Thus, the forty-seventh Act to be passed in the year 1978, namely 'An act to make new provision for contribution between persons who are jointly or severally, or both jointly and severally, liable for the same damage and in certain other similar cases where two or more persons have paid or may be required to pay compensation for the same damage; and to amend the law relating to proceedings against persons jointly liable for the same debt or jointly or severally, or both jointly and severally, liable for the same damage' is referred to as the Civil Liability (Contribution) Act 1978. It is divided into sections (abbreviated as S) and, if necessary, into sub-sections and may be even sub-sub-sectioned. In the margin, opposite each section is what is termed the marginal note. This indicates briefly the contents of the particular section, but is not strictly a part of the statute. Very long Acts are divided into chapters and each chapter into parts.

A statute

Set out on the next page, as an example of a statute, is an extract from the Civil Liability (Contribution) Act 1978.

It is included simply to illustrate the way an Act is structured and to give you the flavour of the language used.

CIVIL LIABILITY (CONTRIBUTION)

ACT 1978

CHAPTER 47

ARRANGEMENT OF SECTIONS

Proceedings for contribution

Section
1   Entitlement to contribution.
2   Assessment of contribution.

Proceedings for the same debt or damage

3   Proceedings against persons jointly liable for the same debt or damage.
4   Successive actions against persons liable (jointly or otherwise) for the same damage.

Supplemental

5   Application to the Crown.
6   Interpretation.
7   Savings.
8   Application to Northern Ireland.
9   Consequential amendments and repeals.
10   Short title, commencement, and extent.

SCHEDULES:

Schedule 1 - Consequential amendments.
Schedule 2 - Repeals.

CIVIL LIABILITY (CONTRIBUTION)

ACT 1978

1978 CHAPTER 47

An Act to make new provision for contribution between persons who are jointly or severally, or both jointly and severally, liable for the same damage and in certain other similar cases where two or more persons have paid or may be required to pay compensation for the same damage; and to amend the law relating to proceedings against persons jointly liable for the same debt or jointly or severally, or both jointly and severally, liable for the same damage.   (31st July 1978)

Be it enacted by the Queen's most Excellent Majesty, by and with the advice and consent of the Lords Spiritual and Temporal, and Commons, in this present parliament assembled, and by the authority of the same, as follows:

Proceedings for contribution

1   (1)   Subject to the following provisions of this entitlement to contribution section, any person liable in respect of any damage suffered by another person may recover contribution from any other person liable in respect of the same damage (whether jointly with him or otherwise).

Entitlement to contribution

(2) A person shall be entitled to recover contribution by virtue of subsection (1) above notwithstanding that he has ceased to be liable in respect of the damage in question since the time when the damage occurred, provided that he was so liable immediately before he made or was ordered or agreed to make the payment in respect of which the contribution is sought.

(3) A person shall be liable to make contribution by virtue of subsection (1) above notwithstanding that he has ceased to be liable in respect of the damage in question since the time when the damage occurred, unless he ceased to be liable by virtue of the expiry of a period of limitation or prescription which extinguished the right on which the claim against him in respect of the damage was based ...

Codification and consolidation

Consolidation is the bringing together, under one head as it were, of scattered enactments relating to a particular branch of the law and an Act accomplishing this end is known as a consolidating statute. A codifying statute on the other hand is an enactment bringing together in statutory form the whole law including the case law on a particular subject; such process being known as **codification**.

1.3.3 Delegated legislation

Reference has already been made to the fact that Parliament may delegate its legislative power to other bodies and that the rules so made by those bodies are known as delegated legislation.

Delegated legislation is an inevitable development in the modern state and has the following advantages.

(a) It relieves pressure upon Parliamentary time. Parliament has so much to do and so little time in which to do it that it is convenient, indeed essential, to delegate legislative powers to make more detailed rules.

(b) Parliament is not always in session and its procedure is slow whereas delegated legislation has the advantage of speed.

(c) The medium of delegated legislation enables rapid changes to be made in the law so as to accommodate new and possibly unforeseen circumstances at the time when the enabling legislation was passed.

(d) Subordinate legislation is more flexible than supreme legislation.

(e) Legislation on technical topics necessitates prior consultation with experts and interests concerned. The giving of power to make regulations to Ministers facilitates such consultation. Further, it keeps the statute book clear of such highly technical provisions, which only experts in the field concerned can readily understand.

Delegated legislation has been criticised as giving too much power to civil servants, who are not elected representatives. They are not, it is argued, subject to the control of the electorate. However, it must be remembered that, firstly, Parliament exercises control over the use of these powers through the ministers responsible; and secondly, there is a significant element of judicial control through the doctrine of *ultra vires*, that is, a body to which Parliament has delegated legislative power is confined legislatively to the area delegated to it.

The principal forms of delegated legislation are:

(a)   *Orders in council* - These are enacted under powers delegated to the Privy Council.

(b)   *Ministerial regulations* - Such are known as statutory instruments and are made by individual Ministers within some limited sphere relating to their departmental responsibilities.

(c)   *By-laws* - Local authorities are given powers by many Acts of Parliament to make by-laws operative within their own geographical areas.

Statutory instruments, the most common form of delegated legislation, are cited: S1 1985 No 1 etc. Thus, the Family Provision (Intestate Succession) Order 1972 made by the Lord Chancellor under the Family Provision Act 1966 on 21st June 1972 may be cited as S1 1972 No 916 being the 916th statutory instrument made in the year 1972.

A statutory instrument

Set out below, as an example of a statutory instrument, is the Solicitors Act 1965 (Commencement No 4) Order 1972.

STATUTORY INSTRUMENTS

1972 No. 642 (C.10)

SOLICITORS

The Solicitors Act 1965 (Commencement No. 4) Order 1972
Made - - - -   21st April 1972

The Lord Chancellor, in exercise of the powers conferred on him by section 30(2) of the Solicitors Act 1965(a), hereby makes the following Order:

1   This Order may be cited as the Solicitors Act 1965 (Commencement No 4) Order 1972.

2   The following provisions of the Solicitors Act 1965 shall come into operation on 1st June 1972:
      sections 1 and 2;
      Schedule 3, so far as it relates to section 54
      of the Solicitors Act 1957(b);

Schedule 4, so far as it relates to sections
3(2) and 40 to 45 of the Solicitors Act 1957.

Dated 21st April 1972.

Hailsham of St. Marylebone, L.C.

EXPLANATORY NOTE

(This Note is not part of the Order)

This Order brings into operation on 1st June 1972 the
provisions of the Solicitors Act 1965 which extend the
powers of the Law Society to make regulations
regarding the education and training of those seeking
admission as solicitors.

Statutory interpretation

Interpretation or construction is the process by which the courts seek to ascertain the meaning of
the legislature through the medium of the authoritative forms in which it is expressed.

In the main, the English courts adopt what may be termed the literal approach - the duty of the
court being to interpret the words that the legislature has used and to discover from them its
intention. Parliamentary debates must not be referred to but dictionaries and text-books of
learned writers may be consulted and judicial decisions in similar context will be followed. The
courts use three methods of construction:

(a) *The literal rule* - According to this rule, the words of a statute must be interpreted
according to their literal meaning and sentences according to their grammatical
meaning. Thus, in *IRC v Hinchy (1960)* a taxpayer declared only part of his Post Office
interest. The Income Tax Act 1952 S25(3) provided that a person who failed to deliver
a correct income tax return should forfeit 'the sum of £20 and treble the tax which he
ought to be charged under this Act'. The House of Lords held that in addition to the
penalty of £20, he was liable to pay treble the whole tax chargeable for the year and not
merely treble the tax on the undeclared income.

(b) *The golden rule* - This principle follows on from the literal rule, in that the plain,
ordinary meaning of the words is taken, unless it would be absurd or repugnant. In *Adler
v George (1964)*, for example, it was held that persons who obstructed HM forces in a
prohibited place were guilty under the Official Secrets Act 1920 of obstructing HM
forces 'in the vicinity' of a prohibited place.

(c) *The mischief rule* - In this rule, the courts try to discover the reason for the Act. The
courts look for the defect or the mischief which the Act was trying to remedy and then
they interpret the words accordingly. In *Corkery v Carpenter (1951)*, for example, a pedal
cyclist under the influence of drink was held to have been legally arrested without a
warrant under the Licensing Act 1872, which provided that a person who was drunk in
charge of a carriage on the highway might be arrested without warrant.

Further, there are various so-called maxims of interpretation such as the *ejusdem generis* rule, whereby general words used by way of summary, after the enumeration of particulars forming a category, are taken to refer only to things of the kind which fall within that category. Thus, in *Evans v Cross (1938)* it was held that the word 'device' following signals, warning signposts, direction posts and signs, did not include a white line painted on the road; and noscitur a socis, whereby the words within a section must be read in their context and a statute must be read as a whole, for one section may be explained or modified by another: if certain items are expressly excluded, it follows that items not so excluded are still to apply (*expressio unius est exclusio alterius*); and words having a doubtful meaning may be clarified from their use in the particular context (*noscitur a sociis*).

In addition there are certain presumptions or rules of evidence which must also be borne in mind. These presumptions apply to the construction of a statute unless there are express words to the contrary. Thus, an Act is presumed only to apply to the United Kingdom; the Crown is presumed not to be bound by an Act of Parliament; and a presumption against an Act having retrospective effect.

Finally, there are statutory rules which may be utilised in the process of interpretation. Most statutes contain an interpretation section specifically defining the words and terms used in the statute, and the Interpretation Act 1978 interprets many general words and terms that are used in Acts. Thus, the Act provides, for example, that unless contrary intention appears words importing the masculine gender shall include females, and words in the singular shall include the plural, and words in the plural shall include the singular. In so far as such as these are found in the Act itself, for example, interpretation section they are termed intrinsic aids and, in so far as they are to be found outside the Act, for example, the Interpretation Act 1978 they are termed extrinsic aids.

1.4   Custom and authority

1.4.1   The nature of custom

Custom is usage recognised by law. Usage is the general acceptance over a lengthy period by a community of a course of conduct and is no doubt the earliest form of law making. As a state becomes organised, customary observances which until then had been enforced by public opinion, become laws under the authority of the state. Customs are not laws as they arise, but they are adopted into law by state recognition.

Custom exists as law in all countries, although it is losing its importance. In England, it is the Common Law or the custom of the realm, the existence of which is proved by showing that it has been affirmed by the courts or is contained in the writings of early legal historians. New customs may yet arise owing the the progress of science and the development of civilisation, and customary observances now being followed may find themselves eventually incorporated into law. Thus custom will continue to form one of the sources of law.

Types of custom

(a)   *General custom* - Such customs are to be found mainly in mercantile transactions. The cases show a conflict, and it is not certain whether it is still possible to incorporate new mercantile customs into the common law. The tests which the courts apply in establishing general custom is universality of observance rather than commercial antiquity.

(b)   *Local custom* - Local custom is that which prevails in some defined locality only, such as a borough or county, and constitute a source of law for that place only. As such, a local custom is always an exception to the general law, but it must not be contrary to a statute or to a fundamental principle of the common law.

In order that an alleged custom may be recognised by the courts as a binding legal custom, it must fulfill the following conditions:

(i)   Antiquity - The custom must have existed at the commencement of legal memory - 'from the time when the memory of man runneth not the contrary'. Actually, the limit of legal memory is arbitrarily fixed at 1189, and existence from this date will be readily presumed. In practice, however, it is sufficient if the person alleging the existence of a custom brings evidence that it has existed for a substantial period, and this will shift the burden of proof on to the person who asserts that the custom did not exist in 1189: *Simpson v Wells (1872)*.

(ii)   Continuity - The custom must have been in existence continuously, and the right to exercise it must not have been interrupted: *Wyld v Silver (1963)*.

(iii)   Certainty - The custom must be certain in nature and scope.

(iv)   Peaceable enjoyment - The custom must have been exercised *nec vi, nec clam, nec precario*, that is without force, stealth or permission. Thus in *Mills v Colchester Corporation (1867)* the plaintiff failed to establish the existence of a custom as the so-called custom had been exercised by licence.

(v)   Reasonableness - The courts will not recognise a custom which is manifestly unreasonable: *Bryant v Foot (1868)*.

(vi)   Recognition as compulsory - People must must feel bound to observe the custom: *Beckett (Alfred F) v Lyons (1967)*.

(vii)   Consistency - Customs must be consistent with each other: *Aldred's Case (1610)*.

(c)   *Conventional customs* - Conventional customs are are a source of rights and duties by reason of being impliedly incorporated into contracts. Being terms of a contract, they only bind the parties.

In order to establish such a custom the plaintiff must show that it is reasonable, certain, not contrary to the general law and universally accepted by the particular trade or profession.

Thus, in *Smith v Wilson (1832)* oral evidence was admitted that by a local custom 1,000 rabbits meant 1,200.

1.4.2   Books of authority

Legal authority - the use of textbooks in court

The general rule applied by English courts is that textbooks, however eminent their authors, are not to be treated as authorities. This does not mean that the views of such persons do not form the basis of counsel's argument or of the judge's decision, but that the expression of such views would stand or fall by their intrinsic merits. It may be that the lowly position of the jurist in English law may be ascribed to its pre-eminently judicial character and the weight attached to judicial decisions.

However, despite this general attitude, some of the earlier textbooks are treated by the courts as authoritative statements of the law of their time, and of present law if it is not shown to have been changed, which may be quoted and relied on in court on the authority of their authors. The attainment by a textbook of such authoritative status depends on the reputation of the author and the time when it was written, and is determined by professional tradition and practice. The ranks of such authors are sparse; included amongst their number are Glanvill, Bracton, Britton, Fleta and Hengham.

1.5   European law

1.5.1   The European Community

The European Community is an association of 12 European nations, including the UK.

The most important feature of the Community is that the territory of its member states is a 'common market' - that is, no customs duties are charged on goods moved from one member state to another, and goods imported from outside the Community are charged with the same import duties wherever they enter the Community. In addition, efforts are made to remove differences between member states' rules governing trade and commerce so that economic activity may be pursued just as easily in one member state as another.

Sources of Community law

The European Community is governed by its own law, the sources of which are:

(a)   Treaties made between the member states, of which the most important is the Treaty Establishing the European Economic Community (known as the EEC Treaty) which was made in 1957.

(b)   Regulations made by the Council or by the Commission. The Council consists of one member from the government of every member state, and is commonly called the Council of Ministers. Certain decisions of the Council must be unanimous but in general it acts by majority. The Commission is a team of international civil servants who are appointed by the governments of the member states but are required to perform their duties without regard to the special interest of any particular member state. In practice regulations are concerned with customs duties and with the market for agricultural produce in the Community.

(c)   The case law of the European Court of Justice (ECJ), which is also known as the Court of Justice of the European Communities (CJEC).

(d)   Directives adopted by the Council. A directive requires member states to make their laws on a particular topic approximately the same, and specifies what those laws should provide.

Direct effect of Community law

In each member state, Community law has effect as if it were part of the member state's internal law. As far as the UK concerned, Parliament made Community law a part of UK law, ie, a part of

English law, of Scots law and of Northern Ireland law) by enacting the European Communities Act 1972, S2(1).

It is important that Community law should be applied uniformly in all member states. Article 177 of the EEC Treaty therefore empowers any court in a member state to refer to the CJEC for an opinion on any point of Community law involved in a case.

It is possible for Community law to be in conflict with the national law of a member state. For example, national law may require payment of a customs duty that has been prohibited by Community law. The CJEC has repeatedly said that Community law must be given precedence in such a case. In practice the governments of member states have always acted to remove inconsistencies between national and Community law, though sometimes with reluctance. For example, in *Re Equal Pay for Equal Work (EC Commission v UK, case 6/81) (CJEC 1982)* it was held that the UK had failed to implement fully a Council directive of 1975 because under UK law job evaluation may be used to establish that work done by women and men is of equal value only with the employer's agreement. The CJEC held that the UK should introduce a procedure by which an employer can be required to have job evaluation performed. Regulations to implement the Court's ruling were subsequently laid before Parliament.

1.5.2   The Council of Europe

The Council of Europe is a larger and older association than the European Community and the two are not connected, though they have members in common. The Council of Europe has 21 members, including the UK. The executive organ of the Council is the Committee of Ministers, which consists of the Foreign Ministers of the member states.

Human rights law in Europe

The European Convention for the Protection of Human Rights and Fundamental Freedoms is an international treaty between 21 European nations, including the UK. The Convention was drafted under the auspices of, and is administered by, the Council of Europe. All the present members of the Council have ratified the Convention. The Convention sets out a number of rights and freedoms of persons which signatory states are required to secure for every person in their jurisdiction.

If a person or group claims that a signatory state has failed to secure for it one of the specified rights and freedoms then a complaint may be made to the Secretary-General of the Council of Europe. (The offices of the Secretary-General are in Strasbourg, France.) Some of the signatory states (including the UK) have accepted that such complaints may be laid against them by the alleged victims themselves, but the remaining signatory states have insisted that any complaint against them may only be made by another signatory state. In practice, of course, it is very rare for one government to complain about another.

A complaint against a state may be considered only if all legal processes available to the complainant within that state have been exhausted. A complaint must be presented within six months of the final judgment in legal proceedings.

A complaint is first considered by the European Commission of Human Rights. There is one commissioner for each signatory state but commissioners are not government representatives: they do their work as individuals. The vast majority of applications are rejected by the Commission. Of those not rejected, many can be settled after correspondence with the complainant and with the government involved. The Commission is required to work in camera.

In a very few cases the Commission is unable to bring about a settlement between the complainant and the government, and in those few cases the Commission may bring the matter before the European Court of Human Rights. The Court has one judge for each member state of the Council of Europe.

If the Court finds against a defending government then it may order compensation to be paid to the complainant. Such an award cannot be enforced by court action but failure by a government to pay it would be such a serious breach of treaty obligations that it would probably be expelled from the Council. While it was a military dictatorship, Greece preferred to resign from the Council rather than defend allegations (by other states) that it had violated the Convention.

Unlike Community law, the Convention on Human Rights is not a part of English law, and so no English statute could be ruled by the courts to be invalid because inconsistent with the Convention. However, the courts must assume that the Crown, when legislating, does not contravene its international obligations. Therefore, the courts will interpret legislation in a way that is consistent with the European Convention (*R v Secretary of State for the Home Department (ex parte Bhajan Singh)*).

1.6   Law reform

There are a number of official bodies that have been established to consider and make proposals for law reform. The first bodies of this kind were the Law Revision Committee, set up in 1934 and reconstituted in 1954 as the Law Reform Committee, and the Criminal Law Revision Committee formed in 1959. These committees, however, proved inadequate because their powers of review were limited and they worked on a part-time basis. The deficiency was met by the Law Commission Act of 1965 which set up a full-time **Law Commission** to promote the reform of English Law. The Lord Chancellor appoints the members of the Commission, on a full-time basis, from among persons holding judicial office, experienced barristers and solicitors and university teachers of law. The duty of the Commission is to keep under review the whole of the English Law with a view to its systematic development and reform, including the codification of such law, the elimination of anomalies, the repeal of obsolete enactments and generally the simplification and modernisation of the law.

1.7   Forms of liability

1.7.1   The nature of criminal and civil liability

Whether a law has its origin in case law or statute law, its breach may give rise to criminal and/or civil liability and in the latter case to liability in contract and/or tort.

The distinction between criminal and civil liability

The difficulty in distinguishing between criminal and civil liability lies in the fact that a wrong may give rise to both criminal and civil liability. Thus, if A takes B's watch by deception, A may be prosecuted in a criminal court and sent to prison; B may also sue A in a civil court to recover the value of the watch.

The distinction lies not in the nature of the wrong concerned, though this may not be completely ignored, but rather in the proceedings arising therefrom and the aim with which they are taken. Criminal law is concerned with the protection of the community and is aimed, by means of punishment, at deterring or reforming criminals and thus preserving peace and order. Civil law is concerned with the conduct of individuals towards one another. It is administered in civil courts and is aimed at giving compensation to those injured by its breach.

The nature and elements of a crime

There is no statutory definition of a crime and, indeed, any attempt to define a crime in the sense of enabling one to recognise an act as criminal or not, encounters the difficulty that it is not so much the act itself but rather its legal consequences that are the determining factor as to whether an act is classifiable as criminal or not. In the words of Lord Atkin in *Proprietary Articles Trade Association v AG for Canada (1931)* 'The criminal quality of an act cannot be discerned by intuition; nor can it be discovered by reference to any standard but one: is the act prohibited with penal consequences.'

The elements of a crime are *actus reus* (a wrongful act) and *mens rea* (a guilty mind) and before a man can be convicted of a crime it is usually necessary for the prosecution to prove beyond reasonable doubt:

(a)   that a certain event or a certain state of affairs which is forbidden by the criminal law, has been caused by his conduct (the *actus reus*); and

(b)   that this conduct was accompanied by a prescribed state of mind (the *mens rea* of the crime).

This principle of common law is expressed in the common law maxim *actus non facit reum, nisi mens sit rea* (an act does not make a person guilty unless the mind is guilty).

The classification of civil law

Civil law is primarily concerned with the rights and duties of individuals towards each other. It is aimed at compensating the party injured rather then punishing the wrongdoer. Civil law may be further broken down and classified under the following sub-headings:

(a)   *Law of contract* - A contract is a legally enforceable agreement and the law of contract is concerned with the formation of such agreements and their legal consequences.

(b)   *Law of tort* - A tort may be defined as a civil wrong, for which the remedy is an action for damages, and which is not solely the breach of a contract or the breach of a trust or other merely equitable obligation.

(c)   *Law of property* - In law the term property is not used to identify the physical asset concerned, but rather the interest of a person therein. Thus the law of property is that part of the law which determines the nature and extent of the rights which people may enjoy over land and other property.

(d)   *Law of succession* - Such is concerned with that part of the law which determines the devolution of property on the death of the former owner and in certain other events.

(e)   *Family law* - Family law is concerned with the determination of the rights, duties, and status of husband and wife, parent and child etc.

1.7.2   Liability in contract and tort

The distinction between contract and tort

The law of contract is designed to protect agreements that individuals make with each other. In a contract the interests that are protected and corresponding obligations exist only because the parties who make the contract consent to them. Obligations in contract are not imposed by the law, they are imposed by agreement between the parties. Contractual obligations are only enforced by the law.

The law of tort is designed to protect certain interests of individuals from various kinds of harm. These protected interests and the obligations not to violate them are laid down by the law. The obligations imposed by the law of tort are binding by law upon every individual for the benefit of every other individual.

The nature of tortious liability

'Tort' is the French word for 'wrong', and in English law it is used to cover certain kinds of civil wrongs and the rules which prohibit them. In modern society it is inevitable that some people will be injured or annoyed by their neighbour's activities. This may take the form of physical injuries (from car accidents, defective goods); or injury to reputation (from, say, an erroneous newspaper report); or diminution in the value of one's property, because of the obnoxious pursuits of the man next-door; or perhaps loss of or damage to property, as where an employee of a firm of dry-cleaners steals the plaintiff's mink coat. In all these and many other situations the law of tort governs the question of whether the injured party, the plaintiff, may sue the party responsible for the injury, the defendant, to recover compensation for his loss, and if so how.

However, although it is possible to describe the purpose for which the law of tort exists, it is less easy to define a tort, for, as stated earlier, the same factual situation may give rise to various forms of liability. Such being the case it is obvious that it cannot be the act itself which determines the form of liability, but rather the viewpoint from which that act is regarded and in particular its procedural consequences. Hence, the definition of the term tort, by reference to the origin of the rule and the legal consequences of its breach, as a civil wrong for which the remedy is a common law action for unliquidated damages, and which is not exclusively the breach of a contract or the breach of a trust or other merely equitable obligation.

Damage and liability

As regards tortious liability the law distinguishes between two concepts:

(a)   *Damnum* - which means the damages suffered; and
(b)   *Injuria* - which is an injury having legal consequences.

Sometimes, but not always, the two go together.

There are, however, cases of *damnum sine injuria* and *injuria sine damno*:

(a)   *Damnum sine injuria* - There are many forms of harm of which the law takes no account and the mere fact that a person has suffered damage does not entitle him to maintain an action in tort. The harm suffered must be caused by an act which is a violation of a right which the law rests in the plaintiff or injured party. Damage so suffered is known as *damnum sine injuria*. Thus, A may suffer damage as the result of the negligent act of B, but, if he cannot establish that B owes him a duty of care the damage suffered is not redressible by legal action.

(b)   *Injuria sine damno* - Here the behaviour concerned is actionable as a tort, although it has been the cause of no damage at all: *injuria sine damno*. Thus, the tort of trespass, whether it be to land, goods or person is actionable per se - without proof of damage, for a person has an absolute right to his property, to the immunity of his person and to his liberty. On the other hand, in the case of a qualified right, that is a right to be saved from loss, no action lies for any infringement without proof of damage: thus, in actions for negligence, damage is an essential requirement and must be proved.

Thus when a person has suffered what in the eyes of the law is looked upon as a legal duty, he must have a corresponding right of action even though he has suffered no harm. On the other hand, if a person suffers damage by the act of another he has no right of action unless there has been an infringement of what the law looks upon as a legal right. In the vast majority of cases both *damnum* and *injuria* continue to support the claim of the plaintiff.

1.8   Revision exercise

In order to assess your assimilation of the material contained in this session attempt the following questions. Check your answers against the references given.

(1)   What do you consider the characteristics of English law?   **(Solution: 1.1.1)**

(2)   Outline the nature of our legal system prior to the Norman Conquest.

                                                                          (Solution: 1.1.2)

(3)   What factors accounted for the evolution of our common law?   **(Solution: 1.1.3)**

(4)   What was the significance of the premature rigidity of the common law?

                                                                  (Solution: 1.1.3 to 1.1.5)

(5)   What was the main effect of the Judicature Acts 1873-5?   **(Solution: 1.1.7)**

(6)   What do you understand by the following terms?

        (a)   Sources of law.   **(Solution: 1.2.1)**
        (b)   Common law.   **(Solution: 1.2.2)**
        (c)   Equity.   **(Solution: 1.2.3)**

(7)   What do you understand by the term 'case law'?   **(Solution: 1.2.4)**

(8)   Explain the term 'judicial precedent'.   **(Solution: 1.2.4)**

(9)   Differentiate between binding and persuasive precedent.   **(Solution: 1.2.4)**

(10)   What factors are required to exist if the system of binding judicial precedent is to operate?   **(Solution: 1.2.4)**

(11)   Differentiate between the terms *res judicata*, *ratio decidendi* and *obiter dicta*.

                                                                          (Solution: 1.2.4)

(12)   Examine the nature of legislation.   **(Solution: 1.3.1)**

(13)   Differentiate between supreme and subordinate legislation.   **(Solution: 1.3.1)**

(14)   What do you understand by the term delegated legislation?   **(Solution: 1.3.1)**

(15)   Examine the three basic approaches to statutory interpretation.   **(Solution: 1.3.2)**

(16)   What are presumptions of interpretation?   **(Solution: 1.3.2)**

(17)   What is custom?   **(Solution: 1.4.1)**

(18)   When does custom become law?   **(Solution: 1.4.1)**

(19)   Differentiate between general and local customs.   **(Solution: 1.4.1)**

(20)   What tests determine the validity of local custom?   **(Solution: 1.4.1)**

(21)   Discuss the effect of the works of jurists on the development of English Law.
                                                                                               (Solution: 1.4.2)

(22)   What are the sources of Community law?   **(Solution: 1.5.1)**

(23)   What is the direct effect of Community law?   **(Solution: 1.5.1)**

(24)   What is the significance of the European Convention for the Protection of Human
         Rights and Fundamental Freedoms?   **(Solution: 1.5.2)**

(25)   Examine the role of the Law Commission.   **(Solution: 1.7.1)**

(26)   What is a crime?   **(Solution: 1.7.2)**

(27)   How does tortious liability differ from contractual liability?   **(Solution: 1.7.3)**

(28)   What is the purpose of the law of tort?   **(Solution: 1.6.3)**

1.9   Conclusion

Having studied this session you should now have an understanding of the nature, development and sources of English law and the various forms of liability. In particular, you should have an understanding of the role of the judiciary and Parliament in the making of our law.

1.10   Questions

Objective test questions

(1)   Which of the following terms is used to describe the reasoning behind a judicial decision?

A   *Per incuriam.*
B   *Obiter dicta.*
C   *Res judicata.*
D   *Ratio decidendi.*

(2)   Delegated legislation may be challenged in the courts on the grounds that it is:

A   Unreasonable.
B   *Ultra vires*.
C   Not *bona fide*.
D   *Intra vires*.

(3)   The term 'equity' technically means:

A   Natural justice.
B   The law administered in the Chancery Division of the High Court.
C   The law administered in the Court of Chancery prior to 1875.
D   Fairness.

(4)   The aim of civil law is:

A   Punishment.
B   Compensation.
C   Retribution.
D   Deterrence.

(5)   In *Evans v Cross (1938)* the words 'signals, warning signposts . . . signs or other devices' in the Road Traffic Act 1930 were held not to include lines painted on the road. This applied:

A   The literal rule.
B   The *ejusdem generis* rule.
C   The Interpretation Act 1978.
D   The golden rule.

(6)   The term 'disapproval' describes the situation where:

A   A superior court in the course of its judgement expresses doubt as to the validity of some previous rule but does not expressly overrule it.

B   A higher court decides a similar case on the basis of a different legal principle.

C   An appeal court reverses a decision given in a lower court from which the appeal emanated.

D   The judge is able to point to some material difference which justifies him in refusing to apply a rule of law previously laid down.

(7)   Unless it provides otherwise, an Act of Parliament becomes law:

      A   On approval by the House of Lords.
      B   On receipt of the Royal Assent.
      C   One month after its publication.
      D   Two months after it receives the Royal Assent.

(8)   Which of the following is not a form of delegated legislation?

      A   Orders in Council.
      B   By-laws.
      C   Ministerial regulation.
      D   Codifying statutes.

(9)   Which of the following is not a legal source of English law?

      A   Legislation.
      B   Conventional custom.
      C   Judicial precedent.
      D   Custom.

(10)   English law has various characteristics which distinguish it from others. Which of the following is not one of those characteristics?

      A   Its judicial character.
      B   Its codified nature.
      C   Lack of Roman influence.
      D   The independence of the legal profession.

Written test questions

1.1   Common law and equity

Explain the difference between common law and equity. In what ways do common law rights differ from equitable rights?

1.2   Judicial precedent

Explain the English doctrine of judicial precedent. What are the advantages of this system?

1.3   Delegated legislation

What do you understand by 'delegated legislation'? Explain the reasons for the increased delegation of legislative powers by Parliament in modern times. Outline some of its advantages and disadvantages. To what extent, if at all, is it subject to control by the courts and by Parliament?

SESSION 2

Administration of the law and the settlement of disputes

Careful study of this session will give you:

- a knowledge of the structure of the court system;

- a knowledge of the composition and jurisdiction of the courts;

- an appreciation of civil and criminal procedure;

- an awareness of the role of the various forms of tribunal and the use of arbitration as a means of dispute settlement;

- a knowledge of the personnel of the law.

2.1   The courts

2.1.1   Development

The present basic structure of the court system dates from the Judicature Acts 1873-5 which established the Supreme Court of Judicature. This court, now named the Supreme Court, consists of the Court of Appeal, the High Court of Justice and the Crown Court: S1(1) of the Supreme Court Act 1981. Prior to the Judicature Acts there had been a considerable number of courts. There were three common law courts - the Court of Queen's Bench, the Court of Common Pleas and the Court of Exchequer - having jurisdictions which differed in some respects and overlapped in others. There was the Court of Chancery, established in the fourteenth century and concerned with the administration of equity. There was the High Court of Admiralty, which administered Admiralty law, and the Court of Probate and the Divorce Court. Appeals were to the Court of Exchequer Chamber or to the Court of Appeal in Chancery. Appeals from Colonial, Admiralty and Ecclesiastical Courts were to the Judicial Committee of the Privy Council. To rationalise the jurisdiction of these numerous and overlapping courts and, in particular, to fuse the administration of law and equity, the Judicature Acts 1873-5, as stated earlier, established the Supreme Court of Judicature to which was transferred the jurisdiction of all the superior courts of law and equity except the Chancery Courts of the Counties Palatine of Lancaster and Durham which were unaffected.

2.1.2   The Supreme Court

Governed now by the Supreme Court Act 1981, the Supreme Court consists of the Court of Appeal, the High Court of Justice and the Crown Court.

The Court of Appeal

The Court of Appeal is the appellate branch of the Supreme Court. It sits in two divisions - Civil and Criminal.

The High Court of Justice

Though a single court, the High Court is, for administrative purposes, divided into three divisions - Chancery, Family and Queen's Bench.

(a)   *Chancery Division* (within which the Patents Court is a specialist section) hears cases concerning land, trusts, estates of deceased persons, patents, trademarks, copyright, guardianship of minors, contentious probate business, partnership, companies, and bankruptcy (if the person against whom the bankruptcy petition is presented has resided or carried on business in London during the preceding six months, or is not resident in England or Wales, or if his residence cannot be ascertained). Certain judges specialise in company law, and most of the bankruptcy business is heard by court officials. In theory the president of the Chancery Division is the Lord Chancellor, but he never has time to devote to this office and the effective head is a senior judge called the Vice-Chancellor.

(b)   *Family Division* which hears cases concerning matrimony, legitimacy, adoption, and consent to the marriage of a minor (though in practice minors seeking such consent usually prefer to ask a Magistrates' Court), and deals with non-contentious probate business. The head of the division is called the President of the Family Division.

(c)   *Queen's Bench Division* (within which the Admiralty Court and the Commercial Court are specialist sections), which deals with cases concerning contract, tort, admiralty and commercial law, and the applications for judicial review. The Lord Chief Justice is president of the Queen's Bench Division.

The Crown Court

The Crown Court is a single court, organised on a national basis and able to sit anywhere in England and Wales, replacing the former Courts of Assize and Quarter Sessions which were organised on a local basis. Whereas the High Court is essentially a court of civil jurisdiction, the Crown Court is primarily a court of criminal jurisdiction.

The House of Lords

The House of Lords was not included in the Supreme Court of Judicature and it was envisaged by the Judicature Acts that the Court of Appeal would be the final court of appeal within the system. However, the House of Lords jurisdiction as the final court of appeal was restored by the Appellate Jurisdiction Act 1876 which also provided the House with trained judges.

County and Magistrates' Courts

In addition to the superior courts that have already been mentioned, reference should also be made to the County and Magistrates' Courts which are inferior courts exercising civil and criminal jurisdiction respectively.

Summary

The above information concerning the present structure of the court system is presented in Figure 2.1 in diagrammatic form.

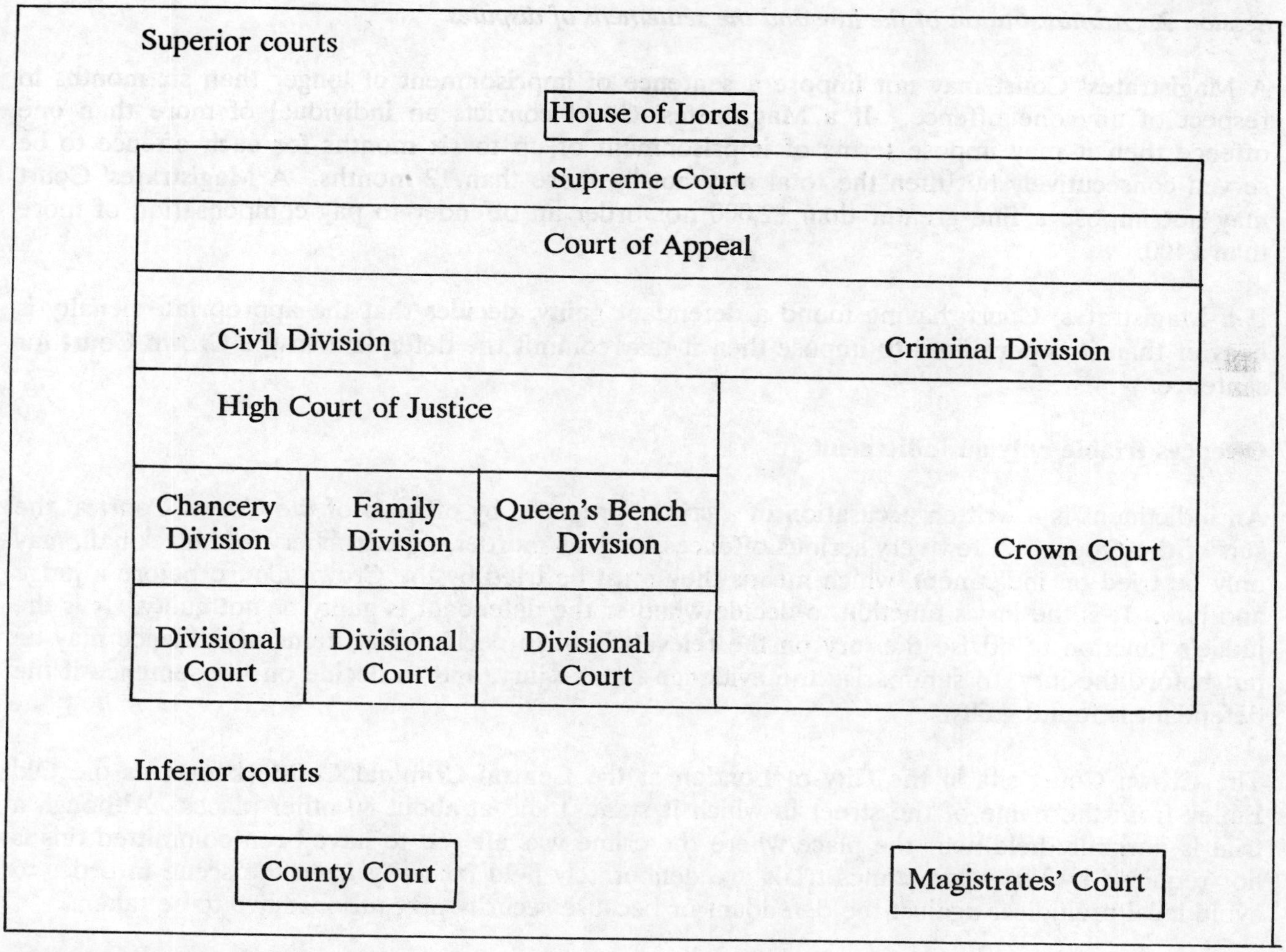

Figure 2.1: The court system

2.1.3   Crown Court and Magistrates' Courts

Trial of criminal cases

Criminal offences are divided into three classes by the Criminal Law Act 1977, S14:

(a)   offences triable only summarily;
(b)   offences triable only on indictment;
(c)   offences triable either way.

Offences triable only summarily

Minor criminal offences, such as wilfully obstructing free passage along a highway (Highways Act 1980, S137), or unlawfully assaulting an individual without causing bodily harm (Offences against the Person Act 1861, S42) are triable only summarily - that is, they must be tried by a Magistrates' Court. A Magistrates' Court can only hear a case arising in the geographical district with which it deals.

In some Magistrates' Courts a case is heard by a full-time salaried judge, who is appointed by the Crown and is called a stipendiary magistrate. In the vast majority of courts a case is heard by between three and seven justices of the peace (JPs). A JP is a local person of respectable character appointed by the Lord Chancellor on the advice of a local advisory committee. A JP is paid expenses and may be entitled to compensation for loss of earnings.

A Magistrates' Court may not impose a sentence of imprisonment of longer than six months in respect of any one offence. If a Magistrates' Court convicts an individual of more than one offence then it may impose terms of imprisonment of up to six months for each offence to be served consecutively but then the total may not be more than 12 months. A Magistrates' Court may not impose a fine greater than £2,000 nor order an offender to pay compensation of more than £400.

If a Magistrates' Court, having found a defendant guilty, decides that the appropriate penalty is heavier than it is permitted to impose then it may commit the defendant to the Crown Court for sentence.

Offences triable only on indictment

An indictment is a written accusation of a crime, prepared by officials of the Crown Court at the suit of the Queen. A few very serious offences, such as murder, rape, robbery and blackmail, may only be tried on indictment, which means they must be tried by the Crown Court, before a judge and jury. It is the jury's function to decide whether the defendant is guilty or not guilty. It is the judge's function to advise the jury on the relevant law, to decide what items of evidence may be put before the jury, to summarise the evidence for the jury, and to decide on the sentence if the defendant is found guilty.

The Crown Court sits in the City of London at the Central Criminal Court (known as the Old Bailey from the name of the street in which it stands) and at about 80 other places. Although a trial is normally held near the place where the crime was alleged to have been committed this is not required by law. Sometimes trials are deliberately held far away from the scene in order to avoid local prejudices against the defendant or because security precautions have to be taken.

Most of the judges of the Crown Court are circuit judges - so called because they are appointed to hear cases at all courthouses within a particular region called a circuit. In addition, High Court judges sit in the Crown Court to hear the most serious cases. A murder trial, for example, is always conducted by a High Court judge. Until recently only judges from the Queen's Bench Division went 'out on circuit' to the Crown Court, but in an effort to clear the backlog of cases, judges from other Divisions have recently been sitting in the Crown Court.

There are also some part-time judges of the Crown Court called recorders. An individual may be appointed a recorder (by the Crown on the advice of the Lord Chancellor) if he is a barrister or a solicitor of at least 10 years' standing. Circuit judges must be either barristers of at least 10 years' standing or must have held the office of recorder for at least three years. At the Central Criminal Court, one of the circuit judges has the title of Common Serjeant to preserve an ancient City of London tradition.

In principle, when a circuit judge or a recorder is hearing a case, between two and four JPs should sit with him. If that happens,the sentence is decided by a majority of the members of the court (though if there is an even number, the circuit judge or recorder has a casting vote). In practice justices very rarely have time to spare to sit in the Crown Court, except in appeals.

Before a case is heard by the Crown Court there must be a committal hearing before a Magistrates' Court. In principle the evidence against the defendant should be presented to the Magistrates' Court which should decide whether there is a *prima facie* case for the defendant to answer. In practice defendants very rarely challenge the prosecution's case at a committal hearing and magistrates very rarely refuse to commit for trial. The main function of a committal hearing nowadays is that it ensures that a person held in custody is brought before a court which can satisfy itself that there is a good reason for holding him.

Offences triable either way

Many offences consist of doing an act, such as stealing, which on some occasions may be a major crime and on other occasions a comparatively trivial matter. There is a three-stage process for deciding whether to try an offence of this kind at the Crown Court or in a Magistrates' Court:

(a)   Prosecution of a serious offence is usually undertaken by the Director of Public Prosecutions (DPP). If the DPP asks for trial at the Crown Court, the defendant will be indicted.

(b)   If the DPP does not intervene or does not apply for trial on indictment, the case must be considered by a Magistrates' Court. It hears representations from both prosecutor and defendant and, after considering the gravity of the alleged offence, decides whether to try the case itself or to conduct a committal hearing only, on the assumption that it will commit the accused to the Crown Court for trial.

(c)   If the Magistrates' Court decides to try the case itself, it must explain this decision to the accused, who then has a final opportunity to demand trial by the Crown Court. If the accused makes that demand, he will be indicted.

Appeals in criminal cases

There are two methods of appeal from the decision of a Magistrates' Court in a criminal case:

(a)   A defendant who has been convicted may ask the Crown Court to hear the case again, provided he notifies the Magistrates' Court and the prosecutor within 21 days of his conviction. The defendant does not get a trial at the Crown Court, but the circuit judge or recorder who re-hears the case must sit with justices of the peace. On a re-hearing the Crown Court has power to find the defendant guilty or not guilty and, if found guilty, to impose any sentence it thinks fit. It can even impose a sentence greater than the one originally imposed by the Magistrates' Court but it cannot impose a sentence which would have been beyond the powers of the Magistrates' Court. A defendant may only obtain a re-hearing in the Crown Court if he pleaded not guilty in the Magistrates' Court.

A defendant who has been convicted by magistrates may ask the Crown Court to review the sentence imposed (even if he pleaded guilty in the Magistrates' Court). In this type of appeal the Crown Court does not hear any evidence concerning the facts of the case. Again the circuit judge or recorder must sit with justices, and again the Crown Court can increase the original sentence.

(b)   Either prosecutor or defendant may appeal against a decision of a Magistrates' Court to a divisional court of the Queen's Bench Division on the ground that the decision was wrong in law. The divisional court makes no enquiry at all into the facts of the case. The Magistrates' Court has to 'state a case', which means that it must summarise its finding of fact and state its opinion of the legal consequences which flow from the facts it found.

The divisional court will hear and determine the questions of law arising, after argument by counsel for the parties. The court may allow argument on a point not raised in the court below or even consider a new point in its judgment, provided the new point involves only a point of law not requiring any evidence. The court may reverse, affirm or amend the decision that has been appealed, or it may remit the case to the Magistrates' Court with its opinion. If a case is remitted to a Magistrates' Court the magistrates may proceed to acquit or convict the defendant on the basis of the divisional court's ruling concerning the law.

A defendant who has appealed from a Magistrates' Court to the Crown Court may further appeal to a divisional court on the grounds that the Crown Court's decision was wrong in law: in other words, it is possible to gain a re-hearing of the evidence in the Crown Court and then argue about the law in the divisional court.

2.1.4   County Courts

Composition and jurisdiction

There are 267 County Court districts in England and Wales. The Lord Chancellor is required to assign one or more circuit judges to every County Court district, and to appoint a registrar for each district.

County Courts, like Magistrates' Courts, are intended to be local courts and can only deal with a case if it arises within their district. Only about a third of the courts deal with bankruptcy or divorce and have correspondingly larger districts for these purposes. A registrar may try any disputed claim if the amount involved is not above £500, and neither party objects. A registrar may deal with any undisputed claim. The County Court for the City of London is called the Mayor's and City of London Court. In any action in a County Court, either a solicitor or a barrister may appear as an advocate.

It is quite common for a statute to require that certain minor questions arising under its provisions must be determined in a County Court. Apart from these restrictions a plaintiff may bring an action either in a County Court or in the High Court but the County Court is available to him only if his claim is within certain financial limits. However, a County Court will hear a claim outside the limits if both parties agree in writing.

An action may be transferred from the County Court to the High Court and vice versa, and this may be necessary if the amount of the claim is unclear at the outset. If a plaintiff pursues a claim founded on contract or tort in the High Court when it could have been heard by the County Court, and recovers less than £600 then he will not be entitled to claim his costs from the defendant.

County Courts deal mainly with the following matters:

(a)   actions in contract or tort (with a limit of £5,000);

(b)   equity matters (with a limit of £30,000);

(c)   actions affecting the title to and/or possession of land (where the rateable value does not exceed £1,000);

(d)   bankruptcies (other than those which must be heard in the High Court);

(e)   company liquidations (for companies with paid-up share capital not exceeding £120,000, provided the court concerned has bankruptcy jurisdiction);

(f)   probate proceedings (for estates of £30,000 or less);

(g)   certain Admiralty matters (but this applies only to certain courts, and is limited to cases not exceeding £5,000, or £15,000 for salvage);

(h)   most matrimonial proceedings.

Appeal from the County Courts lies to the Court of Appeal (Civil Division).

2.1.5 High Court of Justice

Judges

The Crown may, on the advice of the Lord Chancellor, appoint up to 85 Justices of the High Court. They are known as puisne (pronounced 'puny') judges. An individual cannot be appointed as a puisne judge unless he has been a barrister for at least 10 years. It is conventional to identify a puisne judge in writing by his or her surname followed by a capital J; for example, Smith J.

Divisions

The High Court has to deal with a wide range of legal problems. In practice both judges and barristers tend to specialise in particular aspects of the law, and this is reflected in the organisation of the High Court into three divisions - Chancery, Family and Queen's Bench. The Lord Chancellor assigns judges to particular divisions according to their previous experience and expertise.

Composition and venue

A case in the High Court is normally heard by a single judge. A judge may sit with expert assessors if he needs advice on technical matters, and this is often done in the Patent and Admiralty Courts. On some occasions trial is by judge and jury.

Most sittings of the High Court are at the Royal Courts of Justice in the Strand in London. It may also sit at 24 other towns in England and Wales.

Divisional courts

For a wide range of cases the High Court has jurisdiction as an appeal court. Most appeals are from decisions of Magistrates' Courts, though the Chancery Division hears appeals from County Court decisions in bankruptcy matters, and the Queen's Bench Division hears some appeals from the Crown Court.

An appeal is heard by a **divisional court**, which must consist of at least two judges, and is usually three. In the Queen's Bench Division a hearing of an application for judicial review is usually by a divisional court. A divisional court may adopt a majority decision.

2.1.6 Court of Appeal

Composition

The Crown may appoint up to 28 Lords Justices of Appeal. It is conventional in writing to identify a Lord Justice of Appeal by his surname followed by the letters LJ; for example, Smith LJ. The Court of Appeal consists of the Lords Justices plus the Master of the Rolls (who is president of the Civil Division of the court) and the Lord Chief Justice (who is president of the Criminal Division). The Lord Chancellor, the Vice-Chancellor and the President of the Family Division are ex officio members of the Court of Appeal but in practice do not sit in it.

An appeal in the Civil Division must be heard by an odd number of judges and by at least three judges unless all parties consent to a hearing by two judges. An appeal in the Criminal Division must be heard by an odd number of judges and by at least three judges unless the appeal is against sentence only, when it may be heard by two judges.

The Lord Chancellor may require puisne judges of the High Court to sit in the Court of Appeal. In practice High Court judges do not sit in the Civil Division, but in the Criminal Division a court consists of either the Lord Chief Justice, a Lord Justice of Appeal and a puisne judge, or a Lord Justice of Appeal and two puisnes. The Criminal Division replaced the Court of Criminal Appeal in 1966: only the Lord Chief Justice and puisne judges of the Queen's Bench Division sat in the Court of Criminal Appeal. Lawyers have often expressed disquiet that it is assumed that civil cases require better judges than criminal cases. (Until the Court of Criminal Appeal was established in 1907 it was practically impossible to appeal in any criminal case tried by jury.)

The Court of Appeal may adopt a majority decision.

The Civil Division hears appeals against decisions of the High Court (including those of divisional courts), County Courts (except in bankruptcy and a few other matters in which appeals go to a divisional court), the Employment Appeal Tribunal, and (when there are any) the Restrictive Practices Court. It also hears appeals against decisions of the Lands Tribunal, which decides questions relating to compensation for compulsory purchase of land and valuation for rating.

The Criminal Division hears appeals by persons convicted on indictment by the Crown Court. If a prosecutor is dissatisfied with the legal grounds involved in an acquittal in the Crown Court then the Attorney-General may refer the point of law involved to the Criminal Division for consideration; a reference by the Attorney-General is not a re-hearing of the facts of the case - a person acquitted by the Crown Court cannot be convicted as a result of the reference and, indeed, the defendant's name is normally not disclosed.

The Court of Appeal always sits at the Royal Courts of Justice in London, though in theory it could sit anywhere the High Court can.

Appeals in the Civil Division

The right to appeal to the Civil Division is virtually unlimited. The court hears the arguments of counsel again but it does not hear witnesses give their evidence again: it relies on the trial judge's notes or the official transcript. Because it does not see witnesses give their evidence the Civil Division normally will not disagree with the findings of fact made by the trial judge. So in practice appeals in the Civil Division concern only points of law. The Civil Division will hear new evidence but only if it is significant and only if it was not reasonably practicable to produce it at the original trial.

The Civil Division of the Court of Appeal does not have power to reverse the verdict of a jury. An appeal against the verdict of a jury must, therefore, take the form of a request for a new trial before a different jury. This is of limited importance now that trial by jury in civil cases has become so rare. The Civil Division may order a new trial if satisfied that the judge misdirected the jury, or allowed evidence to be put before them which should have been ruled inadmissible, or rejected evidence which was in fact admissible, or if the judge wrongly withdrew a question from the jury (that is, decided that the jury did not have to give a verdict on the question because it could be decided as a matter of law). However, the Rules of the Supreme Court provide that a new trial may be ordered on these grounds only if the Court of Appeal is of the opinion that some substantial wrong or miscarriage has been occasioned.

It is possible for the Civil Division to order a new trial on the ground that the jury's verdict in the original trial was perverse - meaning that no jury of reasonable people, properly directed, could have decided the matter in the way that the jury did. It may be shown, for example, that there was no evidence in support of material fact, or that what evidence was produced could not reasonably be believed.

The Civil Division will not normally alter a jury's decision on the amount of damages, unless the amount was so entirely erroneous that no reasonable jury could have awarded it. However, the Civil Division does consider appeals against amounts awarded by judges sitting without juries, and its supervision of such awards has enabled the High Court to develop a generally agreed 'scale' of damages for matters like personal injuries.

Whether or not there was a jury at the original trial, a new trial may be ordered where necessary to consider the fresh evidence, or where there was a misconduct by the judge, jury, counsel, court officers or other persons, or where the original verdict was obtained by fraud, or where there was surprise - that is, the appellant was unprepared for the arguments or evidence adduced by another party.

Appeals in the Criminal Division

An appeal in the Criminal Division may be made in any case on a point of law, but only with the leave of the Court of Appeal on a question of fact or a question of mixed law and fact. Application for leave to appeal is made to a single judge of the Court of Appeal but if he refuses leave then the application may be pursued before a court of three judges. The Criminal Division may allow an appeal against conviction if they think that:

(a)   under all the circumstances of the case the conviction is unsafe or unsatisfactory; or

(b)   the judgment of the court below should be set aside on the ground of a wrong decision of any question of law; or

(c)   there was material irregularity in the course of the trial.

These three conditions are specified now in the Criminal Appeal Act 1968, but there is a proviso that the Court may decline to allow an appeal if they think that no miscarriage of justice has actually occurred.

As in the Civil Division the trial witnesses are not heard again in a criminal appeal. The Criminal Division hears fresh evidence if there is a reasonable explanation for it not being given at the trial.

If the Court of Appeal accepts that new evidence, had it been put before the jury at the original trial, might have persuaded the jury to acquit the appellant then the Court of Appeal must quash the appellant's conviction. However, it has a power, in these circumstances, to order that the appellant be tried again (Criminal Appeal Act 1968 S7). This statutory provision is an exception to the common-law rule that a person cannot be tried twice for the same crime. In practice the Court of Appeal has rarely exercised its power to require an appellant to be retried.

In exceptional cases the Court of Appeal may find that an appellant's original trial was conducted so irregularly that it may be regarded in law as not having been a trial. In such an event the Court of Appeal may order *venire de novo*, meaning that the accused must be tried again, this time properly. The circumstances in which *venire de novo* may be ordered are very limited. An example was where a trial was conducted on the basis that the defendant had pleaded guilty whereas in fact he had pleaded not guilty (*R v Scothern 1961*).

By S36 of the Criminal Justice Act 1988 if it appears to the Attorney-General:

(a)   that the sentencing of a person in a proceeding in the Crown Court has been unduly lenient; and

(b)   that the case is one for an offence triable only on indictment or for an offence of a description specified in an order under S35 of the Act,

he may, with the leave of the Court of Appeal, refer the case to them for them to review the sentencing of that person; and on such a reference the Court of Appeal may:

(a)   quash any sentence passed on him in the proceeding;

(b)   in place of it, pass such sentences as they think appropriate for the case and as the court below had power to pass when dealing with him.

2.1.7   House of Lords

Appellate committee

An appeal to the House of Lords may be made from a decision of the Court of Appeal, and from a divisional court of the Queen's Bench Division in criminal cases, and from equivalent courts in Scotland and Northern Ireland. It is also possible to appeal direct from a decision of the High Court if an appeal to the Court of Appeal would be a waste of time because that court is bound by precedent.

The Crown may appoint up to 11 Lords of Appeal in Ordinary. Appointment is made on the advice of the Prime Minister though in practice the advice presumably comes from the Lord Chancellor. Lords of Appeal in Ordinary are given life peerages so that they are members of the House of Lords. (They never take part in debates of a political nature though they often contribute to debates on bills affecting the administration of justice.) They must have either held high judicial office for two years or have been practising barristers for 15 years.

An appeal to the House of Lords must be heard by at least three members of the House who are either Lords of Appeal in Ordinary or who hold, or have held, high judicial office. One of the three may be the Lord Chancellor. In theory other members of the House may sit with the judicially qualified members but none has done so since the nineteenth century (when, it seems, they were usually ignored by the judicial members). In practice an appeal is usually heard by five Lords of Appeal. Almost all cases heard by the House are in civil litigation.

Right of appeal

(a)   From the Court of Appeal, Civil Division, an appeal may only be made if leave to appeal is given either by the Court of Appeal or by an Appeals Committee of the House of Lords (Administration of Justice (Appeals) Act 1934, S1).

(b)   From the Court of Appeal, Criminal Division, an appeal may only be made if the Court of Appeal certifies that a point of law of general public importance is involved in the decision, and leave to appeal is granted (Criminal Appeal Act 1968, S33).

(c)   From a Queen's Bench divisional court, an appeal may only be made if the divisional court certifies that a point of law of general public importance is involved and leave to appeal is granted (Administration of Justice Act 1960, S1).

(d)   An appeal direct from the High Court may only be made if the High Court judge who heard the case certifies that there is a point of law of general public importance either involving the construction of a statute or involving a point where the Court of Appeal is bound by precedent but there are grounds for believing the precedent could be reconsidered.

Form of decision

An appeal in the House of Lords is heard by a committee of the House which recommends a resolution to be adopted by the House. If the appeal is successful then the resolution instructs the court from which the appeal was heard to make a new order embodying the House's decision.

Although it is not expressly required, appeals are always heard by an odd number of lords, who may adopt a majority decision.

2.1.8   Summary

The above information relating to the English courts exercising civil and criminal jurisdiction is presented in diagrammatic form in Figures 2.2 and 2.3.

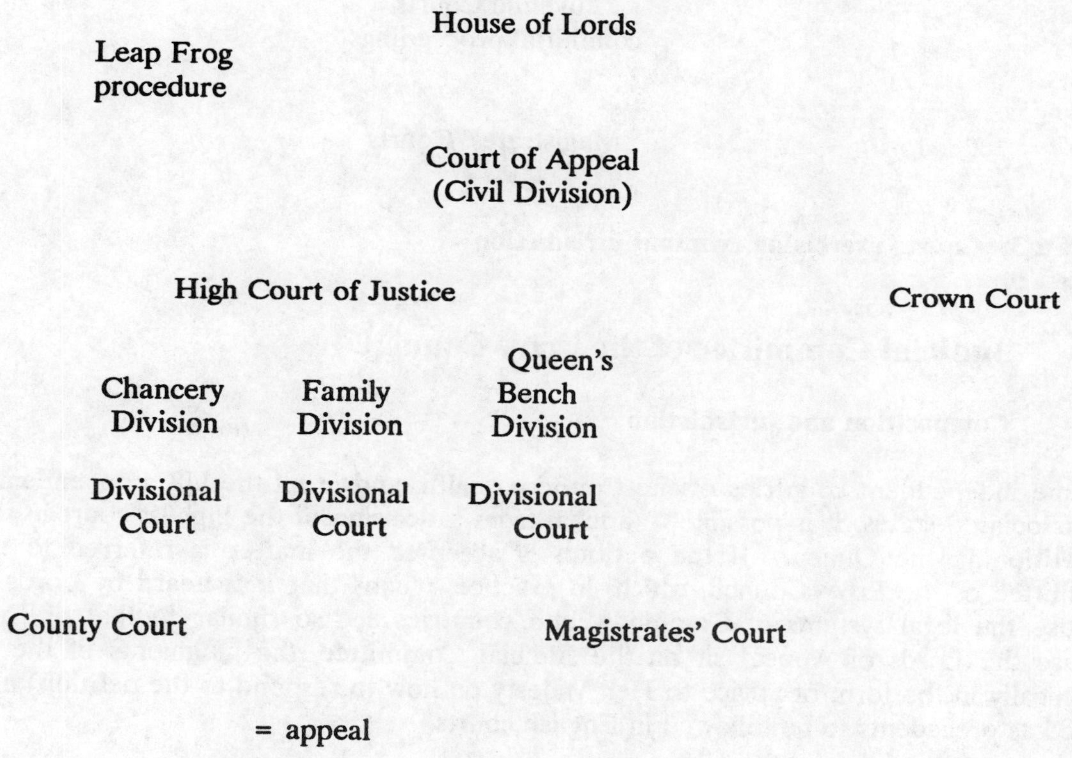

House of Lords

Leap Frog
procedure

Court of Appeal
(Civil Division)

High Court of Justice   Crown Court

Chancery   Family   Queen's
Division   Division   Bench
                                  Division

Divisional   Divisional   Divisional
Court   Court   Court

County Court   Magistrates' Court

= appeal

Figure 2.2:   Courts exercising civil jurisdiction

House of Lords

Court of Appeal
(Criminal Division)

Queen's Bench Division   By way of
                                                                    Crown Court
Divisional Court   case stated

By way of case stated   Committal for sentence   Committal for trial

Petty Sessions and
Juvenile Courts
committal proceedings

Magistrates' Courts

Figure 2.3: Courts exercising criminal jurisdiction

2.2   Judicial Committee of the Privy Council

2.2.1   Composition and jurisdiction

In some independent countries of the Commonwealth, and in all the UK's dependent territories and associated states, it is possible to appeal from a decision of the highest court in the territory by petitioning the Queen. If the petition is accepted the matter is referred to the Judicial Committee of the Privy Council, which, in practice, means that it is heard by Lords of Appeal. Because the legal systems of Commonwealth countries are so similar to that of England, and because the Lords of Appeal sit on the Judicial Committee, the judgments of the Committee (technically in the form of advice to Her Majesty on how to respond to the petition) are normally treated as precedents to be followed in English courts.

The Judicial Committee has some functions in relation to English legal proceedings:

(a)   It hears appeals in some matters from ecclesiastical courts of the Church of England.

(b)   It hears appeals from the statutory disciplinary bodies for the medical, dental and optical professions and the professions ancillary to medicine.

(c)   It can hear an application for a declaration that a Member of Parliament is subject to a statutory disqualification.

(d)   In time of war it hears appeals from the Admiralty Court (in the Queen's Bench Division) on matters relating to prize (that is, enemy property captured at sea).

The Judicial Committee does not act on the rule that it is bound by its own decisions, but it will differ only with great hesitation.

2.3 Court of Justice of the European Communities

The court, generally known as the European Court, ensures the observance and recognition of Community rules with regard to legal interpretation and application. It is concerned with disputes between member countries over Community matters. It hears appeals from member countries, individuals and the Community institutions on matters relating to the treaties, and its rules are binding. The Court is the final arbiter in all matters of law that lie within the scope of the treaties. The Court of Justice consists of judges representing each of the Community members and is assisted by Advocates-General whose duties are to present publicly, with complete impartiality and independence, reasoned conclusion on cases submitted to the Court with a view to assisting the latter in performance of its duties.

Judges and Advocates-General are chosen 'from among persons of indisputable independence who fulfil the conditions for the holding of the highest judicial office in their respective countries or who are jurists of recognised competence'.

2.4 Proceedings in the High Court

2.4.1 Starting proceedings

The most usual way of doing this is by **writ of summons**, used in most actions in tort or contract. The writ is a form stating a summary of the plaintiff's claim, requiring the defendant to take part in the action by formally acknowledging that the writ has been served on him, and warning him that if he does not do so the plaintiff can enter judgment against him (ie, he will lose the case by default).

The writ is valid for 12 months after it has been issued, and can only be served thereafter by leave of the court. The method of service is either (1) personally handing it to the defendant, or (2) posting it to him, or (3) leaving it at his address. With it is served a form for acknowledging service, which the defendant must complete and send to the court within 14 days of service. If he does not do so, or if he states on the acknowledgment that he does not intend to defend the proceedings, the plaintiff may at once enter judgment against the defendant, and proceed to enforce the judgment just as if the case had been tried in court. Such a judgment ('judgment in default') may be set aside by the court on the defendant's application, but he will usually have to show that he has an apparent defence to the claim which ought to be tried. If, however, he has some good reasons for not acknowledging service, eg, if the writ went astray in the post, the judgment will be set aside as of right.

There is a time limit for issuing the writ as well as for serving it. In actions in contract and tort, proceedings must be begun within six years of when the claim arose. Various other limitation periods apply to other classes of action, eg, 12 years for possession of land (so that a squatter gets title to the land after that time), and three years in actions for negligence etc, causing personal injury, though for such actions the court may allow an action to proceed after the three years have expired. Apart from the discretion in personal injury cases, an action commenced after the limitation period has expired will inevitably fail, however unanswerable the plaintiff's claim otherwise is.

2.4.2   Pleadings

Within 14 days of acknowledgment of service (though this period can be, and usually is, extended by agreement of the parties or leave of the court) the plaintiff must serve on the defendant a **statement of claim**. In fact this is often served with the writ, indorsed on the back of it. This is the first of the documents called 'pleadings', which have the purpose of defining the issues (the questions of fact and law which are in dispute) which have to be tried and concerning which evidence may be given at the trial. So the statement of claim is a document setting out, in numbered paragraphs, the allegations of fact which are the basis of the plaintiff's claim, and stating the nature of the defendant's liability together with the remedies sought by the plaintiff. Upon receipt of the statement of claim, the defendant must, in theory within 14 days, serve a **defence** on the plaintiff. This will state, referring to the numbered paragraphs of the statement of claim, which of the plaintiff's allegations he is admitting and which he is denying, and any further facts which assist his defence. Failure to serve either of these documents will entitle either the defendant to have the action struck out or the plaintiff to enter judgment, as the case may be.

If the defendant wishes to claim a contribution from someone else whom he alleges is jointly liable to him with the plaintiff, or to claim against a third person a similar remedy as the plaintiff seeks against him, or to have some question tried between himself and a third person as well as the plaintiff, he must serve a **third-party notice** on that person, who will then be brought into the action, and then seek the court's directions on whether the third party should be added as a defendant.

If the defendant has himself a claim against the plaintiff, he will add to his defence a **counterclaim** saying how the plaintiff is liable to him, eg, if in an action for breach of contract the defendant wants to sue for damages for fraud, he will not bring a separate action but will serve a counterclaim for fraud with his defence. If he disputes any matter raised in the defence or counterclaim the plaintiff will serve a **reply** and/or **defence to counterclaim**. Finally, if either party finds a pleading ambiguous or defective, he may request **further and better particulars** of it, and if they are not supplied get the court to order them; these too form part of the pleadings.

Joining parties and causes of action

There is no reason why several plaintiffs and/or defendants should not be parties to an action, provided there is a sufficient connection between them and the subject matter of the action. Similarly, where there are two or more parties, they may join several different claims in a single action. The court has power to order that different issues and claims be tried separately, and that persons cease to be parties to an action, and conversely to join separate actions in a single action, and add new parties at their request, if it is just and convenient to do so.

Amendment

Any party may amend his pleadings once without the leave of the court, provided he serves the amended pleading on all other parties, who may then amend their pleadings accordingly. But any subsequent amendment, and any amendment which alters the parties (eg, adding a new defendant) or causes of action, requires leave of the court. This is usually given, on terms that the party pay the costs incurred, but since the amended pleading dates back to the date of the original pleading, leave will not be given if any relevant limitation period has expired since that would prevent the defence of limitation being raised.

2.4.3   Summary judgment

It may be that although a defendant has given notice of intention to defend proceedings the plaintiff does not believe him to have a genuine defence. In such a case he may generally obtain judgment after a summary hearing before a Master under Order 14 of the Supreme Court Rules, without having the delay and expense of a full trial. This procedure is not available if the proceedings were not begun by writ nor with certain types of action, eg, libel. The plaintiff must serve on the defendant a **summons** requiring him to attend the hearing, with an **affidavit** swearing that he has a good claim (and giving details of it) and that he does not believe there is a defence to it. The defendant may serve an affidavit in reply giving details of his defence. At the hearing the Master will read the affidavits and hear the parties' arguments, and may make any of these orders:

(a)   Judgment for the plaintiff, if the defendant cannot show that there is an issue which ought to be tried. This is enforceable as an ordinary judgment of the court.

(b)   Leave to defend, if the Master thinks there is an issue that ought to go to trial. If he is very doubtful, he may grant leave to defend conditional upon the defendant's paying money into court as security. The case will then continue to proceed as usual.

(c)   Dismiss the summons, if it ought not to have been issued, eg, if it is a libel action or the plaintiff knew all along that there was a triable defence; the plaintiff will be ordered to pay the costs of the summons.

2.4.4   Preparing a civil case for trial

Discovery of documents

The court has a discretionary power to order parties to disclose and produce to each other documents relating to matters in question in the action which are or were in their possession, custody, or power. Such orders are called orders for **discovery**. In most High Court actions rules have been made for this to take place automatically, but where this does not happen (eg, where the action was not begun by writ, or was begun in a County Court, or a party neglects to make automatic discovery) a party may apply to the court for an order. When automatic discovery applies the parties must within 28 days of service of the defence serve on each other a form listing (in schedule 1 of the form) all relevant documents which they have or formerly had (schedule 2), saying where the latter have gone to. The documents they must disclose are those relating to a matter in question: meaning documents that would help the case of the party on whom the list is served, or harm his adversary's, or might fairly lead to a train of inquiry which would have one of these consequences (*Compagnie Financiere et Commercial du Pacifique v Peruvian Guano Co 1882*), but they do not have to be used in that party's evidence and may even not be admissible in evidence.

Schedule 1 of the list is further divided into two parts: the second part contains documents which the party refuses to produce for inspection on the grounds of **privilege** (eg, advice on the case from a solicitor, or a letter admitting to a criminal offence, or secret Government files).

The list must state a time and place within seven days where the documents in schedule 1, part 1 may be inspected and photocopied; the court may vary this if it is unreasonable. If a party fails to serve a list, or serves a defective one, or claims privilege for a document which is not or may not be privileged, or fails to disclose particular relevant documents, or fails to allow inspection, the other side must apply to the Master for an order for disclosure and/or production for inspection; discovery being discretionary. However, the order will only be made if it is necessary to dispose fairly of the case or to save costs. The purpose of discovery is to assist the parties to prepare their cases and to ensure a fair trial; consequently any use of the documents or copies of them for other purposes is a contempt of court (*Distillers Co (Biochemicals) Limited v Times Newspapers Limited 1974*) and punishable as such, and any action founded on such a document will be struck out as an abuse of process (*Riddick v Thames Board Mills Limited 1977*). Failure to comply with an order for discovery or production is also a contempt, and in addition the court may give judgment against the recalcitrant party or order his action to be struck out.

Interrogatories and notices to admit

A party may apply to a Master for an order requiring another party to answer questions relating to the subject matter of the action. As with discovery of documents, this will only be ordered if it is necessary to dispose fairly of the case or to save costs, and in addition the Master must take into account any offer by the other party to furnish the facts required by producing documents or making admissions or giving particulars. If the order is made, the questions (called 'interrogatories') are served on the other party who must answer them on affidavit, so that failure to give true answers is perjury. The affidavit may be used in evidence at the trial. Interrogatories are rare and are normally ordered only when a party has peculiar knowledge of certain facts of which there is no documentary evidence.

A party may serve on his opponent a **notice to admit facts**, requiring him to admit facts stated in the notice. If he does so, the admission thus obtained may be given in evidence. If he does not, the court will not order him to do so but if the facts are proved at the trial the court will normally order that he pays the costs of proving them.

A party may also serve a **notice to admit the authenticity of documents**; if the admission is made then authenticity does not have to be proved at the trial. However, where there is automatic discovery the parties are deemed to admit the authenticity of documents in their lists; if they wish to dispute this they must give **notice of non-admission** requiring authenticity to be proved at the trial.

Discovery of documents and facts from non-parties

Generally only a party can be compelled to disclose documents or answer questions or to allow inspection. To this there are three exceptions:

(a)   Since 1970, the rules have permitted someone who is likely to be a party to proceedings arising from personal injuries or death to obtain discovery of documents from a likely defendant by applying to the court for an order. Similarly when the action has begun any person may be ordered to give discovery to a party. The documents must be relevant and be in the possession, custody, or power of the non-party, and since an order is needed discovery must be necessary. The non-party is entitled to claim privilege as if he were a party.

(b)   Since 1969, it has similarly been possible to apply for an order for the inspection, preservation, or detention of property likely to be the subject matter of an action or relevant to an action, and the same remedy is available once the action has commenced against non-parties as well as parties.

(c)   In 1973 the House of Lords in *Norwich Pharmacol Co v Customs & Excise Commissioners* that where a person innocently got involved with the wrongful acts of another so as to facilitate the other's wrongdoing, that person had a duty to disclose the identity of the wrongdoer to the person aggrieved. In that case the defendants were ordered to disclose the identity of importers who were infringing the plaintiffs' patent in this country. This remedy is equitable and so discretionary; in particular it will be refused if compliance with it would expose the defendant to a criminal charge (*Rank Film Distributors Limited v Video Information Centre, 1981*).

2.4.5   Regulating the parties' rights pending trial

Since a High Court action may take 18 months or more between writ and judgment, it is often necessary for the court to make orders to deal with the parties: property and other rights connected with the action pending the trial. The most important such orders are as follows:

An **interlocutory injunction** may be obtained ordering the defendant to refrain from doing some particular act, pending the trial when it will be determined whether a final injunction to the same effect should be granted. (Rarely, an injunction may require an act to be performed.) Application is made in the Queen's Bench Division by **summons** to a judge sitting 'in chambers' (in private), or in the Chancery Division by **motion** in open court, depending on whether publicity is sought.

The summons or notice of motion is accompanied by an affidavit giving details of the plaintiff's case, and the defendant may file an affidavit in reply. In emergencies, an application may be made for a temporary injunction lasting a few days. Such an application may be made *ex parte*: this means the other side is not informed of the hearing. Since the only evidence the judge has is the unsupported assertions of the parties in their affidavits, the judge should not try to adjudicate on the merits of the case but should grant or refuse the injunction according to the 'balance of convenience', ie, which party will, if at the trial the decision at the interlocutory stage turns out to have been wrong, suffer the greater loss for which he cannot be compensated in money terms (*American Cynamid Co v Ethicon Limited, 1975*). For this reason whenever an interlocutory injunction is granted the plaintiff is required to undertake to compensate the defendant in damages, should it turn out the injunction should not have been granted. But since very often the interlocutory stage settles the matter and the action never goes to trial, it is often proper to take into account the strength of the parties' cases as part of the balance of convenience, eg, where industrial disputes are involved (*NWL Limited v Woods, 1979*).

A so-called **Mareva injunction** (named after a case in which such an order was made in 1975), a special form of interlocutory injunction, may be granted restraining the defendant from removing property from the jurisdiction of the High Court (ie, England and Wales). The purpose of the order is to prevent the defendant from stultifying any judgment for money which the plaintiff would get if he succeeded at trial, by removing property out of which the judgment could be satisfied. The defendant need not himself be foreign, provided he is likely to take his property out of the country.

The court has wide powers to order the **detention and preservation of property** which is or relates to the subject matter of the action, and also to order a party be allowed to inspect such property which is in the other party's possession. If it is feared the possessor may interfere with or destroy the property, eg, in order to get rid of material damaging to his case, the court may make an order *ex parte* so that he is taken by surprise. If, however, the order would expose him to criminal, rather than civil, liability, it will not be made (*Rank Film Distributors Limited v Video Information Centre, 1981*).

Because of the delay in coming to trial a plaintiff may be almost certain to obtain a substantial award of damages at the trial but be suffering financial hardship meanwhile. Accordingly the court has power to order the defendant to make **interim payments** to the plaintiff if either (1) the defendant has admitted liability (but is disputing the amount of damages) or (2) the defendant has been judged to be liable (but the award of damages has yet to be determined) or (3) it appears that if the case were tried the plaintiff would get substantial damages. Interim payments were formerly only made in personal injury cases, but are now available in all types of action.

2.4.6   Summons for directions

Within 14 days of discovery the plaintiff must issue a summons requiring the defendant to attend before a Master who will give directions about the conduct of the case. The directions he may give are wide-ranging and include most of the orders mentioned above. In addition he may make orders:

(a)   to transfer the action to the County Court (if within its jurisdiction);

(b)   to order the plaintiff to give security for costs, ie, pay money into court to ensure that if he loses then the defendant will get his costs paid;

(c)   to admit *affidavit* or hearsay evidence;

(d)   to order the evidence of a witness who cannot attend the trial to be taken on examination;

(e)   to limit the number of expert witnesses and require the parties to disclose to each other the substance of their expert evidence;

(f)   to fix the mode (with or without a jury) and place of trial and the day when the action is to be set down for trial, ie, when the writ and pleadings are to be lodged with the court and the case entered on the list.

In practice such orders are usually made on separate applications by the parties and the summons for directions is a formality in which the Master simply fixes the mode and place of trial (typically by a judge alone in London) and the time for setting down (typically 42 days after inspection of documents).

2.4.7   Striking out actions and pleadings

Striking out for want of prosecution. Sometimes a plaintiff, through his own or his solicitors' negligence, or as a delaying tactic, fails persistently to keep to the timetable laid down by the rules or indeed to comply with orders of the Master. If this happens, eg, he fails to take out a summons for directions, or to set the action down for trial, the defendant can apply for an order that the action be struck out. The order will be made if the plaintiff's delay has been inexcusable and prejudices the fair trial of the action (because witnesses' memories have faded, etc). However, an order of this kind will not normally be made until the limitation period has expired, because the plaintiff could always bring another action for the same claim (*Birkett v James, 1977*). There is a similar power to give judgment for the plaintiff if the defendant is in default, eg, of serving a defence; and compare the powers that exist for default in discovery.

Striking out pleadings may be ordered if a pleading discloses no reasonable cause of action or defence, or is 'scandalous, frivolous, or vexatious', or will prejudice the fair trial of the action, or is otherwise an abuse of the process of the court. If a pleading is struck out and no satisfactory replacement served, the action itself could be struck out.

2.4.8   The trial and its consequences

Procedure at the trial

In civil actions, trial by jury is now practically confined to libel cases and it is trial by judge alone that is considered here. When the case comes on the judge will have before him only the pleadings and (sometimes) an agreed bundle of documents which he will not have had time to read, so the facts and the issues must be explained clearly in the opening speech.

The **opening speech** is given by counsel for the plaintiff unless the burden of proof on all issues is on the defendant. He must:

(a)   explain the nature of the case, often going through the facts in chronological order;
(b)   go through the pleadings; and
(c)   go through relevant documents in the bundle.

Sometimes, in a difficult case, he may outline his legal arguments at this stage.

This is followed by **the case for the plaintiff** in which he presents his evidence, which may be:

(a)   *Oral evidence on oath of witnesses.* After being sworn a witness is **examined in chief** by counsel for the plaintiff, who will ask questions designed to elicit answers favourable to his case; he may not, however, ask leading questions or contradict the witness by referring to a previous statement of his inconsistent with what he now says. Counsel for the defence may **cross-examine** a witness to try to discredit the evidence given in chief or elicit answers favourable to his case, and he may contradict the witness and ask leading questions. Finally counsel for the plaintiff may **re-examine** the witness on matters which have arisen during cross-examination.

(b)   *Documentary evidence.* This may be in the agreed bundle of documents or be produced by a witness in the course of giving evidence. It is generally necessary to produce the original of a document, but a copy may be used if the original has been destroyed or lost, or production is otherwise impossible; also if one party has disclosed a document in his list on discovery, he must produce it if called on to do so by the other, and if he does not a copy may be produced.

(c)   Depositions taken on examination and affidavits are read to the court.

It is in theory possible when the plaintiff has closed his case for the defendant to submit that there is **no case to answer**, on the same grounds *mutatis mutandis* as in a criminal case (see below). But since it is the practice for the judge to refuse the rule on such a submission unless the defendant agrees not to call evidence if he loses it, this is hardly ever done.

The defence has a right to open his case if he is calling evidence. The procedure for examining witnesses is exactly the same as with the plaintiff's evidence.

Closing speeches. The defendant's counsel addresses the judge first, and if the judge has decided to find for the plaintiff, counsel for the latter will not be called on to reply. Argument on points of law is generally confined to the closing speeches, since such points depend on the facts of the case which will only be fully before the court when the evidence has been heard.

The judge will then give a reasoned judgment setting out his findings of fact from the evidence; if he is in doubt on any issue he must find against the party bearing the burden of proof (see below). He will deal with all legal points which could be relevant in an appeal, and announce his decision on all relevant issues, eg, if in an action for damages he rules that the defendant is not liable, he will normally still decide what damages the plaintiff would have received if he had decided the other way, because the Court of Appeal might decide the defendant was liable, whereupon damages would have to be paid.

Costs

Once the judge has given judgment, counsel for both sides (the successful side first) make submissions on costs, ie, the expense incurred by reason of the action taking place. The question of costs is entirely in the discretion of the judge, and his decision on costs will only be interfered with on appeal if his discretion has been wrongly exercised, not merely because his decision was not one which the Court of Appeal would have made. Nonetheless there are some rules that are generally followed by the court. The general principle is 'costs follow the event': the successful party has the costs he has incurred paid by the unsuccessful one. The principal exceptions to this are as follows:

(a)   If the defendant makes a **payment into court** ie, a formal offer to settle the action if the plaintiff accepts a sum of money which is paid into the court office, and the plaintiff does not accept it, and on judgment the plaintiff is awarded damages equal to or less than the payment in, the defendant will generally be awarded his costs incurred since the date of payment in.

(b)   If any application at the interlocutory stage (pending the trial) was unnecessary, or conversely made necessary only by the default of the other side, the party at fault will generally be ordered to pay the costs of it **in any event**, even if he wins the action. Usually the costs of interlocutory matters are ordered to be **costs in cause**, to form part of the whole costs of the action.

(c)   If a successful plaintiff recovers less than £600 he will generally be given no costs at all, ie, there will be **no order as to costs** but either side will be left to pay the costs they have incurred. If he recovers less than £3,000 but £600 or more he will be awarded costs only on the County Court scale, which will leave him substantially out of pocket.

(d)   The Legal Aid Act 1988 contains specific provisions limiting costs against assisted persons: S17; and dealing with the question of the costs of successful unassisted parties in proceedings with assisted parties: S18.

It should be noted that even a successful party who comes within none of these exceptions will not recoup from the loser all the expense he has incurred. This is because the costs are **taxed** (that is, examined by a master) and only those costs which were necessary for the conduct of the action will be allowed. Unfortunately, during litigation a party often incurs costs preparing to prove matters which the opponent eventually admits without dispute Similarly other costs are incurred which strictly were not necessary to fight the action, and these will not be recovered from the losing party since it is not fair that he should have to pay for the 'luxuries of litigation'.

Execution

The enforcement of a judgment is known as **executing** the judgment. This section is primarily concerned with the enforcement of money judgments, for which there is the greatest variety of methods of execution.

Writ of fieri facias ('that you cause to be made'). This writ authorises the sheriff of the country where the judgment debtor (the person ordered to pay money by the judgment) lives to send his bailiffs to seize and sell the debtor's personal property and pay the judgment debt and the cost of execution out of the proceeds. The moment judgment has been recorded the creditor can obtain the writ from the court office by producing a copy of the judgment with a formal request for the writ. The writ is then sealed and delivered to the under-sheriff of the debtor's county, or the county where the property is which is to be seized. There are a number of difficulties which make this a less efficient method of execution than it might seem:

(a)   The debtor can always apply for execution to be stayed, in which case leave of the court is needed for the issue of the writ; and this will be done generally on condition that the debt is paid by instalments.

(b)   Even if execution is not stayed there may be insufficient property to satisfy the judgment debt; even if the debtor has a car it may in fact be being bought on hire-purchase. Also certain property is exempt from seizure; including wearing apparel and bedding to a value of £100, and tools and implements of the debtor's trade to £150.

(c)   There may be dispute about who owns the property; such a dispute can be resolved by a summons to the court, but this will add to expense and delay.

Garnishee order. This can be made where there exists a debt due to the judgment debtor; the person owing the debt ('garnishee') is ordered to pay it direct to the creditor to satisfy the judgment debt and the costs incurred in obtaining the order. The procedure is as follows:

(a)   The creditor applies *ex parte* (so that the debtor and garnishee are ignorant of the application) for an order forbidding the garnishee to pay the debt and requiring him and the debtor to attend before the master to show why the order should not be made absolute (this order is called a **garnishee order nisi**).

(b)   If on the face of it there appears to be a debt owing, the order nisi is drawn up and served on the debtor and garnishee at least seven days before the hearing.

(c)   At the hearing the order will be made absolute unless it can be shown there is no debt owing or that the claims of other persons would be prejudiced (eg, if the debtor were about to go bankrupt and his creditors would lose out), and it will order the garnishee to pay the money to the judgment creditor. This method is most frequently used against money in the judgment debtor's bank account.

Charging order on land or securities. By this procedure the creditor is given a charge on the debtor's land (or securities, but these will not be considered here) which places him in the same position as a mortgagee of the land. The debtor will thus be inhibited from dealing with the land, which will induce him to pay the debt, and the creditor can in any event apply for the land to be sold. The procedure for getting the order is similar to garnishee proceedings, with orders nisi and absolute. Since the creditor is secured once the order is made, the fact that the debtor is about to go bankrupt may inhibit the court from granting the order in such a case.

Attachment of earnings order. This may be obtained when the debtor is in employment and has defaulted in one or more instalments under a judgment ordered so to be paid. For administrative convenience the creditor applies to the debtor's local County Court, even when the judgment was a High Court one. The application is sent to the debtor with a questionnaire requiring him to give details of his means and to attend for a hearing before the County Court registrar. At the hearing the registrar, if he makes the order, must specify the rate at which deductions are to be made from his earnings to satisfy the judgment debt, and also a level of 'protected earnings' from which no deduction may be made. The employer is then ordered to make the appropriate deductions, on pain of a fine, until the debt is paid off or the employment ceases.

Bankruptcy, and **winding up a company**, may also be used as methods of execution. In both cases the debtor is served with a notice requiring him to pay the debt, and if he does not do so a petition is issued followed by an inquiry or hearing as the case may be. The effect in either case is that the assets of the bankrupt or company are distributed among his or its creditors, so that normally the creditor will not ever be paid in full. These methods are therefore most often merely threatened to induce the debtor to pay up.

There are a number of ways of enforcing a judgment other than for money, eg:

(a)   A judgment for the possession of land is enforced by a **writ of possession** authorising the sheriff's officers to enter on the land and dispossess the occupier.

(b)   A judgment for the delivery of goods wrongly held by someone is enforced by a **writ of specific delivery**, for which the leave of the court is needed.

(c)   A judgment or order requiring a person to do an act within a specified time, or to restrain someone from doing an act (eg, a **Mareva** injunction, or indeed any injunction) is enforced by committing him to prison for contempt if he fails to obey the order: this is usually for a specific period such as 14 days. In the case of a body corporate such as a limited company the method of enforcement is by sequestrating its assets so that it cannot deal with them. Either imprisonment or sequestration may be replaced by a fine.

2.4.9   Procedure in the County Court

Issue and service of the summons

An ordinary action is commenced by the filing in the court office of a request for the summons setting out the names, addresses and descriptions of all the parties and the nature and amount of the claim. Particulars of claim and the sum claimed with a copy for each defendant must also be filed. When these documents have been filed the registrar of the court issues to the plaintiff a plaint note containing the title of the action, the reference number of the plaint and a date and time for the return day. He also prepares, from the plaintiff's request, and issues a summons to which are annexed the particulars of the claim. The summons and particulars are then served on every defendant at least 21 clear days before the return day. The defendant is also served with forms of admission, defence and counterclaim.

Usually the summons is served by the county court bailiff, though there are other methods of service.

Defence

Service of the summons opens to the defendant the following courses of action:

(a)   He may, within 14 days of service, pay into court, the whole or any part of the claim together with costs on a fixed scale;

(b)   The defendant may admit the whole or any part of the claim but express his desire for time to pay;

(c)   If the defendant denies liability or wishes to plead a set-off or counter-claim he must within fourteen days, file the forms of defence and counterclaim if appropriate. Copies of these will be served upon the plaintiff by the registrar;

(d)   The defendant may appear on the return day without having filed a defence and dispute the plaintiff's claim.

Pre-trial review

In the case of an ordinary action the return day on the summons will be, unless the court otherwise directs, a day fixed for the preliminary consideration of the action by the registrar, known as a 'pre-trial review'. The function of the registrar at this review is to consider the course of the proceedings and give all such directions as appear to him necessary or desirable for securing the just, expeditious and economical disposal of the action. The action may be disposed of at this review, or it may be settled prior to trial or it may simply be discontinued.

Trial

If the plaintiff does not appear on the day fixed for the trial then when the case is called the action will be struck out and he will have to apply to have it reinstated at another time. If the defendant does not appear the trial may proceed in his absence and judgment may be entered against him. The exact mode of trial, whether it be before the registrar, the judge or the judge and jury depends on the amount claimed and the nature of the action involved. The conduct of the trial is similar to that in the High Court.

If the defendant admits the plaintiff's claim or does not appear judgment will be entered for the plaintiff. Where this judgment is for the payment of money the court may order the sum to be paid forthwith or within a specified time, or may order payment by fixed instalments.

If the plaintiff does not succeed in proving his case the court may either give judgment for the defendant or non-suit the plaintiff. The latter course of action is not an affirmative decision against the plaintiff and he may therefore bring a subsequent action on the same facts.

Execution and enforcement of judgment

Execution and enforcement of the judgment rests with the plaintiff.

2.5   Criminal procedure

2.5.1   Arrest and bail

A private person or a police officer may arrest without warrant any person who he reasonably suspects to be, or who is, committing an arrestable offence, or who is committing a breach of the peace. A police officer may arrest without warrant anyone who he reasonably believes has committed or is about to commit such an offence; a private person only if such an offence has been committed. Any other arrest without warrant is unlawful and whoever makes an unlawful arrest is liable both criminally and to an action for damages. A magistrate (justice of the peace) may by warrant authorise any officer to arrest someone, though he will be liable to be sued if the person arrested is acquitted and the magistrate had acted without jurisdiction, or maliciously and without reasonable cause. An arrestable offence is essentially one for which the sentence is fixed by law (treason or murder) or for which the maximum sentence is five years' imprisonment or more (such as theft, rape, criminal damage, arson, assaults causing actual bodily harm - most offences of any degree of seriousness). The person arrested must be told the specific reason for his arrest and any warrant must name the offence for which he is to be arrested.

The person arrested must be taken to a police station designated for the detention of arrested persons and his detention therein must be strictly in accordance with the provisions of Part IV of the Police and Criminal Evidence Act 1984 and any codes of practice issued thereunder. This Act also establishes rules governing the questioning and treatment of persons by the police. 'On bail' means that he is under a duty to attend court at a particular time. When he is brought before a court (a Magistrates' Court) he will be remanded either on bail or in custody pending the trial of his case. He cannot be remanded in custody for more than eight days, at the end of which his case must again be considered by the court. The court may impose conditions for the grant of bail to ensure that he does not abscond, commit offences while on bail, or interfere with witnesses; for example he may be required to report daily to a police station, or keep away from a particular area. If he fails to comply with these conditions he may be arrested, and if he fails to attend court at the stated time without reasonable cause he is guilty of an offence.

The magistrates may refuse to grant bail to an accused on the same grounds as they may impose conditions; so they may refuse it because the offence is a serious one (and so he has an incentive to abscond), or has numerous previous convictions for the same offence (and so is likely to commit more offences). They may also refuse bail if they think he should be kept in custody for his own protection. He can also be required, as a condition of being released on bail, to produce a **surety** - someone who will forfeit a fixed sum of money if the accused fails to turn up at court. If bail is refused, an appeal can be made to a High Court judge sitting in chambers.

As described earlier, a criminal offence may be tried either in a Magistrates' Court (summarily) or in a Crown Court (on indictment).

2.5.2   Summary trial

Proceedings commence by the laying of an information or the making of a complaint, whereupon the justices issue a summons requiring the person to attend before them. If after proof of service the accused fails to appear, the justices may, on the complaint or information being supported on oath, issue a warrant to arrest the accused or hear the matter ex parte. The hearing must be in an open and public court to which the public have access, and the first step is for the Clerk of the court to read out the offence with which the accused is charged. If the offence is one triable either summarily or on indictment, the accused is given the option of electing to be tried by jury, and if he does not so elect, the case proceeds as a summary trial.

The accused is next called upon to plead guilty or not guilty, and on the latter plea, the prosecution opens its case and calls witnesses who may be cross-examined. When the case for the prosecution is closed, the accused may submit that there is no case to answer, and if this is not accepted by the court the accused proceeds to state his case.

On hearing both sides the court considers whether to dismiss the case or convict and in the latter case enquires into the accused's previous record and hears him in mitigation. It will then decide upon sentence.

2.5.3   Trial on indictment

Indictment and joining offences and offenders

An indictment contains one or more **counts**, each of which must charge a single offence, and each of which has a **statement of offence**, eg, 'Theft contrary to section 1 of the Theft Act 1968', or in the case of a common law offence, simply 'Murder'; and also **particulars of offence**, eg, 'John Doe on 25 December 1980 in the City of London stole an umbrella, the property of Richard Roe'. Two or more defendants may be charged in a single count, but only of one offence. Several counts may be included in a single indictment, so that they will be tried together, provided that the charges are founded on the same facts, or form or are part of a series of offences of the same or similar character (Indictment Rules 1971). Even so, the court may **sever** an indictment with many charges and have the counts tried separately if it thinks the accused is prejudiced or embarrassed by the joinder, but in practice it will usually do so only if the evidence on one or more of the charges is scandalous or the trial would become intolerably complicated and the jury confused (*R v Novac, 1976*).

Similar principles apply to charging several defendants in a single count or indictment. They may be joined if they have jointly committed the same offence, or their offences are so linked that they ought in the interests of justice to be tried together (eg, where the offences are part of a general conspiracy and the real nature of the offences will be disclosed only if they are tried together). The judge has a discretion to order defendants indicted together to be tried separately if he thinks they would be prejudiced by a joint trial, such as if one defendant had made a statement implicating the other, but the discretion is infrequently exercised because the judge will usually trust in his summing-up to the jury to remedy any prejudicial effect.

If the indictment is defective, ie, it discloses no offence known to the law, or the court has no jurisdiction to try the offence (eg, it was committed in Scotland), or a count is bad for **duplicity** (it charges more than one offence), the defence may **move to quash** the indictment. However, the court will normally not quash but merely amend unless this cannot be done without injustice.

2.5.4   Arraignment and pleas

When the day comes when the accused is to stand trial, he must attend in person or he is liable to arrest and he may be punished for a criminal contempt of court. He will be brought into the dock and the clerk of the court will address him by name, read out the charges in indictment and ask him in relation to each count whether he pleads guilty or not guilty to it. This is the **arraignment**, when the accused is formally told what are the issues joined between the Crown and himself which have to be tried. He must then plead, and the following pleas are open to him:

(a)   *Guilty of the offence charged*. This plea must be made orally by the accused. There is now no issue between the Crown and the accused, and the court proceeds directly to sentence.

(b)   *Guilty of another offence not charged in the indictment*. This may be done when the allegations in the indictment amount to or include (expressly or by implication) an allegation of another offence which is within the court's jurisdiction (ie, not an offence triable only summarily). So if charged with murder he could (usually) plead guilty to manslaughter, or when charged with robbery, guilty of theft. However, this plea must be accepted by the court, which the judge may refuse to do, so that he has to stand trial on the greater charge in the indictment (as in *R v Sutcliffe, 1981*). In those circumstances, if he is found not guilty of the greater charge then he cannot be sentenced for the lesser offence, despite his rejected plea of guilty to it. If the plea is accepted the court proceeds directly to sentence.

(c)   *Any of the special pleas in bar*. These are legal objections to being tried. They are rarely pleaded but the most important is that another court has already judged whether he is guilty or not guilty of the offence now being tried and he may not be tried twice for the same or substantially the same offence. The effect of a successful plea in bar is the same as an acquittal.

(d)   *The accused may stand silent*. If this happens a jury must be sworn to try the preliminary issue of whether he is **mute of malice**, ie, deliberately refusing to plead.

The burden is on the prosecution to prove beyond all reasonable doubt that he is mute of malice, and the issue is tried in exactly the same way as a trial of an indicted crime, with witnesses, examination by counsel, etc. If the jury finds he is mute of malice then a plea of not guilty to the indictment will be entered by the court, and the indictment itself will be tried by a new jury, to avoid prejudice. If it finds his silence is due to some physical cause (he is **mute by visitation of God**) the jury will have to determine whether he is **fit to plead**. The question of fitness to plead may be raised even if the accused makes a plea. It may be raised by either side at any time during the trial up to the end of the prosecution's case. The issue of fitness is tried in the normal way, and if he is found unfit to plead the judge must commit him to a mental hospital until such time, if ever, as he recovers. For this reason it is the usual practice to postpone trial of the issue until the close of the prosecution case, so that the defence can submit there is no case to answer, because if that submission is accepted then the accused will be acquitted. If the jury finds him fit to plead he is presumably dumb and he will have to plead through an interpreter.

(e)   *He pleads not guilty.* This puts the burden on the Crown to prove the allegations on the indictment beyond all reasonable doubt and a jury must be sworn to try this, the general issue.

2.5.5   The jury

When a jury is required to be sworn, a panel of more than 12 jurors comes into court. The defence is told it has a right to challenge the jurors, and then the names of the jurors, selected by drawing lots, are read out as they come to be sworn. Before each is sworn, the accused or his counsel may challenge the juror. Three jurors may be challenged without giving any reason ('peremptory challenge') and the juror thus challenged must leave the box and be replaced by another person from the panel. After three challenges a reason must be given ('challenge for cause'): this might be that the juror is biased (has been known to assert the accused is guilty, for example) or might be biased (a challenge 'for favour', eg, that he is a relative of the victim of the crime). The prosecution also has the right to challenge for cause, but not to make a peremptory challenge; but it may instead ask a juror to **stand by**, ie, be excluded unless a complete jury cannot be made from the panel, and since the prosecution is in a better position to know a juror's background than the defence (it can use police records to vet them), this right is perhaps more useful to it than the defence right to peremptory challenge. Either side can also **challenge the array**, ie, the whole panel, on the grounds that the officer responsible for summoning the jurors is biased or has acted improperly, but this is now unknown. The jurors may not normally be questioned before being challenged. If after the challenges there are not enough in the panel to form a complete jury of 12, qualified persons in the vicinity of the court may be called on to serve (this is called 'praying a tales').

Once the jury has been sworn to try the issues between the Crown and the defendant faithfully and to give a true verdict according to the evidence, the clerk reads the indictment to the jury, tells them the accused has pleaded not guilty to the counts in it, and says that it is their charge, having heard the evidence, to say whether he be guilty or not guilty.

2.5.6   Trial of the general issue

When the accused has been put in charge of the jury, counsel for the prosecution begins his opening speech. His task is not quite the same as that of the plaintiff's advocate in a civil case, because he is addressing a jury of laymen as well as the judge. He must explain that the burden is on him to prove the accused is guilty beyond all reasonable doubt, he must explain to them what the elements of the offence charged are, and he must show how the facts he is alleging amount to that offence. He is not to try to obtain a conviction by all means, but to put before the jury the facts which compose his case, and to see that the jury can apply the law to them. So, for example, if he has a statement from a witness which is favourable to the accused's case, he should show it to the defence, and if the defence says it intends to dispute the admissibility of certain evidence, he should not mention it in his opening speech.

The prosecution then calls its evidence. All those whose statements or depositions were tendered at the committal proceedings should be called, unless they were only conditionally bound and no notice has been served requiring their attendance. They can tender evidence not tendered at the committal, provided they give notice to the defence.

The same rules apply to the examination of witnesses as in a civil case (see above). If there is a dispute over the admissibility of any evidence, eg, a confession which the defence argues was not voluntary, counsel for the prosecution should indicate this to the judge, who will usually send the jury out of court so that they do not hear the evidence in dispute. The point is then argued before the judge, and evidence heard on the issue if necessary; the judge rules whether the evidence may be admitted, and if he rules that it may not the jury are let back into court unaware of its existence.

Counsel for the defence will cross-examine the prosecution witnesses and must put to them every point in which the defence case differs from that of the Crown. His duty is to do everything he can properly do to secure an acquittal, though he must avoid deceiving the court. In cross-examination he may use the statements and depositions made at the committal to show inconsistency.

At the end of the prosecution case the defence may submit to the judge that there is no case to answer. The ground for this submission may be either that the prosecution has failed to prove an essential element of the offence or that the prosecution evidence is so weak, or has been so discredited in cross-examination, that no reasonable jury could convict on it.

If the judge accepts the submission then he must withdraw the case from the jury and direct them to acquit the defendant. (In principle, the jury may decide at any time after the close of the prosecution's case that they will acquit the defendant without hearing any more of his case.)

If the judge rules there is a case to answer, the defence case is heard. Provided counsel for the defence is calling witnesses as to the facts other than the accused (ie, not merely character witnesses) he may make an opening speech. He then calls his evidence: if the accused gives evidence he must do so first. He has, however, the right to remain silent or to make an **unsworn statement** from the dock, which although it is not evidence may be taken into account by the jury. The prosecution may not comment on failure by the accused to give evidence, and although the judge may, he may not suggest that it is capable of being evidence of guilt (*R v Bathurst, 1968*).

At the end of the defence case, counsel for the prosecution , and then counsel for the defence, address the jury. Occasionally, if evidence is adduced during the defence case which raises an issue that the prosecution could not have foreseen, the prosecution will be allowed at this stage to call evidence in rebuttal. But the defence always has the final word.

2.5.7 Summing up

The judge must now explain to the jury its function, the law relating to the case, and the issues between the two sides. Accordingly he must:

(a)   explain that they must accept the law from him but they are the sole judges of fact and they may disregard any comment he makes about the facts;

(b)   remind them that it is the duty of the prosecution to prove its case beyond all reasonable doubt, and do so throughout his review of the evidence;

(c)   when there is more than one accused, require the jury to consider the case of each separately and, in particular, direct the jury where a piece of evidence is evidence against only one accused. Similarly when one accused faces several charges;

(d)   warn the jury of the danger of convicting on the evidence of certain witnesses (eg, accomplices) without corroboration. A similar warning is necessary when the prosecution case depends largely on identification evidence;

(e)   review fairly the evidence called by both sides and explain how it relates to the elements of the offence charged, and in particular deal with every point raised by the defence;

(f)   tell the jury that it must try to reach a unanimous verdict and that the time has not yet come when he will accept a majority verdict.

At the conclusion of the summing up the jury retires to the jury room under the supervision of the jury bailiff. It is not normally allowed to separate until it has reached its verdict, and if during retirement a juror is found outside the jury room it may be a ground for quashing the conviction on appeal. On the other hand, proceedings in the jury room are completely secret and the Court of Appeal will not even hear evidence that, say, four of the jurors disagreed with a purportedly unanimous verdict (*R v Roads, 1967*).

2.5.8   Verdict

The jury's verdict must be unanimous in the first place, but since 1967 it has been possible to accept a majority verdict provided that:

(a)   the jury has had two hours for deliberation (in practice 10 minutes extra is allowed), or such longer period as the judge thinks fit having regard to the nature and complexity of the case; and

(b)   at least 10 of the jurors (nine if, through the discharge of two jurors, the number has fallen to 10) are in agreement on the verdict.

When the judge decides he is willing to accept a majority verdict, he recalls the jury and directs them to try to reach one. When they return to court, the clerk asks them whether they have reached a verdict on which at least 10 of them are agreed, and if they say yes and it is not guilty the accused is acquitted with nothing further said, so that is it not known whether the acquittal was by a majority. But if it is guilty the clerk must find out how many were in agreement with the verdict or it is a nullity. It is also a nullity if a majority verdict is accepted before the two hours are up, or indeed if the judge puts pressure on the jury to reach a speedy verdict. These rules are permissive only: the judge is never bound to accept a majority verdict and may, if the jury cannot agree, discharge them and have a new trial before a new jury. He will have to do this anyway if not even 10 agree. If a second jury cannot agree an accused is in practice not tried again.

The verdicts a jury may return are guilty, not guilty, or guilty of some offence not charged in the indictment but to which the accused could have so pleaded. They may also return a special verdict stating particular facts which they have found, but this is now done only when they find the accused is insane, when the verdict is 'not guilty by reason of insanity'.

2.5.9   Sentence

When an accused person has been acquitted it is like a defendant being found not liable in a civil action: all that remains to be decided is the question of costs. In the Crown Court these are normally ordered to be paid out of central funds, unless the prosecution has acted maliciously, in which case it pays, or the defendant has brought suspicion on himself or been acquitted on a technicality, when he will be left to pay his own costs.

When he has been convicted of the offence charged or of some other offence, the court must proceed to sentence him for that offence. The sentences which may be imposed are numerous and the provisions concerning them, especially with regard to offenders under 21, extremely complex. It is here proposed to deal with the procedure for determining sentence and then to consider very briefly the possible orders that can be made.

If the offender was convicted on his own plea of guilty, the prosecution must outline the facts of the offence. If the defence admits guilt but disputes the prosecution's account of the facts, the judge will have to determine where the truth lies from the depositions and statements and the offender's character; only in rare cases does he hear evidence on the issue.

When this has been done, or, where there has been a trial, immediately after the jury has returned its verdict, the prosecution gives evidence of the defendant's character and previous convictions. If he is alleged to be in breach of a probation order or conditional discharge or suspended sentence, this must be put to him and if he denies it then it must be proved.

The defendant may ask the court to take into consideration, in deciding on sentence, other offences he has committed but not been tried for. The court will normally agree to do so; the resulting sentence may be more severe than it would have been but it cannot be for more than the maximum for the offence on the indictment. In practice the offences taken into consideration are not subsequently prosecuted.

In most cases a social enquiry report is made available to the court. It is prepared by a social worker and its purpose is to indicate factors in the defendant's circumstances which may have led to the offence and his likely response to various sentences. Other reports may be received by the court.

The defendant or his counsel is always allowed to plead in mitigation immediately before sentence. The purpose of the plea is to show any circumstances of the offence or of the offender which would justify leniency: eg, the offence was impulsive, the offender played a minor role in it, he showed contrition by making restitution to his victim, this was his first offence.

The judge proceeds to sentence the offender. There are a number of factors which may play a part in his decision: punishing the offender in proportion to his desert, protecting the public from dangerous and anti-social offenders, reforming the offender's behaviour, and deterring people from committing similar crimes. An individual over the age of 21 who is convicted of murder must be sentenced to imprisonment for life (Murder (Abolition of Death Penalty) Act 1965, S1) unless he was under 18 at the time the offence was committed, in which case he must be sentenced to be detained during her Majesty's pleasure. The following are the chief sentences a judge can impose on other offenders aged 21 or over:

(a)   **Imprisonment** up to a maximum term fixed for the offence by statute; if there is no statutory maximum then imprisonment may be for any length provided it is not inordinate.   In fact the usual sentence passed in the absence of unusually serious features is much less than the maximum (this is called the 'Tariff'). Typical maxima are: manslaughter, rape, wounding with intent - life; burglary - 14 years; theft, criminal damage - 10 years; wounding, assault - five years. An offender who has not been sent to prison before should be sentenced to imprisonment only if no other way of dealing with him is appropriate.

The time that an offender has spent in prison before being sentenced is counted as a part service of any term of imprisonment imposed as a sentence, unless he was in a prison serving a sentence imposed for a previous conviction.

Variations on such, in the form of attendance centre orders, detention centre orders and youth custody, are available in respect of young offenders.

(b)   A sentence of imprisonment for a term of not more than two years may be **suspended** for between one and two years.   This means that the offender does not serve the sentence unless he is convicted of another crime within the suspension period and the court which convicts him of that second crime orders him to serve the sentence imposed for the first.   The second court may decide not to activate the sentence if, for example, the second crime is trivial.

It is possible (if the offender is over 21) to suspend only part of a prison sentence (between 28 days and three-quarters of the term of the sentence) and require the rest to be served immediately.

(c)   A **probation order** may be made and requirements of residence or treatment attached to it, with the offender's consent.   It will mean he is under the supervision of a probation officer for up to three years.   If he breaks a requirement of the order or commits a further offence he is liable to a fine or sentence for the original offence.

(d)   A **community service order** requiring him to do unpaid work for the community may be made with his consent. Similar rules about breach apply as for a probation order.

(e)   He may be **fined** an unlimited amount (unless statute restricts it), though the amount must be appropriate to his means as well as to the offence; usually he must be given time to pay, and a prison sentence fixed in default of payment.

(f)   He may be given an **absolute** or **conditional discharge**.   The latter will be for a certain period (up to three years) during which he must commit no further offence or he will be liable to sentence for the original offence.

In addition the court may make ancillary orders for the payment of costs and compensation, disqualification from driving, deportation, etc, in suitable cases.

2.6   Tribunals and arbitration

2.6.1   Types of tribunal

Industrial tribunals

An industrial tribunal has a legally qualified chairman drawn from a panel of chairmen appointed by the Lord Chancellor.   There are also two lay members, one drawn from a panel of representatives of employees' organisations (in practice, persons nominated by the TUC) and one drawn from a panel representing employers' representatives (in practice nominated by the CBI). The Lord Chancellor also appoints the President of the Industrial Tribunals (England and Wales), who, in collaboration with regional chairmen, decides when and where tribunals are to sit and assigns members to each tribunal.

In practice the main function of industrial tribunals is to hear claims by employees that they have been unfairly dismissed. The tribunals also determine many other questions under employment protection law (see Sessions 14 and 15).

A tribunal adopts a majority decision. Proceedings before industrial tribunals are required to be informal. Legal aid is not available for proceedings before an industrial tribunal.

Employment Appeal Tribunal

For most of the matters with which industrial tribunals deal, an appeal on a point of law may be made to the Employment Appeal Tribunal. This consists of a number of High Court judges, one of whom is president, and representatives of employers' and employees' organisations. An appeal is heard by a judge and four lay members (two from each side of industry) though all parties can consent to a hearing with only two lay members. It seems that the judge's opinion must prevail over that of the lay members since the tribunal is concerned only with questions of law.

On some minor matters, an appeal from an industrial tribunal goes to a divisional court of the Queen's Bench Division.

Administrative tribunals

These tribunals assist in the administration of the provisions of Acts of Parliament (and of statutory instruments thereunder), by dealing with disputes arising from the application of those provisions. Examples are rent tribunals, VAT tribunals, and Special Commissioners of Income Tax.

The advantages of tribunals are that: they relieve the ordinary courts of additional work; expert knowledge is available, as each tribunal is composed of specialists; and they are informal, cheap and speedy (due to the absence of counsel, formal pleadings and normal court procedures). Several disadvantages exist, however. Tribunals may possibly be capricious. In some cases no reason is given for a particular decision. Sometimes the party appearing before the tribunal is not professionally represented. Legal aid is often not available. With some tribunals, there are no rights of appeal against a decision. There is a lack of publicity in cases where public comment might be warranted. However, tribunals are controlled by the High Court by means of prerogative orders (see 2.6.2).

Domestic tribunals

These are usually disciplinary committees or boards of:

(a)   professional bodies (eg, the Association of Certified Accountants, the Institute of Cost and Management Accountants);

(b)   particular professions (eg, the Law Society, and the General Medical Council);

(c)   trade organisations (eg, the Milk Marketing Board).

They, too, are controlled by the High Court by means of prerogative orders.

2.6.2 Prerogative orders and writs

The following are methods available to a Divisional Court of the Queen's Bench Division to control excessive or *ultra vires* acts by tribunals, government departments, or inferior courts.

(a) *Mandamus* - an order addressed to a person or body (eg, an inferior court or administrative or domestic tribunal) commanding the performance of a particular duty.

(b) *Prohibition* - an order to a public body or person, preventing the latter from exceeding its jurisdiction. Available against the Crown but not against private persons or clubs.

(c) *Certiorari* - an order to an inferior court to remit the particular matter to a superior court. For this purpose, inferior courts include administrative and domestic tribunals, and even (on occasion) the decisions of ministers. The order is available in the following circumstances: want or excess of jurisdiction; denial of natural justice; an error of law.

(d) *Habeas corpus* - a writ designed to obtain the release of a person confined without legal justification and against his wishes.

(e) *Injunction* - to prevent the implementation of decisions of those tribunals which have not observed the rules of natural justice.

(f) *Declaratory judgment* - requested by parties aggrieved by decisions of inferior tribunals, so that the High Court may state the legal position.

2.6.3 Arbitration

Nature

Arbitration is the reference of a matter in dispute to one or more persons called arbitrators. Arbitration, with the secrecy of its proceedings, is becoming more and more common in the commercial world as a means of settling disputes.

Advantages and disadvantages

Reference has already been made to the secrecy of arbitration and such is its great advantage. Further advantages are its convenience - arbitration being held at a place and time convenient to the parties; speed - the delays often encountered in litigation are avoided; informality - technical procedural rules of a court of law are not rigidly applied; expert knowledge on the part of the arbitrator; expenses are generally less than the costs of litigation. The disadvantages of arbitration are the potential lack of legal expertise where the issue hinges on a difficult point of law and the unpredictability of decisions through a lack of precedent.

2.7 Legal personnel

2.7.1 Judges

Definition

The term judges is in general used to mean full-time paid judges of the High Court, Lords Justices and Law Lords, and the new-style circuit judges and part-time recorders. The last two are often referred to since the Courts Act 1971 as 'lower tier judges', whilst the other judges are referred to as 'superior judges'.

The judges

(a)   *The Lord Chancellor* - The Lord Chancellor occupies a special position; he is a Minister of the Crown, appointed by the government of the day. He is Speaker of the House of Lords, is always a member of the Cabinet, and, in a curiously English way, is head of the judiciary for most purposes. He may preside over the sittings of the Lords of Appeal in Ordinary and give judgment with them. He receives a peerage on appointment and is paid as a government minister, but the tenure of his office is sometimes short, for when the government changes he is out of office automatically with a pension to console him and a conventional obligation to make himself useful in judicial work. But whilst in office he exercises powerful patronage as regards other judicial appointments.

     Constitutionally the Lord Chancellor is the one and only superior judge appointed on a political basis; he must be a barrister of some standing who is usually a peer or a Member of Parliament.

(b)   *The Lord Chief Justice* - He is appointed by the Crown on the advice of the Prime Minister. He is head of the Criminal Division of the Court of Appeal and the Queen's Bench Division. He is a member of the House of Lords.

(c)   *The Master of the Rolls* - Appointed by the Crown on the advice of the Prime Minister, he is deputy to the Lord Chancellor and is head of the Court of Appeal (Civil Division) and of the Chancery Division. He supervises the admission of solicitors to the Rolls of the Supreme Court.

(d)   *The President of the Family Division* - Appointed by the Crown on the advice of the Prime Minister, he is responsible for the work of the Family Division.

(e)   *The Lords of Appeal in Ordinary* - The Lords of Appeal in Ordinary - the Law Lords - are appointed by the Crown on the advice of the Prime Minister from amongst existing judges or barristers of 15 years' standing. They are life peers and can adjudicate in appeal cases heard in the House of Lords.

(f)   *Lords Justices of Appeal* - These are the judges of the Court of Appeal. They are appointed by the Crown on the advice of the Prime Minister from among existing judges or barristers of at least 15 years' standing.

(g)   *Judges of the High Court* - Known as puisne judges, the judges of the High Court are appointed by the Crown on the recommendation of the Lord Chancellor from amongst barristers of at least 10 years' standing.

All the judges referred to above, other than the Lord Chancellor, hold office 'during good behaviour' and may be removed by the Crown on an address presented by both Houses of Parliament. Their salaries are fixed by statute and form a charge on the consolidated fund. These rules reinforce the concept of judicial independence: a vital feature in the administration of law and justice within the State.

(h)   *Circuit Judges* - These judges are appointed by the Crown on the advice of the Lord Chancellor to serve in the Crown and County Courts. A circuit judge must be a barrister of 10 years' standing or a person who has held the office of recorder for five years.

(i)   *Recorders* - Recorders act as part-time judges of the Crown Court. Appointments are made by the Lord Chancellor from barristers or solicitors of 10 years' standing.

Circuit judges and recorders can be removed from office by the Lord Chancellor on the grounds of incapacity or misbehaviour.

2.7.2   Magistrates

The town magistrates include both the professional stipendiary magistrates and the unpaid lay justices of the peace.

Stipendiary magistrates

Such are full-time professional judges who must be either barristers or solicitors of seven years' standing. They are appointed by the Crown on the advice of the Lord Chancellor. Stipendiaries always sit alone in London and more often than not in the provinces. There are some 15 stipendiaries in the provinces and some 40 in London.

Lay justices

Lay justices are appointed by the Lord Chancellor on the advice of a local advisory committee whose composition is kept secret to avoid the embarrassment of canvassing by citizens who want the honour of becoming justices without necessarily having the qualities required.

The formal qualifications of magistrates are few. On appointment a magistrate must be over 21 and under 60 (50 in the case of those who will be on the juvenile court bench), and must normally reside within 15 miles of the area in which he is to act. There is no formal requirement of good character (other than that bankruptcy and conviction for treason are disqualifications) though the process of selection outlined above ensures that only persons of good character will be appointed. They must retire at 70 (65 in the case of the juvenile bench) and may be removed for misconduct. Training schemes for magistrates have been required since 1966 under the general direction of the Lord Chancellor, and are organised by the county commission of the peace. These schemes are aimed at training magistrates to understand the nature of their duties rather than the substantive law they administer. In addition to training, the Home Office issues circulars giving guidance on new legislation and such details as average sentences for motoring offences, etc. In court the magistrates receive advice on procedure and points of law from the justices clerk: the clerk is not entitled to take part in their deliberations as to guilt or sentences.

The Lord Chancellor possesses power to remove a justice from office if he thinks it expedient.

2.7.3   Masters and registrars of the High Court

In the course of most actions in the High Court it is necessary for a great many minor matters to be settled between the parties which do not require a decision on any point of law. The decisions on these matters are usually given by court officials called masters (in the Chancery and Queen's Bench Divisions) or registrars (in the Family Division). If it is necessary for counsel to argue a matter before a master or registrar the hearing is in private instead of in a public courtroom. It is usually possible to appeal to a judge against a decision of a master or registrar.

There are also taxing masters whose main job is to approve the amount of costs claimed when the court has ordered that an unsuccessful party in proceedings should pay costs of other parties.

2.7.4   The legal profession

Division of the legal profession

An unusual feature of the legal profession in England, and in Scotland and Ireland, is its division into solicitors and barristers. (In Scotland, barristers are called 'advocates'.) The two branches of the profession are entirely separate and both are protected by rules that give them a monopoly over certain kinds of work.

Solicitors

The main work of a solicitor is to provide legal advice and to conduct negotiations on behalf of persons who fear they may suffer legal wrongs. Solicitors also act as advocates for parties in Magistrates' Courts and County Courts. In order to practise as a solicitor an individual must have a practising certificate issued by the Law Society. This certificate is given only to an individual who has completed a course of training prescribed by the Society, including working with a practising solicitor and passing examinations.

Solicitors have monopolies on doing certain kinds of legal work for gain, such as drawing up documents relating to ownership of land, and it is an offence for someone who is not a solicitor to do such work. It is also an offence for an unqualified person to pretend to be a solicitor. Many of the fees charged by solicitors are fixed by orders made under the Solicitors Act 1974. A client always has the right to ask a High Court taxing master to rule on whether a solicitor's bill of charges is correct.

Barristers

The principal work of a barrister is to act as an advocate for parties in court, and in general only a barrister may appear as an advocate in the High Court (except in bankruptcy matters). In addition to advocacy work, many barristers acquire special expertise in particular aspects of the law and are consulted by solicitors who require expert advice. By custom, a barrister will only take instructions from a solicitor: it is not possible for a person to consult a barrister directly.

It is necessary to be a barrister in order to be appointed a judge of the High Court. (A solicitor may become a circuit judge, but only after serving for three years or more as a recorder.) In principle it is for judges to determine who will be heard in court, and a part of the courtroom is set off by a 'bar' which may only be crossed by officers of the court (which includes solicitors), the parties in a case and their advocates. The grant of general permission to act as advocate in the Supreme Court is by a procedure known as 'calling to the bar'.

As the professions of barrister and judge are so closely linked the judges have always left it to the professional associations of barristers to determine who shall be called to the bar. These associations are called Inns of Court. (Originally they provided living accommodation for barristers practising in the Royal Courts.) The four Inns are Lincoln's Inn, the Inner Temple, the Middle Temple and Gray's Inn. Regulations concerning who may be called to the bar are now made by a body called the Senate of the Inns of Court and the Bar, which includes senior members of the Inns. The principal conditions for being called to the bar are the passing of examinations and maintaining student membership of one of the Inns for at least two years. Barristers may not form partnerships (that is, agree to share the profits of their work) though they do form associations to hire offices (called 'chambers') and share administrative services.

There is an important rule that giving instructions to a barrister does not form a contract with the barrister. The legal results of this rule are that a barrister has no enforceable entitlement to be paid for his work and a barrister cannot be sued for negligence in performing his work. Payment to a barrister is an honorarium. A barrister is entitled to refuse to act unless and until an honorarium is paid, but normally barristers rely on the fact that the Law Society requires the solicitors who are its members to be personally responsible for paying barristers they instruct, whether or not the ultimate client pays.

2.7.5 Juries

The jury system

Juries are normally required for the more serious criminal cases and for those civil actions involving fraud or defamation. A jury usually consists of 12 persons, although the number can be smaller (nine in criminal cases and eight in civil cases); however, in trials for murder, treason and arson, the number must be 12. Qualifications for a juror are now as follows:

(a)   jurors must be between 18 and 65 years of age;

(b)   they must be included in the Register of Electors for parliamentary and local government elections;

(c)   they must have been resident in the United Kingdom, the Channel Islands or the Isle of Man for at least five years since the age of 13;

(d)   they are ineligible if they have ever received a prison sentence of five years or more, or any custodial sentence within the last 10 years, or a probation order within the last five years;

(e)   they must not be aliens, traitors, of unsound mind, deaf or blind.

Persons exempted from jury service include peers, Members of Parliament, doctors, clergymen, other lawyers and members of HM forces. In addition, persons may be excused jury service in future if they have already served on a jury (particularly in a long and difficult case).

In criminal cases, the jury may bring in an alternative verdict. This must be less severe (ie, more advantageous to the accused) than the verdict pressed for by the prosecution. In civil and criminal cases, the verdict of the jury need not now be unanimous (Juries Act 1974 and Courts Act 1971 for criminal and civil cases respectively). The verdict stands if supported by at least 10 jurors (where there are 11 or more), or by nine jurors (where there are 10 on the jury). In criminal cases, a verdict of guilty will not stand unless the foreman states in open court the number of jurors respectively voting for and against the verdict. However, if a 'not guilty' verdict is delivered, the foreman must not indicate whether it was unanimous or not.

The pros and cons of the jury system

The following criticisms of the jury system have been made:

(a)   there is no physical or educational test for jury service;
(b)   jurors may be too easily impressed and swayed by advocacy of experienced counsel;
(c)   juries are too prone to leniency in criminal cases;
(d)   local prejudice may exist in certain trials and this may be reflected in local jurors;

(e)   jurors are susceptible to corrupt influences, threats and intimidation from outside parties; and

(f)   the physical, mental and financial burden inflicted on jurors by long trials is too great.

Against these factors, however, must be weighed the advantages of jury trial. These may be listed as follows:

(a)   jurors are independent of the parties to a trial;

(b)   juries represent the verdict of ordinary people of common sense, and this fact can be corrective of the harshness of the law;

(c)   there is public confidence in jury trials; and

(d)   in jury trials the judge explains the facts to be proved and the law to be applied, which tends to clarify the issues verbally. The public thus sees that justice is done.

2.8   Revision exercise

In order to assess your assimilation of the material contained in this session attempt the following questions. Check your answers against the references given.

(1)   What courts constitute the Supreme Court?   **(Solution: 2.1.2)**

(2)   What are the divisions of the High Court of Justice?   **(Solution: 2.1.2)**

(3)   What is the basic nature of the Crown Court?   **(Solution: 2.1.2)**

(4)   What are the divisions of the Court of Appeal?   **(Solution: 2.1.2)**

(5)   What is the final court of appeal in the English court system?   **(Solution: 2.1.2)**

(6)   What are the inferior civil and criminal courts?   **(Solution: 2.1.2)**

(7)   How may criminal offences be classified for the purposes of trial?   **(Solution: 2.1.3)**

(8)   Outline the criminal jurisdiction of Magistrates' Courts.   **(Solution: 2.1.3)**

(9)   Examine the composition and jurisdiction of the Crown Court.   **(Solution: 2.1.3)**

(10)   Outline the methods of appeal from the decision of a Magistrates' Court in a criminal case.
                                                                                         (Solution: 2.1.3)

(11)   What is the jurisdiction of the County Courts?   **(Solution: 2.1.4)**

(12)   Outline the composition of the High Court.   **(Solution: 2.1.5)**

(13)   What are the Divisional Courts?   **(Solution: 2.1.5)**

(14)   Outline the civil and criminal jurisdiction of the Court of Appeal.   **(Solution: 2.1.6)**

(15)   How does the House of Lords exercise its legal functions?   **(Solution: 2.1.7)**

(16)   What are the rights of appeal to the House of Lords?   **(Solution: 2.1.7)**

(17)   Outline the composition and jurisdiction of the Judicial Committee of the Privy Council.
         (Solution: 2.2.1)

(18)   What is a writ of summons?   **(Solution: 2.4.1)**

(19)   What is the aim of pleadings?   **(Solution: 2.4.2)**

(20)   Explain the concept of summary judgment.   **(Solution: 2.4.3)**

(21)   What rules govern discovery of documents?   **(Solution: 2.4.4)**

(22)   What are interrogations?   **(Solution: 2.4.4)**

(23)   What is a summons for directions?   **(Solution: 2.4.6)**

(24)   How may a High Court judgment be enforced?   **(Solution: 2.4.8)**

(25)   Outline the procedure involved in an ordinary action in the County Court.
         (Solution: 2.4.9)

(26)   Outline the procedure involved in a summary trial.   **(Solution: 2.5.2)**

(27)   In what circumstances may a person be lawfully arrested?   **(Solution: 2.5.3)**

(28)   What do you understand by trial on indictment?   **(Solution: 2.5.3)**

(29)   Outline the procedures governing majority verdicts in criminal cases.
         (Solution: 2.5.8)

(30)   What is the main role of industrial tribunals?   **(Solution: 2.6.1)**

(31)   What are administrative tribunals?   **(Solution: 2.6.1)**

(32)   In what ways do the courts control tribunals?   **(Solution: 2.6.2)**

(33)   What are the pros and cons of arbitration?   **(Solution: 2.6.3)**

(34)   What are the functions of the Lord Chancellor?   **(Solution: 2.7.1)**

(35)   Who may act as a Law Lord?   **(Solution: 2.7.1)**

(36)   What are the formal qualifications required of a magistrate?   **(Solution: 2.7.2)**

(37)   What is the role of a Master of the High Court?   **(Solution: 2.7.3)**

(38)   Differentiate between the functions of solicitors and barristers.   **(Solution: 2.7.4)**

(39)   Who may act as a juror?   **(Solution: 2.7.5)**

(40)   Discuss the pros and cons of the jury system.   **(Solution: 2.7.5)**

2.9   Conclusion

You should now have a practical knowledge of the way the English legal system operates and in particular the composition and jurisdiction of the courts of law.

2.10   Questions

Objective test questions

(1)   X has just been convicted on indictment. He wishes to appeal against sentence. To which court would his appeal lie?

A   The Crown Court.
B   The Court of Appeal (Criminal Division).
C   The House of Lords.
D   The County Court.

(2)   Which of the following is not a constituent element of the Supreme Court?

A   The Court of Appeal.
B   The Crown Court.
C   The House of Lords.
D   The High Court.

(3)   Which of the following is a prerogative writ?

A   Prohibition.
B   Habeas corpus.
C   *Certiorari*.
D   Mandamus.

(4)   In which court would a petition for an order to wind up a company having paid up share capital of £150,000 be heard?

A   The Queen's Bench Division.
B   The County Court.
C   The Chancery Division of the High Court.
D   The Crown Court.

(5)   In which of the following courts would you not find a jury?

A   Crown Court.
B   Queen's Bench.
C   Chancery Division.
D   County Court.

(The judges of the Court of Appeal are known as:

A   Lords of Appeal in Ordinary.
B   Puisne judges.
C   Recorders
D   Lord Justice of Appeal.

(7)   In which of the following would a claim for unfair dismissal be heard?

    A   A Magistrates Court.
    B   A County Court.
    C   An Industrial Tribunal.
    D   The Queen's Bench Divisional Court.

(8)   The Commercial Court is a specialist court within:

    A   The Chancery Division.
    B   The Court of Appeal.
    C   The Queen's Bench Division.
    D   The Crown Court.

(9)   Proceedings in the High Court are generally commenced by:

    A   Originating summons.
    B   A summons for directions.
    C   A writ of summons.
    D   Pleadings.

(10)   The Admiralty Court is a specialist court within:

    A   The House of Lords.
    B   The County Court.
    C   The Judicial Committee of the Privy Council.
    D   The High Court.

Written test questions

2.1   Judicature acts

How was the judicial system in this country remodelled by the Judicature Acts 1873-5?

2.2   Criminal appeal

State the circumstances in which an appeal is made to the Criminal Division of the Court of Appeal. In what circumstances will the Criminal Division not follow its previous decisions?

2.3   Prerogative orders

Write short notes on the prerogative orders.

SESSION 3

Law of contract 1

Careful study of this session will give you:

- an understanding of the phenomenon of agreement;

- an awareness of the concept of intention to create legal relations;

- an understanding of the doctrine of consideration;

- an awareness of the law regarding formality of contract;

- a knowledge of contractual capacity;

- an appreciation of the origin and significance of contractual terms;

- an ability to assess the validity of exclusion clauses.

3.1 Nature of a contract

3.1.1 Introduction

A <u>contract is a legally binding agreement</u> and the law of contract is that branch of our civil law which is concerned with the determination of whether or not a promise or set of promises is legally binding. The idea of agreement as the basis of contractual obligation, however, evolved slowly, and even today cannot be accepted without qualification.

3.1.2 Free negotiation

In medieval times the royal courts did not enforce agreements as such, although there were various forms of action which could be used in contractual situations. It was only in the course of the fifteenth and sixteenth centuries that a truly contractual action, known as *assumpsit*, evolved to remedy breaches of informal promises.

Around the basis of this action the courts gradually evolved rules for the determination of the validity of particular promises. Many of these rules developed in the atmosphere of the nineteenth century economic doctrine of *laissez-faire*. In consequence, the underlying theory is that the parties to a contract represent two equal bargaining powers who enter into the agreement of their own free will and as a result of negotiations in which each of them is free to accept or reject the terms of the other. However, this nineteenth century idea of agreement as a freely negotiated bargain must now be viewed with qualification.

In the first place the law is often more concerned with the fact of agreement. In general the attitude of the law is objective and pays more regard to the actions of the parties than with the state of their minds. Second, although the parties' agreement may be the basis of the contractual relationship between them, there may be implied into that agreement terms to which they did not expressly agree, and may never have considered, such as those of the Sale of Goods Act 1979, an act which implies into contracts for the sale of goods various terms for the protection of the buyer.

Indeed, today even this fundamental requirement of agreement is under attack, for in commercial agreements one of the parties is frequently economically superior to the other and will only be willing to contract on his own terms. In particular, he will seek by the means of terms excluding his liability to exclude or limit his liability to the other party in the event of certain contingencies. Though, both the judiciary and, subsequently, the legislature have sought to redress the balance between the parties and restrict the ability to exclude liability.

Finally, it should be appreciated that there are certain contractual relationships where even the apparent basic agreement present in the situation mentioned above is absent. Thus, a person whose property was compulsorily purchased by a government agency can hardly be said to have freely agreed with the acquiring authority.

In spite of these qualifications, it is still broadly true to say that the law of contract is concerned with the criteria an agreement is to satisfy if it is to be legally binding.

3.1.3   The essential characteristics of a contract

There are seven essentials of a valid contract:

(a)   there must be an offer and acceptance, that is an agreement;
(b)   there must be an intention to create legal relations;
(c)   there must be consideration (except for certain contracts under seal);
(d)   there is a requirement of written formalities in some cases;
(e)   the parties must have capacity to contract;
(f)   there must be genuineness of consent by the parties to the terms of the contract;
(g)   the contract must be legal and possible.

All these points will now be examined in detail.

In the absence of one or more of these essentials, the contract may be void, voidable, or unenforceable. A void contact is a contract which does not, and has never in fact existed nor been enforceable either in part or in whole.

A voidable contract is one which one of the parties may affirm or reject at his option and is valid until rejected. This may arise, for example, through fraud, and whereas no rights may be acquired under a void contract, third parties may acquire rights under a voidable contract before the contract is avoided.

Thus, for example, in *Lewis v Averay (1971)* Lewis (L) agreed to sell his car to a crook who, before the sale, gave the impression that he (the crook) was a famous actor (Richard Green). L allowed the crook to take the car after the latter had given him a cheque signed 'R A Green'. The cheque was false, but before L discovered this fact the crook had sold the car to Averay (A). It was held that the contract between L and the crook was voidable for fraud, not void for unilateral mistake. The crook was therefore able to pass on a title to the car to A.

An unenforceable contract is one which is valid but, owing to the lack of the necessary legal evidence, it is incapable of legal proof and therefore cannot be sued upon.

Contracts of guarantee are required by S4 of the Statute of Frauds 1677 to be evidenced in writing and unless so evidenced are unenforceable.

3.2   Offer and acceptance

3.2.1   Introduction

The phenomenon of agreement. The first essential of a contract is that there must be an agreement between the parties. The phenomenon of agreement is usually expressed in the terms of offer and acceptance. It must be shown that an offer was made by one party (the offeror) and that that offer was accepted by the other party (the offeree) and that legal relations were intended.

3.2.2   The offer

An offer is an expression of willingness to contract on certain terms made with the intention that it shall become binding as soon as it is accepted by the person to whom it is addressed.

An offer may be made to a specific person, to a group of people, or to the world at large. In *Carlill v Carbolic Smoke Ball Co (1893)*, the defendants offered to pay £100 as reward to anyone who used their smoke ball as prescribed and subsequently contracted influenza. The plaintiff bought and used a smoke ball but still contracted influenza. She sued the company and it was held that she was entitled to the £100 reward. The judgement decided that:

(a)   While acceptance must be made specifically to a particular offeror, the offer itself may, on occasion, be to the world at large.

(b)   The consideration which must support a simple contract was in the present case the plaintiff's suffering inconvenience by using the smoke ball.

(c)   While acceptance must usually be communicated to the offeror, there are occasions (as in the present case) where the performing of an act by the person receiving the offer constitutes in itself sufficient acceptance.

An offer may be conditional but must be certain. It may be express or implied; public transport is an example of an implied offer. Finally, it must be communicated to (ie, it must reach) the offeree. A person who returns property without knowing that a reward had been offered would not be entitled to the reward.

3.2.3   Invitation to treat

An offer must be distinguished from an invitation to someone to make an offer (often referred to as an invitation to treat). In the case of an offer, the agreement is complete when the offeree agrees unconditionally to the terms of the offer. However, with an invitation to treat it is the person to whom the invitation is directed who may make the offer, which the party issuing the invitation (now the offeree) is free to accept if he wishes to do so. No agreement (and hence no contract, if the other essentials are also present) arises until acceptance is made by the party originating the invitation.

An invitation to treat is essentially an attempt to elicit an offer from the person to whom it is addressed.

Examples of invitations to treat include notices in shop windows, prospectuses for the issue of company shares, mail order 'bargain offers', and the display of goods in a supermarket. This is illustrated in the following two cases.

In *Pharmaceutical Society of Great Britain v Boots Cash Chemists (Southern) Limited (1953)*, goods were sold in certain of B's shops under the self-service system. Customers selected their purchases, put them in a basket, and paid for them at a cash desk. The Society brought an action against B for selling certain drugs without a qualified pharmacist being present. It was held that the contract in cases such as this occurs at the cash desk, not before. In other words, Boots were simply making an invitation to treat by displaying the goods. The customer made the offer at the cash desk, which Boots accepted. As it was shown that there was a qualified pharmacist present at the cash desk to check if the relevant statutes were being observed, there had been no infringement in the sense of a sale without proper supervision.

In the case of *Fisher v Bell (1960)*, a shopkeeper displayed a flick-knife in a shop window. He was charged with offering an offensive weapon for sale but acquitted because it was only an invitation to treat. (As a result, the Restriction of Offensive Weapons Act 1961, S1, made it an offence to expose, or have in one's possession, an offensive weapon for the purpose of sale or hire.) In both these cases, the display is the invitation to treat (or to make an offer), and the selection of the item is the offer (to purchase).

Auction sales form an important example of invitations to treat. Notice of an auction and the subsequent putting up of items for bids are both invitations; the bids constitute a series of offers, one of which (usually the highest) is accepted by the auctioneer when he drops his hammer. As a bid is an offer, it may be withdrawn at any time before it has been accepted by the fall of the auctioneer's hammer.

3.2.4   Lapse of offer

The offer lapses in either of the following cases:

(a)   On the death of the offeror or the offeree before acceptance, though in the former case where the offer is non-personal, death may only cause revocation on notification.

(b)   If it is not accepted within:

(i)   the time prescribed in the offer for acceptance; or

(ii)   a reasonable time (determined on the facts in each case) if no time for acceptance has been prescribed.

In *Ramsgate Victoria Hotel Co v Montefiore (1866)*, M applied (ie, offered) to take shares in the R company on 8 June, but he heard nothing from the company until 23 November, when he received a letter of acceptance. M refused to take the shares and was sued by the company. It was held that M was entitled to refuse to take the shares as the acceptance came so long after the offer that the offer could be said to have lapsed before 23 November; accordingly it could not be accepted on that date.

3.2.5 Revocation of offer

This may take place in the following ways. The offer may be revoked by the offeror at any time before it has been accepted. The revocation must reach the offeree before he has accepted. In *Byrne v Van Tienhoven (1880)*, VT posted a letter in Cardiff to B in New York on 1 October, offering to sell B some tinplate. On 8 October VT wrote to B revoking their offer. On 11 October B received VTs' offer and immediately telegraphed acceptance. On 15 October B confirmed acceptance by letter. On 20 October B received VT's letter of revocation dated 8 October, and by this time VT had contracted to sell the tinplate elsewhere. It was held that a revocation of an offer is not effective unless it reaches the offeree before he has accepted the offer. The mere posting or other form of notifying the offeree that the offer is revoked is not sufficient; it must actually be communicated to (ie, reach the attention of) the offeree before he proceeds to accept the original offer.

An offer which is expressed to be open for a certain time may nevertheless be revoked before the expiry of that time unless: the offeree has already accepted it or, there was consideration by the offeree for the offeror's promise to keep the offer open (eg, the case of an option).

An offer may be revoked via a third party who ought reasonably to be believed. In *Dickinson v Dodds (1876)*, Dodds offered by letter to sell property, the offer to be left open 'until 9am Friday'. On the day preceding (Thursday) Dickinson learnt from X that Dodds was negotiating to sell the property to B. On the same evening Dickinson left a letter of acceptance at the place where Dodds was staying but the letter never reached Dodds. On Friday morning (at 7 am, two hours before the original deadline) X, acting as Dickinson's agent, handed Dodds a duplicate of the letter of acceptance. Meanwhile, during the previous evening Dodds had completed the contract of sale with B. It was held (in an action brought by Dickinson) that:

(a) Dodds was free to revoke the offer at any time before acceptance, because there was no consideration for any promise by Dodds to keep the offer open.

(b) Dickinson's learning through X of Dodd's negotiations with B before Dickinson had accepted the original offer constituted sufficient notification of Dodd's revocation of his offer.

3.2.6 Rejection of offer

An offer may be rejected in the following ways. The offeree may notify the offeror that he does not wish to accept the offer. If the offeree makes a counter-offer, then this destroys the previous offer. In *Hyde v Wrench (1840)*, W offered to sell his farm for £1,000. H's agent made W an offer of £950 and W requested a few days leave to consider it. W then wrote saying he could not accept £950 whereupon H wrote purporting to accept the original offer of £1,000, W refused to be bound and was sued by H for specific performance. (Specific performance is the enforcement of the act in question.) It was held that H's offer of £950 constituted a counter-offer which effectively rejected the original offer of £1,000 by W. Hence there was no contract.

However, a mere inquiry by the offeree for further information is not in itself a rejection of the offer. Thus, in *Stevenson v McLean (1880)*, M offered to sell iron to S at 40s per ton. S telegraphed 'please wire whether you would accept 40s per ton for delivery over two months or, if not, the longest limit you are prepared to give'. M did not reply, and S telegraphed acceptance. It was held that this acceptance was valid, the offer was not terminated by S's prior telegram which was meant only as 'a mere inquiry, which should have been answered, and not treated as a rejection of the offer'.

3.2.7 The acceptance

Acceptance is a final expression of assent to the terms of an offer. In order to be effective, the acceptance of an offer must be made in accordance with the following rules. It must be made while the offer is still in force, ie, before it has been revoked or before it has lapsed. It must be absolute and unqualified; if the terms of the offer are altered then there has been a counter-offer.

The acceptance must be communicated to the offeree in cases where notification of acceptance is specifically or tacitly required, although mere performance may, on occasion, be sufficient without the communication (see 3.2.2, *Carlill's case*). Furthermore, the offeror may not make the offeree's silence amount to acceptance. In *Felthouse v Bindley (1862)*, F offered to buy his nephew's horse for £30 by writing to him; in the letter F said, 'If I hear no more I shall consider the horse to be mine for £30'. The nephew made no reply but he told the auctioneer (B) who was selling a number of the nephew's horses not to sell that particular animal. However, B inadvertently sold the horse and was sued by F. It was held that F had no claim against B (or the nephew) because F's original offer had not been accepted by or on behalf of the nephew.

The acceptance must be made in whatever form (if any) has been prescribed by the offeror. If it is made by post (where the use of the post is permitted by the offeror), it is effective from the moment the letter is posted, even if it never reaches the offeror. In *Household Fire Insurance Co v Grant (1879)*, G applied for shares in the H Company and a letter of acceptance (allotment) was duly despatched to G. However, it never reached him. Subsequently, the company was wound up and the liquidator claimed from G the balance due on the partly-paid shares allotted. G refused to pay claiming that as he had never received a notification of acceptance he was not liable, the contract having failed through non-acceptance of G's offer. It was held (by a majority) that G was liable to pay as a contributory, because acceptance took place at the moment the allotment letter was given to the Post Office who acted as agent for both parties. If, however, the letter of acceptance is merely handed to a postman the operative time of acceptance is usually when the letter reaches the offeror.

An 'acceptance' which is subject to a formal (or proper) contract is conditional and will become effective only if and when the relevant contract has been executed and (where appropriate) exchanged. The phrase 'subject to contract' used in house purchase prevents the oral offer and acceptance from being binding.

3.3 Certainty and intention

3.3.1 The need for certainty

A contract may fail to come into existence, even though there is offer and acceptance, because of uncertainty as to what has been agreed. In *Scammell v Ouston (1941)*, for example, the parties agreed that Ouston should acquire from Scammell a new motor-van 'on hire-purchase terms'. It was held that the agreement was too vague to be enforced, since hire-purchase terms were many and various, and it was impossible to decide on which hire-purchase terms the parties intended to contract.

3.3.2   Attitude of the courts

The courts will however, if possible, implement and not defeat the reasonable expectations of the parties. This is illustrated by the following cases:

Hillas v Arcos (1932)

The courts upheld an agreement for the purchase of timber 'of fair specification'; holding that in the light of the previous course of dealing between the parties, and in the light of legal implication in contracts of what is 'reasonable' the words used were sufficiently certain.

Nicolene Limited v Simmonds (1953)

There was an agreement for the sale and purchase of a large quantity of steel bars. The terms were perfectly clear except for a statement that the transaction was to be subject to 'the usual conditions of acceptance'. It was held that, there being no 'usual condition of acceptance' the words were meaningless and must be ignored.

3.3.3   Intention to create legal relations

Even if an accepted offer creates an agreement it does not automatically make the agreement a contract. If one of the parties wishes to invoke the aid of the law in enforcing the terms of the agreement against the other party, he must show, *inter alia*, that there had been an intention by both parties that the agreement was to create legal relations. In social or domestic agreements there is a presumption that legal relations are not intended. In commercial agreements there is a presumption that legal relations are intended. Both of these presumptions may be rebutted by evidence to the contrary.

Agreements between spouses living together are usually assumed to be of a domestic nature only. In *Balfour v Balfour (1919)*, a husband agreed to pay his wife £30 per month while he was abroad. It was held that this agreement was not legally enforceable. Where the agreement is made at a time when a husband and wife have decided to separate, there will be a stronger presumption that the agreement is intended to be contractual.

The agreement between a football pools competitor and the promoting company is not a binding contract where the company has expressly indicated that the pool was not to be legally enforceable but if two or more persons agree to 'go shares' in the stake for a pools entry (or for any other type of open competition), the person who wins must share the prize money with the other(s) even though the winning entry was in his sole name. In *Simpkins v Pays (1955)*, P and his granddaughter agreed with S, their paying boarder, that they would jointly enter a weekly competition in a newspaper, using P's name as competitor. On one occasion their entry won £750 which was paid to P, the named competitor. S sued for his one-third share but P claimed that there was no intention to create a legal relationship with the joint weekly entry. It was held that there was an intention that the participation in the competition was to constitute a joint business enterprise. S was therefore entitled to his share.

If a business agreement includes an 'honourable pledge' clause, ie, one that expressly states that the agreement is not to be legally binding, then this will prevent it being legally enforceable.

3.4 Consideration

3.4.1 The doctrine of consideration

It is a fundamental principle of the English law of contract that before there may be a binding simple contract (ie, one made other than under seal in a deed (see 3.5)), **both parties must have agreed to provide something of value to the other.** In other words, each must have bought the agreement of the other in some way, and the price which each is to pay must be capable of measurement in monetary terms. This price is known as consideration and converts the mere promises of the parties into bargains enforceable by the courts.

Consideration may be executory, where the parties exchange promises to perform acts in the future, ie, both acts are in the future; or it may be executed, where one party promises to do something in return for the act of another, rather than for the mere promise of future performance of an act, ie, one act is performed now and the other is in the future.

3.4.2 Rules of the doctrine of consideration

The following are the rules applicable to the doctrine of consideration.

(a) *Simple contracts must be supported by consideration* - If A promises to give B his car and B agrees to accept it, we do have an agreement (offer and acceptance) but there is no contract because there is no consideration. If A changes his mind, B has no contract on which he can sue. For there to be a contract each party must have bought the agreement of the other. In the above example, A has promised to surrender his car, but B has offered nothing of value in return. If however, A offers to sell his car to B for £3,000 and B accepts, then this is a contract because there is consideration; both parties are providing something of value to the other.

Note that the consideration need not be a physical object; it may be a service provided or it may be the promise not to perform an act. Thus if A promises not to play loud music if B pays £1,000 then there is a contract: B is promising £1,000 which is of value to A, and A is forbearing to do something which is of value to B.

(b) *Consideration need not be adequate but must have some value, however slight* - The common law will only enforce a promise for which some value has been given. But it does not, in general, ask whether value has been given or whether the agreement is harsh or one-sided. It is for the parties themselves to determine whether or not the consideration is adequate and the bargain fair.

In *Chappell and Co Ltd v Nestle (1960)*, Nestle offered a record for sale at a price of 1s 6d plus three wrappers from their 6d bars of chocolate. When the wrappers were received by Nestle they were thrown away. However, it was still held that they were part of the consideration for the contract between the record buyers and the chocolate manufacturers. It would logically follow that if these wrappers could be part of the consideration, they could just as easily in an appropriate case be the entire consideration. However the consideration must have some economic value, and mere natural affection of itself is not enough: *White v Bluett (1853)*.

In this case White, the executor of Bluett's father's estate, alleged that Bluett had not paid a promissory note given to his father during his lifetime. Bluett admitted that he had given the note to his father, but said that his father had released him from it in return for a promise not to keep on complaining about the fact that he had been disinherited. The court held that the defence failed and that the defendant was liable on the note. The promise not to complain was not sufficient consideration to support his release from the note. Nevertheless, the act or omission involved, even if of a trivial nature, may be sufficient to support a contract.

(c)   *Consideration must be sufficient* - Although consideration need not be adequate, it must be sufficient and the promisee must promise more than he is legally bound to do. Thus, the discharge of a public duty imposed by law is not consideration. In *Collins v Godefroy (1831)*, a promise to pay a witness who had already been subpoenaed, was held unenforceable. The witness already had a legal duty to attend court and was therefore not offering anything of value over and above his legal duty. However, it is clear that a person can recover a promised payment for doing more than he is by law obliged to do. In *Glasbrook Bros Limited v Glamorgan CC (1925)* mine owners who feared violence from strikers asked for a greater degree of police protection than the police reasonably thought necessary and promised to pay for it. It was held that his promise was enforecable - the police were doing more than they were obliged by law.

This same principle results in the rule that an agreement by a creditor to accept less than the sum owed will not normally be binding because the debtor provides no fresh consideration for the agreement to discharge. In *Foakes v Beer (1889)*, B obtained a judgment against F for £2,090. F asked for time to pay and it was agreed that B would not take further proceedings if F paid the amount due in stated instalments. After F had paid the whole of the debt B sued him on the judgement for interest. F pleaded that B had agreed not to take further proceedings, but B contended that no consideration had been furnished for this agreement by F. It was held that B was entitled to recover interest.

However, if there is anything different in the method of payment, it might be held that there had been true satisfaction (by means of fresh consideration) for the complete discharge of the debtors' obligation. Examples of such differences are:

(i)   payment by means of an asset other than cash, but this does not apply to payment by cheque;

(ii)   payment before the due date;

(iii) payment by a third party;

(iv)   payment of a smaller sum in cases where the amount of the debt (or the debt itself) is in dispute;

Further in this context the general principle of sufficiency must be viewed in the light of the development of the doctrine of promissory estoppel (see 3.4.3).

(d)   *Consideration must be legal* - An illegal consideration makes the whole contract void (see session 4).

(e)   *Consideration must not be past* - The consideration for a promise must be an act done (or promised) in return for a promise.

The act offered as consideration must be performed after the agreement is made. In *Re McArdle (1951)*, M left a life interest in his estate to his widow and the residue to his children. The wife of one son improved, during the widow's lifetime, a bungalow on the estate in which she and the son lived. After the repairs were carried out the five children agreed in writing that they would repay the money spent on repairs. On the widow's death the son's wife asked for the money, but the children (apart from her husband) had changed their minds. It was held that the agreement was not enforceable because the consideration was past; the improvements were carried out before the agreement to pay was made.

However, there are exceptions to this rule and, where, for example, services are rendered at the express or implied request of the promiser in circumstances which raise an implication of a promise to pay, the subsequent promise to pay may be regarded as fixing the value of the services provided.

In *Stewart v Casey (1892)*, Casey was asked to 'push' certain patents. He worked on the project for two years. The joint owners of the patents then agreed to pay him one-third share of the patents. It was held that the previous request for his services raised an implied promise to pay. The subsequent agreement to pay was enforceable.

(f)   *Consideration must move from the promisee* - The person to whom the promise is made must give some consideration for it, ie, it must move from the promisee. This arises from the doctrine of privity of contract, whereby a contract cannot, as a general rule, confer rights or impose obligations under it on any person except the parties to it. In general third parties cannot sue for the carrying out of promises made by the parties to a contract (see 6 below). Thus, in *Tweddle v Atkinson (1861)*, T married the daughter of G. In order to provide for T and his wife, G promised T's father that if the latter paid T £100 he (G) would give T £200. An agreement was drawn up by the parties concerned, giving T the right to sue either promisor for the relevant sum promised. G did not make his payment during his lifetime and T sued A, G's executor. T's action failed because he had not given any consideration to G in return for the promise to pay £200. Without consideration the provision in the agreement was of no effect.

Without doubt the most common example of the doctrine in operation is to be found in contracts for the sale of goods. Its operation restricts the enforcement of the buyer's contractual right, and in particular his rights under the Sale of Goods Act 1979, to actions against the buyer (see Session 7).

3.4.3   Promissory estoppel

Estoppel is a general principle of English law. It deals with a situation in which one person makes a statement to another which misrepresents the facts, and the other person then acts on the assumption that what he has been told is correct. In subsequent legal proceedings the maker of the misstatement may not be allowed to rely on the true state of affairs; he will be required to stand by what he said and will have to suffer the consequences of his misrepresentation; he is said to be 'estpopped' (meaning 'precluded') from saying that his statement was not true. Estoppel can only be invoked if the maker of the misstatement ought to have realised that people would act on the assumption that the statement was true.

Generally, estoppel can only be invoked to deal with a statement that misrepresents facts as they existed at the time the statement was made.

Suppose A and B have made a contract. A then promises that he will not require B to carry out some of his obligations under the contract though B provides no consideration and A does not make his promise under seal. Suppose A later changes his mind and takes legal action to enforce B's obligations under the contract. Should a court ignore A's promise because it was made without consideration (and so force B to carry out his obligation) or should the court hold that A is estopped from denying that his promise was to be relied on (and so refuse to enforce B's obligations)? Estoppel relating to a promise is called 'prommissory estoppel' and the cases so far show that the courts adopt the following attitude. **Promissory estoppel will be invoked if the maker of the promise ought to have known that the other party would alter his position in reliance on the promise.** However, the maker of the promise is entitled to give notice to the other party that the promise is to be withdrawn and, provided the period of notice is reasonable, the other party will have to accept this withdrawal unless the change in position made in reliance on the promise cannot be reversed. This statement of the doctrine of promissory estoppel was made by the Privy Council in *FA Ajayi v R T Briscoe (Nigeria) Limited (1964)*.

The doctrine may be illustrated by reference to the facts of *Central London Property Trust Limited v High Trees House Limited (1947)*. The plaintiffs let a block of flats to the defendants at £2,500 pa. In 1940, because of the war, the defendants found it impossible to let all the flats, so the plaintiffs gratuitously agreed to reduce the rent to £1,250. In 1945, the plaintiffs sued the defendants claiming that the rent should be readjusted to £2,500 and arrears of rent which had accrued at the full rate. It was held that the plaintiffs were entitled to reinstate the rent to its original level from a current date, but they were not entitled to claim arrears of rent at the full rate because their promise not to do so had been relied on in letting the flats at reduced rents down to that time.

3.5   Formality

3.5.1   The requirement of formality

A legal system is said to require that a contract shall be made in a certain form if it lays down the manner in which the conclusion of the contract is to be marked or recorded in order to make it binding. In this respect the general rule of English law is that contracts can be made quite informally; and the form in which a contract is made does not matter and will have no effect upon the validity of the contract. There are, however, certain exceptions:

(a)   contracts which must be made by deed;
(b)   contracts which must be in writing; and
(c)   contracts which must be evidenced in writing.

Contracts requiring a deed

A document written on paper (or on parchment or vellum, delivered by the person who is to be bound by it and bearing that person's seal and signature (unless the person is a corporation in which case a signature is unnecessary) is called a 'deed'.

A seal is a symbol of adoption of a document as the deed of the person whose seal it bears. A seal may be in the form of a piece of wax or lead, or a disc of red paper (called a 'wafer'), attached to the document. Alternatively it may be a design impressed on the document by placing it between dies. A corporation does not have a signature, only a seal. However, any individual, acting under the authority, express or implied, of a corporation, may sign a document on behalf of the corporation (Companies Act 1985, S37; Corporate Bodies' Contracts Act 1960, S1). If a document stating an obligation of a corporation bears the seal of the corporation then it does not also require a signature (Law of Property Act 1925, S73), though usually the rules of corporation require that officers who put the corporation's seal on a document must also sign the document.

It is possible for a document to be recognised as a deed, even though it does not bear a seal, if it is expressed to be a deed. The traditional words, 'Signed, sealed and delivered' put above a signature may be sufficient (*First National Securities Limited v Jones (1978)*).

In order to be enforceable the following types of contract must be stated in deeds.

(a)   Any contract which imposes an obligation on one party for which no consideration is receivable.

(b)   A bill of sale of goods given by way of security (Bills of Sale Acts 1978-82) unless given by a corporation.

(c)   A transfer of a British ship.

A contract recorded in a deed is called a 'specialty'.

A transfer or grant of a legal estate in land is effective only if made in a deed (Law of Property Act 1925, S52). However, if the owner of a legal estate has contracted to transfer it, or grant a lease, then, usually, the contract may be enforced by a decree of specific performance which may require the execution of the necessary deed, or may order it to be executed by someone else.

A lease of land (which is a contract between landlord and tenant) will not grant the tenant a legal estate in the land unless it is stated in a deed; however, this does not affect the enforceability of the contract between landlord and tenant.

Contracts which must be in writing

The following simple contracts are required to be wholly in writing.

(a)   Policies of marine insurance.
(b)   Regulated agreements under the Consumer Credit Act 1974.
(c)   The transfer of shares in a limited company.
(d)   Bills of exchange and cheques.
(e)   Legal assignments of choses in action.
(f)   Most contracts for land under the Law of Property (Miscellaneous Provisions) Act 1989.

The effect of non-compliance varies, depending on the type of agreement. Usually the contract will be void, but in the case of regulated agreements under the Consumer Credit Act 1974 the effect of non-compliance by the seller is to make the agreement unenforceable against the debtor unless the creditor obtains a court order: S127 Consumer Credit Act 1974.

Contracts which must be evidenced in writing

S4 of the Statute of Frauds 1677 requires that contracts of guarantee, ie, promises to answer for the debt, default or miscarriage of another must be evidenced in writing and that if this requirement is not satisfied any such agreement shall be unenforceable by legal action.

3.6   Capacity

3.6.1   General rule

The general rule is that any person, of whatever nationality or sex, may enter into binding contractual relations. To this rule there are certain exceptions. There are special rules of common law and statute law formed for the protection of certain classes of persons who by reasons of want of age or deficiency in mental ability or understanding might be taken advantage of by experienced and mature adults. Furthermore, there are special rules regarding the contractual capacity of artificial (or juristic) person such as registered companies.

Minors

The Family Law Reform Act, 1969, S1 reduced the age of majority from twenty-one to eighteen years and any person under that age is now termed a minor. The contracts of a minor may be divided into four classes:

(a)   *Contracts for necessaries* - 'Necessaries' in this sense means 'goods suitable to the condition in life of such minor and to his actual requirements at the time of sale and delivery'. The term is not restricted to things which are required to maintain a bare existence but includes articles which are reasonably necessary to the minor having regard to his station in life. The term even extends beyond goods and would, for example, include hire of a motor car.

When the necessaries are goods, the minor is only liable when the goods are:

(i)   suitable to the condition in life of the minor;

(ii)   necessary to the minor's requirements at the time of the sale;

(iii)   necessary to the minor's requirements at the time of delivery; and

(iv)   goods with which the minor was not sufficiently supplied at the time of sale and delivery.

Finally, even if the goods are necessaries and the four requirements set out above are satisfied, the minor need pay only a reasonable and not necessarily the contractual price for them.

In *Nash v Inman (1908)*, for example, I, a minor ordered a number of fancy waistcoats from N. At that time he already had an adequate wardrobe. N sued I for the price but it was held that as I was a minor and the waistcoats did not constitute necessaries, he was not liable to pay for any of them.

(b)   *Beneficial contracts of service* - A minor is bound by contracts of service such as those for training, education and apprenticeships provided they are overall for his benefit. However, a contract which is in general for the minor's benefit will not be enforced if its terms are onerous, although the court will look at the whole contract not merely at isolated terms, and will arrive at its decision on the total effect of the agreement. In *Doyle v White City Stadium Limited (1955)*, for example, the plaintiff (a professional boxer) entered into a contract which contained a clause that if disqualified he would lose the prize money. He was disqualified but claimed that as a minor the contract was not binding on him. It was held that although this particular clause appeared onerous, the contract taken as a whole was for his benefit.

In *Roberts v Gray (1913)* an infant would-be billiards professional was held liable to honour a contractual promise to contribute to his manager's expenses in training him.

(c)   *Contracts which are generally beneficial* - The courts will, on occasion, uphold contracts which are neither for necessaries, nor beneficial contracts of service, but which are beneficial *in specie*.

For example, in *Chaplin v Leslie Frewin (Publishers) (1965)* Chaplin, infant son of the famous comic actor, made a contract with publishers for the ghosting of his memoirs. Once written, he disliked the volume and sought to avoid the contract. It was held that when the contract was made it was for Chaplin's (general) benefit. He could not avoid it.

(d)   *Voidable contracts* - These are contracts by which the minor enters a contract of a continuing nature. Included in this category are contracts made by a minor for a lease, contracts for the acquisition of shares and contracts of partnerships. Such contracts bind the minor unless he takes active steps to avoid them either during his minority or within a reasonable time thereafter. If he does take the necessary steps he ceases to be liable on the obligations under the contract. However, he may only recover money paid under the contract if there has been a total failure of consideration (ie, he has received **no** benefit at all under the contract) (*Steinberg v Scala (Leeds) Limited (1923)*).

(e)   *Unenforceable contracts* - The contracts falling into this residual category were originally regulated by the common law. However, in 1874 they were brought into the realm of statute law by the Infants Relief Act of that year. By S1 of that Act three types of minors' contracts were '**absolutely void**'. These were loan contracts; contracts for the supply of goods other than necessaries; and accounts stated (ie, debts acknowledged by minors with an implied promise to pay (eg, IOUs)). Much case law accrued round the meaning of 'absolutely void'. The courts were prepared to grant some legal effect in such contracts (eg, it seemed that property passed under them to a minor and hence to third parties, and that a minor could recover money paid where there had been a total failure of consideration). Due to the uncertain meaning of the 1874 Act and its interaction with the common law, and the fact that it made the law unduly favourable to minors, it has been wholly repealed by the Minors' (Contracts) Act 1987.

As a result of this, these contracts are now governed by the pre-1874 common law rules, and are enforceable **by** the minor as at common law, though unenforceable **against** him.

S2 of the 1874 Act did two further things: it prevented a person from ratifying any promise or contract made during infancy, and it also prevented him from making a fresh agreement to pay a debt contracted during minority. A creditor will no longer be concerned with the distinction between ratification and a fresh agreement, since S2 of the 1874 Act is repealed by the 1987 Act which makes effective any new agreement after majority and any security given to repay a previously void loan. A fresh agreement and an act of ratification made after majority are both equally binding.

Remedies for third parties

Under S3 of the 1987 Act where a contract is unenforceable against the defendant (or he repudiates it) because he was a minor when the contract was made, then the court, may, if it is just and equitable to do so, require the defendant to transfer to the plaintiff any property acquired by the defendant under the contract, or any property representing it.

Where the minor has induced the other party to enter into the contract by stating that he (the minor) is of full age, the other party may not bring an action on the contract (unless it is in itself binding, ie, of a necessary or beneficial kind); nor may he sue the minor in tort for fraud, because if he were allowed to do so he would indirectly be enforcing the contract.

In *R Leslie Limited v Sheill (1914)*, S, a minor, borrowed £400 from L, stating that he was of full age. He did not repay the money and L sued for either fraudulent misrepresentation, or money had and received to S's use. The court held that to allow either of L's claims would be to enforce the contract indirectly, and therefore L failed.

Where a minor commits a tort in the course of performing his part of a contract he may not be sued for breach of contract or in tort. However, the other party may have an action in tort if the tortious act of the minor was not concerned with the terms of the contract. This distinction is illustrated by the following two cases.

In *Jennings v Rundall (1799)*, a minor hired a horse, rode it badly and injured it. It was held that he could avoid the contract because of his minority. In *Ballett v Mingay (1943)*, however, B hired a microphone and amplifier to M, a minor. M sold the goods and was therefore unable to return them when asked to do so. B sued for the return of the goods or their value. M pleaded minority as his defence. The court held that B should succeed and that minority was no defence since the act of selling the goods was outside the terms of contract.

Aliens

Aliens normally have full capacity to contract, but they may not have an interest in a British ship (except as a member of a British limited company).

Contracts with enemy aliens are illegal. With regard to a contract made during peacetime with a person who subsequently becomes an enemy alien (eg, through the outbreak of war):

(a)   the contract is cut short, and gives rise to no rights after the end of the war;

(b)   rights and liabilities outstanding in respect of matters under the contract performed before the outbreak of war are effective, but actions thereon are stayed until the war ends.

Foreign sovereigns and diplomats are generally not subject to English legal processes, except to the extent that they submit to the jurisdiction of the courts.

Drunkards and persons suffering from mental disorder

Since the passing of the Mental Health Act 1958, now the Mental Health Act 1983, the contractual position of persons suffering from mental disorder, and drunkards, is somewhat similar. It differs in those cases where the mental disorder is of such an advanced state that the persons concerned are regarded as being totally incapable of managing their affairs, when this is done for them through the Court of Protection.

In respect of contracts entered into by drunkards and by persons suffering from mental disorder who nevertheless are allowed to manage their own affairs, the general law is as follows:

(a)   The contracts are voidable by them, but only if the other party was aware of their disability at the time the contract was executed.

(b)   Even if the contract may be avoided, the drunkard or mental patient may have to pay a reasonable (not necessarily the contract) price for necessaries supplied under the contract.

3.7   Terms and exclusion clauses

3.7.1   Terms and representations

Terms, as applied to contracts, must be carefully distinguished from representations. A representation is a statement of fact which is made before a contract is executed, with a view to persuading a party to enter into contract. A term is an integral part of the contract itself, although it may be in a form identical to a representation made previously. Terms of a contract may be classified as conditions and warranties, and express terms and implied terms.

Conditions and warranties

A condition is a term which is so vital to a contract that its breach entitles the other party to claim that, without the condition, there is no true contract. The word 'condition' was defined in *Wallis v Pratt (1910)* as:

> 'An obligation which goes so directly to the substance of the contract (or, in other words, is so essential to its very nature) that its non-performance may fairly be considered by the other party as a substantial failure to perform the contract at all.'

A warranty has been defined as: 'an agreement which is collateral to the main purpose of the contract' (Sale of Goods Act 1979); and 'an obligation, which though it must be performed, is not so vital that a failure to perform it goes to the substance of the contract' (*Wallis v Pratt*).

It is often difficult to know whether a particular term is a condition or a warranty, yet it is important to determine the difference. A breach of condition by one party entitles the other (injured) party to repudiate the contract and claim damages. A breach of a warranty by one party, however, entitles the injured party to claim damages only.

In *Poussard v Spiers and Pond (1876)*, P agreed to sing in an operetta, the first performance of which was scheduled for 28 November 1874. On 23 November 1874 she became ill and could not appear until 4 December. S needed a substitute but found that the only way to obtain a suitable person was to engage the substitute to perform for the whole period. When P appeared on 4 December, S refused her services. P then sued S for breach of contract. It was held that P's failure to perform the contract from the start (28 November) was a breach of condition, which entitled S to rescind the contract with P.

In *Bettini v Gye (1876)*, B agreed to sing in Great Britain for a period beginning on 30 March 1875, and to be in London for rehearsals six days before that date. B fell ill, and was unable to reach London before 28 March 1875, when G refused to accept B's services, treating B's absence from rehearsals as a breach of condition. B sued G for breach of contract. It was held that the clause referring to rehearsals was subsidiary to the main agreement, and its breach was no more than a breach of warranty. G was therefore liable to B for breach of contract, although G might have a counterclaim for any additional costs incurred because of B's non-attendance at some of the rehearsals.

Innominate terms - In recent years the courts have tried to avoid too rigid a classification of terms on the lines set out immediately above and recognise an intermediate category described as innominate terms: *The Mihalis Angelos (1970)* and *Hansa Nord (1976)*. In the latter, Citrus pulp pellets were sold for £100,000. One of the conditions of the contract was that 'shipment to be made in good condition'. On arrival not all the pellets were in good condition, and their market value was reduced to £80,000. However, even if all the pellets had been sound the market value, which had fallen between sale and delivery, was only £86,000. The buyers wished to reject the goods, the goods were sold and eventually reacquired by the original buyers for £34,000.

On the question of whether the buyers' rejection had been justified, the Court of Appeal held that the provision as to shipment in good condition was neither a condition nor a warranty, but an intermediate stipulation and the effect of the breach was not sufficient to justify repudiation. The buyers only remedy was in damages, ie, the difference in value of the sound goods and the defective goods.

An intermediate stipulation or innominate term is neither a condition nor a warranty at the time the contract is made, but one must consider the effects of a breach of that term. If serious, ie, if it substantially denies the injured party of what he contracted for, then remedies as if it were a breach of condition should be granted. If less serious, ie, if the injured party still substantially gets what he contracted for, then only remedues for breach of warranty can be obtained.

Express and implied terms

The contents of a contract depend primarily on the words used by the parties. These make up the express terms of the contract. A contract may further contain a number of terms which are not expressly stated, but which are implied because the parties so intended, or by operation of law, or by custom or usage, ie, implied terms.

(a) *Express terms* - If the contract between the parties is wholly oral, the determination of the express terms of the contract is a matter of fact to be decided by the court from the evidence presented to it. If the parties have reduced their agreement to writing then it is the written word that is the determining factor and, in general parol evidence will not be permitted to add to, vary or contradict, the written agreement. This rule is known as the Parol Evidence Rule. The rule is, however, subject to various exceptions and, for example, as in *Humphrey v Dale (1857)*, oral evidence may be admitted to prove a trade custom or usage.

(b) *Implied terms* - These may originate in custom, have their origin in statute or arise as a result of judicial interpretation.

    (i) *Customary implied terms* - Any contract may be deemed to incorporate any relevant custom of the market or locality in which it is made, unless the custom is inconsistent with the express terms or nature of the contract. *Hutton v Warren (1836)* may be quoted as an example. In that case the lease of a farm was determined and the lessee claimed to be entitled to a reasonable sum in respect of tillage, sowing and cultivation. The lesee, as an off-going tenant, relied upon the custom of the country as the foundation of his claim, the lease itself making no provision for any such payment. The court held that the lesee was entitled to recover as custom required a tenant to plough and sow and a landlord to pay for his work.

    (ii)   *Statutory implied terms* - Various terms having their origin in custom have graduated, as it were, through the courts, to being terms implied by statute. The most significant of these are to be found in the Sale of Goods Act 1979. This Act implies into every contract for the sale of goods various terms; these will be studied in detail in Session 7.

    (iii)   *Judicial implied terms* - The court may imply a term into a contract whenever it is necessary to do so in order that the express terms decided upon by the parties shall have the effect which was presumably intended by them. In *The Moorcock (1889)*, the appellants (A) had possession of a wharf and jetty while the respondent (R) was the owner of the steamship Moorcock. It was agreed between the parties that the ship would be unloaded and loaded at the wharf and moored alongside the jetty. Both parties realised that when the tide was out the ship would rest in the mud on the bed of the river. However, unknown to R, there was a harsh ridge under the mud, and the ship sustained considerable damage when it settled on that ridge. It was held that although A had given no express warranty concerning the suitability of the river bed as a temporary resting place for the vessel, such a warranty should be implied. A was therefore liable in damages for breach of such a warranty.

3.7.2   Exclusion clauses

Standard-form contracts and exclusion clauses

One of the products of the standardisation of commercial and industrial life resulting from the industrial revolution was the introduction of the standard-form contract and its more or less obligatory contents the exclusion clause.

A standard-form contract is one utilised in every bargain dealing with the same product or service with every client or customer, the individuality of the parties being irrelevant. These contracts are also frequently contracts of adhesion for the party seeking to use the standard contractual form will be the stronger economically and will be able to dictate terms to the other. In particular, he will seek to exclude or limit his liability in the event of certain contingencies and will thereby introduce into the contract terms excluding or limiting that liability known as exclusion clauses.

Validity of exclusion clauses

Such clauses have frequently been the target of judicial and legislative activity and in determining the validity of any particular exclusion clause the following questions must be considered:

  (a)   *Is the clause a term of the contract?* - It is essential that the particular document relied on as containing notice of the exclusion clause be an integral part of the contract:

Chapleton v Barry UDC (1940). It may be integrated either by signature: *L'Estrange v Graucob Limited (1934)* or by giving reasonable notice of its provisions: *Richardson Steamship Co v Rowntree (1894)*. As regards integration by signature the basic rule is that if a document containing an exclusion clause is signed it will be exceedingly difficult to deny its contractual character and evidence of notice is irrelevant. With reference to integration by notice it should be noted that a belated notice, ie, one given after the contract has been made is valueless: *Olley v Marlborough Court Limited (1949)*.

Chapleton v Barry Urban District Council (1940): C, wishing to hire some deck chairs, went to a pack of such chairs behind which was a notice 'Hire of chairs 2d per session of three hours'. C took and paid for two chairs and received two tickets which he put in his pocket without really looking at the wording. On the back of each ticket was a notice - 'The council will not be liable for any accident or damage arising from hire of chairs'. One chair collapsed and C was injured. C sued the council, who sought to rely on the exclusion clause on the ticket. It was held that the council was liable to C, because it had made no attempt to bring its 'exclusion of liability' notice directly to C's attention, while C, for his part, had not noticed the clause.

L'Estrange v Graucob Ltd (1934): The plaintiff ordered an automatic slot machine by signing a printed form supplied by the defendant for this purpose and on this form in very small print were certain special terms. One of these terms provided that 'any express or implied condition, statement or warranty . . . is hereby excluded'. The machine did not work satisfactorily and the plaintiff, who contended that she was not bound by the condition as she had not read it and knew nothing of its contents, claimed damages. The court held that here action must fail as, having signed the contract, in the absence of misrepresentation, she was bound by its terms and the provision in the contract had successfully excluded the defendants' liability under the implied warranty that the machine was fit for the purpose for which it was sold.

Richardson, Spence and Co v Rowntree (1894): The respondent paid the appellants passage money for a voyage on their steamer and was handed a folded ticket which purported to exclude liability in respect of loss or injury exceeding £100. No writing was visible unless the respondent unfolded the ticket. The jury found that the respondent knew there was writing or printing on the ticket, but did not know that it related to the terms of the contract of carriage. The court held that the appellants did not do what was reasonably sufficient to give the respondent notice of the condition and for this reason she was not bound by them.

Olley v Marlborough Court Limited (1949): O and his wife went to M's hotel as guests and paid in advance for a room. On a wall in the room was a notice saying that M would not be liable for items lost or stolen unless handed to the manageress for safe custody. Some of Mrs O's belongings were stolen and O sued M, who relied on the notice as a term of the contract. O succeeded in his claim because he had completed his part of the contract (by paying for the room in advance) before he reached the room in which the notice was displayed. He (and his wife) were accordingly not bound in the terms of the notice.

Thornton v Shoe Lane Parking Ltd (1971): T drove his car up to the automatic barrier of a multi-storey car park, where a notice stated 'all cars parked at owners' risk'. After obtaining his ticket from the machine which then automatically raised the barrier, T drove his car into the car park. The ticket referred to other conditions which were displayed inside the building. One of these conditions exempted the proprietors from liability for possible physical injury sustained by users of the car park, but T (who had not used the car park before) did not read the conditions. T was injured when leaving the car park and sued the defendants as proprietors of the park. It was held that the defendants were liable as T was bound only by the notice at the barrier. He had already accepted the contract (by taking the ticket and entering the premises) before the extra conditions (including the one excluding liability for physical injury) were brought to his attention (even if he had read and understood them).

(b)   *Does the clause cover the loss or damage which has occurred?* - Exclusion clauses are interpreted *contra proferentem* in that any ambiguities in such a clause will be construed against the party seeking to exclude his liability. Thus, in *Andrews v Singer (1934)*, P contracted to buy some 'new Singer cars' from D. By a clause in the written contract 'all conditions, warranties and liabilities, implied by statute, common law or otherwise' were excluded. One of the cars, when delivered, turned out to be a used car. P sued for damages and was successful. The court held that though the term 'new Singer car' was a condition, it was not an implied, but an express, condition, and therefore the exemption clause, since it purported only to protect the sellers from liability for breach of implied conditions, did not apply to it.

(c)   *Are there any grounds on which the clause may be declared inoperative?* - In *Curtis v Chemical Cleaning and Dying Co (1951)*, for example, it was held that an exclusion clause in a signed document could be avoided as the plaintiff had been misled as to the effect of its nature; and, in *Adler v Dickinson (1955)*, that an employee could not take the benefit of an exclusion clause contained in a contract between his employer and one of his employer's customers, though, in *New Zealand Shipping Co Limited v AM Satherwaite and Co Limited (1975)*, it was held that a properly drafted clause could provide such protection.

More significantly, an exclusion clause may be ineffective on the grounds that some statutory provision prohibits or restricts the exclusion of liability in such circumstances. In particular, the Unfair Contract Terms Act 1977 severely limits the ability of a person to exclude his liability. The main provisions are:

(i)   Generally, a business cannot exclude or restrict by contract or by notice, liability for negligence resulting in death or personal injury.

(ii)   A business cannot so exclude or restrict liability for negligence resulting in any other loss or damage except in so far as such contractual term or notice is reasonable.

(iii)   A contract may not exclude or restrict a business' liability for breach of contract or claim that it may perform the contract in a way substantially different from what was agreed.

(iv)   In contracts for the sale and hire-purchase of goods implied terms as to title cannot be excluded at all; implied terms as to conformity of goods with description or sample or as to their quality or fitness for a particular purpose cannot be excluded as against a person dealing as consumer, and, as against non-consumers, can only be excluded subject to such exclusion being reasonable.

The provisions of the Unfair Contract Terms Act 1977 in so far as they relate to the sale of goods will be dealt with in Session 7.

3.8   Revision exercise

In order to assess your assimilation of the above information attempt the following questions. Check your answers against the references given.

(1)   What is a contract?   **(Solution: 3.1.1)**

(2)   To what extent is agreement the basis of contractual liability?   **(Solution: 3.1.2)**

(3)   What are the essentials of a valid contract?   **(Solution: 3.1.3)**

(4)   Differentiate between the terms void and voidable.   **(Solution: 3.1.3)**

(5)   Define an offer.   **(Solution: 3.2.2)**

(6)   In what circumstances does an offer lapse?   **(Solution: 3.2.4)**

(7)   Define an acceptance   **(Solution: 3.2.7)**

(8)   What are the 'postal rules'?   **(Solution: 3.2.7)**

(9)   Explain the need for there to be certainty of terms.   **(Solution: 3.3.1 - 3.3.2)**

(10)   What do you understand by intention to create legal relations?   **(Solution: 3.3.3)**

(11)   What is consideration?   **(Solution: 3.4.1)**

(12)   'Consideration need not be adequate but it must be sufficient.' Explain.
                                                                               (Solution: 3.4.2)

(13)   What is past consideration?   **(Solution: 3.4.2)**

(14)   'Consideration must move from the promisee.' Explain.   **(Solution: 3.4.2)**

(15)   Explain the doctrine of promissory estoppel.   **(Solution: 3.4.3)**

(16)   What do you understand by the requirement of formality?   **(Solution: 3.5.1)**

(17)   What is the general rule in English law as regards formality of contract?
                                                                               (Solution: 3.5.1)

(18)   Explain the phrase 'signed, sealed and delivered'.   **(Solution: 3.5.1)**

(19)   What contract does the law require to be evidenced in writing?   **(Solution: 3.5.1)**

(20)   Explain the term 'necessaries' as used with regard to the contractual capacity of minors.
                                                                               (Solution: 3.6.1)

(21)   In what circumstances does a contract for necessaries bind a minor?   **(Solution: 3.6.1)**

(22)   Explain the term 'beneficial contract of service' as used when speaking of a minor.
                                                                               (Solution: 3.6.1)

(23)   What contracts fall within the category of being voidable by a minor as a result of his lack of contractual capacity?   **(Solution: 3.6.1)**

(24)   What contracts are unenforceable when entered into by a minor?   **(Solution: 3.6.1)**

(25)   Differentiate between terms and representations.   **(Solution: 3.7.1)**

(26)   Distinguish between conditions and warranties.   **(Solution: 3.7.1)**

0065x

(27)   What is an innominate term?   **(Solution: 3.7.1)**

(28)   What are implied terms?   **(Solution: 3.7.1)**

(29)   What is a standard-form contract?   **(Solution: 3.7.2)**

(30)   Define an exclusion clause.   **(Solution: 3.7.2)**

(31)   What questions must be considered in determining the validity of a particular exclusion
         clause?   **(Solution: 3.7.2)**

(32)   Outline the main provisions of the Unfair Contract Terms Act 1977.   **(Solution: 3.7.2)**

3.9   Conclusion

You should now have a knowledge of those factors that raise the moral obligation of agreement to
the legal obligation of contract. You should also have an appreciation of the law regarding the
terms of a contract.

In particular you should have an ability to:

●   determine in relation to factual situations when an agreement has been concluded;

●   state and apply to problematical situations the rules for determining whether or not an
      agreement is supported by consideration;

●   assess the validity of particular exclusion clauses.

3.10   Questions

Objective test questions

(1)   A offers to sell certain goods to B for £150. B responds by sending a cheque to A for
        £140 and giving instructions for delivery of the goods. What is the effect of B's
        response?

        A   It constitutes an acceptance of A's offer.
        B   It causes A's offer to lapse.
        C   It frustrates A's offer.
        D   It amounts to a counter-offer and thereby destroys A's offer.

(2)   Assuming that both parties contemplate the post as the means of communication
        between them, when is an acceptance by post effective?

        A   On delivery.
        B   On being read by the offeror.
        C   On posting.
        D   On the letter of acceptance being signed by the offeree.

(3)   Which of the following would constitute an offer?

    A   An advertisement in a newspaper.
    B   A display of goods in a ship window.
    C   A bid at an auction.
    D   A display of goods in a ship window indicating the price of the goods.

(4)   Which of the following rules regarding consideration is incorrect?

    A   Every simple contract must be supported by consideration.
    B   Consideration must move from the promisee.
    C   Consideration must be adequate.
    D   Consideration must be sufficient.

(5)   A enters into a partnership agreement with B, a minor. This agreement is:

    A   Absolutely void.
    B   Unenforceable.
    C   Binding upon both parties.
    D   Voidable by the minor during his infancy and within a reasonable time thereafter.

(6)   Which of the following contract must be evidenced in writing for it to be enforceable?

    A   An indemnity.
    B   A contract of insurance.
    C   A contract for the sale of land.
    D   A bill of exchange.

(7)   Breach of a condition entitles the injured party:

    A   To claim damages only.
    B   To sue on a *quantum meruit*.
    C   To repudiate the contract and claim damages.
    D   To repudiate the contract only.

(8)   A and B wish to enter into an agreement for the sale and purchase of certain goods. However, they do not wish their agreement to be legally enforceable. In which of the following ways may they achieve this desire?

    A   By making their agreement under seal.
    B   By including in their agreement a clause to that effect.
    C   By not recording their agreement in writing.
    D   By not having their agreement witnessed.

(9)   A number of children, by their father's will, were entitled to a house after their mother's death. During the mother's life, one of the children and his wife lived with her in the house. The wife made various improvements to the house, and at a later date all the children signed a document addressed to her, stating that 'in consideration of your carrying out certain alterations and improvements to the property, we hereby agree that the executors shall repay to you from the estate, when distributed, the sum of £488 in settlement of the amount spent on such improvements'. The agreed sum was not paid. The wife's action to recover the sum will fail on the ground that:

A   There was no intention to create legal relations.
B   Past consideration is no consideration.
C   The document should have been registered.
D   The contract was illegal.

(10)   The legal effect of a trading contract entered into by a minor is that the contract is:

A   Absolutely void.
B   Binding.
C   Unenforceable.
D   Binding on the minor if overall for his benefit.

Written test questions

3.1   White and Black

(a)   Why is it important in the law of contract to distinguish an 'offer' from

(i)   an invitation to treat, and
(ii)   a statement of intention?

(b)   By letter dated 21 June, White offers to sell his house to Black for £50,000. On 23 June Black receives the letter and on the same day posts a reply accepting the offer. On 22 June, White had a heart failure and died. Black is not aware of White's death when he posts his reply. In there a binding contract to sell and buy White's house. If yes, how may the contract be executed? Give reasons for your answer.

3.2   Tim

Tim who is sixteen years of age has just entered into the following:

(a)   a contract with Arthur, a bespoke tailor, to supply him with three suits costing £120 each;

(b)   a partnership agreement with Peter and Paul.

Advise Arthur and Peter and Paul, as regards their legal position.

3.3   Jack, Derek and Christopher

(a)   What is the difference between a condition and a warranty? What is the practical importance of the distinction?

(b)   Jack told Derek that Christopher had a 1974 Range Rover for sale. It was true Christopher had a Range Rover for sale but it was a 1973 model. Derek telephoned Christopher and agreed to buy 'the Range Rover' without any mention of its date of manufacture. When Christopher delivered the Range Rover Derek discovered the mistake and refused to accept it.

Advise Christopher.

SESSION 4

Law of contract 2

This second session on contract examines factors, known technically as vitiating or destructive factors, that may destroy a contractual bond. Careful study of this session will give you:

- a knowledge of the effects of mistake on a contract;

- an understanding of the law regarding misrepresentation;

- an appreciation of duress and undue influence as relevant to contractual liability;

- a knowledge of the law regarding illegality of contract and, in particular, contracts in restraint of trade.

4.1   Genuineness of consent

One of the essential requirements of any contract is the genuine consent of each party to assume the rights and obligations resulting from his becoming a party to the contract. Genuineness of consent in relation to contract may be considered under the principal headings of mistake and misrepresentation. However, before considering these vitiating factors, it is advisable to note carefully the distinction between the words void, voidable, unenforceable and illegal.

Distinction between void, voidable, unenforceable and illegal contracts

A void contract is one which is destitute of legal effect; in fact, it is no contract at all. This means that no rights, duties or liabilities arise out of the 'contract', with the result that:

(a)   neither party is under any obligation towards the other;

(b)   moneys and other property may be recovered by the party (the owner) who transferred them under the 'contract';

(c)   if the transferree has passed property onto a third party, the original transferor (owner) may recover the property even though the third party took it in good faith and for value;

(d)   unless the contract was also illegal, collateral contracts connected with the void contract may be valid, and hence enforceable in the courts.

A voidable contract is one which is valid unless and until the party entitled to avoid it actually does so. If the contract is avoided, the party repudiating it is entitled to recover from the other party any property which he had transferred to the latter, but only if it is still under the transferee's control. If, before the contract was avoided, the other party had sold it to an innocent third party, the purchaser would have acquired a good title to the property even as against the original owner. Thus the position of a third party who has purchased goods from a seller with a void title is quite different from one who has purchased from a seller with a voidable title. If the seller's title was void, the purchaser's title is void and the goods may be claimed from him by the true owner. If the seller's title was voidable (and the owner had not avoided the original contract), then the purchaser will acquire a good title and the true owner will not be able to recover his goods.

An unenforceable contract is one which, although valid, may not be enforced in court because of the absence of some written evidence (required by certain statutes), or because the time stipulated by the Limitation Act 1980 for bringing actions has elapsed. If the technical defect can be remedied (eg, by the plaintiff's being able subsequently to obtain a note or memorandum evidencing the debt, or by the debtor's knowledging a statute-barred debt), the plaintiff will be able to bring an action on the contract.

An illegal 'contract' is not only itself void, but contracts collateral thereto will also be void if the main 'contract' was strictly illegal (ie, contrary to law) at the time of its execution.

4.2   Mistake and misrepresentation

4.2.1   Classification of mistake

If regard is had to the factual situation involved, there are three possible types of mistake:

(a)   *Common mistake* - in this situation each party makes the same mistake.

(b)   *Mutual mistake* - in this situation both parties make a mistake but a different mistake; they are at cross-purposes.

(c)   *Unilateral mistake* - in this situation only one of the parties is mistaken and the other knows, or must be taken to know, of his mistake.

Legally, however, there are only two categories of mistake, for in common mistake the presence of an agreement is admitted whereas in mutual and unilateral mistake the existence of the agreement is denied. However, the distinction between mutual and unilateral mistake cannot be ignored, for in the former the judicial approach is objective whereas in the latter it is subjective.

Finally, it must be realised that a mistake is only relevant if of fact. A mistake of law is no ground for relief from a transaction.

Common mistake

A common mistake has no effect whatsoever at common law unless it is such as to eliminate the very subject matter of the agreement: *Bell v Lever Bros Ltd (1932)*.

The cases in which this has been held to occur seem to fall into two categories - those of *res extincta* and those of *res sua*. In the former what has happened is that the subject matter of the so-called agreement is in fact non-existent and thus the agreement has been emptied of all content. In *Strickland v Turner (1852)* a person bought and paid for an annuity upon the life of another person who, unknown to the buyer and seller, was already dead. A further example is *Couturier v Hastie (1856)*. In that case C was employed by H's London agent to sell corn on behalf of H. C sold some corn to a buyer, but at the time of the sale, the goods (unknown to the parties) had perished. The buyer repudiated the contract, and H sought to sue C, a del credere agent, for the loss arising out of the repudiated contract. (A del credere agent is one who guarantees payment for goods he sells.) It was held that H's action against C failed, because the sale between C (on H's behalf) and the buyer presupposed that the goods were in existence at the time of the sale; as these goods had ceased to exist there had, in fact, been no contract.

In cases of *res sua*, the agreement between the parties is again emptied of all content for one of the parties contracts to buy from the other something which, unknown to either of them, already belongs to the purchaser. In *Cooper v Phibbs (1867)*, for example, one of the parties to a contract contracted to buy from the other a lease of a fishery which, unknown to either of the parties, already belonged to the purchaser.

In contrast with the common law, in equity certain other cases of common mistake may result in the court treating the contract as voidable. However, the remedy is merely discretionary and the court may require the party seeking to avoid the contract to comply with terms proposed by the court.

In *Solle v Butcher (1950)*, B agreed to lease a flat to S for seven years, at a yearly rental of £250, this figure being accepted by S because both parties believed the property to be decontrolled (ie, not affected by the Rent Acts). In fact, the flat was controlled, and when S learnt of this he sought to recover overpaid rent (the controlled rent figure being £140 pa) for his two years' occupation and permission to remain in residence for the remainder of the lease at an annual rental of £140. B counterclaimed for rescission of the lease. It was pointed out that although, for the controlled property, the maximum yearly rent was £140, B could have also claimed eight per cent of repairs and improvements if he had served the relevant statutory notice on S before the lease was executed. This would have brought the total up to approximately £250. It was held that the mistake was one of fact, a bilateral mistake of quality which would not invalidate the contract at common law - therefore S was entitled to succeed with his claim. However, the Court held that, in equity, the contract could be rescinded. The Court offered S the following alternatives: (a) to surrender the lease; or, (b) to remain in possession, but only as a licensee, until B had time to draw up a new lease, after serving the requisite notice, when he would be able to add the sum for repairs to the figure of £140 per annum (thus bringing the total for lawful rent up to £250 per annum).

Equity may also order **rectification** of the terms of a contract where common mistake has occurred, the contract not expressing the true intentions of the parties, but only where it can be shown that:

(a)   There was complete agreement between the parties on all major items at the outset.

(b)   The original agreement continued unchanged until it was reduced to writing.

(c)   It was the writing which did not accurately express what the parties had already agreed.

Mutual mistake

Mutual (non-identical bilateral) mistake occurs where one party refers to a particular item while the other party thinks that another item is being considered. In this case, there is no consensus from the start (unlike cases of common mistake where the parties at least have the same item in mind). It applies even where a third party was responsible for the mistake.

In *Raffles v Wichelhaus (1864)*, W agreed to buy goods from R which were to arrive 'ex Peerless from Bombay'. There were two ships called Peerless sailing from Bombay, one leaving in October and the other two months later. W thought the goods were sailing on the October vessel, whereas R intended the goods to sail on the December vessel. W refused to accept the later delivery and was sued by R. It was held that because there was a mistake as to the subject matter of the contract, there was no effective contract between the parties. R therefore had no action against W.

A feature of cases involving mutual mistake is that, wherever possible, the courts will try to find 'the sense of the promise' and may, on occasion, enforce the contract on the terms understood by one of the parties. However, if this 'sense of promise' cannot be detected, the contract will be void on the grounds of uncertainty, In equity, a contract will not be enforced in a case involving mutual mistake (even if the 'sense of the promise' can be determined) if the court considers that to enforce it would cause hardship to the defendant.

These points are illustrated in the case of *Wood v Scarth (1855)*. S agreed to lease a property to W at a stated annual rental. S intended to charge W a further £500 as premium on W's taking up the lease, but the agent acting on S's behalf, although knowing about the premium, had forgotten to mention it to W. After talking to the agent W wrote to S offering to take the lease 'on the terms already agreed' and S accepted the offer. Here there was a mutual or non-identical bilateral mistake.

Initially, W sued for specific performance when S refused to grant the lease, but the Court, exercising its equitable jurisdiction, refused to grant specific performance, because it was felt to be too hard on S. However, later, when W sued for damages at common law, the Court awarded him damages on the ground that where a case is involved with mutual or non-identical mistake, the Court can find the 'sense of the promise' and treat the contract as having been made on those terms. As it was reasonable for W to be unaware of the premium as a condition for the granting of the lease W was entitled at common law to treat the terms given him by S's agent as the only ones applying to the contract.

Unilateral mistake

Unilateral mistake arises where one party is mistaken as to some material fact concerning the contract, and the other party knows, or ought to know, that the mistake exists. Knowledge by the other party of the mistake's existence is essential, otherwise the first party is liable under the contract. The principal cases of unilateral mistake are those concerning mistakes as to the identity of one of the parties. This sort of mistake is nearly always induced by fraud. A person is persuaded to enter into the contract through a belief that the other party is someone he is not. In this event the contract will only be void if the identity of the other party really mattered. The plaintiff must prove that he only intended to deal with the person whom the other party pretended to be. If the plaintiff cannot do this, he will only have an action against the rogue for misrepresentation. This distinction may be seen by comparing *Cundy v Lindsay (1878)* with *Phillips v Brooks Limited (1919)* and *Lewis v Averay (1971)*.

In *Cundy v Lindsay (1878)*, Blenkarn, a crook, ordered handkerchiefs from Lindsay (L) requesting delivery to 37 Wood Street; in his order his signature was written as Messrs. Blenkiron, a well-known firm situated at 132 Wood Street. L knew of Blenkiron but did not know the firm's address. The goods were sent to 37 Wood Street, and Blenkarn then sold them to Cundy (C) who bought them in good faith. It was held that L had intended dealing with Blenkiron. There had been an operative mistake as to the party with whom they were contracting, and therefore the contract with Blenkarn was void. Consequently, Blenkarn could pass no title to C, who therefore was liable in conversion to L.

In the case of *Phillips v Brooks Limited (1919)*, a rogue went into a jeweller's shop and purported to buy some valuable rings. He then asked if he could take one ring with him for his wife's birthday, at the same time volunteering the information that he was Sir George Bullough of St. James's Square. Phillips, the jeweller, checked the name and address in the telephone directory, and then allowed the rogue to take the ring away. The rogue then pledged the ring with Brooks Limited (B) who were pawnbrokers. P brought an action against B for the recovery of the ring. It was held that, as P had intended dealing with the actual person in the shop (the rogue's assertion that he was Sir George Bullough merely influencing P's decision to let him take a ring away before paying for it), the contract was voidable, not void. The rogue was therefore able to pass on a good title to B (who had acted in good faith) before P sought to rescind the contract. Consequently, P was unable to recover the ring.

In *Lewis v Averay (1971)*, Lewis (L) agreed to sell his car to a crook who, before the sale, gave the impression that he (the crook) was a famous actor (Richard Green). L allowed the crook to take the car after the latter had given him a cheque signed 'RA Green'. The cheque was false, but before L discovered this fact the crook had sold the car to Averay (A). It was held that the contract between L and the crook was voidable for fraud, not void for unilateral mistake. The crook was therefore able to pass on a good title to the car to A.

If the contract with the rogue is voidable not void, the goods may not be recovered from the innocent third party.

Non est factum

This is a specialised form of mistake whereby a party to a contract seeks to deny the contract on the ground that it is not my deed (*'non est factum'*). However, this plea will not be lightly entertained by the courts. While the age and/or infirmity of the pleader may, on occasion, be accepted by the courts as evidence of the mistake, it will not always be so. The general rules which indicate to what extent the plea of *non est factum* will be entertained are:

(a)   The signer of the document forming the basis of the plea should not have been negligent (although infirmity - eg, illiteracy, blindness or senility - may be accepted in mitigation of the pleader's carelessness).

(b)   The document actually signed must be fundamentally different from that which the signer believed it to be - if the end result is basically the same as that which the signer thought would be achieved, he may not plead *non est factum*.

These rules were laid down in *Saunders (Executrix of the estate of Rose Maud Gallie) v Anglia Building Society (previously known as Gallie v Lee) (1971)*. Mrs Gallie (G), a widow of 78, signed a document which Lee (L) told her was a deed of gift of her house to her nephew. (G did not read the document, relying on what L had told her.) The document was actually an assignment of her leasehold interest in the house to L, who later mortgaged that interest to the Anglia Building Society (A). G brought an action against L and A for the recovery of the leasehold interest, and succeeded in the lower court, where it was held:

(a)   The assignment to L was void (on the grounds of *non est factum*).

(b)   Although G had been negligent, she was not liable to A, there being no privity of contract.

The Court of Appeal, on appeal by A, reversed the decision and held that *non est factum* was not available to G. On appeal by G's executrix to the House of Lords, the decision of the Court of Appeal was upheld. The House of Lords restated the law regarding avoidance of documents on the grounds of mistake as follows:

(a)   Non est factum as a plea is rarely available to a person with full capacity who signs a legal document without bothering to read its contents.

(b)   The decision in *Carlisle and Cumberland Banking Co v Bragg (1911)*, has been overruled - in future carelessness on the part of someone signing a document will prevent him from successfully pleading *non est factum*.

4.2.2   The meaning of representation

A representation is a statement made by one party to the other before or at the time of contracting with regard to some existing fact or to some past event which is one of the causes that induces the contract.

This definition should be learnt and the following related matters appreciated:

(a)   A representation of law cannot found an action merely because it happens to be wrong.

(b)   A representation of intention is not actionable unless it implies a statement of fact.

In *Edgington v Fitzmaurice (1885)* a company issued a prospectus inviting the public to subscribe for its debentures. The company stated that the money raised was to complete alterations to the company's premises, to purchase horses and vans and to develop trade. The plaintiff advanced money, but it turned out that the real object of the loan was to enable the directors to pay off pressing liabilities. It was held that the misstatement of the purpose for which the debentures were issued was a material misstatement of fact which rendered the directors liable in deceit.

(c)   · A statement of opinion will not constitute a representation, unless it can be shown that the person making the statement had no such opinions.

In *Smith v Land and House Property Corporation (1884)*, for example, a vendor described his property as being 'let to Mr Frederick Fleck (a most desirable tenant) at a rental of £400 a year (clear of rates, taxes, insurance, etc) for an unexpired time of 27½ years, thus offering a first-class investment'.

In fact the Lady Day rent had been paid by instalments under pressure and no part of the midsummer rent had been paid. It was held that the description of Mr Fleck as 'a most desirable tenant' was not a mere expression of opinion. It was an untrue assertion that nothing had occurred which could be regarded as rendering him an undesirable tenant.

(d)   A representation must be by positive words or conduct. Silence or non-disclosure by one or both of the parties does not normally affect the contract. However, it may do so in the following circumstances:

     (i)   Where the statement is a half-truth:

          In *R v Kyslant (1932)*, the chairman of a company was convicted under a section of the Larceny Act (since repealed), because his company put out a prospectus with some very relevant facts omitted. The prospectus stated that the company had paid out dividends every year for a number of years, which was true. It did not say, however, that these had been paid from reserves, etc, and the company had actually suffered substantial losses in those years.

     (ii)   Where the statement was true when made but becomes false before the contract is concluded:

          In *With v O'Flanagan (1936)*, O wished to sell his medical practice and, in January 1934, he informed W (Who was interested in buying the practice) that the annual income from the practice was £2,000. Shortly afterwards, O fell ill and his practice's receipts fell to £5 per week. In the meantime W had agreed to buy the practice, relying on the original information given by O). The contract for sale was not executed until May 1934, when no mention was made by O of the marked fall in income. W subsequently sought rescission of the contract. It was held that he was entitled to do so, because the representation concerning the annual income was of a continuing nature until the contract was completed. W was therefore entitled to be advised of any change in the rate of income, and O's silence accordingly constituted a misrepresentation of a fundamental term.

     (iii)   Where there is a fiduciary or confidential relationship between the parties.

     (iv)   Where the contract is one uberrimae fidei (that is, of utmost good faith). This concept is dealt with below.

(e)   Trade puffs do not amount to representation.

Contracts uberrimae fidei

As already stated, the general rule is that silence is not misrepresentation. However, there are certain contracts where, from the very necessity of the case, one party alone possesses full knowledge of all the material facts and in which therefore the law requires him to show *uberrimae fides* - utmost good faith. He must make full disclosure of all the material facts known to him, otherwise the contract may be rescinded.

The classic example of such contracts is that of insurance. It is the duty of the person insured to disclose to the insurer all facts which might affect the premium: *London Assurance v Mansel (1879)*. If, therefore, the insured omits the information required, the insurer may rescind the contract.

Also within the scope of the concept *uberrimae fidei* are contracts between members of a family designed to preserve the harmony, to protect the property and to save the honour of the family: *Greenwood v Greenwood (1863)*.

In addition, there are certain other contracts, such as those to take shares in a company under a prospectus, analogous to contracts *uberrimae fidei* but which in truth are not strictly speaking of utmost good faith.

The meaning of inducement

In order to operate as an inducement the representation must be made with the intention that it should be acted upon by the person misled. In *Peek v Gurney (1873)*, Peek bought shares in a company, from an existing shareholder, on the strength of certain statements by directors of the company included in a prospectus. Some of the statements were false, and Peek sued the directors. It was held that Peek's action failed because he was a purchaser, and not an original allottee, of the shares he acquired. He could not therefore rely on statements in the prospectus which were only intended to mislead the original allottees.

The statement must actually induce the contract: the person making the claim to have misled must not have relied on his own skill and judgement. In *Redgrave v Hurd (1881)* a man was induced to buy a solicitor's practice by a misstatement of its value. He was given an opportunity to examine the accounts. If he had examined the accounts he would have discovered the truth. He did not examine them, preferring to rely on what he had been told. The misstatement was held to be an operative misrepresentation.

The representation must be material, in the sense that it affected the plaintiff's judgement. In *Smith v Chadwick (1884)*, for example, a prospectus contained a false statement that a certain important person was on the board of directors, but the plaintiff frankly admitted in cross-examination that he had been in no degree influenced by this fact. The plaintiff was held unable to recover.

Finally, if it is to induce the transaction it must be known to the plaintiff. In *Horsfall v Thomas (1862)*, T bought a gun from H, who had made it. Soon afterwards, the gun broke and it was shown that the breech was defective, and that a plug had been inserted to hide the defect. T refused to pay and H sued him; T pleaded fraud on H's part. H succeeded and T's defence failed because T had never examined the gun, so the concealment of the defect was immaterial and unknown to T. It could not have induced the transaction.

Types of misrepresentation

Misrepresentations may be:

(a) *Fraudulent*, if the party making the statement intended to mislead or did not honestly believe it to be true or made it recklessly without caring whether it was true or false.

(b) *Innocent*, if the party making it honestly believed it to be true. Innocent misrepresentation may be:

  (i) *innocent but negligent*, where the person making the statement, although unaware that it was false, nevertheless uttered it without having reasonable grounds for believing it to be true;

  (ii) *innocent and non-negligent*, where the person making the statement had reasonable grounds for believing it to be true.

Remedies

For fraudulent misrepresentation:

(a) rescission of the contract by the party misled;

(b) refusal by the injured party to perform his part of the contract;

(c)   in addition to (a) or (b), an action in damages by the injured party for any loss suffered by him.

For innocent but negligent misrepresentation:

(a)   rescission of the contract (but the judge or arbitrator may at his discretion refuse to permit rescission and may award damages in lieu);

(b)   refusal by the injured party to perform his part of the contract;

(c)   damages for loss (in addition to any damages granted in lieu of the plaintiff's right to rescind the contract).

For innocent, non-negligent misrepresentation:

(a)   rescission (but subject to the judge's or arbitrator's discretionary power to award damages in lieu);

(b)   refusal by the injured party to perform his part of the contract.

It should be noted that, with innocent, non-negligent misrepresentation, the plaintiff has no common law or statutory right to claim damages for any loss suffered. The only damages he might be awarded are those granted by the judge or arbitrator in lieu of the plaintiff's right to rescind the contract.

A contract may not be rescinded where:

(a)   The injured party has taken a benefit under the contract, or has in some other way affirmed it.

(b)   There has been too great a lapse of time, a form of implied affirmation (*Leaf v International Galleries (1950)*).

(c)   The parties cannot be restored to their original positions.

(d)   Third party rights have accrued (*Phillips v Brooks Limited (1919)* and *Lewis v Averay (1972)* - see above).

Moreover, as mentioned earlier, a plaintiff will lose his right to rescind a contract on the grounds of innocent misrepresentation if the judge or arbitrator awards damages in lieu of rescission.

In addition to the civil law remedies referred to in the preceding paragraphs, the Trade Descriptions Act 1968 prescribes certain criminal penalties for which a person may become liable if he falsely or misleadingly describes goods which he is selling.

4.3   Duress and undue influence

Duress means actual violence, or threats of violence, to the person (not merely to property), or imprisonment or the threat of criminal proceedings to the person coerced or to those near and dear to him. There is, however, authority recognising economic duress as a vitiating factor if the duress amounts to a coercion of will negativing consent.

Undue influence is a doctrine which was developed by equity, and refers not only to the person but also to his property.

The law governing the effects of duress and undue influence on contracts is today virtually the same. The party threatened or unduly influenced may treat the contract as voidable, subject to the following rules:

(a)   There is a presumption of undue influence where there is some form of confidential relationship between the parties which the law regards as putting one of the parties under the influence (if not the control) of the other - eg, parent and child, trustee and beneficiary, solicitor and client, and guardian and ward (but not husband and wife).

(b)   There may also be a presumption of undue influence if it can be shown that, although none of the special relationships in (a) prevails, nevertheless:

    (i)   a gift is so large, or of such a nature, that it would not ordinarily have been made; and

    (ii)   there exists such a relationship between the donor and the recipient as to raise the presumption that the former was under the influence of the latter.

(c)   Where undue influence is presumed, the onus is on the person assumed to have exercised the influence to prove that, in fact, he did not do so (eg, by showing that the other party was independently advised).

(d)   In other cases, it is the party seeking to avoid the contract who must prove that he has been subjected to duress or undue influence.

(e)   *Laches* (ie, delay on the part of the person influenced in bringing his action) may defeat his claim to have the contract set aside.

(f)   A third party contracting with a person known to him to have been subjected to undue influence by another is in the same position as if he, the third party, had exercised the undue influence himself.

    In *Lancashire Loans Limited v Black (1934)*, a girl of 18 married and lived with her husband in his home. However, for some years after her marriage she raised funds to enable her mother, an extravagant person, to pay off her debts. The mother and daughter signed a joint and several promissory note in favour of the plaintiffs, and in due course the plaintiffs sued mother and daughter on the note. The daughter did not appreciate the nature of the transactions (including charging property to which she was entitled) which she was persuaded to enter into, and her only adviser was a solicitor who acted for the mother and the plaintiffs. It was held that the daughter was able to avoid liability on the note on the grounds that she was under the undue influence of her mother (despite the fact that she was married, was by then of full age, and had her own home), and that the plaintiffs were aware of this undue influence.

As with other forms of voidable contract, a contract procured by undue influence may not be avoided after affirmation (express or implied) or as against third party purchasers. However, if he has not affirmed the contract, the party influenced may avoid it as against:

(a)   persons knowing him to have been subjected to undue influence;
(b)   third persons receiving the property transferred without having purchased it.

4.4 Types of invalid contract

4.4.1 Illegal contracts

Nature and effect

A contract may be illegal because it is expressly prohibited by law, or because it is deemed to be contrary to public policy (ie, not in the public interest).

Illegality by statute

The nature and effect of contracts declared illegal by statute depend on the terms of the Act concerned. A few statutes declare the whole contract illegal and thus void as are contracts collateral thereto. The Life Assurance Act 1774 makes a contract to insure a life in which the proposer has no insurable interest illegal. Other statutes declare certain terms in a contract to be illegal; the remainder of the contract will be valid.

Illegality at common law

Illegal contracts regarded at common law as being against public policy include contracts:

(a)   *For the commission of a crime, tort or fraud* - In *Gray v Barr (1970)*, for example, B accidentally shot and killed G (who was Mrs B's lover) after having menaced G with a loaded shotgun. B admitted liability and paid damages to G's estate. He tried to obtain indemnity under an accident liability insurance policy, but his action failed because it was held that his threatening G with a loaded gun was unlawful, and it would have been against public policy to allow him to benefit under the policy. In *Dann v Curzon (1911)* Dann agreed for reward to commit a breach of the peace (in modern terms, in fact, to 'streak') to publicise a play to be performed at Curzon's theatre. He was unable to enforce the promise of payment, the purpose of the contract having been the commission of a crime.

(b)   *For immoral purpose (sexual or otherwise)* - The case of *Pearce v Brooks (1866)* illustrates a contract of this type. P hired a carriage to B, who was known by P to be a prostitute and to need the vehicle for her profession. P brought an action against B for sums due under the contract for hire. The action failed because the contract was illegal, due to the fact that at the time the contract was made, P knew the carriage was to be used for immoral purposes.

(c)   *Prejudicial to the safety of the public* (eg, trading contracts with persons in enemy countries in time of war).

(d)   *Prejudicial to the proper administration of justice.*

(e)   *Liable to cause corruption in public life* - It was held that the contract in *Parkinson v The College of Ambulance Limited and Harrison (1925)* was illegal, being liable to cause corruption in public life. H, as secretary of the college, agreed with P that if P paid a donation to the college (a charity), the charity might be able to obtain for P some suitable honour (eg, a knighthood). P paid £3,000 but received no honour. P sued the college and H for the recovery of the sum paid. His action failed, as the agreement between P and H (for the college) was against public policy and illegal.

(f)   *Intended to defraud the Revenue or other taxation bodies* - In *Alexander v Rayson (1936)*, A sublet a flat to R on condition that R paid £450 a year as rental and a further £750 for services to be provided by A. In fact, it was shown that A had no intention of providing the services referred to - the second agreement was intended to mislead the local rating authority into assessing the rateable value of the flat on the basis of an annual rental of £450 instead of the more realistic £1,200. After a period during which £300 a quarter was paid by R, R paid the rental of £112.50 for a quarter but refused to pay for the 'services'. A sought to recover the amount outstanding. His action failed because the agreement for services was illegal.

Effects of an illegal contract

If a contract is strictly illegal at the moment it is made:

(a)   the contract is void, so that neither party may bring an action;

(b)   money or property transferred may not be recovered; however, there are certain exceptions to this rule, namely:

  (i)   where the parties are not equally at fault the innocent party may recover money paid under the contract;

  (ii)   if the illegal purpose has not been substantially performed, a party who has paid money under a contract may recover it if he has repented;

  (iii)   where one has an illegal intent unknown to the other and the contract is lawful in its inception;

  (iv)   where the action for recovery of property is independent of the illegal contract;

(c)   collaterial contracts are also illegal;

(d)   if executed abroad, it cannot be enforced in England (even if it was legal in the country of execution).

Illegal contracts are treated more severely by the courts than any other type of contract, as shown above, and they should therefore be carefully distinguished from the contracts dealt with below which are sometimes called 'illegal contracts'.

4.4.2   Void contracts

Nature and effect

Void contracts (as distinct from those which are strictly illegal) include contracts which are:

(a)   prohibited by statue:

  (i)   wagering contracts under the Gaming Act 1845 - a wager is an agreement between two persons whereby on the happening or non-happening of some uncertain event in respect of which neither party has an interest other than the wager itself (contrast insurance contracts) one party will win and the other will lose;

(ii)   restrictive trade agreements under the Restrictive Trade Practices Act 1976;

(iii)   certain resale price maintenance agreements under the Resale Prices Act 1976;

(b)   contrary to public policy, at common law:

(i)   contracts intended to oust the jurisdiction of the courts, ie, agreements which purport to deprive a party of the right to submit questions of law to the court;

(ii)   contracts which are prejudicial to the status of marriage (eg, those in total restraint of marriage, and marriage brokage contracts);

(iii)   contracts in restraint of trade.

The effects of a contract being void, though not illegal, are:

(a)   the terms of the contract are unenforceable, but only insofar as they are contrary to public policy;

(b)   if certain provisions are lawful and severable, they may be enforceable;

(c)   money and other property transferred may be recoverable;

(d)   subsequent or collateral promises may be actionable;

(e)   if the contract was legal in its country of execution, it may be enforceable in England;

4.4.3   Contracts in restraint of trade

Nature

A contract in restraint of trade is one whereby a person who has entered into a contract agrees to suffer some restriction as to carrying on his trade, profession or calling. A contract in restraint of trade (partial or general) is prima facie void and may not be enforced unless the restraint is considered reasonable in the interests of the parties and of the public at large.

Types

Contracts in restraint of trade are of three main types:

(a)   Agreements where an employee undertakes that he will not, after leaving his present employment, compete with his employer either by setting up a business of his own or by entering the service of another employer.

(b)   Agreements where merchants or manufacturers combine for the purpose of regulating their trade relations.

(c)   Agreements between the vendor and purchaser of the goodwill of a business, whereby the vendor promises that he will not carry on a similar business in competition with the purchaser.

The courts are more likely to uphold categories (b) and (c) where the parties' bargaining positions are likely to be balanced.

Rules governing

The modern law regarding such contracts dates from the decision of the House of Lords in *Nordenfelt v Maxim Nordenfelt Guns and Ammunition Co (1894)* and may be summarised as follows:

(a)   If a contract is classifiable as in restraint of trade it is prima facie void and cannot become binding unless the test of reasonableness is satisfied.

(b)   The restraint must be reasonable in the interest of both parties and also in the public interest.

(c)   To be reasonable between the parties, the restraint must be no wider than is reasonably necessary to protect the covenantee's interest.

(d)   Whether a restraint is reasonable is a question for the court to decide.

As stated above the courts are more willing to uphold a restraint on the vendor of a business than one on an employee, for a purchaser of a business must be entitled to protect the asset he has bought against competition by the vendor. However, it will not be enforced unless it is connected with some proprietary interest in need of protection.

Accordingly, there must be a genuine, not merely a colourable sale of a business by the covenantor to the covenantee: *Vancouver Malt and Sake Brewing Co Ltd v Vancouver Breweries Ltd (1934)*; and it is only the actual business sold by the covenantor that is entitled to protection: *British Concrete Co v Schelff (1921)*.

An express covenant in such a case may, therefore, be valid, but only if it is no wider than is necessary for the adequate protection of the proprietary interest acquired by the purchaser. In considering this question, the court pays special attention to the two factors of time and area.

As regards restraints imposed on an employee, these are never reasonable unless there is some proprietary interest of the employer which required protection. The only matters in which he will be held to have such an interest are his trade secrets (if any): *Forster and Sons Ltd v Suggett (1978)* and his business connection: *Fitch v Dewes (1921)*.

In determining whether an agreement is reasonable, the courts pay regard to the class of business of the employer; the status and class of work of the employee; the area covered by the restriction; and the duration of the restraint clause in the agreement.

The factors outlined above are examined in the cases set out below.

In *Morris & Co v Saxelby (1916)*, S was employed by M and covenanted not to engage anywhere in the UK in business of a nature similar to that of M, during the seven years following his leaving M's employment. When M sought to enforce the covenant it was held that their action failed, because the area and length of the restraint were unreasonable, having regard to the protection of M's interests. The restraint effectively debarred S from working anywhere in the United Kingdom in the business in which he was skilled, even though M's offices were situated in only a few cities.

In *Esso Petroleum Limited v Harper's Garage (Stourport) Limited (1967)*, H owned two garages (M and C), each of which were tied to E by 'solus agreements' (whereby a garage buys all its petrol from one supplier). As regards the M garage, the agreement provided that H would buy E's products from time to time at E's scheduled prices, and also that in the event of H's selling the garage H would persuade the buyer to enter into a similar solus agreement with E. The agreement was to continue for about four and a half years. As regards the C garage, there was a similar solus agreement, coupled with a mortgage under which E lent £7,000 to assist H with the purchase and improvement of the garage. The agreement was for a period of 21 years, and forbade redemption of the mortgage during that period. When H sought to redeem the mortgage after a year E refused to accept repayment. When H decided to sell a rival company's fuel at both garages, E sought injunctions to prevent him doing so.

It was held that:

(a)   The solus agreement in respect of garage M was reasonable (as regards the nature and duration of the restraint) and was binding on H.

(b)   The agreement in respect of garage C concerning the tie for 21 years, and the mortgage for a similar period, was unreasonable, and the injunction sought by E could not be granted.

Another case, illustrating the question of the duration of the restraint is *Fitch v Dewes (1921)*, in which D was employed as managing clerk by F, a solicitor, whose office was at Tamworth. In his contract of service D agreed that if he left F's employment he would never practise as a solicitor within seven miles of Tamworth. In an action brought by F, it was held that the agreement was valid, because it was reasonable that D should be prevented indefinitely from using confidential knowledge concerning F's clients, gained by D while working for F, to the detriment of F.

This case also shows that sometimes a restraint may be for a very long period of time and yet still be reasonable in the eyes of the court.

In *Attwood v Lamont (1920)*, L, an employee of A (who carried on a business as a tailor, draper and general outfitter in Kidderminster) agreed that if he left A's employment he would not at any time carry on any of a wide range of activities within ten miles of Kidderminster. However, after leaving A's employment L set up a tailoring business on his own near Kidderminster, and took orders from some of A's customers. A sought an injunction to prevent L's continuing as a tailor. His action failed because:

(a)   The restraint in respect of tailoring was not severable (see below) from the rest of the wide range of activities listed in the covenant executed by L.

(b)   Even if it had been severable it would not be enforceable because it involved L's skill rather than any trade connection, and an employee cannot be prevented from competing against his ex-employer where the threat to the employer is merely the ability of his ex-employee.

Severance

If the restraint consists of a number of clauses which are severable, the courts may apply the 'blue pencil' test, ie, they may uphold certain of the clauses if they remain, unamended, after the offending clauses have been deleted or 'severed'.

In *Nordenfelt v Maxim Nordenfelt Gun Co (1894)*, N, an inventor and manufacturer of guns and ammunition, sold his business to M and agreed that, for a period of 25 years, he would not make guns or ammunition anywhere in the world, and would not compete with M in any way. In an action, it was held that:

(a)   The restraint concerning the manufacture of guns and ammunition was reasonable, because the market for those products was worldwide.

(b)   The restraint covering other forms of competition was unreasonable.

As these restraints were severable, (a) could be enforced although (b) was void.

In *Scorer v Seymour Jones (1966)*, S sought an injunction to prevent SJ, (an ex-employee who had covenanted not to work in competition within five miles of K or D for three years after leaving the plaintiff's employment), from practising near K. It was held that the injunction should be granted as regards SJ's practising near K because although SJ's office was outside a five mile radius of D, the restraint clause could be severed so as to exclude the reference to D but to be effective in respect of K. However, if the clauses are not severable, none of the restraint will be upheld, because it is not the duty of the courts to make a contract for the parties.

Finally, if an employee is wrongfully dismissed, his employer may not enforce a restrictive agreement against him. In *General Billposting Co v Atkinson (1909)*, A was employed by the X Company, and covenanted not to carry on a similar business within a certain radius of Newcastle while employed by X or during the two years following his leaving X's employment. X dismissed A who brought a successful action against X for wrongful dismissal. He then set up a rival business within the stated area. G, who had bought X's business, sought an injunction to prevent A from competing. It was held that as the courts had supported A's action for wrongful dismissal, A was entitled to treat his original contract (and its covenant) as having been repudiated. He was therefore no longer bound by the terms of the covenant.

4.5   Revision exercise

In order to assess your understanding of the above session attempt the following questions. Check your answers against the references given.

(1)   Define the term 'common mistake'.   **(Solution: 4.2.1)**

(2)   Differentiate between mutual and unilateral mistake.   **(Solution: 4.2.1)**

(3)   Explain the concepts *res extincta* and *res sua*.   **(Solution: 4.2.1)**

(4)   In what circumstances is a mutual mistake operative?   **(Solution: 4.2.1)**

(5)   In what circumstances does a unilateral mistake of identity render a contract void?
                                                                                                              (Solution: 4.2.1)

(6)   Differentiate between duress and undue influence.   **(Solution: 4.3)**

(7)   What contracts are regarded at common law as being illegal?   **(Solution: 4.4.1)**

(8)   What contracts are regarded at common law as being void on grounds of public policy?
                                                                                                              (Solution: 4.4.2)

(9)   What are the effects of a contract being void, though not illegal, at common law?

(Solution: 4.4.2)

(10)   What is a contract in restraint of trade?

(Solution: 4.4.3)

(11)   What are the main types of contract in restraint of trade?

(Solution: 4.4.3)

(12)   Outline the rules governing contracts in restraint of trade.

(Solution: 4.4.3)

(13)   What is the doctrine of severance?

(Solution: 4.4.3)

4.6   Conclusion

You should now have a practical knowledge of those factors that may vitiate a contract. In particular, you should be able to deal with problems involving all or any of the forms of mistake, misrepresentation and, as regards illegality, determine the validity or otherwise of particular contracts in restraint of trade.

4.7   Questions

Objective test questions

(1)   An operative unilateral mistake of identity will render a contract:

A   Voidable.
B   Void.
C   Unenforceable.
D   Irregular but valid.

(2)   Which of the following statements regarding the remedy of rescission is incorrect?

A   Rescission is available as of right.
B   Rescission is not available if *restitutio in integrum* is impossible.
C   The remedy of rescission must be pursued quickly.
D   The intervention of third party rights is a bar to rescission.

(3)   On 5 November A entered into a contract to sell a painting to B. Unknown to either party the painting had been destroyed by fire on 4 November. The destruction of the painting:

A   Renders the contract voidable by B.
B   Brings about the frustration of the contract.
C   Has no effect on the contract.
D   Renders the contract void on the ground of common mistake.

(4)   A contract in restraint of trade is:

A   Void.
B   Valid.
C   *Prima facie* void except insofar as reasonable.
D   Voidable.

4.17

(5)   Which of the following can never constitute a misrepresentation?

     A   A statement of opinion.
     B   Silence.
     C   A statement of intention.
     D   A statement of law.

(6)   Which of the following would render a contract illegal?

     A   An understanding to the effect that the parties do not intend their agreement to be legally enforceable.

     B   An undertaking to the effect that the parties do not intend their agreement to be legally enforceable.

     C   An agreement to oust the jurisdiction of the courts.

     D   An agreement that the parties shall make arrangements to defraud the Inland Revenue.

(7)   A fraudulent misrepresentation renders a contract:

     A   Void.
     B   Voidable.
     C   Illegal.
     D   Absolutely void.

(8)   Humphrey contracts with John to purchase from him a consignment of wool being delivered to the UK on flight TE001 from New Zealand. Unbeknown to either party, during the course of the flight, shortly before the time at which the contract was made, the wool was destroyed due to adverse conditions in the aircraft hold. The contract is:

     A   Void for mutual mistake.
     B   Void for common mistake.
     C   Voidable for common mistake.
     D   Enforceable, the sense of the promise being detectable.

(9)   Duress renders a contract:

     A   Voidable.
     B   Illegal.
     C   Unenforceable.
     D   Void.

(10)   A successful plea of *non est factum* renders a contract:

     A   Unenforceable.
     B   Illegal.
     C   Void.
     D   Voidable.

Written test questions

4.1   James and Robert

(a)   When can a person who has paid money under a contract which has turned out to be illegal, recover the money so paid?

(b)   James paid £1,000 to Robert, a civil servant employed in a government department, in return for Robert's promise to use his position to secure a valuable government contract for James. On the procurement of the relevant contract James was to pay Robert a further £2,000. However, before the contract could be placed, Robert was dismissed from his job and was thus unable to help James in obtaining the contract. James now claims that he has repented of his arrangement with Robert and is seeking to recover the £1,000 he has already paid to Robert.

Advise James.

4.2   Bernard's Garage Limited

(a)   What is meant by a contract in restraint of trade? In what circumstances (if any) will the courts give effect to such contracts?

(b)   Bernard's Garage Limited owned a garage and had entered into a solus agreement with Basso Oil Co Limited whereby the garage company agreed:

(i)   to buy all its motor fuel from Basso Oil Co Limited;

(ii)   to keep the garage open at all reasonable hours; and

(iii)   not to sell the garage without ensuring that the purchaser entered into a similar agreement with Basso Oil Co Limited.

The garage was mortgaged to the oil company in return for an advance of £20,000, and the mortgage was not redeemable before the end of a period of twenty-five years.

Bernard's Garage Limited wish to challenge the validity of the agreement. Advise them.

4.3   Sykes

(a)   (i)   In the law of contract, what are the meaning and effect of 'operative mistake', and how is it classified?

(ii)   Briefly describe the meaning and effect of unilateral mistake.

(b)   A rogue, Sykes, presented himself at a shop dealing in radios and other electrical goods, and announced that he was Lord Rich and wanted to buy a tape recorder as a present for his daughter. The shopkeeper sold him a tape recorder and the rogue said he would pay later. The rogue then took the tape recorder to a dealer in second-hand goods who gave him £25 for it.

Can the original vendor recover the tape recorder from the dealer?

SESSION 5

Law of contract 3

This session concludes your study of the law of contract.

After careful study of this session you should have a knowledge of:

- the ways in which a contract can be discharged;

- the law regarding discharge of contract by frustration;

- the remedies available for breach of contract, with particular reference to damages;

- the doctrine of privity of contract and the exceptions to the doctrine.

5.1   Discharge of contract

A contract may be discharged, that is brought to an end, in any of the following ways: agreement; performance; breach; subsequent impossibility (frustration); lapse of time; and operation of law.

5.1.1   Discharge by agreement (accord and satisfaction)

The parties may decide before either of them has performed his side of the contract that they will not perform it. Their agreement to discharge the contract will be valid without any formality. The consideration is their mutual release. This is known as **bilateral discharge**.

Sometimes, one party will agree to excuse or release the other party from performance, even though he himself has already performed his part of the contract. This agreement to discharge must be supported by fresh consideration or be made in a deed. This is known as **unilateral discharge**. For example, A delivers goods in accordance with a contract to B. The agreed price is £200. The parties agree that instead of paying £200, B will give A £100 plus ten hours of gardening work. The contract to pay £200 is discharged by the subsequent agreement. B's consideration is the promise to do the gardening work. The agreement is known as **accord**, and the consideration as **satisfaction**.

New agreement

A new agreement may be entered into by the parties to the original contract, whereby the earlier contract is replaced by the later one. This is termed **novation**. However, this will be effective only if both parties had still to perform their obligations under the earlier contract. An example of novation occurs when an incoming partner agrees with the existing creditors of the firm to be responsible for the debts in place of an outgoing partner.

Provision for discharge

A provision may be incorporated in a contract whereby the contract will automatically be discharged if:

(a)   A condition is not fulfilled, which is termed a condition precedent (see *Head v Tattersall*, below).

(b)   A certain event occurs, which is termed a condition subsequent.

(c)   The contract contains a term that either party may terminate by notice (eg, contracts of employment).

In *Head v Tattersall (1871)*, T sold a horse to H, and warranted that it had hunted with the Bicester hounds. T also gave H the right to return the horse by a specified date if the warranty was bad. The horse was injured, but this was through no fault of H who returned it to T by the specified date, having discovered that it had not hunted with the Bicester hounds. It was held that H, having returned the horse in time and because of the breach of warranty, was entitled to treat the contract as discharged. It should be noted that by itself, the breach of contract would not have enabled H to rescind the contract. However, T's giving H the right to return the horse if the warranty was bad constituted a condition; namely, that the contract was at an end if, because of the breach of warranty, H returned the horse within the specified time.

Form of agreement to discharge

An agreement to discharge does not normally require any particular form; indeed, a contract under seal may be discharged by an oral agreement. However, a contract which must be evidenced in writing (eg, sale of an interest in land) must be varied in writing.

5.1.2   Discharge by performance

In general, a contract is not discharged by performance unless and until both parties have completed their part of the bargain. In *Cutter v Powell (1795)*, C was employed as second mate on a ship whose master was P. The contract of employment provided that C was to receive a stated sum on completion of C's duties for the whole of the journey from Jamaica to Liverpool. C died on the journey, and his widow sought to obtain a share of the wages for the period up to C's death. It was held that the contract was for satisfactory performance of the whole contract, and as C had not completed the whole of the agreed services an action on a quantum meruit for part performance could not be upheld (The Merchant Shipping Act 1970 now provides for the payment of wages for partial performance where the contract cannot be completed because of death, injury, sickness, etc suffered by the employee.)

However, the following are exceptions to the general rule:

(a)   *Where the contract is divisible*, the courts may enforce certain portions thereof if:

(i) the portions in question are identifiable, severable and complete in themselves; and

(ii) the plaintiff has fully performed his obligations in connection with those portions.

(b) *Where a partial performance has been accepted*, the party who has made the partial performance may sue on a quantum meruit if the other party has actually accepted the benefit of that performance. For example, X contracts to supply ten rosebushes. He delivers five which Y accepts. Y must pay for those five bushes. If the other party has no choice but to accept performance he will not have to pay for it. Thus, in *Sumpter v Hedges (1898)* S agreed to build property on H's land and after S had partially performed his side of the contract H paid him some of the contract price. S then told H that, owing to his having been out of funds, he was unable to finish the contract. H then got somebody else to complete the work, and materials, belonging to S, lying on the site were used for this purpose. In an action brought by S it was held that:

(i) he was entitled to recover the value of the materials used;

(ii) he could not succeed with his claim for work done, because quantum meruit claims are granted only where the defendant was free to accept (or reject) the work done. In the present case, H had no option but to accept the work done (ie, partial construction on his own land);

(c) *Where performance is prevented by one party*, the other party can claim on a quantum meruit for the amount of work done by him to the date when the other party prevented him from continuing. In *De Bernady v Harding (1853)*, for example, D agreed to act as H's agent for the preparation and issue of certain notices intended to encourage the sale of tickets for the funeral of the Duke of Wellington. The agreement provided that D was to be paid a commission of ten per cent on the proceeds of sale of the tickets. After D had completed work on the notices, H withdrew D's authority to sell tickets, thus depriving D from earning his commission. D bought an action against M, claiming on a *quantum meruit* for work done, and it was held that he should succeed.

(d) *Where there has been substantial performance*, the plaintiff may sue on the contract for the work he has performed (although the defendant will be able to counter-claim for work not done or done badly). Thus, in *Hoening v Issacs (1952)* I employed H to decorate I's flat and to supply furniture for a total of £750. I made two payments of £150 each, after which H claimed the balance of £450 when he asserted the decorating was complete. I claimed that the work done by H was faulty, but nevertheless sent H a further £100, at the same time moving into the flat and using the furniture supplied by H. H then sued for the balance of £350, I's defence being that the contract was not complete. The court held that the contract was not substantially completed and I was liable for the balance of £50 less the cost (approximately) of £56 for putting the faulty workmanship right.

Time of performance

The general rule is that time is not of the essence of a contract, but it will be if the contract specifically provides for it to be so. Where a specified time for completion is provided for in a contract, failure by the party concerned to complete this obligation within that period constitutes a breach of contract. If no time is stipulated, the law will presume that the parties intended performance to be within a reasonable time.

5.1.3   Discharge by breach

A party may fail to perform his side of the contract altogether or he may fail to perform part of his side of the contract. The other party may only treat himself as discharged if the failure amounts to a breach of condition.

If a party renounces his obligations in advance of the date for performance this is known as anticipatory breach. The case of *Hochster v De La Tour (1853)* is an example. In April 1852 D agreed to engage H as courier, H's duties to begin on 1 June 1852. On 11 May 1852 D wrote to H saying that he (D) no longer needed H's services. H started his action for breach of contract on 22 May 1852 and it was held that he was entitled to do so, on the ground of anticipatory breach of contract, even though the date fixed for H to start his duties had not yet occurred. If there has been an anticipatory breach, the innocent party may act on the breach immediately or he may wait until the time for performance. It is advisable to act quickly in case frustration (see below) occurs. In *Avery v Bowden (1855)*, B chartered A's ship and agreed to load her at Odessa within 45 days of the agreement. The ship arrived at Odessa, where it stayed for most of the relevant period. B told the ship's captain that he was not going to load the vessel after all, and advised the captain to leave Odessa at once. However, the ship remained at Odessa (her captain hoping that B would change his mind and load after all). Before the end of the relevant period the Crimean War began, after which it would have been illegal for the loading to have been carried out. It was held that, although A could have treated B's refusal to load as an anticipatory breach of contract, A's captain remaining at Odessa constituted a waiver of that right and, because of the intervening event (the Crimean War), the contract had been frustrated. A's action therefore failed.

A party may refuse to accept an anticipatory breach, perform his part and then sue for the full contract 'price'. This happened in the case of *White and Carter (Councils) Limited v McGregor (1961)*. In 1957 M's sales manager, with apparent authority to do so, agreed on behalf of M to engage W to prepare and display certain bill hoardings during the following three years. On the same day, M (on learning of his manager's action) wrote to W, asking for the contract to be cancelled. W refused to cancel the agreement and performed their part of the contract for three years, at the end of which they sued for the full contract price. It was held that W were entitled to succeed because they were not bound to accept the attempted repudiation by M. Having satisfactorily performed their part of the contract they could legitimately call upon M to pay the agreed sum.

5.1.4   Discharge by frustration or subsequent impossibility

The nature of frustration

A contract is discharged by frustration when its performance is rendered impossible by external causes beyond the contemplation of the parties. After the parties have made their agreement, unforeseen contingencies may occur which prevent the attainment of the purpose they had in mind. It may also be said that a contract is frustrated (and therefore terminated), if, between the time that a contract is made and when it is completed, an event occurs which destroys the basis of the contract, but which is not the fault of either party. Under the doctrine of frustration the parties may be discharged from their obligations, the performance of which has become impossible or sterile.

The rule as to absolute contracts and frustration

The doctrine of frustration is of fairly recent origin. The basic common law rule is that the contract is not discharged merely because its performance has become more onerous or expensive due to unforeseen happenings. In *Davis Contractors Limited v Fareham UDC (1956)* the plaintiffs could not treat as frustrated a contract which they had taken 22 months rather than 8 months to complete.

The general rule laid down in *Paradine v Jane (1647)* is that, when the law casts a duty upon a man which, through no fault of his own, he is unable to perform, he is excused for non-performance; but if he binds himself by contract absolutely to do a thing he may not escape liability for damages by proving that, as events turned out, performance is futile or even impossible. The party to a contract may of course guard against such unforeseen contingencies by an express stipulation in the contract. The doctrine of frustration is an exception to the rule as to absolute contracts enunciated in *Paradine v Jane*. It mitigates the harshness of the above rule by introducing a number of exceptions to it.

In general, if an event is to frustrate and thus discharge a contract it must be:

(a)   not contemplated by the parties, when the contract was formed;
(b)   one which makes the contract fundamentally different from the original contract;
(c)   one for which neither party was responsible; and
(d)   one which results in a situation to which the parties did not originally wish to be bound.

Frustrating events

The circumstances where frustration may apply can be tabulated as follows:

(a)   *Where the subject matter of the contract has been destroyed* - In *Taylor v Caldwell (1863)*, C agreed to let T have the use of a music hall in which to hold four concerts. Before the date of the first concert the hall was destroyed by fire. T sued C for damages, claiming breach of contract by C in not having the hall ready. It was held that the contract was impossible to perform, and C was not liable.

(b)   *Where the object of the contract has been destroyed* - In *Krell v Henry (1903)* K agreed to let one of his rooms to H on a particular date to view the procession for King Edward VII's coronation. Because of the illness of the King the coronation did not take place, but K sued H for the letting fee. It was held that H was not liable as the contract had become impossible to perform, as the viewing of the procession formed the basis and whole point of the contract for both parties.

In contrast in *Herne Bay Steam Boat Co. v Hutton (1903)* a steam boat was chartered to see the naval review at the time of the coronation of Edward VII and to cruise around the fleet. The review was cancelled. The defendants did not use the boat and claimed that the contract was frustrated. It was held that the whole point of the contract had not been destroyed since it had still been possible to cruise around the fleet. Hence there was no frustration.

(c)   *By action of the state* - The clearest example of this is where an outbreak of a war renders the contract impossible. In *Finelvet A.G. v Vinara Shipping Co. Ltd (The Chrysalis) (1983)* a ship was trapped in the Shat-al-arab river by the outbreak of the Iran-Iraq war on 22 September 1980. No-one knew how long the war would last and how long neutral ships using the river would be affected. In arbitration, the arbitrator held the contract had become frustrated by the 24 November 1980. From that date, hire charges ceased to be payable. The court upheld the arbitrator's decision.

A variety of other state actions, particularly those taken in wartime, may affect performance and lead to a plea of frustration. Examples are: requisitioning the materials and calling up the labour force which was building a reservoir (*Metropolitan Water Board v Dick, Kerr and Co. Ltd (1918)*), and making illegal a contract for a sale of timber under wartime regulations (*Denny, Mott and Dickinson v Fraser (1944)*).

(d)   *Through incapacity of a party* - Contracts involving personal services, such as contracts of employment, are discharged by the death of either party. Likewise such contracts may be discharged through illness. Thus in *Condor v Barron Knights Ltd (1966)* a member of a pop group was advised by his doctor that his health would be seriously endangered if he continued to fulfil the group's demanding schedule. His contract was held to be frustrated.

The contract may also be discharged if a party becomes temporarily incapable, although the outcome will depend largely on the specific circumstances. The court would consider whether, should the contract continue, it would be radically different from what was originally envisaged. In *Morgan v Manser (1948)*, the defendant ('Cheerful Charlie Chester') engaged the plaintiff to act as his manager for ten years. Two years later, in 1940, the defendant was called up and it was held that the contract was discharged by frustration at that point as it was likely that Manser would be in the army for a considerable time.

(e)   *Frustration of economic purpose* - In *Jackson v Union Marine Insurance Co (1874)* it was held that the delay consequent upon the stranding of a ship which had been chartered to a third party released both owner and charterer from the contract. The particular voyage envisaged by the parties was no longer possible, and the contract was therefore frustrated.

Limits to the doctrine

As already indicated, a contract is not frustrated if it merely becomes unexpectedly more expensive or burdensome to one of the parties.

In *Davis Contractors Limited v Fareham UDC (1956)* the plaintiffs agreed to build houses for the defendants for a price of £92,425. The construction period was agreed at eight months, but in the event D took 22 months to complete (owing to lack of materials and labour). D claimed for the extra cost of £17,651, asserting that the original contract was frustrated and that they were entitled to the extra monies on a *quantum meruit*. It was held that the contract was not frustrated even if it had become more onerous. Hence D were entitled only to the agreed figure of £92,425.

Frustration does not apply where the frustrating event is self-induced. Thus, in the *Eugenia (1964)* a charterer ordered a ship into a war zone in breach of contract. The ship was delayed. It was held that the charterer could not rely on the delay as a ground for frustration.

Finally, frustration will not apply where the parties have expressly provided for a contingency which has occurred. It is a means by which risk is allocated and loss apportioned in circumstances which neither party has foreseen.

Legal consequences of frustration

The occurrence of the frustrating event brings the contract to an end forthwith, automatically and without further action.

The contract is not void from the outset but is terminated as to the future only. These contracts are perfectly valid when they are entered into but are abruptly terminated by the happening of the frustrating event.

The rule on automatic termination previously led to harsh results in some cases as it was held that any loss stayed where it fell on the happening of the frustrating event. It was not possible, therefore, for money paid to be recovered, even though there was a failure of consideration.

The harshness of this rule was slightly mitigated by the decision in *Fibrosa SA v Fairbairn Lawson Combe Barbour Limited (1942)*. Fairbairn Lawson had contracted to supply machinery to Fibrosa, a Polish firm, which paid £1,000 with the order. Britain then declared war on Germany and Poland was occupied by the Germans. Fibrosa sued for the return of the £1,000 advanced with the order. It was held by the House of Lords that the money was recoverable; the contract was not void, but there had been a total failure of consideration.

This was only a slight relaxation of the harshness of the rule: it only permitted recovery where there was a total failure of consideration, so that if the payer of the money had received anything in return, recovery would not be possible. There was also still no means of catering for a payee who had incurred pre-contractual expenses but could still be ordered to return the whole payment.

The Law Reform (Frustrated Contracts) Act 1943

This legislation was introduced in order to regulate the situation. It provides that:

(a)   all sums paid before the frustrating event are recoverable, and further sums payable are no longer due;

(b)   the court has the discretion to decide what expenses may be claimed or retained (from sums already held) by the parties; and

(c)   the court may award on a *quantum meruit* if the party claiming has performed part of the contract from which the other party has received a benefit.

The Act, however, draws a distinction between cases where money has been paid under a contract which subsequently becomes frustrated and cases where no money has been paid. If the latter is the case, the party who has incurred expenses cannot recover them from the other party unless it can be shown that that other party has received some valuable benefit by virtue of the expenditure.

The 1943 Act excludes some types of contract:

(a)   Contracts for the sale of specific goods (ie clearly identifiable and separable goods) which are governed by the Sale of Goods Act 1979;

(b)   charterparties;

(c)   contracts of insurance (as premiums cannot be recovered once the risk has attached); and

(d)   contracts for the sale of specific goods which have perished.

5.1.5   Discharge by lapse of time

Lapse of time as applied in the law of contract has the following meanings:

(a)   The period contained in the contract for performing the contract has passed, without the performance having been completed: here, the lapse of time indicates that the party concerned has broken the contract, so that the contract is really discharged by breach.

(b)   The period mentioned in the contract as being the duration of the contract (eg, a lease) has expired, so that the contract is discharged by performance.

(c)   Rights of one of the parties cannot be enforced because the relevant period under the Limitation Act 1980 has expired; however, this is not really a discharge of the contract because statute-barred actions may be revived.

Under the Limitation Act 1980 the limitation periods are, from the date the action accrued:

(a)   for actions on simple contract: six years;

(b)   for actions on specialty contracts (ie, under seal): 12 years;

(c)   for actions for the recovery of land: 12 years in normal cases and 30 years in cases involving the Crown.

The action accrues from the date of the breach for most contracts. For cases involving a loan, it is the date that the loan was made, unless the contract provided for a specific repayment date, when that becomes the date from which the limitation period begins. Where an action is based on fraud or mistake, the period starts on the day when the plaintiff discovered (or could with reasonable diligence have discovered) the existence of the fraud or mistake.

A debt which is statute-barred (ie, one where the period for bringing an action has expired) does not become void, voidable or illegal, but no action may be brought on it. However, the right to bring an action may be revived in one of two ways:

(a)   by a written acknowledgment of the existence of the claim, signed by the person to be charged (or his agent) and addressed to the claimant;

(b)   by the claimant's receiving from the other party or his agent a payment which is clearly referable to the claim.

5.1.6   Discharge by operation of law

Contracts may be discharged by operation of law in the following circumstances:

(a)   Merger, whereby the relevant contract is merged into another document (eg, a deed).

(b)   Material alteration (eg, one on a cheque or deed) without the agreement of one party entitles that party to treat the contract as discharged.

(c)   Death of either party will discharge a contract for personal services, but other forms of rights or obligations survive for or against the estate of the deceased party.

(d)   Bankruptcy of a party may discharge a contract, although the general rules are:

        (i)   the rights of the bankrupt against the other party survive, but are enforceable by the trustee in bankruptcy;

(ii) the rights of the third party against the bankrupt are, in some circumstances, voidable at the option of the trustee;

(iii) certain types of contract, such as a contract of employment, are not affected by the bankruptcy and therefore these are not discharged when one of the parties becomes bankrupt.

5.2 Remedies for breach of contract

The following remedies may be available to the injured party in a case of breach of contract: damages; specific performance; an injunction; rescission of the contract; a refusal of any further performance by himself; and a right to sue on a quantum meruit.

5.2.1 Damages

The injured party has a common law right to claim for damages in any case where the other party has broken a term of the contract. As a general rule, the object of an award of damages is to place the plaintiff in the same position as if there had been no breach; it is not intended to enable the plaintiff to make a profit from the breach (other than any profit arising from the contract itself).

The court may award the following types of damages:

(a) *Ordinary damages*, payable for losses arising naturally from the breach.

(b) *Special damages* - In tort, these will be awarded for specific, provable losses, but in contract they will be granted only if shown to have been contemplated by both parties.

(c) *Exemplary damages*, which are today rarely awarded in actions for breach of contract, although they are, on occasion, granted in cases of tort where the court considers that the defendant needs to be punished although he has not committed a criminal offence.

(d) *Aggravated damages* - Additional damages awarded (usually in tort) against a defendant whose wrongful action is considered to have caused the plaintiff additional injury or suffering in an unpleasant manner.

(e) *Nominal damages*, awarded to the plaintiff in cases where, although he had a right to sue, he did not in fact suffer any real loss.

(f) *Contemptuous damages* may be awarded in a case where the court disapproves of the plaintiff's bringing the action (although the plaintiff had a right to do so).

Normally the court will award 'ordinary damages' and it is this type of damages which will now be considered in depth.

The court, when making an award of damages, will consider two matters. First of all, it has to ask itself whether the damage suffered was too remote. Then it will consider the amount of the award.

Remoteness of damage

The plaintiff may not recover for all the consequences of the defendant's breach. The law states that this would be unreasonable as there would be no definable end to the defendant's liability. Two tests laid down in the case of *Hadley v Baxendale (1854)* (see below), still form the basis of the rules governing remoteness of damage:

(a)   Natural loss is not too remote. This is loss which arises naturally from the breach and which is reasonably foreseeable.

(b)   Special loss is not too remote. This is loss, not arising naturally from the breach, but which was within the contemplation of both parties at the time the contract was made.

All other types of loss are too remote. These principles are illustrated in the following cases.

In *Hadley v Baxendale (1854)*, H, a miller, engaged B, a carrier, to take a broken driving shaft from his mill to the makers for repair. B took an undue length of time in delivering the shaft and, as a result, the mill was idle for longer than would have been necessary if B had been more efficient. H sued B for the loss of profits for the additional delay. It was shown that B was not aware that H did not have a spare shaft and H did not even indicate that the shaft was that applicable to the mill. H's claim for damages failed as the injury (ie, loss of profits) was too remote.

The effect of late delivery was considered in *Victoria Laundry v Newman Industries (1949)*. V bought from N a boiler for use in V's laundry. Delivery was agreed for 5 June but was not made until five months later. V sued N, claiming:

(a)   loss of profit of the laundry during the period of delay;
(b)   loss of extra profit from two highly profitable dyeing contracts.

It was held that V would succeed under (a), but the loss under (b) was too remote, N not having been advised of the particular contracts when the boiler was ordered.

Similarly, in *Diamond v Campbell-Jones (1961)* the defendants contracted to sell leasehold premises in Mayfair to the plaintiff for £6,000. The defendants wrongfully repudiated the contract. The plaintiff sued and claimed the profit he would have made if he had converted the ground floor into offices and the four upper floors into maisonettes. The defendants, while they acknowledged that such a conversion was a possible use of the premises, denied that they knew or should have known that the plaintiff had bought with this intention. It was held that he could recover only the difference between the purchase price and the market value at the date of the breach of contract.

The measure of damages

In assessing the amount of damages payable, the courts will observe the following rules:

(a)   Under the doctrine of restitution, the plaintiff is entitled to damages measured by the value to him of the contract broken, and not by the cost of performance to the defendant. Arising from this:

(i)   In a contract for the sale of goods, the measure of damages is the difference between the market price at the date of the breach and the contract price, so that only nominal damages will be awarded to a plaintiff buyer or plaintiff seller if the price at the date of breach was respectively less or more than the contract price.

(ii) If the plaintiff is a buyer of goods for which he has found a customer, and the seller knows of this, the damages will be the profit on the buyer's sale if alternative goods are not available, or the additional cost (if any) to the buyer of purchasing alternative goods where they are available.

(iii) In fixing the amount of damages, the courts will usually deduct the tax (if any) which would have been payable by the plaintiff if the contract had not been broken.

(b) Difficulty in assessing the amount of damages should not prevent the injured party from receiving them.

(c) The injured party should seek to minimise the damages by trying to find an alternative method of performance of the subject matter of the contract.

On this last rule, the court will expect the injured party to take all reasonable steps to reduce his loss. If he does not then he cannot expect to receive full compensation. In *Brace v Calder (1895)*, the plaintiff had been employed as a manager in a business with four partners. Two of the partners died. The surviving partners wished to continue in business so they gave the plaintiff a technical dismissal linked with an offer of re-employment. The plaintiff resented the dismissal and refused the offer. He sued for wrongful dismissal. It was held that the plaintiff would receive nominal damages only. He had not mitigated his loss.

Liquidated damages and penalties

If a contract includes a provision that, on a breach of contract, damages of a certain amount or calculable at a certain rate will be payable, the courts will normally accept the relevant figure as a measure of damages. Predetermined damages of this type are called **liquidated damages**. However, a court will ignore a figure for damages put in a contract if it is in fact a **penalty** - that is, a sum in excess of the reasonably foreseeable loss that a breach would cause.

A court will not be influenced by the fact that a sum payable on breach is called liquidated damages if it is, in fact, a penalty and not a genuine pre-estimate of the damage. This could be the case where:

(a) The prescribed sum is extravagant in comparison with the maximum loss that could follow from a breach.

(b) The contract provides for payment of a certain sum but a larger sum is stipulated to be payable on a breach.

(c) The same sum is fixed as being payable for several breaches which would be likely to cause varying amounts of damage.

All of the above cases would be regarded as penalties. The court will not enforce payment of a penalty, and if the contract is broken only the actual loss suffered may be recovered. However, a sum fixed as liquidated damages will be payable, whether this is greater or less than the actual damage incurred.

As an illustration of these rules, reference should be made to *Ford Motor Co (England) Limited v Armstrong (1915)*. In this case, the defendant, a retailer, in consideration of receiving supplies from the plaintiff company, agreed not to sell any car or parts below the listed price, not to sell Ford cars to other motor dealers, and not to exhibit any car supplied by the company without their permission. He also agreed that for every breach of this agreement he would pay permission. He also agreed that for every breach of this agreement he would pay £250 as being 'the agreed damage which the manufacturers will sustain'. It was held the provision was a penalty. It was not only substantial but was arbitrary and fixed *in terrorem* for, since it was made payable for various breaches differing in kind, its very size prevented it from being a reasonable estimate of the probable damage.

5.2.2   Specific performance

Specific performance is an equitable remedy (as a substitute for damages), and is only granted by the court at its discretion. A decree of specific performance will not be issued where:

(a)   Damages would provide an adequate remedy, eg, most contracts for the sale of goods; a unique item, eg, a painting or rare antique, is the type of item for which this remedy will be granted.

(b)   The court cannot adequately supervise performance; for instance, where the contract is one for personal services, or in the case of a building contract.

(c)   There is no consideration.

(d)   One of the parties is a minor.

(e)   The contract is for the loan of money.

(f)   The plaintiff was himself unable to carry out his part of the contract.

5.2.3   Injunction

An injunction (another equitable remedy) is an order of the court restraining a person from doing some act. In tort, the act complained of may be a nuisance or defamation, but in contract it usually takes the form of an enforcement of a negative stipulation. For example, the court may order that a person shall not work in a particular industry for anyone other than the plaintiff. In such a case the injunction may be a means of encouraging the defendant to work for the plaintiff. However, if the plaintiff seeks an injunction preventing the defendant from working anywhere, it will not be granted. It will only be granted when it does not amount to the same thing as a decree of specific performance.

Injunctions fall into the following categories:

(a)   *Interlocutory injunction*, which is issued before the case is heard, and where the plaintiff undertakes responsibility for any damage (arising from its issue) caused to the defendant, should the plaintiff subsequently lose the case.

(b)   *Perpetual injunction*, which is granted after and arising out of the decision in the case.

(c)   *Prohibitory injunction*, which is an order that something must not be done.

(d)   *Mandatory injunction*, which is an order that something must be done.

5.2.4 Rescission

This is also an equitable remedy. It is a court order which sets aside the contract and restores the status quo. It is most commonly used for misrepresentation or breach of contract. The remedy has already been considered under misrepresentation. If the plaintiff succeeds in having the contract rescinded, he must usually return to the defendant moneys or other property transferred as part of the contract (unless the payment he had received was a guarantee for due performance by the other party who subsequently forfeited the sum because of his breach).

5.2.5 Refusal of further performance

This is a passive remedy in that the injured party will be allowed to set up the breach as a defence should the party in breach attempt to sue him for failing to complete his obligations under the contract. The injured party is entitled to augment this remedy by bringing an action for the rescission of the contract.

5.2.6 Quantum meruit

A claim on a *quantum meruit* is a claim for the value of work done by a party to a contract whereas a claim for damages is for compensation in respect of loss suffered consequent on a breach of contract. The general rule is that if a contract provides for services to be rendered in return for payment of a lump sum, nothing may be claimed unless the work has been completely performed (see *Cutter v Powell, 5.1.2). Exceptionally, however, a claim may be made under a quantum meruit* in the following cases:

(a)   The innocent party has elected to accept the benefit of the work done (eg, where a lesser quantity than is stipulated in the contract has been delivered, and accepted, under a contract for the sale of goods).

(b)   The contract is divisible (eg, where goods are to be delivered by instalments but the contract has not been completed).

(c)   Complete performance has been prevented by the wrongful act of the other party.

A *quantum meruit* claim is also appropriate if the plaintiff has rendered services under a contract which is later found to be void. An example is where the managing director of a company was employed under a service agreement made on behalf of the company. The agreement was found to be void since none of the directors had taken up their qualification shares within the necessary time but the managing director sued the company on a *quantum meruit* for reasonable remuneration in respect of the services which he had rendered to the company. He succeeded in quasi-contract (*Craven-Ellis v Canons Limited (1936)*).

5.2.7 Promissory estoppel

This has already been examined.

5.3 Quasi-contract

5.3.1 Nature

Quasi-contract refers to situations where one person has received a benefit to which he is not entitled, and at the expense of another. Although there is rarely a contract between the parties concerned, the courts will usually order the person enriched to account for the property in question to the other person, ie, they will apply the same rules as would apply to contracts.

The following are typical examples of quasi-contract:

(a)   Where one person has paid money for the use of another, the latter is usually obliged to repay a similar amount to the former (see *Brook's Wharf and Bull Wharf Limited v Goodman Bros (1937)*, below).

(b)   Where there exists an account stated (ie, where there is mutual indebtedness, a balance agreed by the parties), the net debtor is obliged to pay the creditor the agreed balance, without reference to the individual debts.

(c)   Where money has been paid on a consideration which has wholly failed, the payer may usually recover the sum paid from the recipient.

(d)   Where money has been paid under a mistake of fact, it may be recovered by the payer but not where the mistake was one of law.

(e)   Where money has been received by one person to the use of another (ie, which should have gone to another), the former is liable to account for the amount involved to the latter (see *Reading v Attorney-General (1951)*, below).

(f)   Claims on a *quantum meruit* (see above).

In *Brook's Wharf and Bull Wharf Limited v Goodman Brothers (1937)*, the defendants agreed to warehouse certain goods with the plaintiffs. Not due to any negligence by B, the goods were stolen before the customs duty was paid. B was under an obligation to pay the customs duty, which they did and sued for the sum paid. It was held that they should succeed.

In *Reading v Attorney-General (1951)*, R, a sergeant in the British Army, received large monetary payments for agreeing to sit, in uniform, in the front seat of loaded lorries passing through Cairo so that they would not be inspected. It was held that, quite apart from any criminal liability incurred by R, he was to pay the Crown the moneys he had received, because he had obtained them through the use of his uniform and the opportunities and facilities attached to it.

5.4   Privity of contract

5.4.1   The doctrine

Reference has already been made (in Session 3) to the doctrine of privity of contract whereby a contract cannot confer rights or impose obligations arising under it on any person except the parties to it. To permit a person who had no part in the original agreement whatsoever to obtain benefits or to impose upon such a person an obligation to which he was not a party or had never agreed, would be clearly contrary to the basic rules of justice.

In *Dunlop Pneumatic Tyre Co Limited v Selfridge and Co Limited (1915)* Dunlop sold tyres to Dew and Co on condition that the latter would not re-sell Dunlop's tyres below a certain price and that they (Dew and Co) would obtain a similar agreement from any of their customers. Selfridges bought tyres from Dew & Co and agreed not to sell tyres below list price. Selfridges sold some tyres below the list price in breach of the agreement between Selfridges and Dews. The manufacturer, Dunlop, sued Selfridges on the breach of the agreement. It was held that Dunlops could not enforce the agreement between Selfridges and Dews, because Dunlops were not party to the agreement and could not therefore obtain rights under it.

5.4.2   Exceptions to the doctrine

There are cases in which a person is allowed to sue upon a contract to which he is not a party:

(a)   *Covenants concerning land* - The position in land law is that benefits and liabilities attached to or imposed on land may, in certain circumstances, follow the land into the hands of other owners. For example, a lease through a contractual arrangement also creates proprietary rights. Suppose A grants a lease of land to B. The lease will contain a number of covenants (or promises) by the tenant and the lord. As between A and B there is privity of contract, so there is no difficulty about the enforcement of the covenants. But suppose A sells the freehold of the land to X, and B assigns the lease to Y. The law is that, although there is no privity of contract between X and Y, either may enforce a covenant in the original lease against the other.

Likewise, when a freeholder sells his land, he can, subject to certain conditions, impose restrictions on its use which will be binding, not only on the immediate purchaser, but also on his successors in title. Such restrictions, technically known as restrictive covenants, were first recognised in *Tulk v Moxhay (1848)*. In that case the purchaser of the garden in the centre of Leicester Square entered into a covenant with the vendor promising not to build on the garden. The covenant was held to be binding in equity on a subsequent purchaser of the land.

(b)   *Agency* - Agency is the relationship which arises where one person, the principal, authorises another, the agent, to act on his behalf and the agent agrees to do so. In such circumstances the principal, even if undisclosed, may sue on a contract made by an agent. Agency is dealt with in Session 6.

(c)   *Assignment* - The assignee of a debt or chose in action may, if the assignment is a legal assignment, sue the original debtor.

(d)   *Trusts of promises* - This exception is based on the equitable doctrine of the constructive trust. Thus, in *Tomlinson v Gill (1756)*, the defendant promised a widow to pay her late husband's debts. It was held that the widow was trustee of the promise for the husband's creditors, who could thus enforce the promise against the defendant.

(e)   *Covenants in a marriage settlement* - A covenant to settle after-acquired property contained in a marriage settlement, can be enforced by all persons 'within the manage consideration': *Hill v Gomme (1839)*.

(f)   *Statutory exceptions* - These fall into the following categories:

    (i)   Price maintenance agreements - Under the Resale Prices Act, 1976, S26 the supplier of goods is given a statutory cause of action, so that he may enforce against a person not a party to a contract of sale a condition as to re-sale price. However, the re-sale price agreement must have been approved under the provision of the Resale Prices Act, 1976, otherwise there can be no enforcement of it.

(ii) Insurance - S11 of the Married Women's Property Act 1882 provides that if a man insures his life for the benefit of his wife and/or children or a woman insures her life for the benefit of her husband and/or children a trust is created in favour of the objects of the policy, and the policy moneys are not liable for the deceased's debts, other than capital gains tax.

Other exceptions under this head are to be found in S149 of the Road Traffic Act 1972 and the Third Parties (Rights against Insurers) Act 1930.

(iii) Bills of exchange - Under the Bills of Exchange Act 1882 a third party may sue on a bill of exchange (including cheques and promissory notes). This gives statutory recognition to the concept of negotiability: see Session 9 of the pack.

(iv) Law of Property Act, 1925, S56 - This provides that 'a person may take an immediate or other interest in land or other property, or the benefit of any condition, right of entry, covenant or agreement over or respecting land or other property, although he may not be named as a party to the conveyance or other instruments'.

Lord Denning sought to interpret this provision so as to evade the doctrine of privity. However, in *Beskwick v Beskwick (1967)*, the House of Lords refused to accept this wide interpretation of the section and held that it was limited to cases concerning real property.

5.5   Revision exercise

In order to assess your understanding of the above session attempt the following questions. Check your answers against the references given.

(1)   Explain the terms bilateral and unilateral discharge.   **(Solution: 5.1.1)**

(2)   What do you understand by the concept of accord and satisfaction?   **(Solution: 5.1.1)**

(3)   Differentiate between the terms 'condition precedent' and 'condition subsequent'.
                                                                                (Solution: 5.1.1)

(4)   What is the general rule as regards discharge by performance?   **(Solution: 5.1.2)**

(5)   What exceptions are there to this general rule?   **(Solution: 5.1.2)**

(6)   In what circumstances is time of the essence of a contract?   **(Solution: 5.1.2)**

(7)   What is an anticipatory breach?   **(Solution: 5.1.3)**

(8)   In what circumstances may a breach of contract constitute its discharge?
                                                                                (Solution: 5.1.3)

(9)   Explain the doctrine of frustration.   **(Solution: 5.1.4)**

(10)   In what circumstances may a contract be discharged by frustration?   **(Solution: 5.1.4)**

(11)   What are the legal consequences of frustration?   **(Solution: 5.1.4)**

(12)   Explain the terms ordinary and special damages as used in the law of contract.

(Solution: 5.2.1)

(13)   What rules govern remoteness of damage in contract?

(Solution: 5.2.1)

(14)   What rules govern the measure of damages in contract?

(Solution: 5.2.1)

(15)   What are liquidated damages?

(Solution: 5.2.1)

(16)   Examine the nature of the remedy of specific performance.

(Solution: 5.2.2)

(17)   What do you understand by rescission?

(Solution: 5.2.4)

(18)   Explain and illustrate the concept of quasi-contract.

(Solution: 5.3.1)

(19)   Explain and illustrate the doctrine of privity of contract.

(Solution: 5.4.1)

(20)   What exceptions are there to the doctrine in land law?

(Solution: 5.4.2)

(21)   Give four statutory exceptions to the doctrine.

(Solution: 5.4.2)

5.6   Conclusion

This session will have given you a knowledge and understanding of:

•   the ways in which a contract can be discharged;

•   the doctrine of frustration;

•   the remedies available for breach of contract;

•   the doctrine of privity of contract and the exceptions to it.

5.7   Questions

Objective test questions

(1)   Which of the following contracts could be enforceable by an order of specific performance?

    A   A contract with a minor.
    B   A contract of employment.
    C   A contract for the purchase of land.
    D   A contract for the sale of goods.

(2)   Which of the following is not an equitable remedy?

    A   Rescission.
    B   Specific performance.
    C   Damages.
    D   Injunction.

(3)   The effects of frustration of a contract for the sale of specific goods which have perished are provided for by:

A   The common law.
B   The Law Reform (Frustrated Contracts) Act 1943.
C   Equity.
D   The Sale of Goods Act 1979.

(4)   The general rule for a contract to be discharged by performance is that performance must be exact and precise. However, to this rule there are certain exceptions. Which of the following is not one of them?

A   Substantial performance.
B   Divisible contracts.
C   The doctrine of part performance.
D   Acceptance of partial performance.

(5)   A entered into a contract with B whereby B agreed to manufacture and deliver certain goods to A by June 5. On May 23 B notified A that he was unable to perform his part of the agreement. B's action constitues:

A   Frustration of the contract.
B   An anticipatory breach of contract.
C   An actionable misrepresentation.
D   Breach of a fundamental term.

(6)   The doctrine of privity of contract means:

A   A contract is not legally binding if it is a private agreement.
B   Only the parties to a contract can enforce it.
C   The terms of an agreement are primarily the concern of the parties.
D   An ambiguity in an exclusion clause will be interpreted against the party seeking to exclude liability.

(7)   The Limitation Act 1980 lays down various periods of limitation. The period specified in relation to a simple contract is:

A   Three years.
B   Twelve years.
C   Six years.
D   Five years.

(8)   Remoteness of damage in contract is determined according to the rule established in:

A   *Ford Motor Co (England) Limited v Armstrong.*
B   *Lewis v Averay.*
C   *Hadley v Baxendale.*
D   *Flight v Bolland.*

(9)   On 1 January 19X1 Sharon lends Darren £500. Darren signs a note promising to repay the sum on 1 January 19X2. He fails to do so and Sharon forgets all about it until February 19X7. She writes to Darren but receives no reply. However, Sharon's brother Warren receives a postcard from Darren saying 'What am I going to do about the £500 I owe your sister? Do you think you could persuade her to give me a bit more time?'

What are Sharon's rights?

A   The loan is statute-barred and Sharon may not claim it.

B   The loan will not be statute-barred until 12 years from January 19X1 and Sharon therefore has a good claim.

C   The postcard has revived the debt and Sharon may claim at any time in the next six years.

D   The loan will not be statute-barred until January 19X8 and Sharon therefore has a good claim.

(10)   Which of the following does not constitute discharge of a contract?

A   Breach of a condition.
B   Frustration.
C   Breach of a warranty.
D   An unagreed material alteration to a deed.

Written test questions

5.1   Barber and Foot

(a)   (i)   What is meant by frustration of contract?

(ii)   In what circumstances will a contract be discharged by frustration?

(iii)   How are the rights of the parties to a contract adjusted following frustration?

(b)   (i)   Barber and Co Limited agreed to install a new machine, manufactured by them, in the factory of Foot & Co Limited. In furtherance of this contract Foot & Co Limited gave £500 to Barber & Co Limited in part payment of the price of the machine and also the cost of the installation. After Barber & Co Limited had built a platform (costing them £200) in Foot & Co Limited's factory, but before the machinery was installed on that platform, the factory was completely destroyed by fire.

Advise the two company how they should adjust their losses under the contract.

(ii)   What would have been your advice if Foot & Co Limited had not made the part payment of £500?

5.2   Contractual remedies

(a)   Distinguish between a penalty clause and a liquidated damages provision.

(b)   What is a claim on a *quantum meruit* and in what circumstances can such a claim be made?

5.3   Exceptions to privity of contract

In what circumstances may a person sue upon a contract to which he is not a party?

SESSION 6

Agency

This session will provide you with:

- an understanding of the concept of agency;

- a practical knowledge of the ways in which agency may arise;

- a detailed knowledge and understanding of the authority of agents and the effects of contracts made by agents especially as regards partnerships and companies;

- an understanding of the relationship between principal and agent with particular reference to the obligations that arise from the relationship;

- an awareness of the circumstances in which an agency may be terminated and the effects of its termination.

Note: This Session incorporates the Companies Act 1989 (so far as it is relevant) and has been written on the basis that the provisions of that Act are fully operative.

6.1   The concept of agency

6.1.1   Definition

In business the word 'agent' is used in a wide variety of contexts to describe a person who transacts business on behalf of others. For example, a literary agent sells his clients' work to publishers, film producers and so on; a travel agent makes travel arrangements for his clients; and estate agent finds buyers for his clients' houses. In law, however, the word 'agent' has a special technical meaning, and this session is concerned only with the technical legal concept of agency. This concept has probably been described best by the High Court of Australia in *International Harvester Co of Australia Pty Ltd v Carrigan's Hazeldene Pastoral Co (1958)* in which it was said that:

> Agency is a word used in the law to connote an authority or capacity in one person to create legal relations between a person occupying the position of principal and third parties.

In law, then, agency is a relationship between two persons, called principal and agent, which empowers the agent to act on behalf of the principal for the purpose of binding the principal to legal commitments. For example, an agent may be able to sell the goods or services of his principal, or commit his principal to the purchase of goods or services; he may be able to make his principal a party to a contract, he may be authorised to put his principal's signature on documents. The relationship of agency depends on there being an agreement between principal and agent that the agent can function as a substitute for the principal for the purpose of putting the principal into legal relationships. The agreement between principal and agent defines the matters in which the agent may act for the principal: that is, it defines the extent of the agent's authority to act for the principal.

An agent has the same legal capacity as his principal. For example, if an individual under the age of 18 makes a contract then, in general, the courts will not enforce the contract against him, and a contract would not become enforceable merely because it was made by an adult agent on behalf of the minor. On the other hand an adult may employ a minor as agent and will be bound by any contracts the minor makes as his agent: *G(A) v G(T) (1970)*.

6.2 Creation of agency

6.2.1 Methods of creation

Agency may be created by express agreement; by implication; by necessity; by ratification; and by estoppel.

(a) *By express agreement* - The agent may be appointed orally, in writing, or by deed. If he is appointed orally, he may act for his principal in respect of any type of simple contract, even for contracts which must be in writing or which need to be evidenced by writing. However, an agent may not, as such, execute a deed unless he has been appointed by a deed. An agent appointed by deed is called an **attorney** and the deed appointing him is called a **power of attorney**.

(b) *By implication* - Even though the parties have not expressly agreed to become principal and agent it may be possible to find an implied agreement based on their conduct or relationship. If the parties have so conducted themselves towards one another that it would be reasonable for them to assume that they have consented to act as principal and agent, then they are principal and agent. For example, the agent of a finance company or an insurance company may also be held to be the agent of the party seeking finance or insurance if the circumstances warrant an implication of agreement to such an agency relationship: *Newsholme Bros v Road Transport and General Insurance Co Ltd (1929)*. An implied agreement to agency by virtue of the relationship of the parties arises in the case of husband and wife. A wife has authority to pledge her husband's credit for household necessaries even if he has not expressly appointed her his agent: *Debenham v Mellon (1880)*.

Since there is no express appointment in this case, the authority which the principal bestows upon the agent is implied authority; but, as with agents expressly appointed, agents impliedly appointed may have the power to bind the principal to contracts with third parties by virtue of usual or ostensible authority. These forms of authority are discussed in section 6.3.

(c) *By necessity* - This form of agency arises when an individual is in possession of property belonging to another, and it becomes necessary for the holder to do something in connection with the property or in some other way to protect the owner's interests.

The feature of agency of necessity is that a person is dealing with property belonging to another without first getting the owner's permission. The courts will not readily concede that an agency of necessity exists. Therefore, before the individual in possession of someone else's goods does anything with them in such a way as to deprive the true owner of his title to them, the following conditions must have been observed:

(i) The 'agent' must prove that it was not possible to obtain the owner's instructions (see *Great Northern Railway Co v Swaffield (1874)*, below).

(ii) There must have been a valid reason why the 'agent' had to act as he did - usually an emergency which endangers the goods.

(iii) The 'agent' must have acted bona fide on behalf of the owner.

In *Great Northern Railway Co v Swaffield (1874)*, the plaintiffs had carried a horse to its destination station but there was nobody there to collect it. As there was no suitable accommodation at the station the horse was put in some nearby stables and the relevant charges were paid by the plaintiffs. In an action brought against the owner of the horse, it was held that, although the railway company had no express or implied authority to incur such charges, it had acted as agent of necessity in an emergency and could therefore claim indemnity from the defendant as owner of the horse.

(d) *By ratification* - If an 'agent' purports to make a contract with a third party on behalf of a principal, although at the time of the contract the 'agent' has not been authorised to do so by the principal, the principal may do one of two things. He may refuse to ratify the contract, thereby incurring no personal liability. In this case, the third party would be entitled to sue the agent for breach of warranty of authority (see 6.4.5).

Alternatively, he may ratify the contract, thereby creating a contractual relationship between himself and the third party. Ratification is the express adoption by the principal of the contract, and includes conduct showing unequivocally that he is adopting the contract made by the agent.

Ratification is possible only if:

(i) The 'agent' specifically informs the third party that he is acting for the principal, and identifies the principal. In *Keighley, Maxsted & Co v Durant (1901)*, K authorised R (his agent) to buy wheat at a stipulated price, but R exceeded his authority by buying wheat at a higher price from D. R bought in his own name, although he intended to buy for K. K agreed with R to take delivery but did not do so. It was held that K was not obliged to take delivery because K was not liable to D as they could not ratify R's contract with D.

(ii) The principal would have been capable of making the contract at the time when it was made. In *Kelner v Baxter (1866)*, Kelner, a wine-merchant, agreed to sell wine to Baxter and two associates who intended to incorporate their business association as a registered company.

It was held that, as the company was not in existence at the time the contract was entered into, it could not subsequently ratify the contract. Baxter and his associates were personally liable to Kelner on the contract.

(iii)   The principal ratifies the contract within any period of time fixed for ratification, but if none has been fixed then within a reasonable time.

(iv)   The principal, before ratification, is aware of all the material facts.

(v)   The principal ratifies the whole contract; partial ratification of only those parts of the contract that are beneficial to the principal is ineffective.

(vi)   The contract itself is valid (ie, if the contract as executed by the agent was void, the principal cannot make it effective by ratifying it).

The legal effect of ratification is to make the contract as binding on the principal as if the agent had had the authority of the principal right at the start before the contract was made. A ratified contract is therefore effective from the date the contract was made by the agent. In *Bolton Partners v Lambert (1889)*, Lambert made an offer to an agent of Bolton Partners which the agent, who did not have authority, accepted. Lambert then sought to revoke his offer before this acceptance was ratified. It was held that the contract was valid. The ratification related back to acceptance and therefore the revocation was too late.

(e)   *By estoppel* - Agency by estoppel is usually regarded as one of the ways by which the relationship of principal and agent may be created. Under the doctrine of estoppel, if one person allows the impression that another person is acting on his behalf, he may not later deny the authority of that other person to act on his behalf. For instance, if P stands by and allows A to tell T that A is P's agent, then P will be bound by any contract A negotiates with T.

6.3   The nature of the agent's authority

6.3.1   The nature and types of authority

As a general proposition, the principal is bound to the third party by the acts of the agent which are within the agent's authority. If the agent acts outside of his authority, the principal is only bound by such acts if he ratifies them.

However, because the agency relationship is created in different ways, there are various types of authority: express, implied, usual, apparent and by ratification.

(a)   *Express authority* - The principal may give the agent express authority orally or in writing. In the latter case, it may be under hand or under seal. If under seal, it is termed a power of attorney.

(b)   *Implied authority* - The agent, in addition to the express authority just described, has an implied authority to do everyting that is necessary for, or incidental to, his express authority.

Thus, if an agent is expressly authorised to find a purchaser for certain property he is impliedly authorised to describe the state of the property to the prospective purchaser (*Mullens v Miller (1882)*) and is also impliedly authorised to accept a deposit from him (*Ryan v Pilkington (1959)*). However, everything depends on the construction of the words of the express authority.

(c)   *Usual authority* - If you appoint an estate agent to sell your house, it is to be expected that in attempting to do so, he will engage in certain activities in which it is usual for an estate agent to engage (eg, to advertise the property), unless you forbid him from doing so. Thus, the general rule is that an agent has implied authority to perform those acts which are usual to his profession, trade, or business, unless the principal restricts such authority. What is 'usual' is a question of fact, often of expert evidence. Customs often prevail in certain situations.

Usual authority is an aspect of implied authority which relates, in particular, to certain speical types of agents. Thus a factor is an agent who is entrusted with the possession of goods for the purposes of sale. He has authority to sell the goods in his own name; unless the principal instructs him to sell in his own name: to warrant the goods if it is customary to warrant the goods he is selling; to give credit if this is reasonable. He has no authority, however, to pledge or barter the goods, but if he does so, the pledgee may have acquired good title under S2 of the Factors Act 1889.

If the principal restricts the agent's usual authority, this restriction will not affect the third party if the third party is unaware of it.

In *Watteau v Fenwick (1893)*, H, who owned a public house, sold it to F, but it was agreed that H should stay as manager. W, who knew nothing of F or of the sale to him, sold cigars on credit to H for use in the public house. F had expressly forbidden H to buy cigars on credit. W was unable to get payment from H, but having by then learnt of the sale of the public house he then sued F as owner. It was held that, as the cigars were an item that would normally be supplied to a public house, and H was acting within his implied authority as manager in ordering cigars, F was unable, as against W, to set up any secret limitation of authority.

Restricted usual authority is sometimes termed apparent authority, though this term is more usually used as descriptive of ostensible authority. Ostensible authority is to be discussed next.

(d)   *Ostensible authority* - In this situation the principal makes a representation which gives the third party the impression that the agent has authority for his activities. The agent does not, in fact, have such authority, but because the principal has represented to the third party that the agent has such authority, the principal is estopped from denying that the agent has this authority. Essentially, as with all forms of estoppel, there must be a representation, reliance on that representation and an alteration of the third party's position resulting from such a reliance.

6.4   Effect of contracts made by agents

The position will depend upon whether the agent informed the third party that he was acting for a principal. A principal may be disclosed and named to the third party, disclosed but not named or undisclosed altogether.

6.4.1   Identity of principal disclosed

If the agent reveals to the third party the identity of the principal, the agent usually has no rights or liabilities under the contract, the principal and the third party normally being the parties who are liable. Exceptions to this rule include the following instances in which the agent may also be liable:

(a)   Where the agent expressly agrees to be liable.

(b)   Where the custom of the trade makes him liable.

(c)   Where the agent executes a deed or a bill of exchange in his own name - he will be personally liable on the bill or deed.

6.4.2   Identity of principal not disclosed

If the agent does not inform the third party of the identity of the principal at the time the contract is executed, although he makes it clear that a principal exists, the agent will not as a general rule incur personal liability on the contract. The principal may make known his identity to the third party, at which point the agent drops out of the picture. The legal position is similar to that pertaining when the identity of the principal is disclosed. However, the third party may have a claim upon the agent if the latter has executed the contract in his own name without expressly describing himself as agent. For example, in *Davies v Sweet (1962)*, it was held that if estate agents sign a receipt in their own names, without referring to themselves as being the vendor's agent, the receipt may be taken to be a sufficient memorandum to identify the contracting parties as being the purchaser and the agents (not the vendor). See also *Keighley Maxsted and Co v Durant (1901)* (above).

6.4.3   Existence of principal not disclosed

Here the position is radically different from that in 6.4.1 and 6.4.2 above. If an agent acts for an undisclosed principal, it is the agent himself who is primarily liable under the contract negotiated, and is entitled to enforce it by taking legal action against the third party to the agreement.

However, the undisclosed principal may reveal his identity and enforce the contract in his own name. This is an anomalous right allowed by law so that the needs of the business community resorting to this device may be met. The right is subject to some limitations:

(a)   The undisclosed principal has no right of action if the terms of the contract expressly exclude an agency of this type. In *Humble v Hunter (1848)*, the plaintiff's son entered into a charter party with the defendant, the son describing himself as owner of the vessel. It was held that evidence was not admissible to allow the son to show that he was only an agent of the plaintiff. Such evidence would contradict the express term of the contract in which he stated that he was the owner. Therefore the plaintiff could not sue on the contract.

(b)   The undisclosed principal may not sue if it is evident that the personality of the agent was vitally important to the third party. For example, a trader may have been willing to contract only with selected clients, and may have given credit terms to the agent personally, because he could be trusted to settle his indebtedness. The trader is unwilling to extend credit to a principal of whom he knows nothing.

(c)   The undisclosed principal may not acquire better rights under the contract than those possessed by the agent. The third party may have a right to set off his indebtedness under the contract against the agent's indebtedness to him in respect of a previous transaction. The undisclosed principal is bound by such third party rights unless, when dealing with the agent, the third party realised that the agent might be contracting for an undisclosed principal but did not enquire further into this matter.

When the principal has been disclosed, the third party may sue the principal or the agent, but not both. If he has already begun proceedings against the agent, he may continue to sue him or may sue the principal instead (on first learning of the latter's existence). Once judgement has been given against the agent, the third party cannot sue the principal, even though the judgement does not give full satisfaction.

6.4.4 Non-existent principal

In this case, if an agent purports to act for a principal who is either not in existence or not legally capable of contracting at the time the contract is executed, the agent is personally liable on the contract.

6.4.5 Breach of warranty of authority

In the four situations described above, the principal is only liable to the third party if the agent had authority by express authorisation, or by implication, or by necessity, or by ratification, or by estoppel. If a person claims to act for a principal and he has no authority then the 'principal' is not liable to the third party. However, the third party may sue the 'agent', who will be liable. The relevant action is for breach of warranty of authority.

Deceit does not have to be proved by the third party; it is sufficient that the defendant claimed to have authority to act as an agent when he had no such authority. In *Yonge v Toynbee (1910)*, a firm of solicitors were instructed to defend a case against the plaintiff. After this instruction was given, but by the time the case came to court, their client had become insane, unknown to the solicitors. Insanity terminates an agency contract. It was held that the solicitors were liable for breach of warranty of authority.

6.5 Agency in partnership

6.5.1 Definition and nature of partnership

'Partnership is the relation which subsists between persons carrying on a business in common with a view of profit' S1(1) Partnership Act 1890 (PA 1890). Partnership is a form of unincorporated association. Each partner is at one and the same time both the principal and agent of the others in relation to the business they have agreed to carry on and has unlimited liability in respect of debts thereby incurred.

6.5.2 Authority of partner: liability of partners in contract

A partner's authority may be:

(a)   *Actual* - Where a partner makes a contract which he is authorised to make. The result will be that the firm is bound.

(b)   *Apparent* - If the partner enters into a transaction on behalf of a firm without authority, the outsider may nevertheless hold the firm bound under the provisions of S5 PA 1890, which gives partners some apparent authority. Under this section, however, apparent authority is confined to acts connected with the business and the court decides what can be regarded as connected. Thus, in *Mercantile Credit Co Limited v Garrod (1962)* A and B had entered into an agreement for the letting of garages and the execution of motor repairs, but expressly excluding the buying and selling of cars. A, without B's knowledge, purported to sell a car to a hire purchase company for the sum of £700, which was paid into the partnership account, the owner of the car not having consented to the sale. Mocatta J, in holding that the firm was accountable for the £700 to the hire purchase company, dismissed the argument that the transaction was not binding because of the exclusion of buying and selling in the partnership deed, looking at the matter instead from 'what was apparent to the outside world in general'. A's act was consistent with the kind of the business carried on by persons trading as a garage.

In addition, the act in question must not only be within the scope of the business carried on by the firm but must also be executed 'in the usual way' of such business. Thus, in *Higgins v Beauchamp (1914)* acceptance by a partner of a bill of exchange which was incomplete in the sense that it lacked the drawer's name was sufficiently unusual to put the acceptance beyond the usual way of carrying on business so that the firm was not bound.

As regards dormant partners, if the dormant partner has actual authority to enter into the transaction (which may be a contradiction in terms since he is supposed to be inactive) then the firm is bound. If the dormant partner has no actual authority so that the outsider relies on apparent authority under S5 PA 1890, then the position is as follows:

(i)   If the outsider knew that the dormant partner was a member of the firm, the dormant partner and the firm would be bound.

(ii) If, as is likely, the outsider did not know that the dormant partner was a member of the firm, the firm is not bound and it seems that the dormant partner is not bound in a personal capacity either, since he did not intend to contract for himself but on behalf of the firm.

Situations of apparent authority as laid down by case law

The courts have over the years laid down in decided cases a number of areas in which a partner has apparent authority. These are as follows:

(a)   **Powers available to all partners, regardless of the nature of the business**

(i)   To sell goods or personal chattels of the firm. Thus in *Dore v Wilkinson (1817)* the firm was held bound when a partner without authority sold the partnership books.

(ii) To purchase on account of the firm goods necessary for, or usually employed in, the business. Thus in *Bond v Gibson (1808)* A and B were in partnership as harness makers and B bought bits to be made into bridles on the firm's account. B later pawned them and kept the money, and it was held that the firm was liable to pay the person from whom B bought the bits.

(iii) To receive payment of debts due to the firm and give valid receipts (*Stead v Salt (1825)*). It should be noted that there is no converse rule so that payment to the firm will discharge a separate debt due to a partner unless the firm has authority to receive it (*Powell v Brodhurst (1901)*).

(iv) To engage employees for the business (*Beckham v Drake (1841)*) and also to discharge them unless the other partners object (*Donaldson v Williams (1833)*).

(v)   To employ a solicitor to defend the firm should an action be brought against it (*Tomlinson v Broadsmith (1896)*).

(b)   **Additional powers where there is a trading partnership**

Partners in trading firms have wider powers than those in non-trading firms. There appears to be no good reason for this, but the distinction has by now occurred in many cases and cannot be ignored. Although he was not purporting to give an exhaustive definition of what constitutes a trader, Ridley J in *Wheatley v Smithers (1906)* said: 'One important element in any definition of the term would be that trading implies buying or selling.' On this basis he held that an auctioneer was not a trader because he does not buy goods and, although he sells, he sells goods belonging to other people rather than to himself. This distinction as regards trading firms was approved in *Higgins v Beauchamp (1914)*, in which it was held that a partner in a firm of cinema and theatre proprietors had no power to borrow on the credit of the firm. The partnership agreement expressly negatived any such power to borrow and the non-trading character of the firm prevented an implied power to borrow from arising. In the course of his judgment Lush J said: 'In my opinion it would be wrong to say that every business which involves spending money is a trading business. To my mind a trading business is one which carries on the buying and selling of goods.'

If therefore, the firm is engaged in trade, the additional implied powers of the partners are as follows:

(i)   To draw, issue, accept, transfer, and endorse, bills of exchange, either by signing the firm's name or the partner's own name 'for and on behalf of' the firm. In a non-trading firm this authority will not exist unless there has been a course of dealing where the firm has in the past honoured instruments signed by one partner. Thus in *Hedley v Bainbridge (1842)*, where there was no such course of dealing, a solicitor was held to have no power to bind his firm by promissory note, even in respect of a debt which was due from the firm.

(ii)   To borrow money on the credit of the firm irrespective of any private limitation of authority between the partners unless of course, such limitation is known to the third party. Borrowing includes the overdrawing of a bank account (S7 PA 1890).

(iii) To secure the loan:

-    by pledging personal property of the firm (*Gordon v Ellis (1844)*); or

-    by depositing title deeds of land, whether freehold or leasehold, so as to create an equitable mortgage. A legal mortgage requires a deed and the consent of all the partners (*Harrison v Jackson (1797)*).

(c)   **Cases in which there is no implied power regardless of the nature of the firm**

No partner, whether in a trading firm or not, has apparent authority in the following areas:

(i)   He cannot bind the firm by deed unless the other partners have given him express authority under seal. The fact that the partnership agreement is under seal does not suffice for this purpose (*Harrison v Jackson (1797)*).

(ii) He cannot give a guarantee so as to bind the firm, even in relation to the firm's business. The subject was considered in *Brettel v Williams (1849)*, where the defendants, who were railway contractors, made a sub-contract for the performance of part of certain work which they had undertaken. The sub-contractor required a quantity of coal to enable him to get on with the job and one of the defendants, in the name of the firm, guaranteed to the plaintiffs, who were coal merchants, payment for coals to be supplied by them to the sub-contractors. It was held that this guarantee did not bind the partners of the contractor signing it on the grounds that it is not usual for persons in business to make themselves answerable for the conduct of other people.

(iii) He cannot compromise a debt by taking something else instead of money, eg, shares in a company (*Niemann v Niemann (1889)*). However, he may take a cheque, which is not regarded as a compromise of the debt (*Tomlins v Lawrence (1830)*).

(iv) He cannot bind the firm by submitting a dispute to arbitration (*Adams v Bankhart (1835)*).

(v)   He cannot open a bank account in his own name for the partnership business.

The last point was decided in the case of *Alliance Bank Limited v Kearsley (1871)*. James and William Kearsley were in partnership as coachbuilders, trading as George Kearsley & Co. In 1864 James opened an account with the plaintiff bank in Manchester. He said that it was to be a partnership account but that as he was the only partner living in Manchester it had better be in his name. In 1869 the account was overdrawn and the bank sued brother William for the overdraft. The court held that William was not liable because James did not have authority to bind his co-partner to be responsible for the state of his own bank account. Opening a bank account in one's own name for the transactions of a partnership is not an ordinary course of business.

6.5.3   Partners' personal liability for debt and breaches of contract by firm

If, as a result of actual or apparent authority, a partner (or other agent) makes the firm liable in debt or in contract and the firm does not pay the debt or perform the contract, eg, where a partner orders goods and the firm refuses to take delivery, the liability of partners is **joint**, not **several** (S9). So, if A, B and C are in partnership, and X, a creditor, sues A alone and the judgment is not paid, B and C are discharged and X cannot sue them even if he did not know later that they were partners.

The position has now been modified by the Civil Liability (Contribution) Act 1978 (see below), but even before that, this rather harsh rule could be alleviated as follows:

(a)   A deceased partner's estate can be sued if the debt was incurred before his death. This is a contribution of equity and would mean that if, in the example above, B was deceased, X could bring an action against his estate, even though he had already sued A to judgment.

(b)   Separate causes of action are not merged (*Wegg-Prosser v Evans (1895)*).

(c)   Under the Rules of the Supreme Court, order 81, rule 1, if a creditor sues in the firm name and obtains a judgment in the firm name, this operates as a judgment against each individual partner and all are liable on it.

It should be noted that S9 does not prevent rights of contribution between the partners. Thus, if in the example given above, A had paid the judgment, he would be able to ask for a contribution from B and C. Since each partner is liable potentially for all the debts of the firm, this contribution does not appear to be based on capital or profit-sharing ratios. It seems that partners would normally be liable to contribute equally towards a payment made by one of them (but note the provision in S2 of the Civil Liability (Contribution) Act 1978, below). Thus, in the example given above, if A had paid a judgment of £300 he would be entitled to £100 from B and £100 from C. Furthermore, it seems that if, say, C could not pay, the liability would be equal as among the solvent partners, so that A would be entitled to a contribution of £150 from B.

For causes of action arising after 1 January 1979 the Civil Liability (Contribution) Act 1973, S3, now provides that judgment recovered against any person liable in respect of any debt or damage shall not be a bar to an action against anyone who is jointly liable in respect of the same debt or damage. Rights of contribution are preserved by S1 of the 1978 Act, the amount recoverable being such as the court thinks just and equitable (S2 of the 1978 Act). The right to contribution under the 1978 Act can only be excluded by means of an express contractual agreement between the partners to that effect and it is lost after two years from the date when the right to claim it first accrued (Limitation Act 1980, S10(1)).

6.5.4   Liability of partners for torts

The firm may become liable for torts as follows:

(a)   Under S10 PA 1890 the firm is liable for the torts of partners committed in the ordinary course of partnership business (*Hamlyn v Houston & Co (1903)*), but not where the partner acts outside the scope of the firm's activities (*Arbuckle v Taylor (1815)*).

(b)   At common law the firm is liable for the torts of employees acting within the scope of their employment, so that if the firm's van driver injures a pedestrian by negligent driving, both he and the firm would be liable under the doctrine of vicarious liability.

As to the nature of the liability, this is **joint and several** (S12 PA 1890). Thus, a judgment against one partner is no bar to an action against the other. As regards a deceased partner, his estate is liable for the firm's torts committed during his lifetime, subject, as in the case of debt and contract, to the prior payment of his private debts, though if the action is for defamation of character, the deceased partner's liability ends on his death and his estate cannot be sued (Law Reform (Miscellaneous Provisions) Act 1934, S1).

Once again, if one partner pays the damages in respect of a tort he can ask for a contribution from his other partners, the rules being the same as those for debt or contract, which are set out above.

6.5.5   Misapplication of money or property

(a)   *Misapplication by partners* - Under S11 PA 1890 the firm is liable to make good a loss incurred if a partner misapplies the money or property of a third person. However, the partner must have been acting within the scope of his apparent authority when the money or property was received (*Plumer v Gregory (1874)*), otherwise the firm is not liable (*Cleather v Twisden (1884)*). If the firm does not pay, the liability of the partners personally is joint and several.

(b)   *Misapplication by employees* - This is covered by the common law and the firm is liable only if the servant was entrusted with the money or property. The fact that the employee's job helps him to misapply the property is not enough. Thus, if a firm's managing clerk is entrusted with funds as part of his job and he misapplies them, then the firm is liable, but if the office boy misapplies the funds and is assisted in doing this merely because he knows where the safe key is, then the firm is not liable.

Under S11 PA 1890, however, the rule is different for partners. A partner who misapplies property need not have been entrusted with it. Thus, if A and B are in partnership as dry-cleaners, A working at the London branch and B working at the Birmingham branch, and if B comes down to London and steals a fur from the London branch, the firm and A are nevertheless liable.

6.5.6   Improper employment of trust money

Under S13 PA 1890 if a trustee/partner improperly employs trust property, the firm is liable to make good for deficiency only if the other partners knew of the breach, eg, if they all agreed to use the money in the business. If the co-partners were not involved in the breach and had no knowledge of it, the firm is not liable. However, the beneficiaries under the trust are not without a remedy and may trace their property into the assets of the firm. This is based upon the notion that the true owner of property traced to the possession of another has a right to have it restored, not because it is a debt but because it is his property. His right is incidental to his ownership.

Thus, if the trust property is other than money and the beneficiary can identify it in the firm's assets, he can recover it. Thus, if a trustee/partner was using in his office a gold carriage clock which was part of the trust property, the beneficiaries could recover it. As regards money, if this has been placed in a separate account, the beneficiaries may take all of it. If, on the other hand, it is in a mixed account which contains trust money and partnership money, the beneficiaries can recover from that mixed account and in this connection there is an important assumption that trust money is spent last. Thus, if the partnership account stood at £10,000 and the trust money improperly applied was £5,000, the beneficiaries could take £5,000. If, on the other hand, the partnership account stood only at £4,000, the beneficiaries could not obviously recover all the money misapplied but they could take the whole £4,000 in the account.

6.5.7   Partnership by estoppel or holding out

As we have already seen, a person who allows himself to be represented as a partner may become one, but only to an outsider who has relied on the representation and by reason of it has been encouraged to do business with the firm. As regards internal relationships, a partner by estoppel does not necessarily acquire rights and duties in the firm. It is essentially a doctrine to protect outsiders. In connection with holding out, it should be noted that S14(2) PA 1890 prevents the estate of a deceased partner from continuing to be liable to outsiders after death merely because the business is continued for a time in the old firm name.

Continuing guarantees

Firms may become involved in these. Suppose AB & C Co enter into a fidelity bond guaranteeing that CD & Co will faithfully discharge their duties as debt collectors for EF & Co, so that AB &

Co would be liable to make good losses arising from CD & Co's failure to account. Under S18, if there is a change in the membership of CD & Co or EF & Co, the bond is discharged unless there is a contrary agreement between the parties. However, a change in the membership of AB & Co has no effect in terms, at least, of discharging the bond, and the position is as follows:

(a) New partners admitted after the bond was made are not liable on it.

(b) Existing partners are, of course, liable.

(c) Retiring partners continue their liability unless there is a novation or an indemnity.

6.5.8 Other effects of changes in the constitution of the firm

Under S36(1) PA 1890, if X who was a partner in Y & Co leaves the firm and the firm contracts with Z, who knew that X was a member of the firm but does not know that he has left, X will be liable to Z along with the other partners if the firm does not meet its obligations. To avoid this liability X must:

(a) Ensure that individual notices are sent to all customers of the firm while he was a partner.

(b) Advertise the fact of his leaving the firm in the *London Gazette*. This operates as notice to all who had not dealt with the firm before, while he was a partner, but who knew him to be one (S36(2) PA 1890). It should be noted that an advertisement in the *London Gazette* operates even in respect of those persons who have not read it.

In respect of those who had no previous dealings with the firm and did not know that X was a partner, there is no need to advertise in the Gazette and obviously it is impossible to send notice (*Tower Cabinet Co Limited V Ingram (1949)*). It should be noted that under S36(3) PA 1890 the estate of a deceased or bankrupt partner is not liable for debts incurred after death or bankruptcy, as the case may be, even if no advertisement or notice of any kind has been given.

6.6 Agency in registered companies

6.6.1 Definition and nature of a registered company

A registered company is a form of body corporate and, as such enjoys a separate legal identity from those of whom it is composed. It is an artificial legal person, acquiring its status by registration of various documents with the Registrar of Companies under the provisions of the Companies Acts 1985-1989.

6.6.2 Authority of a company's agents

As an artificial legal person, a company can only act through the agency of human beings, its board of directors.

S35A(1) of the Companies Act 1985 provides that in favour of a person dealing with a company in good faith, the power of the board of directors to bind the company, or authorise others to do so, shall be deemed to be free of any limitation under the company's constitution. For this purpose:

(a) a person 'deals with' a company if he is a party to any transaction or other act to which the company is a party;

(b)   a person shall not be regarded as acting in bad faith by reason only of his knowing that an act is beyond the powers of the directors under the company's constitution; and

(c)   a person shall be presumed to have acted in good faith unless the contrary is proved: S35(2) Companies Act 1985.

Under S35(4) a member of a company can bring proceedings to restrain the directors from acting outside their power, and by S35A(5) the protection afforded by S35A(1) does not affect any liability incurred by the directors, or any other person, by reason of the directors' exceeding their authority.

By S35B of the Act a party to a transaction with a company is not bound to enquire as to any limitation on the powers of the board of directors to bind the company or others to do so.

In order to limit the potential for fraud in these provisions, transactions entered into beyond the directors' powers and involving the directors (or persons connected with them) are treated as a special category. S322A Companies Act 1985 provides that such a transaction is voidable at the instance of the company. The directors are liable to be called to account by the company in such a transaction. Where such a transaction involves a third party as well as a director, the transaction is valid, but may be severed or set aside by a court on such terms as the court thinks fit.

6.7   Relationship between agent and principal

6.7.1   Duties of an agent

The duties of an agent towards his principal are:

(a)   He must obey his principal's lawful instructions. In *Turpin v Bilton (1843)*, for example, an insurance broker agreed for consideration to effect insurance cover on T's ship. However, he failed to do so and the ship was lost. As there was no insurance cover T sued B personally for the loss. The court found in favour of T.

Similarly in *Fraser v B N Furman (Productions) Ltd (1967)*, Fraser, an insurance broker, agreed to effect employer's liability insurance cover for the respondents but failed to do so. The respondents were liable for £3,000 on a claim brought by an employee. It was held that Fraser was personally liable to the respondents.

However, as illustrated in *Cohen v Kittell (1889)* the instructions of the principal must be lawful. In that case K undertook to place bets on certain horses on behalf of C. He failed to do so and when some of the horses won C was unable to get the winnings to which he would otherwise have been entitled. C then sued K for the loss of winnings. C's action failed as, by the Gaming Act 1845, the bets themselves and any winnings arising therefrom, would not be recoverable by law.

(b)   He must exercise due care and skill in the performance of his duties. The standard will be 'as skilful and as careful as people in his trade or profession normally are'. For example, if an agent has to sell property, he should obtain the best price reasonably obtainable: *Keppel v Wheeler (1927)*. In that case agents were employed to sell a block of flats. They received an offer from X which the owners accepted 'subject to contract'.

Subsequently the agents received a higher offer from Y. Instead of informing the owners, they arranged a resale between X and Y. It was held that this constituted a breach of duty. The agents were liable in damages to the owners of the flat.

(c)   He must act in good faith for the benefit of his principal, and this includes the following:

    (i)   He must not compete against his principal: *Lucifero v Castel (1887)*. Here, an agent was asked to purchase a yacht for his principal. The agent bought a yacht for himself and then resold it to his principal at a profit. It was held that the agent had broken his duty to the principal and must hand over the secret profit he had made.

    (ii)   He is not permitted to acquire any personal benefit in the course of, or by means of, his agency without the knowledge and consent of the principal: *Grinsted v Hadrill (1953)*. This rule is applied very strictly by the courts. No intention to defraud has to be proved. It is sufficient that the agent makes a secret profit. The principal is entitled to claim the full value of the profit. He may also dismiss the agent without notice and if fraud was involved, he may refuse to pay him his remuneration. If a bribe has been offered to the agent then the principal may repudiate the contract which has been arranged with the third party, as well as taking action against the agent for damages for any loss me may have sustained through entering into the contract, without deducting the amount of the bribe he has recovered from the agent.

    (iii)   He must not misuse confidential information regarding his principal's affairs.

(d)   He must personally carry out the duties entrusted to him: *De Bussche v Alt (1878)*. An agent must not get someone to do things that his principal has chosen him to do, unless the principal gives permission. This is summarised by the Latin maxim, *delegatus non potest delegare* (a delegate cannot delegate). Thus in *John McCann & Co v Pow (1974)*, Mr Pow instructed John McCann & Co, a firm of estate agents, to find a buyer for his flat. They passed details of the flat to another estate agent, Douglas & Co, who advised a Mr Rudd that the flat was for sale. Mr Rudd went to see the flat. Mr Pow said to him: 'Have you come from McCann's?' Mr Rudd said no. Mr Pow and Mr Rudd then agreed a sale. John McCann & Co sued Mr Pow for commission for introducing Mr Rudd. It was held that they were not entitled to delegate the agency and so could not have the commission. There are some exceptions to the rule, which were comprehensively stated in the case of *De Bussche v Alt (1878)*. They are:

    (i)   Where the act delegated is purely ministerial and does not involve confidence or discretion eg, *Allam & Co Ltd v Europa Poster Services Ltd (1968)*. In that case various owners of sites on which advertising posters could be displayed agreed that Europa Poster Services Ltd could act as their agent to terminate existing licences to use their sites. Europa Poster Services Ltd employed a firm of solicitors to send notices terminating the licences. It was held that these notices were valid and effective because Europa Poster Services Ltd was not precluded from delegating a 'purely ministerial act'.

    (ii)   Where, from the conduct of principal and agent, it may reasonably be presumed to have been their intention that the agent should have power to delegate his authority.

(iii)   Where the employment of a sub-agent is justified by the custom of the particular trade or business in which the agent is employed, provided the custom is not unreasonable and does not conflict with an express agreement between principal and agent.

(iv)   Where in the course of the agent's work unforeseen circumstances arise which render it necessary for the agent to delegate his authority.

(e)   He must render an account to his principal when required to do so.

6.7.2   Duties of the principal

The duties owed by a principal to his agent are as follows:

(a)   He must pay the agent the commission or other remuneration as agreed. If no sum has been fixed but payment was implied, a claim may be made on a *quantum meruit* basis.

(b)   He must reimburse the agent for any expenses, losses or liabilities incurred by the agent in the proper performance of his duties.

6.7.3   Rights of the agent against his principal

An agent has the following rights:

(a)   A right of lien, according to the type of agency (eg, auctioneers and factors).

(b)   In certain cases, a right of stoppage against goods in transit to the principal, provided that the agent has assumed liability for payment of the purchase price and, on balance, there is a net amount owing by the principal to the agent.

6.8   Termination of agency

6.8.1   Methods of termination

Agency may be terminated by act of the parties themselves; operation of law; or, completion of the agency agreement.

(a)   *By act of the parties*

(i)   Agency may be terminated bilaterally (by mutual agreement): if both parties agree to end the contract then this will be a binding discharge.

(ii)   Agency may also be terminated unilaterally by either party, subject to the following:

-    Although the principal may instruct the agent not to act for him in the future, the principal will be estopped from denying the agent's continuing authority unless he notifies persons with whom the agent previously dealt on the principal's behalf.

-    If the agent has been engaged for a fixed period, any attempt by the principal to terminate the agency before the end of that period may be regarded by the agent as a breach of contract on which the agent may sue for damages: *Turner v Goldsmith (1891)*. In that case G, a shirt manufacturer, engaged T as a traveller for five years certain on a commission basis. T was required to do his utmost to sell shirts or any other goods made by G. After two years G's factory was destroyed and G did not continue business of any kind. (There was no evidence to show whether or not he would have been able to do so.) T sued G for an amount based on the commission he would probably have earned if the factory had been able to operate for the following three years. T's action succeeded.

- If the agent is an employee of the principal, and receives a regular salary he is entitled to be given reasonable notice before the agency is terminated, unless he is being dismissed for misconduct: *Martin Baker Aircraft Co Ltd v Murison (1955)*. Here the plaintiffs appointed M as their sole selling agent in North America. M was required to devote considerable time and money to his duties and was not allowed to become involved in the sale of competitors' products. There was no time limit provided in the contract. It was held that a term would be implied that either side must give twelve months' notice to terminate the contract.

- The agency may not be terminated unilaterally by the principal if it is irrevocable.

(b)   *By operation of law*

Agency is terminated by operation of law in the following circumstances:

(i)   On the death of either the principal or the agent.

(ii)   On the bankruptcy of the principal (but not necessarily the bankruptcy of the agent).

(iii)   If the subject-matter or the operation of the agency agreement is frustrated or becomes illegal - eg, the property to be dealt with is destroyed, or the agent is compelled to join the armed forces and is consequently not available to carry out his duties as agent.

(iv)   On the insanity of the principal (and probably the agent): *Yonge v Toynbee (1910)*.

If, because of illness, an agent becomes incapable of managing his own affairs then any person who, knowing of the agent's incapacity, allows the agent to make the agent's principal a party to a contract will be unable to enforce the contract.

(c)   *By completion of the agency agreement*

An agency agreement is terminated when:

(i)   The period fixed for the agreement comes to an end.
(ii)   The specific purpose for which the agreement was created is accomplished.

6.8.2   Effect of revocation

If an agent continues to act as though he were an agent after his authority has been revoked then his actions do not bind his principal, and any third party who deals with him in good faith may sue him for breach of warranty of authority. If an agent's authority is given by deed (ie, by power of attorney) then the agent, and persons dealing with him, are protected by S5 of the Powers of Attorney Act 1971 if the agent's authority is revoked without their knowledge (eg, by the death, unknown to them, of the principal).

A donee of a power of attorney who acts in pursuance of the power at a time when it has been revoked shall not, by reason of the revocation, incur any liability (either to the donor or to any other person) if at that time he did not know that the power had been revoked (Powers of Attorney Act 1971, S5(1)). Where a power of attorney has been revoked and a person, without knowledge of the revocation, deals with the donee of the power, the transaction between them shall, in favour of that person, be as valid as if the power had then been in existence (Powers of Attorney Act 1971, S5(2)).

6.8.3   Irrevocable agency

If A authorises B to act as A's agent for the purpose of discharging an obligation owed to B, and the authorisation is stated in a deed or was given for valuable consideration, then it is irrevocable until the obligation is discharged. Such authority is not ended by the death or bankruptcy of the principal and is not ended if, through illness, the principal becomes incapable of managing his own affairs. So, for example, if B lends money to A on condition that A gives him authority to sell an item of A's property and repay the loan out of the proceeds then A cannot revoke the authority until the loan is repaid.

6.9   Revision exercise

In order to ensure that you have understood this session, attempt the following questions, checking your answers against the reference given.

(1)   What do you understand by the concept of agency?   **(Solution: 6.1.1)**

(2)   May a minor act as an agent?   **(Solution: 6.1.1)**

(3)   What is a power of attorney?   **(Solution: 6.2.1)**

(4)   How may an agency arise by implication?   **(Solution: 6.2.1)**

(5)   What criteria must be satisfied before the courts will concede an agency of necessity?
                                                                          (Solution: 6.2.1)

(6)   Explain the concept of agency by ratification.   **(Solution: 6.2.1)**

(7)   What is the legal effect of ratification?   **(Solution: 6.2.1)**

(8)   Give an example of agency by estoppel.   **(Solution: 6.2.1)**

(9)   What do you understand by the concept of usual authority?   **(Solution: 6.5.2)**

(10)   What are the criteria of apparent authority as established by S5 of the Partnership Act 1890?   **(Solution: 6.5.2)**

(11)   What is the liability of partners in tort?   **(Solution: 6.5.4)**

(12)   Examine the liability of incoming and outgoing partners.   **(Solution: 6.5.8)**

(13)   What are the duties of an agent?   **(Solution: 6.7.1)**

(14)   In what circumstances may an agent delegate his duties?   **(Solution: 6.7.1)**

(15)   What duties are owed by a principal to his agent?   **(Solution: 6.7.2)**

(16)   In what circumstances does an agent have a right of stoppage against goods in transit to his principal?   **(Solution: 6.7.3)**

(17)   Examine the law regarding termination of agency by act of the parties.   **(Solution: 6.8.1)**

(18)   In what circumstances may an agency be terminated by operation of law?
                                                                         (Solution: 6.8.1)

(19)   What is the effect of revocation of an agency?   **(Solution: 6.8.2)**

(20)   Explain the concept of irrevocable agency.   **(Solution: 6.8.3)**

6.10   Conclusion

A systematic and thorough study of this session will have given you sufficient knowledge and understanding of agency to clearly explain the concept of agency; to elaborate fully on the ways in which agency can arise; to be able to state and expound upon the authority enjoyed by agents; to detail the relationship between principal and agent and the obligations placed upon them; and to state clearly the circumstances in which an agency may be terminated and the effects of termination.

6.11   Questions

Objective test questions

(1)   The authority which a partner is presumed to enjoy is termed:

A   Actual.
B   Usual.
C   Implied.
D   Apparent.

(2)   A has appointed B his agent. Which of the following events would not necessarily terminate B's authority?

A   The death of A.
B   The death of B.
C   The bankruptcy of B.
D   The destruction of the subject-matter B was appointed to sell.

(3)   If a principal refuses to ratify a contract entered into by an agent on his behalf, but in excess of that agent's authority, the third party concerned may:

A   Sue the principal.

B   Sue the agent or the principal.

C   Sue the agent only.

D   Sue the agent and the principal.

(4)   Partnership is:

A   Carrying on business with a view of profit.

B   The relation which subsists between persons carrying on a business in common with a view of profit.

C   The relation which subsists between persons carrying on a business in common.

D   The relation which arises from sharing the profits of a business.

(5)   Which of the following is not a requirement of agency by necessity?

A   The impossibility of obtaining the owner's instructions.

B   The 'agent' must have acted bona fide on behalf of the owner.

C   There must have been an emergency.

D   The 'agent' must have specifically informed the third party that he was acting for the principal, and identified him as such.

Written test questions

6.1   A, P and T

(a)   How may an agency arise by implication?

(b)   A was P's agent and on P's behalf made several contracts with T over a period of some years. P later terminated A's agency but failed to notify T. A continued to deal with T, in his own name and on his own behalf, but became insolvent. As a result T sustained losses and now claims to be entitled to damages by way of compensation from P. Advise P.

6.2   Thomas, Andy and Peter

(a)   Discuss the doctrine of the undisclosed principal in relation to agency, and examine the rights and duties of all parties concerned where an agent acts for such a principal.

(b)   Thomas sold goods to Andy, who did not disclose that he was purchasing them on behalf of Peter, but Thomas later discovered this.   Thomas's solicitors wrote letters to both Peter and Andy threatening proceedings in respect of the price of the goods. A writ was issued against Peter, who has now gone bankrupt. Thomas wishes to sue Andy. Advise Thomas.

6.3   **X, Y and Z**

(a)   What conditions must be fulfilled before a principal can effectively ratify a contract entered into by his agent without his authority? What is the legal effect of such ratification?

(b)   On 1 June X meets Y (who is Z's chauffeur) and offers to buy Z's car for £1,500. On 2 June Y accepts X's offer on behalf of Z, although he had no actual or apparent authority to do so. On 4 June X purports to revoke his offer and informs Y that he no longer wishes to purchase the car. On 10 June Z ratifies the acceptance of Y.

Advise X whether he is bound by the contract.

Would your answer be different if X and Y had by mutual consent cancelled the unauthorised transaction before ratification?

SESSION 7

Sale of goods

This session will provide you with:

- a knowledge and understanding of what constitutes a sale of goods;

- an indepth knowledge of the terms implied into a contract for the sale of goods by Ss12-15 of the Sale of Goods Act 1979;

- a knowledge of the law regarding the transfer of the property in goods in a contract for the sale of goods;

- an understanding of the law governing performance of a contract for the sale of goods and the position of the parties on a breach of such a contract.

7.1 Nature and definition of a sale of goods

The law relating to the sale of goods was first codified in the Sale of Goods Act 1893. During the 1970s several amendments to this statute were enacted: the Supply of Goods (Implied Terms) Act 1973, the Unsolicited Goods and Services Act 1971, the Consumer Credit Act 1974, the Unfair Contract Terms Act 1977. The subject is of such importance that a new consolidating statute has now been passed so that there will be easy access to the law on this topic. The principal authority is now the Sale of Goods Act 1979.

A contract of sale of goods is defined in S2(1) of the Sale of Goods Act 1979 to be a contract whereby the seller transfers, or agrees to transfer the property in goods to the buyer for a money consideration called the price. If the goods to be sold are in existence at the time the contract is made and the title to those goods is to pass to the purchaser at once, the contract is called a sale. However, if the contract is made at a time when the goods are not yet available (eg, they have not yet been manufactured), or even if available they have not yet been specifically appropriated to the contract, the contract is known as an agreement to sell.

In a sale of goods, the property is generally deemed to pass immediately. Therefore, if the goods were to be accidentally lost or destroyed after the contract had been completed the loss would fall on the purchaser. However, with an agreement to sell, the property does not pass until the goods contracted for are not only available (in the sense of having been manufactured) but have also been specifically appropriated to the particular contract.

For example, if you go into a shop, point to or otherwise identify a certain article, tell the shopkeeper you want to buy it, pay the price and ask the shopkeeper to send it to your home address, you will be the person to suffer if, before this item is delivered, it is stolen, or accidentally lost or damaged (although through no fault of the shopkeeper or his staff). On the other hand, if there were several of these articles in the shop, and you asked the shopkeeper to deliver one of them to your home (leaving him to pick the particular article), the shopkeeper would have to stand the loss if all of his stock of the articles were to be damaged or lost before he had set aside one item for your order.

The foregoing remarks apply to agreements where the subject-matter of the contract was in existence at the time the contract was made. However, if in a contract for the sale of specific goods (ie, a sale proper) the goods are no longer available (eg, they have perished or have been irretrievably lost) at the time the contract was made, and the vendor was not aware of their loss, the contract is void. This also applies if only a part of the subject-matter is lost. In *Barrow Lane and Ballard Ltd v Phillip Phillips & Co Ltd (1929)*, part of a stock of Chinese walnuts had been stolen, although this fact was not known to the owners. A contract for the sale of the whole stock was held to be void, even though some (in fact, the bulk) of the stock was available at the time of making the contract.

Contracts for the sale of goods must be distinguished from contracts for work done or services supplied, and from contracts for hire. In *Beecham Foods v North Supplies (Edmonton) Ltd (1959)*, it was held that when the goods are supplied in returnable bottles, only the contents of the bottles constitute goods sold; the bottles themselves form the subject-matter of a separate contract of hire. In *Lee v Griffin (1861)*, the contract was for the making and supply of a set of false teeth; this was held to be a contract for the sale of goods. However, in *Robinson v Graves (1935)*, the contract was for the painting of a portrait, the artist supplying the canvas and other materials; this contract was held to be one of work and materials, and not for the sale of goods, because the commissioner wanted the portrait to be painted by a particular artist.

It is sometimes difficult to distinguish a contract for work and materials from one for the sale of goods. In *Robinson v Graves (1935)*, Greer LJ laid down the following test:

> 'If you find . . . that the substance of the contract was the production of something to be sold...then that is a sale of goods. But if the substance of the contract, on the other hand, is that skill and labour have to be exercised for the production of the article and that it is only ancillary to that that there will pass . . . some materials . . . the substance of the contract is the skill and experience.'

A contract under which a person agrees to carry out a service is called a contract for the supply of a service and is subject to Part 2 of the Supply of Goods and Services Act 1982 rather than to the Sale of Goods Act. A contract for work and materials is partly a contract for the supply of a service and partly a contract for the transfer of goods. Contracts for the transfer of goods are subject to Part 1 of the 1982 Act.

The Sale of Goods Act 1979 covers only contracts for the sale of **goods**. 'Goods' are defined in S61 of the Act to include all personal chattels apart from things in action and money. The term 'personal chattels' means any property other than land or interests in land. It is traditional to divide personal chattels into 'things in possession' and 'things in action'.

'Things in possession' are physical objects (such as books and tables) and the benefit of ownership of a thing in possession is that the owner can have possession of the object. 'Things in action' are legally enforceable rights (such as the right to payment of a debt) and the benefit of ownership is that the owner can take legal action to enforce the right. It is common for a thing in action to be represented by a certificate or other document but possession of the documentary representation is not the essential benefit of ownership. For example, a cheque is a thing in action because it is a right to payment of a certain sum of money. The printed form on which the cheque is written is merely a means of obtaining payment of the money.

Contracts for the transfer of ownership of money are not covered by the Sale of Goods Act 1979 but a contract for the sale of a particular coin or note as a collector's item is covered by the Act (*Moss v Hancock, 1899*).

A contract for the transfer of goods is subject to the Sale of Goods Act 1979 only if the consideration is money. If the consideration consists entirely of other goods then the contract is one of exchange or barter and will not be subject to the 1979 Act but will be subject to Part 1 of the Supply of Goods and Services Act 1982. If the consideration is partly money and partly goods then the contract will be subject to the Sale of Goods Act if the goods given in consideration can be regarded as representing part of a previously agreed money consideration.

7.2 Formation of the contract

The normal contractual rules apply to a contract for the sale of goods. There must be an agreement, intention to create legal relations, capacity, consideration, formality. The parties may agree express terms about matters such as delivery date, place of delivery, details about the subject matter, payment. The Sale of Goods Act 1979 adds many implied terms to every contract of sale of goods.

7.2.1 Implied terms

Title

Under S12 of the Act, there is an implied condition that the seller has the right to sell the goods. In *Rowland v Divall (1923)*, R bought from D a motor car which he used for four months. In fact, D had no title to the car and finally R had to return it to the true owner. R then sued D for the whole purchase price. It was held that R was entitled to the full price, even though he had had some use of the car, because at no time did he have what he intended to buy, namely the legal title to the vehicle. Thus, if the vendor has no title, the buyer can recover the full purchase price on discovering that fact, even though he has had the benefit of the goods in the meantime.

If the vendor may be stopped by process of law from selling, eg, proceedings for infringement of trademark, he has no right to sell. Thus, the seller undertakes not merely that he owns the goods, but that he is free to sell them.

There is an implied warranty that the goods are free, and will remain free, of any charge or encumbrance not made known to the buyer, and that the buyer will enjoy quiet possession of the goods except so far as it may be disturbed by the person entitled to the charge or encumbrances disclosed.

Description

Section 13 of the 1979 Act provides that:

(a)   Where goods are sold by description there is an implied condition that:

(i)   the goods will correspond with the description;

(ii)   if the sale is by sample as well as by description, the bulk of the goods will also correspond with the sample.

(b)   A sale of goods is not prevented from being a sale by description solely by reason that the goods, being exposed for sale or hire, are selected by the buyer.

A buyer need not accept goods bought by description if the goods as supplied do not tally with the description, even though they may be merchantable in the form supplied. In *Moore & Co v Landauer & Co (1921)*, the vendors were held to have broken the implied condition as to description by supplying goods in cases of 24 tins each instead of the agreed number of 30 tins per case (although the total number of tins supplied agreed with the contract figure).

This condition will apply to nearly all sales as inevitably the goods will be bought by description. In *Beale v Taylor (1967)*, a car was advertised as a '1961' Triumph Herald. The purchaser went to see the vehicle and decided to buy it. After purchase, however, the buyer discovered that only the rear part was 1961. The front part of the car was taken from an earlier model. It was held that this was a breach of S13.

Reference should also be made to *Grant v Australian Knitting Mills Ltd (1936)*. In this case G bought a pair of long woollen underpants from a retailer, the respondents being the manufacturers. The underpants contained an excess of sulphite which was a chemical used in their manufacturer. This chemical should have been eliminated before the product was finished, but a quantity was left in the underpants purchased by G. After wearing the pants for a day or two, a rash, which turned out to be dermatitis, appeared on his ankles and soon became generalised, compelling him to spend many months in hospital. He sued the retailer and the manufacturers for damages. The court held that:

(a)   the retailers were in breach of the equivalent of S14(2) and (3) of the Sale of Goods Act 1979, the article being neither of merchantable quality or reasonably fit for its purpose; and

(b)   the manufacturers were liable in negligence, following *Donoghue v Stevenson (1932)*.

Quality and fitness for purpose

In this respect, S14 of the 1979 Act makes a distinction between private selling and selling in the course of business. Subsection (1) states that there is no implied condition or warranty as to quality or fitness for a particular purpose of goods sold, except as provided by the following subsections (2 and 3) of S14 or by S15 (which deals with sales by sample).

Subsection (2) provides that where goods are sold by the vendor in the course of business, there is an implied condition that those goods are of merchantable quality, except to the extent of defects which:

(a)   are brought specifically to the buyer's attention before the contract is made; or

(b)   ought to have been noticed by the buyer if he had examined the goods before the contract was made.

There are several important points to note about this subsection. The implied condition of merchantable quality will only apply **if the vendor sold in the course of business**. The maxim caveat emptor (let the buyer beware) will apply if the vendor is a private seller.

There is a statutory definition of merchantable quality:

> Goods of any kind are of merchantable quality (for the purposes of S14(2)) if they are as fit for the purpose or purposes for which goods of that kind are commonly bought as it is reasonable to expect having regard to any description applied to them, the price (if relevant) and all the other relevant circumstances: S14(6).

Thus goods described as secondhand or sold at a reduced price may, though less than perfect, be of merchantable quality.

Subsection (3) provides that in cases where the buyer indicates to the vendor the purpose for which he requires the goods, and that he is relying on the vendor's knowledge or skill as to the suitability of the goods for that purpose, there is an implied condition that the goods are reasonably fit for that purpose (whether or not the goods are normally supplied for that purpose), except where it can be shown that the buyer has not relied, or it would have been unreasonable for him to rely, on the vendor's judgment. **Again it should be noted that the sale must be in the course of a business - the subsection does not apply to private sales.**

There is generally no need for the purchaser to make known expressly to the vendor the purpose for which he requires goods. Normally this will be implicit, eg, biscuits are required for eating! If goods are required for a special purpose, eg, make-up for a sensitive skin, then the advice of the retailer must actually be sought. The courts have held that in most cases there will be reliance on the vendor's skill and judgment because the purchaser expects him to select his stock with care.

A case in which the plaintiff was successful in an action brought for breach of this particular implied condition of fitness for purpose was *Frost v Aylesbury Dairy Co (1905)*. The dairy supplied milk to the plaintiff and knew that it was consumed by himself and his wife. The wife drank some contaminated milk and died of typhoid fever. The court held that the defendants were under an obligation to provide milk reasonably fit for consumption.

In contrast to *Frost v Aylesbury Dairy Co (1905)*, reference should be made to *Griffiths v Peter Conway Ltd (1939)* and *Heil v Hughes (1951)*. In the first the plaintiff purchased a tweed coat which caused her to suffer dermatitis. She had an unusually sensitive skin and there was nothing in the coat that would have affected anyone with a normal skin. The court held that as the plaintiff's skin abnormality had not been made known to the seller, the seller was not liable. In the second, a lady and her husband became ill after eating pork chops. Tests indicated that the chops had been insufficiently cooked and that they would have been fit to eat if they had been cooked for a longer period. It was held that the chops were reasonably fit for their purpose.

Although S14(2) deals with merchantable quality and S14(3) with fitness for purpose, there is considerable overlap between them. Often both implied conditions will be broken. The difference between the two subsections becomes apparent when the goods being purchased have more than one possible use. Section 14(2) will not be broken if the goods are fit for any common use. This distinction may be seen by comparing the following two cases.

In *Wilson v Rickett, Cockerell & Co Ltd (1954)*, it was held that a consignment of a certain type of coal was not of merchantable quality because the consignment contained a substance (not an integral part of the coal) which exploded and caused damage.

In *B S Brown & Sons Ltd v Craiks Ltd (1970)*, cloth was bought for the purpose of making dresses although the buyer did not disclose this to the seller. The material was, in fact, not suitable for dresses, but was suitable for other industrial purposes. The court held that if goods can be used for two or more purposes, the goods are of merchantable quality if they are suitable for one or more purpose even though unsuitable for the buyer's (undisclosed) purpose.

Sales by sample

This is dealt with by S15 of the 1979 Act, which provides that there is an implied condition that:

(a)   The bulk will correspond with the sample.

(b)   The buyer will have a reasonable opportunity of comparing the bulk with the sample.

(c)   The goods are free from any defect rendering them unmerchantable which a reasonable examination of the sample would not reveal.

If the sale is by sample and description, the goods must correspond with the sample and the description.

In *Nichol v Godts (1854)*, the sale was by sample of foreign refined rape oil. Although the oil supplied corresponded with the sample, it was not foreign refined rape oil. The implied condition had therefore been broken.

7.2.2   Exclusion of the implied terms

Under the Unfair Contract Terms Act 1977, the implied conditions may not be excluded in the case where the buyer 'deals as a consumer' and any provision purporting to do so is void. This provision covers Ss12, 13, 14(3) and 15 of the Sale of Goods Act 1979. Furthermore, it is illegal to display a notice in a shop attempting to exclude these sections.

A party 'deals as a consumer' if he does not make the contract nor holds himself out as making it in the course of a business; but the other party does contract in the course of a business; and where the goods are of a type ordinarily bought for private use or consumption; but in a sale by auction or by competitive tender the buyer is never to be regarded as dealing as a consumer. The burden of proof is on the seller to show that in a particular sale the other party does not deal as a consumer.

However, the position is different in the case where the buyer does not deal as a consumer. Section 12 may not be excluded but Ss13, 14 and 15 may be excluded subject to a right given to the courts to decide upon the 'fairness' and 'reasonableness' of the particular clause. That is to say, the seller must always have the right to sell the goods, but may exclude, subject to fairness and reasonableness, liability for: the goods corresponding to the description; the quality and fitness for purpose; the sample corresponding to the bulk or the buyer's right relating to samples. The burden of proof is on the seller - he must prove to the courts that it is a fair exclusion clause.

The following criteria, *inter alia*, will be considered by the court when making their decision:

(a)   the relative strength of the bargaining position of the parties;

(b)   to what extent alternative sources of supply are available;

(c)   the inducements offered to the buyer for him to agree to the exemption clause;

(d)   to what extent the buyer was aware of the effect of the clause;

(e)   whether the goods were manufactured, processed or adapted to a special order of the buyer.

Exemption clauses in 'guarantees' (ie, promises to repair faulty goods) given by suppliers of goods may not exclude the supplier's liability for defects while the goods are in consumer use if such defects result from the negligence of the manufacturer or a distributor. Such 'guarantees' are frequently given in contracts for the sale of goods.

Similar provisions on exclusion also apply to contracts of hire, contracts of exchange and contracts for work and materials supplied.

7.3   Transfer of the property in the goods

In this sense, the term 'property' means the legal ownership of (or title to) the goods, which does not necessarily depend upon physical possession. It is necessary to know at what point the ownership is transferred, because if the goods are destroyed or lost, it is the owner who must bear the loss (unless there is an agreement to the contrary). Also, if either party to the sale is made bankrupt, it is necessary to know whether or not the goods in question belong to the trustee of the bankrupt party's estate.

7.3.1   Specific goods

Specific goods are those which are identified and agreed as referring to the particular sale at the time the contract is made. The primary rule is found in S17 of the Sale of Goods Act 1979 - the property passes when the parties intend it to pass. Often, however, their intention is not made clear, and S18 of the Act provides for the situations that may arise, by laying down four rules:

Rule 1 - If the goods are in a deliverable state when the contract is made, the property passes at the time the contract is made. It does not matter whether the goods have been paid for, or whether they have been delivered. Whether goods are in a deliverable state is a question of fact - in other words, a question which the court decides on the basis of the evidence presented to it. This means that a party who bases his case on a claim that goods were in a deliverable state must produce evidence to prove this aspect of his case.

Rule 2 - If the goods are not in a deliverable state and the seller is bound to do something to them for the purpose of putting them into a deliverable state, then the property does not pass until it is done and the buyer has notice of it.

Rule 3 - If the seller is bound to weigh, measure or test specific goods for the purpose of ascertaining the price, property does not pass until this has been done and the buyer has notice of it.

Rule 4 - If the goods are delivered on approval or on 'sale or return', the property passes:

(a)   when the buyer signifies his approval or acceptance to the seller; or

(b)   when the buyer does any act adopting the transaction (eg, by pawning the goods); or

(c)   if, without giving notice of rejection, the buyer retains the goods beyond the time agreed or, if no time has been fixed, beyond a reasonable time - what is a reasonable time is a question of fact, and, furthermore, retention of goods by the sheriff in the course of execution on the buyer's goods is not sufficient to cause the property to pass.

There are a number of cases illustrating the above rules.

In *Tarling v Baxter (1827)*, a contract was made on 6 January for the sale of a specific haystack. Payment was due on 4 February and delivery on 1 May. On 20 January the haystack burnt down. It was held that the property passed under Rule 1 on 6 January and the loss fell on the buyer.

A further example of Rule 1 is found in *Dennant v Skinner and Collom (1948)*. At the auction sale, a car was 'knocked down' to X. X then offered to pay by cheque. The seller agreed on condition that property would not pass until the cheque had been cleared. X sold the car to the defendant. The cheque was not cleared so the seller claimed the car back from the defendant under what is now S17 of the 1979 Act. It was held that Rule 1 applied. Property passed when the car was sold; the subsequent agreement about the passing of property was too late. An intention contrary to Rule 1 must be shown at or before the making of the contract.

In *Kirkham v Attenborough (1897)*, W, to whom jewellery had been delivered by its owner (K) under a sale or return agreement, subsequently pledged the jewellery with a third party (A) who took the goods in good faith. In an action by K for the return of the jewellery from A, the court held that the action failed. Although initially W had no title to the goods, his act of pledging them constituted an adoption of the contract, at which point the title (property) passed to him under Rule 4. W was therefore able to convey a good title to A.

The case of *Weiner v Gill (1906)*, illustrates that the rules only apply if there is no agreement to the contrary. In this case the document under which the goods were delivered on approval stated that they were to remain in the ownership of the deliverer (Weiner) until they had been paid for or charged. A purported transfer of title by the person to whom they had been sent was therefore held to be ineffective since the contrary intention expressed in the contract prevailed over Rule 4.

In *Re Ferrier, Ex parte Trustee v Donald (1944)*, furniture was delivered to F on sale or return within one week, and after two days the relevant items were seized by the sheriff. Although the sheriff retained the goods for a month it was held that the property in them had not passed to F because it was not she who had retained the furniture after the end of the one-week period.

7.3.2   Unascertained goods

These are either goods described but not yet identified or a part (not yet identified) of a larger quantity. By S16 of the 1979 Act no property passes in unascertained goods until they are ascertained. Passing of property is governed by S18 of the Act, Rule 5, which states that the property in unascertained goods does not pass to the buyer until the goods have been unconditionally appropriated to the contract, either by the seller with the consent of the buyer, or by the buyer, with consent of the seller. Delivery of the correct quantity of goods to a carrier for transportation to the buyer will amount to an 'unconditional appropriation'. If the seller reserves the right to dispose of the goods, the property in those goods, whether specific or unascertained, does not pass to the buyer until the right is waived. Such a right is deemed to have been reserved:

(a)   where the goods are shipped, and the bill of lading is to the order of the seller or his agent, and not to the buyer;

(b)   where the seller sends a bill of exchange for the price for acceptance together with the bill of lading, and the buyer does not accept the bill of exchange.

In *Pignataro v Gilroy (1919)*, G sold 140 bags of rice to P. Fifteen of those bags were appropriated by G for the contract, and P was told where he could collect them. Later, the bags were stolen before P had called for them but there was no evidence to show that the theft had been caused by G's negligence. When P tried to recover the price he had paid for the bags, he failed in his action. It was held the G's appropriation of the bags for the contract, without any objection from P, constituted transfer of title to those bags. They therefore belonged to P at the time they were stolen.

In *Federspiel v Charles Twigg (1957)*, F bought 85 bicycles from T under a contract which stipulated that the goods would be shipped to F in June 1953. Before that time, T's assets (including the bicycles) fell into the hands of T's receiver. F claimed that as the contract had been executed before T's assets had been charged to his receiver, the title to the bicycles had passed to him (F). However, the court held that because of the wording of the contract, the intention was that the title of the goods should pass to F at the time of the shipment. The property in the goods was therefore still with T at the date his receiver took possession of the bicycles, and F's action accordingly failed.

7.3.3   Reservation of title

In general, the title to goods passes to the buyer by the time he receives them. Consequently, the following rules will usually apply:

(a)   The seller is unable to recover the goods and must sue the buyer for their price, if unpaid.

(b)   The buyer, once he has sold the goods, is entitled to receive and retain the proceeds from his sale.

(c)   If the buyer is adjudged bankrupt (or, if a company, it goes into liquidation or is involved in a receivership), the seller's debt will rank as an unsecured debt (which usually means that some at least of the moneys owing to him are likely to remain unpaid).

In recent years the numbers of bankruptcies, receiverships and company liquidations have increased significantly, with the result that many suppliers of goods have been left with unsatisfied debts. It has therefore become fairly common practice for vendors to incorporate in their general conditions of sale some clauses providing for the retention of title to the goods by the seller until their price has been paid to him. This is a practice which has been operating in Europe for many years and which is consistent with S17, Sale of Goods Act 1979.

The following is an example of a simple reservation of title clause:

> 'Unless otherwise agreed in writing, all risk in the goods shall
> pass to the customer on delivery but the goods shall remain the
> property of the company until payment in full of the purchase
> price payable by the customer in respect thereof.'

The purpose of reservation of title clauses is threefold:

(a)   To keep the ownership of the goods with the vendor, so that on the occurrence of an event such as bankruptcy or receivership against the buyer, the vendor will be able to reclaim the unsold goods in the buyer's possession from the trustee or receiver.

(b)   To provide that, if the goods of the vendor are processed by the buyer, the vendor obtains the title to the processed goods (even though, in processing, other items not belonging to the vendor have been incorporated).

(c)   To ensure that, to the extent that the vendor's goods (in their original form or after processing) have been sold by the buyer, any proceeds of sale received therefrom by the buyer are held by him as trustee for the vendor (so that, if necessary, they can be traced by the original vendor).

The effectiveness of reservation of title clauses depends on the precise wording of the relevant clauses, which will be influenced by the type of trade concerned.

The leading case on reservation of title is *Aluminium Industrie Vaassen v Romalpa Aluminium Ltd (1976)*. In that case, AIV sold aluminium foil to R, the contractual conditions of sale being:

(a)   that the ownership of the material to be delivered by AIV would only be transferred to the purchaser when he had met all that was owing to AIV, no matter on what grounds;

(b)   that R should store the foil separately;

(c)   that if the foil was used to make new objects, those objects should be stored separately and be owned by AIV as security for payment; and

(d)   that R could sell the new objects but, so long as they had not discharged their debt, they should hand over to AIV, if requested, the claims they had against purchases from R.

R got into financial difficulties and was in debt to its banker to the sum of £200,000. The bank had a debenture secured over R's assets and appointed a receiver under that debenture. At the time of the reciever's appointment, R owed AIV £122,000. In order to recover some of that money at the expense of the bank AIV sought, under their conditions of sale, to recover from R foil valued at £50,000 and the cash proceeds of resold foil of some £35,000.

The proceeds had been received from third-party purchasers from R after the receiver was appointed and he had kept the fund of £35,000 separate so that it was not mixed with R's other funds and was therefore identifiable. The Court of Appeal held that the foil was recoverable and so were the proceeds of sale since there was a fiduciary relationship between AIV and R. Further, the fiduciary duty included the right to trace the proceeds of sale so long as the goods bailed have not been paid for. Accordingly, R was accountable to AIV for the foil and the proceeds of its sale and AIV could trace the proceeds into the hands of the receiver.

7.4   Sale by non-owner

The general rule is that only the owner of the goods (or his authorised agent) may pass a good title: *nemo dat quod non habet* (no-one can give what he does not have). This rule is embodied in S21 of the 1979 Act, but there are many exceptions to it.

7.4.1   Exceptions

(a)   *Estoppel* - If, by his conduct, the true owner allows an innocent purchaser to pay the price of the goods to a third party, under the mistaken belief that the third party is the owner, the property will pass to the purchaser because the true owner will be prevented (i.e. estopped) from denying that the third party had the right to sell the goods.

In *Eastern Distributors Ltd v Goldring (1957)*, M, the owner of a Bedford van, wanted to buy a certain Chrysler car from C, a dealer, but M did not have sufficient money to pay the required deposit. In an attempt to obtain a larger loan from a finance company, M and C agreed that M should complete two loan proposal forms; one of them was for the purchase of the Chrysler car while the other purported to be for the purchase of the Bedford van by M from C. The finance company rejected the application in respect of the Chrysler car, but accepted the proposal for the Bedford van. C 'sold' the van to the finance company, although it remained in M's possession and he 'sold' it having been told by C that the agreement was cancelled, to G. It was held that M was estopped from denying that C was the owner of the van and therefore a good title was passed to the plaintiffs.

(b)   *Factors* - A factor is a mercantile agent who is entrusted with the goods of another person, and who has the power to sell those goods in his own name. The Factors Act 1889 contains provisions to protect a person who deals in good faith with someone he believes to be a factor, and buys goods from him, without knowing that the factor is not really authorised to sell. Such a person will obtain a good title to goods he buys if:

(i)   the goods being sold were in the possession of the factor with the consent of the true owner - this applies even if the consent was obtained by a trick;

(ii)   the factor, in selling the goods, is acting in the ordinary course of business;

(iii)   the third party, to whom the goods are being sold, is unaware of any lack of authority on the part of the factor.

(c)   *Sale by possessor of documents of title* - Where the seller of certain goods retains, with the consent of the buyer, the goods themselves and/or (where applicable) the documents of title to them, the seller may, on the strength of the documents, sell the goods again to another purchaser who takes them in good faith (ie, without being aware of the earlier sale). In such cases, the second buyer obtains a good title to the goods as against the first buyer (although the latter will have an action against the seller for conversion): S24 Sale of Goods Act 1979.

(d)   *Resale by buyer in possession* - If a buyer of goods has possession of the goods (or of the documents of title to them) with the seller's consent and then resells the goods to a second buyer acting in good faith and without notice of any lien, the latter may acquire a good title even though title may not yet have passed from the original seller to the original buyer: S25 of the Sale of Goods Act 1979.

(e)   *Sale by virtue of office* - Where a creditor obtains an order for payment of a judgment debt due to him by a certain debtor, the bailiffs are authorised to sell the debtor's goods in satisfaction of the debt. Such sales are effective in passing to the purchaser of the goods as perfect a title as if the goods had been sold by the debtor (ie, the true owner) himself. It is also possible for the Official Receiver of an insolvent debtor's estate, or the trustee in bankruptcy of the same person, to sell goods which belong to someone else, provided that such goods are held by the debtor (or bankrupt) in his trade or business with the consent of the true owner in such circumstances that it is reasonable to assume that the possessor is the owner of the goods. In such cases, a purchaser in good faith receives a good title, and the original owner has to prove for their value in the bankrupt's estate.

(f)   *Sales in market overt* - A purchaser of goods sold in market overt obtains a good title to them provided that he buys them in good faith and without notice of any defect in the title of the seller: S22 of the Sale of Goods Act 1979. The term 'market overt' means every shop in the City of London where goods are exposed for sale and those goods are of a type usually sold in the particular shop. In places other than the City of London, the term means a market which is held on days prescribed by charter or custom as market days; it therefore applies only in the places where such markets are held (ie, it does not include shops not situated in the market place) and only on the relevant market days.

In order for the buyer to have the protection afforded by a sale in market overt, it must be shown that the sale:

(i)   took place in the shop itself and not in a room not usually open to the public;
(ii)   occurred between the hours of sunrise and sunset;
(iii)   was one by the shopkeeper and not one to him.

(g)   *Sale by person with voidable title* - If the seller of goods has a voidable title to them, and that title has not been avoided (by some party having the right to do so) by the time the sale was effected, the buyer acquires a good title to the items being sold provided that he was unaware of the possible defect in the vendor's title (see *Phillips v Brooks Ltd (1919)* and *Lewis v Averay (1972)* referred to in Sessions 3-5).

If the original seller has avoided the contract, property will not pass. In *Car and Universal Finance Co Ltd v Caldwell (1965)*, Caldwell (C), who owned an expensive car, was persuaded by a rogue to sell the car in exchange for an inferior car and a cheque for the balance of the consideration. The next day C ascertained that the cheque was worthless, and he at once notified the police and the Automobile Association, asking them to recover his original car. Meanwhile, the car had passed through a number of hands after which it was acquired by the plaintiffs, who claimed that, as they had acted in good faith and had given value they were entitled to the property in the car. It was held that, although the rogue had obtained a voidable title in the first instance, and it was normally the responsibility of the original owner in such cases to communicate rescission to any third party involved, in the present case the rogue had absconded, thereby preventing C from contacting any third parties. Furthermore, C's immediately notifying the police and the AA and asking them to help recover the car constituted effective rescission. It was therefore not possible for the plaintiffs to obtain a good title even though they had acted in good faith. Caldwell was therefore able to recover the car.

(h)   *Sale of motor vehicles on hire-purchase* - A further exception to the general rule that nobody may pass a good title to goods unless he himself has a good title, is afforded by the Hire-Purchase Act 1964. If a motor vehicle is sold by the hirer under a hire-purchase agreement to a private person (ie, who is not a car dealer, credit broker or supplier of credit), who takes the vehicle in good faith and without notice of the hire-purchase agreement, the transferee acquires a good title to the vehicle, even as against the original owner (ie, the 'owner/vendor' under the original hire-purchase agreement).

(i)   *Stolen goods* - Where goods have been stolen and the thief is subsequently convicted of any offence connected with the theft, the court by which the offender is convicted may order the person in possession of the goods (eg, a third person to whom the goods have been 'sold') to restore them to the original owner. This is provided by S28(1) of the Theft Act 1968, which superseded S24 of the Sale of Goods Act 1893.

Until 1968, the stolen goods had always to be returned to the original owner if the person who had stolen them was subsequently convicted. The new legislation recognises that there may be occasions when there are two 'innocent' parties (ie, the original owner and the ultimate 'purchaser'). It is, therefore, now left to the courts to decide from the facts of each case which of the two parties concerned should be made to stand the loss (assuming that nothing can be recovered from the thief under the Powers of Criminal Courts Act 1973, Ss35 to 39).

7.5   Performance of the contract

7.5.1   Delivery

Delivery is the transfer of physical possession from one person to another, and may be either actual or constructive. (An example of constructive delivery is the seller's handing to the buyer the key to a warehouse in which the relevant goods are stored, with the view to the buyer's taking them from the warehouse for his own use.)

In the absence of any agreement to the contrary, the rules relating to delivery of goods are as follows:

(a)   The place of delivery is the seller's place of business, if he has one, and, if not, his residence, but if the contract is for specific goods which, to the knowledge of both parties, are in a certain place, that place is regarded as the place of delivery.

(b)   Where the seller is bound to send the goods to the buyer, they must be sent at the agreed time or, if no time has been fixed, within a reasonable time.

(c)   If the goods are in the possession of a third party, there is no delivery until that party acknowledges to the buyer that he holds the goods on behalf of the buyer.

(d)   Where the seller is required to send the goods to the buyer, delivery to a carrier is prima facie delivery to the buyer.

(e)   If the parties have agreed that delivery is to be made to a place other than where the sale was effected, then, in the absence of an agreement to the contrary, the buyer assumes the risk of the goods deteriorating during the transit.

(f)   The expenses of putting the goods into a deliverable state must be borne by the seller.

If the seller delivers to the buyer a larger or smaller quantity of goods, the buyer may (a) reject the whole, (b) accept the whole, or (c) accept the quantity ordered and reject the rest. If the buyer opts for (b), he must pay a price which is pro rata to the original contract price.

If a contract stipulates a certain quantity, which is preceded by the word 'about', or followed by words such as 'more or less' the buyer is normally expected to accept the quantity delivered if it is only slightly different from the quantity mentioned in the contract. What is an acceptable difference depends on the circumstances in each case.

In *Shipton, Anderson & Co v Weil Brothers and Co Ltd (1912)*, the contract was for 4,500 tons (10% more or less) of wheat, and the amount delivered was 4,950 tons 55 lb. The sellers made no charge for the additional 55 lb. It was held that the buyers could not reject the delivery. However, in *Payne and Routh v Lillico & Sons (1920)*, the contract was for the sale of 4,000 tons of meal (2% more or less). The quantity delivered exceeded the agreed variation by a considerable amount, and it was held that the buyers were entitled to reject the whole consignment.

7.5.2   Instalment deliveries

Where delivery is to be made by stated instalments which are to be separately paid for, and there is a breach of contract by either the buyer or the seller, it depends on the circumstances as to whether such breach gives the injured party the right to repudiate the contract or is a severable breach giving a right merely to claim damages: S31(2) Sale of Goods Act 1979. For example, if the buyer fails to pay a particular instalment in such circumstances as might reasonably suggest that he is unlikely to pay for any future instalments, this will be taken to be a total breach, which will enable the seller to refuse to make further deliveries.

In *Robert A Munro & Co v Meyer (1930)*, X sold Y 1,500 tons of meat and bone meal, which were stated to be of a specified quality; the goods were to be supplied by instalments. After about half of the total quantity had been delivered and paid for, Y discovered that it was not of the specified quality, and he refused to accept any further instalments. It was held that he was entitled to do so, as he could not be expected to risk having delivered to him still more goods of the wrong quality. However, in *Maple Flock Co Ltd v Universal Furniture Products (Wembley) Ltd (1934)*, the sellers delivered 15 instalments which were accepted, but the sixteenth instalment (representing 1.5% of the whole order) was defective. The next four instalments were in order but the buyers refused to accept delivery, and sought to repudiate the contract. The court held that they were not entitled to do so. The main tests to be considered in applying S31(2) were held to be:

(a)   the ratio quantitatively which the breach bears to the contract as a whole; and
(b)   the degree of probability or improbability that such a breach will be repeated.

7.5.3   Acceptance

This is very important because the buyer may not reject the goods for breach of condition under Ss13-15 of the Sale of Goods Act 1979 once he has 'accepted' them. Acceptance of the contract is deemed to have taken place when the buyer:

(a)   intimates to the seller that he has accepted the goods; or

(b)   does any act to the goods which is inconsistent with the ownership of the seller; or

(c)   retains the goods, after the lapse of a reasonable time, without intimating to the seller that he has rejected them: S35, 1979 Act.

The seller will not be deemed to have accepted the goods until he has had an opportunity to examine them.

7.6   Rights and remedies

7.6.1   Rights of the unpaid seller

Against the goods

The following are the rights which the unpaid seller has against the goods, notwithstanding that the 'property' in them has passed to the buyer.

Lien

A lien is a right to retain possession of goods (but not to resell them) until the contract price has been paid. It is available when:

(a)   the goods have been sold without any stipulation as to credit;
(b)   the goods have been sold on credit, but the term of credit has expired;
(c)   the buyer becomes insolvent: S41, 1979 Act.

The lien is lost:

(a)   when the goods are delivered to a carrier for transmission to the buyer, without the seller's reserving right of disposal;

(b)   when the buyer or his agent lawfully obtains possession;

(c)   by waiver on the part of the seller: S43, 1979 Act.

Where an unpaid seller, who has exercised his right of lien, resells the goods, the second buyer acquires a good title thereto against the original buyer (see 'Right of resale', below).

Stoppage in transit

This is the right of the seller to stop goods in transit to the buyer, and to regain and retain possession of them until he has received payment. The right is available when the buyer becomes insolvent and the goods are still in transit. The buyer is insolvent if he cannot pay his debts as and when they fall due, but this does not necessarily mean that he is bankrupt: S44, 1979 Act.

The period of transit operates from the time the goods are handed to the carrier until the time that the buyer or his agent takes delivery of them. The transit is at an end if:

(a)   the buyer obtains delivery before the arrival of the goods at the agreed destination (eg, if the carrier hands them to the buyer's agent during transit); or

(b)   if, on reaching the agreed destination, the carrier acknowledges to the buyer that he is holding the goods to the buyer's order (even if the buyer wants them to be delivered to another place); or

(c)   the carrier wrongfully refuses to deliver the goods to the buyer: S45, 1979 Act.

Right of resale

By themselves, the rights of stoppage in transit and lien do not give the seller any right to resell the goods. However, the seller is allowed to resell the goods:

(a)   where they are of perishable nature; or

(b)   where the buyer, having been informed by the seller that he intends to resell the goods, does not within a reasonable time pay for them; or

(c)   where the seller has expressly reserved the right of resale should the buyer make default: S47, 1979 Act.

In connection with (a) and (b), if the seller resells the goods the original contract is rescinded. The seller cannot thereafter recover (from the original buyer) the purchase price, but only damages for any loss sustained by the buyer's default.

Against the buyer himself

In addition to his rights against the goods, the seller may take either of the following actions against the buyer himself:

(a)   He may sue the buyer for the contract price, if the property in the goods has passed to the buyer: S49, 1979 Act.

(b)   He may sue the buyer for non-acceptance, which constitutes a breach of the contract: S50, 2979 Act.

In connection with (b), the measure of damages is the loss caused to the seller by the buyer's breach. This is usually the loss of profit, but it is available only in cases where the seller's stock of the particular goods exceeded the amount required by customers (the buyer's breach resulting in the seller's loss of profit on a sale).

In *Thompson Ltd v Robinson (Gunmakers) Ltd (1955)*, R refused to accept a certain car which he had agreed to buy from T. There were plenty of similar cars available, so R's breach caused T to lose the profit on a sale; the damages awarded to T were therefore based on that lost profit. On the other hand, in *Charter v Sullivan (1957)*, it was shown that the plaintiff seller had more potential customers than the number of cars available; consequently, when the defendant refused to accept the car which he had agreed to buy, the seller was able to resell it immediately to another person. It was held that the seller was entitled to nominal damages only.

In cases where the seller is ready and willing to deliver the goods but the buyer is dilatory in accepting them, the seller is entitled to recover from the buyer a reasonable amount for the care and custody of the goods. This right is in addition to any damages for loss due to the buyer's refusal to take delivery of the goods.

7.6.2   Remedies of the buyer

The buyer has the following remedies against a seller who is in breach of contract:

(a)   He may sue for non-delivery, the measure of damages usually being the difference between the contract price and (where applicable) the higher price of obtaining similar goods elsewhere. However, if the seller knew that the buyer had bought the goods for resale, and there was no alternative supply available, the buyer will be awarded damages as compensation for the loss of the profit he would have made on the resale had the seller not defaulted: S51, 1979 Act.

(b)   He may sue for the recovery of purchase moneys paid to the seller.

(c)   He may sue for specific performance, but only in cases where the goods are specific and where monetary damages would not be an adequate remedy (eg, where the item being bought was an original masterpiece): S52, 1979 Act.

(d)   He may repudiate the contract for breach of a condition by the seller, but he will be unable to do so at a later date if he has previously waived the breach of condition and elected to treat it as a breach of warranty, or if the contract is not severable and the buyer has accepted the goods (or part of them).

(e)   In respect of a breach of warranty, the buyer may either:

(i)   set up the breach against the seller in diminution or extinction of the price; or

(ii)   he may maintain an action in respect of the breach, the measure of damages usually being the difference in value between the goods as delivered and goods answering to the warranty: S53, 1979 Act.

In connection with (e) (ii), the estimated loss must be such as is deemed to arise naturally and directly from the breach.

In *Bostock and Co Ltd v Nicholson and Sons Ltd (1904)*, N sold to B sulphuric acid warranted to be commercially free from arsenic. B manufactured glucose from the acid, and some of that glucose was sold by B to a firm of brewers. Because the acid was in fact poisoned, the beer was also poisoned and caused the death of certain persons who drank it. In an action for damages brought by B against N, it was held that although B could recover the price paid for the acid and the value of the beer which was ruined because of the faulty acid, he was not entitled to recover compensation for the damages which he had to pay to the brewers for the loss of goodwill.

7.7   Export sales

The principal contracts used for the sale of goods to overseas buyers are FOB (free on board) and CIF (cost, insurance and freight).

7.7.1   FOB contracts

Under an FOB contract, the seller's responsibility for the safe custody of the goods ceases when they are put on board the ship, ie, at the moment they are carried over the side of the ship.

(Contrast this with FAS - free alongside ship - contracts, where the seller's responsibility is at an end when the goods are delivered to the quayside where the ship is berthed, or literally alongside the ship where it is anchored in the harbour some way from the quay.)

It is the duty of the seller to see that the goods are put on board the ship selected by the buyer or, failing such selection, the ship chosen by the seller. The cost of loading the goods is borne by the seller, but thereafter the costs of the freight and insurance for the journey, and of unloading at the port of destination, are the responsibility of the buyer.

The property in the goods passes to the buyer when the goods have been put on board, and the buyer has been given sufficient time to effect the appropriate insurance cover.

7.7.2   CIF contracts

Under a CIF contract, the property in the goods passes to the buyer when the seller makes available (ie, tenders) to the buyer the usual documents (namely, the bill of lading, insurance certificate and invoice).

The duties of the seller are:

(a)   to ship goods of the description contained in the contract;

(b)   to procure a contract of carriage by sea, by which goods will be delivered to the agreed port of destination;

(c)   to arrange suitable insurance on the goods for the benefit of the buyer;

(d)   to prepare an invoice of the goods; and

(e)   within a reasonable time after shipment, to tender the documents to the buyer to enable the latter to take delivery of the goods.

The duties of the buyer are:

(a)   to pay the price (excluding the freight charge) as soon as he receives the documents;

(b)   to pay the costs arising from the time the ship reaches the agreed port of destination (ie, for unloading, lighterage and landing, and for the carriage to some destination beyond the port, where applicable); and

(c)   to pay all import duties and wharfage charges which may be due.

7.8   Unsolicited Goods and Services Act 1971

The Unsolicited Goods and Services Act 1971 was passed with a view to checking the increasing practice among some firms of sending goods through the post to private individuals who had not asked for them.

In law, it was always open to the receiver of such goods to return them to the sender, stating that he had not ordered them and did not want them. However, if the recipient attempted to dispose of the unwanted items, he might be sued for conversion (as not being the owner of the goods). Alternatively, he might be liable for their price on the grounds that, having dealt with the goods in a manner which was not consistent with the title still being with the original owner (ie, the sender), he had, in effect, adopted a contract for sale, thereby assuming liability to pay for the goods.

Even if the recipients of unsolicited goods did nothing, some firms had an unpleasant habit of issuing threatening letters informing the recipients that they were liable for the price of the goods and that if they did not pay for them the senders would sue. Although such threats could not have been enforced if the receivers of the goods had not, in fact, accepted them as part of a contract of sale, many private individuals suffered considerable distress as the result of receiving these unwarranted threats.

The 1971 Act stipulates that if the goods are sent to a person with a view to his accepting them, but the recipient did not ask for them and, furthermore, he has no reason to believe that they were sent for use in a trade or business, he has either of the following courses of action open to him:

(a)   He need not take any steps to return the goods or to advise the sender that he is not going to accept them as part of a contract of sale.

(b)   He may notify the sender that he did not ask for them and does not want them.

If the recipient does nothing during the six months following receipt of the goods, and during the same period the sender makes no attempt to collect them or to ask the recipient to return them (paying the recipient for any costs incurred by him), the property in the goods passes to the recipient at the end of the period. If the recipient notifies the sender that he does not want the goods, the sender should arrange for them to be taken off the recipient's hands within thirty days of the notice sent to him. If he fails to do so, the recipient becomes the owner of the goods at the end of the period of thirty days.

When the property passes to the recipient in either of the above ways, he will not have to pay the sender for the goods.

It is, therefore, now possible for the receiver of unsolicited goods to obtain a good title to them without being obliged to accept them as part of a contract.

As a result of the new legislation. the recipient is able to sell the goods to a third party after the expiry of the period of six months or thirty days (as the case may be). However, if the recipient attempts to sell the goods before the end of the relevant period, he will be liable to the sender, either for the price of the goods or for damages for conversion.

If the sender of unsolicited goods demands payment for them, he may be fined up to £200. Furthermore, if he engages in any threats (personally or through agents) for the payment of the goods, he may be fined up to £400.

Similar provisions are contained in the Act in respect of unsolicited entries in trade or business directories.

7.9   Revision exercise

Assess your knowledge of the above session by attempting the following questions. Check your answers against the references given.

(1)   Define a contract of sale of goods.   **(Solution: 7.1)**

(2)   Distinguish between a sale and an agreement to sale.   **(Solution: 7.1)**

(3)   Differentiate between a contract of sale of goods and a contract for work and materials.
                                                                                             (Solution: 7.1)

(4)   What terms are implied into a contract for the sale of goods as regards title?
                                                                                             (Solution: 7.2.1)

(5)   What is a sale by description?   **(Solution: 7.2.1)**

(6)   What condition is implied into a contract for the sale of goods where those goods are sold by description?
                                                                                             (Solution: 7.2.1)

(7)   Examine the scope of S14 of the Sale of Goods Act 1979.   **(Solution: 7.2.1)**

(8)   What do you understand by 'merchantable quality'?   **(Solution: 7.2.1)**

(9)   What is a sale by sample?   **(Solution: 7.2.1)**

(10)   What is the significance of a sale being by sample and description?   **(Solution: 7.2.1)**

(11)   Examine the provisions of the Unfair Contract Terms Act 1977 in so far as they relate to the exclusion of the terms implied by Ss12-15 of the Sale of Goods Act 1979.
                                                                    (Solution: 7.2.2)

(12)   Outline the rules relating to delivery of goods.   **(Solution: 7.5.1)**

(13)   Explain the nature and significance of acceptance.   **(Solution: 7.5.3)**

(14)   In what circumstances is an unpaid seller of goods entitled to exercise a lien?
                                                                    (Section: 7.6.1)

(15)   Explain the concept of stoppage in transit.   **(Solution: 7.6.1)**

(16)   In what circumstances is an unpaid seller of goods entitled to exercise a right of resale?
                                                                    (Solution: 7.6.1)

(17)   What remedies does an unpaid seller of goods have against the buyer?   **(Solution: 7.6.1)**

(18)   What remedies does a buyer have against a seller in breach of contract?
                                                                    (Solution: 7.6.2)

(19)   What is an FOB contract?   **(Solution: 7.7.1)**

(20)   What are the duties of the parties to a CIF contract?   **(Solution: 7.7.2)**

(21)   What are the main provisions of the Unsolicited Goods and Services Act 1971?
                                                                    (Solution: 7.8)

7.10   Conclusion

Having read through and studied this session you should have a sound knowledge of the essential elements of the law relating to the sale of goods. In particular you should be able to:

●   state what constitutes a sale of goods and analyse particular situations to determine whether or not they constitute a sale of goods;

●   give a detailed account of the terms implied into a contract for the sale of goods and apply those terms to particular factual situations;

●   apply the rules governing the transfer of property in goods to specific sales of goods;

●   explain the *nemo dat rule* and recognise the exceptions to it;

●   expound in detail upon the rights of an unpaid seller and the remedies available to a buyer in the event of breach of a contract for the sale of goods.

7.11   Questions

Objective test questions

(1)   The essence of a contract for the sale of goods is the transfer of property in goods from the seller to the buyer.

'Property' in this sense means:

A   Possession.
B   Ownership.
C   The physical goods.
D   Equitable title.

(2)   The rights of an unpaid seller to resell goods under the Sale of Goods Act 1979 only apply in certain circumstances. Which of the following is not one of those circumstances?

A   The goods must be of a perishable nature.

B   The seller must give notice to the buyer of his intention to re-sell and the buyer must not pay or tender the price within a reasonable time.

C   The buyer must be insolvent.

D   The seller must have expressly reserved the right of re-sale in the event of the buyer defaulting.

(3)   Which of the following is not a contract for the sale of goods within the terms of the Sale of Goods Act 1979?

A   A contract for the sale of a particular coin.
B   A contract for the transfer of ownership of money.
C   A contract to purchase a painting.
D   A contract to purchase a motor car.

(4)   S13 of the Sale of Goods Act 1979 implies into contracts for the sale of goods a condition relating to:

A   Merchantable quality.
B   Fitness for purpose.
C   Title.
D   Description.

(5)   Robert heard that Vernon, a coin dealer, wished to acquire a certain rare gold coin. On seeing the coin in Kingsley's shop, Robert persuaded Kingsley to let him have the coin on 'sale or return' terms. Having thus obtained the coin, Robert promptly sold it to Vernon. When did the property in the gold coin pass to Robert?

A   When Kingsley allowed him to take it from the shop.
B   When he sold the coin to Vernon.
C   When he saw it in the shop window.
D   When payment was received by Kingsley.

(6)   Can a seller of goods exclude his statutory obligations regarding title?

       A   Only if it is reasonable for him to do so.
       B   Never.
       C   Only in a non-consumer transaction.
       D   Always.

(7)   Which of the following is not necessarily a consequence of acquiring corporate status?

       A   The ability of the corporate body to own property.
       B   The ability to take legal proceedings in its own name.
       C   The limited liability of its members.
       D   The potential for perpetual existence.

(8)   Michael delivered his car to the Birmingham car showroom of Victor, who agreed to sell it for him at not less than £6,000. Victor sold the car to Katherine for £5,250 and absconded with the money. Michael claims the car from Katherine.

       A   Michael is entitled to the car. Victor had not title and the rule is 'nemo dat quod non habet'.

       B   Katherine is entitled to keep the car since Victor was a mercantile agent given authority by Michael to pass a good title to a bona fide purchaser for value.

       C   Katherine may keep the car. Victor had a voidable title and (until avoided by Michael) can pass a good title to a bona fide purchaser for value.

       D   Katherine is entitled to the car since it was bought in good faith in 'market overt'.

(9)   Priscilla, a dentist agrees to sell her Porsche to her cousin, Adrian, a stockbroker. She gives to Adrian at the time of the sale a piece of paper which reads 'Car Registration Number PLA 124Y bought as seen. All conditions and warranties by statute and common law are hereby excluded'. Adrian drives the car for four months when the police take possession of the car. It had been sold to Priscilla by Martin who had stolen the car from Mark.

       A   Adrian has a good title to the car as he was a bona fide purchaser.

       B   Adrian cannot keep the car but can claim all his purchase monies from Priscilla as she was not able to exclude S12 of the Sale of Goods Act.

       C   Adrian cannot keep the car or take any action against Priscilla as he agreed to exclude the provisions of the Sale of Goods Act at the time of the making of the contract.

       D   Adrian cannot keep the car but can claim the return of his purchase monies from Priscilla less an amount representing four months' use of the car.

(10)   Alec orders from Excel Oil Company 1,000 gallons of oil for his central heating boiler to be delivered to his premises the following day. The property in the oil passes to Alec:

A   When the order is received and the invoice made out.

B   When 10,000 gallons of oil is pumped into the tanker for delivery to Alec and several other customers of Excel.

C   When the oil is pumped into Alec's tank from the delivery tanker.

D   When the tanker arrives at Alec's home.

Written test questions

7.1   Sale of goods contract

(a)   Define a contract for the sale of goods and explain what is meant by 'goods' in this context.

(b)   A agreed in writing to sell a yacht to B, but when the agreement was signed they had not yet fixed a price. What would be the legal position if:

    (i)   the agreement stated that the price shall be mutually agreed at a later date; or

    (ii)   the agreement stated that 'the price shall be fixed by C'; or

    (iii)   no price was mentioned in the agreement at all?

7.2   Smith

Smith signed an order form for a new motor car but refused to take delivery when the dealers received the car from the manufacturers. The dealers then delivered the car to Turner who had signed an order form for the same make of car the previous day. Advise the dealers whether Smith is correct in asserting that he is under no liability to them since they have sold the car elsewhere.

7.3   Unpaid seller

(a)   In what circumstances does an unpaid seller acquire a lien over goods he has sold?

(b)   A sold a consignment of diamonds in London to B for £10,000. B paid £4,000 when the sale was made and agreed to pay the balance of the price on delivery of the stones to his premises in Birmingham. A instructed C, a security messenger, to deliver the stones to B, and to collect the balance of the purchase money. On arrival in Birmingham C was informed that B was insolvent and notified A. A ordered C to withhold delivery. B claims that he is not insolvent and threatens to sue both A and C. Advise A and C.

Consumer credit agreements

This session is concerned with the law regarding consumer credit. Careful study of the session will provide you with:

- an understanding of the various forms of consumer credit arrangements and the distinctions between them;

- an indepth knowledge of the law regarding hire purchase;

- an appreciation of the law regulating the other forms of consumer credit agreements.

8.1   Background

There are many occasions when a dealer wishes to sell goods, but the buyer is not in a position to pay the price in full immediately. Arrangements therefore need to be made to enable the customer to take possession of the goods at once, even though he will have to pay for them by regular instalments in the future. The principal method of providing this arrangement is a hire-purchase agreement.

Whereas contracts for the sale of goods have been regulated by statute since the passing of the Sale of Goods Act 1893, hire-purchase agreements received no statutory recognition until the Hire-Purchase Act 1938. This Act was somewhat incomplete (at least, so far as it covered protection for the customer), and it was supplemented by the Hire-Purchase Act 1964. A year later, the Hire-Purchase Act 1965 was passed, and attempted to consolidate the law relating to hire-purchase agreements (although certain provisions of the 1964 Act were not repealed by the 1965 Act). The current legislation is the Consumer Credit Act 1974 which governs most hire purchase transactions and has repealed the whole of the 1965 Act.

The 1974 Act is extensive, and deals not only with hire-purchase agreements but also with other types of contract involving the transfer of possession (with or without ownership) of goods under personal credit arrangements. Although this session will concentrate mainly on hire-purchase agreements, conditional sale, credit sale, and consumer hire agreements will also be considered.

A consumer credit agreement under the terms of the 1974 Act is a personal credit agreement between an 'individual' (the debtor) and any other person (the creditor) by which the creditor supplies the debtor with credit not exceeding £15,000. The 'individual' may be a private person or a partnership (or other unincorporated association), but not a body corporate (including a limited company). Besides hire-purchase, conditional sale and credit sale, other examples are bank loans, overdrafts and credit cards.

It should be noted that the Act refers to the supply of credit, not the supply of goods. This means that the parties covered by the Act include not only the supplier of goods and his customer, but also those persons who provide the customer with credit facilities. Examples of providers of credit (other than the dealer himself) are finance companies, banks and other moneylenders.

As hire-purchase agreements are usually intended to enable the customer eventually to gain ownership of the relevant goods, such agreements might be expected to be covered by statutory provisions similar to those which apply to ordinary sales of goods where the property passes at once to the buyer. This is, in fact, the case, and it will be seen that many of the provisions of the Sale of Goods Act 1979 apply equally to goods which are subject to hire-purchase agreements.

8.1.1   Distinction between hire-purchase, credit sale and conditional sale

Under a **hire-purchase agreement**, possession of the goods passes at once to the customer (who at that stage is a hirer of the goods and not their purchaser), but the property in the goods remains with the dealer. The agreement provides that when all the instalments have been paid, the hirer will have the option to purchase the goods (with or without a further payment, as the particular agreement provides). The title to the goods passes to the customer only after this option has been exercised. The hirer may terminate the agreement if he so wishes. If, on payment of all sums due, ownership passes automatically, it is a contract for the sale of goods. Until the option to purchase is exercised the hirer (bailee) may not normally transfer a good title to a third party even if that party is an innocent purchaser.

In *Helby v Mattews (1895)*, A, the owner of a piano, agreed to hire it to B, and it was provided that B could terminate the agreement by returning the piano to A. It was also agreed that after paying punctually all instalments due under the contract, the ownership would pass to B but that in the meantime the property in the item was to remain in A. After paying a few instalments, B pledged the piano with C, a pawnbroker. In an action brought by A against C, it was held that B had not 'agreed to buy' the piano within the meaning of S9 of the Factors Act 1889, and what is now S25 of the Sale of Goods Act 1979 (see 7.4 in Session 7), so as to enable him to pass a good title to an innocent third party who had given value. A was therefore entitled to recover the piano from C.

A **conditional sale** is very similar to hire-purchase agreement and most of the provisions of the Consumer Credit Act 1974 apply to a conditional sale. It is an agreement for the sale of goods (as opposed to hire-purchase, which is a bailment of the goods), whereby the purchase price is payable by instalments and ownership remains with the seller until fulfilment of all conditions governing payment of instalments and other matters specified in the agreement. The buyer may be given possession of the goods until ownership is acquired. If the conditional sale is governed by the Consumer Credit Act 1974, the buyer cannot pass on a good title to an innocent third party until payment of the last instalment.

A **credit sale agreement** is one for the sale of goods (the purchase price being payable by instalments) which is not a conditional sale agreement. Under such an agreement the ownership in the goods passes to the buyer immediately the agreement comes into effect, and on general principles the buyer may pass a good title to another person. The 1974 Act applies if the purchase price does not exceed £15,000 and the buyer is not a body corporate.

8.2   Hire-purchase

8.2.1   Nature

It often happens that the dealer is not personally in a position to offer the credit facilities needed for hire-purchase agreements. He will therefore often make an arrangement with a finance company whereby the latter agrees to buy the goods covered by the hire-purchase agreement from the dealer for their cash selling price. As the result, the dealer receives that price (less the deposit which is usually paid by the customer to the dealer) from the finance company, and the property in the goods passes to the company. Thus the parties to the hire-purchase agreement are the hirer (or bailee) and the finance company, and the instalments due under the agreement are paid by the bailee to the finance company (as owner of the goods).

The 1974 Act introduced a system of licensing suppliers of credit, that system being administered by the Director-General of Fair Trading. All persons (including companies) intending to operate a consumer credit business must obtain the appropriate licence. If a hire-purchase agreement is made at a time when the licence is not in force, the terms of the agreement are not enforceable unless, and to the extent that, the Director-General considers those terms to be reasonable. Dealers (referred to as 'credit brokers' in the Act) must also be licensed, and if an agreement is made following an introduction by an unlicensed credit broker, that agreement may be enforced only to the extent that the Director-General considers it to be reasonable.

8.2.2   Rights against third parties

Rights of bailee against third parties

Although the bailee is not the owner of the goods, he has a right to quiet possession of them. If, therefore, a third party attempts to interfere with the goods the bailee is the person who has the right to bring the appropriate action under the Torts (Interference with Goods) Act 1977 against the offending party. If the hire-purchase agreement is concluded in the normal way, and the bailee becomes the owner of the goods, he is entitled to retain the damages awarded against the tortfeasor. However, if the agreement is terminated prematurely (eg, the bailee decides to return the goods, or the owner retakes possession because of the bailee's non-payment of instalments), the bailee must account to the owner for any damages he receives.

Rights of owner against third parties

While a hire-purchase agreement is in operation, the owner of the relevant goods will usually have no action against third parties for interference with the goods because such rights accrue to the bailee. However, if for some reason the agreement ceases to operate, the owner may then bring an action against the relevant tortfeasor.

In *North Central Wagon and Finance Co Ltd v Graham (1950)*, the bailee under a hire-purchase agreement undertook not to sell (or attempt to sell) the car forming the subject-matter of the agreement; if the bailee broke the condition the owners were to be entitled to terminate the agreement forthwith. The bailee handed the car to an auctioneer who sold it on his behalf. The owners then brought an action against the auctioneer for conversion, and it was held that the auctioneer was liable. Whether or not the owners had terminated the agreement they had an immediate right of possession sufficient to support an action for conversion.

If the goods are permanently damaged, or actually destroyed, the agreement must of necessity come to an end, because it is thereafter not possible for the goods, in effective form, to be returned to the owner. If the damage or destruction was caused by the bailee, he may be sued by the owner. If the fault is that of a third party, it is the owner (not the bailee) who may bring the appropriate action in tort.

Lien of third parties

If an owner of goods hands them over to someone else for service or repair, the recipient usually has a lien on the goods until the owner pays the charge for service or repair. If goods subject to a hire-purchase agreement are passed to a third party for some necessary work to be done on them, the repairer will have the normal right of lien as against both bailee and owner.

However, if the agreement has been properly terminated before the goods are handed to the repairer, the owner will not be bound by the repairer's lien whether or not the repairer knew that the agreement had been brought to an end. Similarly, if the agreement provides that the contract will be automatically terminated if damage occurs, any subsequent handing-over of goods to the repairer by the bailee will prevent the repairer's exercising a lien as against the owner.

8.2.3   Exceptions to the rule of nemo dat quod non habet

This rule provides, that in general, a person cannot transfer a good title if he does not have the property in the goods. However, there are exceptions to the general rule, and the following apply where goods forming the subject-matter of a hire-purchase agreement are involved.

Sales in market overt

This exception is best illustrated by the case of *Bishopsgate Motor Finance Corporation v Transport Brakes Ltd (1949)*. X had possession of a car from B (the plaintiff) under a hire-purchase agreement, and took it to Maidstone market, where he gave it to auctioneers to be sold. However, it failed to get the reserve price, whereupon X sold it privately to Y, who took it in good faith. Later, Y sold it to T, the defendant company. The court held that T obtained a good title from Y, who had previously claimed a good title by buying the car in market overt, and in good faith from X. B was therefore unable to recover the vehicle from T.

Assignment by bailee of option to purchase

Unless expressly excluded, there is a right available to the bailee in a hire-purchase agreement to assign his interest in the subject-matter to a third party. If the transferee pays the owner all the outstanding instalments, he is entitled to obtain the property in the goods. It has been ruled that although a bailee's selling (or attempting to sell) goods subject to a hire-purchase agreement automatically brings the bailment to an end, it does not necessarily prevent the bailee from exercising his right to elect to purchase the goods.

Owner's relinquishing of right to repossess goods

The owner may voluntarily relinquish his right to repossess the goods from the purchaser: this will probably occur where the owner is offered the balance of the total price by the purchaser, and prefers to take the cash rather than retake the goods. The action of the owner is referred to as 'feeding the title', and will enable the purchaser (and any subsequent purchaser) to gain the property in the goods.

Purchases of motor vehicles

A 'private person' (ie an individual who is not a car dealer, a credit broker or a supplier of credit), may obtain a good title (even as against the original owner) provided he acts in good faith (part 3 of the Hire-Purchase Act 1964 which is reproduced in schedule 4 to the Consumer Credit Act 1974).

8.2.4   Obligations of the creditor

The provisions of the Supply of Goods (Implied Terms) Act 1973 apply to all hire-purchase agreements, and closely resemble those applying to sale of goods contracts. (Prior to 1973, the owner's obligations were provided by the common law, except to the limited extent that a particular agreement came within the ambit of the then current hire-purchase legislation.) This means that the relevant portions of the 1973 Act will apply even to non-credit transactions and also agreements not covered by the 1974 Act (eg where credit is more than £15,000, or the debtor is a limited company).

Although the 1973 Act is fairly comprehensive, it is not complete as regards protection afforded to the debtor in a hire-purchase agreement. It is therefore necessary to know the common law rules which may still be invoked to the extent that the statutory provisions are inadequate.

Implied terms as to title

Section 8 of the 1973 Act (as amended by the 1974 Act) provides that, in general, there is an implied condition in a hire-purchase agreement that the creditor will have a right to sell the goods at the time when the property therein is to pass. There is also an implied condition that the goods are free from any charge or incumbrance not disclosed to the debtor before the agreement was made and that the debtor will enjoy quiet possession of the goods (except to the extent of the charge or incumbrance disclosed). It is provided by common law that if the debtor, having paid a deposit (and possibly some instalments), then learns that there is a breach regarding the owner's title, the debtor is entitled to recover all moneys paid notwithstanding his having enjoyed possession of the goods for some time.

Implied terms as to quality and fitness for purpose

Section 10 of the 1973 Act (as amended) states that where a creditor bails goods under a hire-purchase agreement in the course of a business:

(a)   There is an implied condition that the goods are of merchantable quality, except to the extent that:

  (i)   defects present are drawn to the attention of the debtor before the agreement was made; or

  (ii)   defects which, if the debtor has examined the goods before the agreement was made, ought to have been seen by him.

(b)   If the debtor makes known to the credit broker or creditor (if a different person) any particular purpose for which the goods are being bailed, there is an implied condition that the goods will be reasonably fit for that purpose (even if one for which goods of that type are not usually supplied), except in cases where it can be shown (by the credit broker or creditor) that the debtor was not relying on the skill or judgement of the broker or creditor.

(c)   An implied condition or warranty as to quality or fitness for a particular purpose may be annexed to a particular hire-purchase agreement by usage.

Section 10 also provides that if the hire-purchase agreement is not made in the course of a business, there is no implied condition or warranty (under the section) as to the quality or fitness of the relevant goods for any particular purpose.

Furthermore, although the section may be invoked against a defaulting dealer (credit broker), the debtor may not rely on it as against a non-dealing creditor if the debtor knew, or ought reasonably to have known, that the creditor was not a person whose skill or judgement (concerning the fitness of goods for a particular purpose) might be relied upon. For example, one would not expect a finance company to be sufficiently expert in the technical content of a process or machine to be able to give a professional opinion as to the suitability of such an item for a particular purpose.

Implied term as to sample

Section 11 of the 1973 Act (as amended) provides that where the bailment under a hire-purchase agreement is made by reference to a sample, there is an implied condition that:

(a)   the bulk will correspond in quality with the sample;

(b)   the bailee will be given reasonable opportunity to compare the bulk with the sample; and

(c)   the goods will be free from any defect (rendering them unmerchantable) that would not be apparent from a reasonable examination of the sample.

Implied term as to delivery

Although the 1973 Act is silent on this point, there appears to be an implied term under common law that the creditor must deliver the goods to the bailee; if no date is fixed for delivery, this should be made within a reasonable time after the agreement was made. Breach of delivery (at all or by the due date) entitles the bailee to repudiate the contract, or to sue for damages. The bailee would not be able to enforce specific performance unless the goods were of a unique or special kind.

Exemption clauses

By S12 of the 1973 Act, any clause in a hire-purchase agreement attempting to exempt the creditor (or broker) from any of the provisions of S8 (as to title) is totally void. Furthermore, clauses which attempt to exclude the provisions of Ss9, 10 and 11 of the Act are also void insofar as they concern consumer agreements (although, if reasonable, they may be upheld insofar as they concern non-consumer agreements).

Remedies available to bailee

In accordance with the general law of contract, if the creditor in a hire-purchase agreement is in breach of a condition (express or implied), the bailee is entitled to treat the contract as discharged and/or to sue for damages. If the bailee treats the agreement as repudiated, he must normally return the goods to the creditor but he is entitled to recover all moneys paid to the creditor (and, where there is a separate credit broker, the deposit paid to that individual). If the bailee does not return the goods within a reasonable time of learning of the breach, he will be taken to have accepted the contract and to have forgone his right to repudiate. Thereafter, his only remedy is to sue for damages.

8.2.5 Obligations of the credit broker (dealer)

If the hire-purchase agreement is made directly between the bailee and the dealer, the points mentioned above regarding the obligations of the creditor will apply equally to the dealer. However, there are many occasions where although the preliminary negotiations are made between the would-be bailee and the dealer, the hire-purchase agreement is actually between the creditor (eg, the finance company) and the bailee, the dealer having sold the goods to the creditor. In this latter case the dealer is not a party to the hire-purchase agreement, yet he was the person likely to have made all the representations (eg, fitness for purpose and quality) which influenced the customer to hire (bail) the goods with the view to eventually owning them.

The Consumer Credit Act 1974 makes it possible for the dealer to be liable in certain situations:

(a)   In any hire-purchase agreement, the dealer (credit broker) is deemed to be the agent of the creditor for the purposes of receiving a notice of revocation, cancellation or rescission: this makes it much easier for the debtor since it means that he may continue to deal with the party with whom he is familiar.

(b)   Where the dealer has arranged with the customer which goods are to be sold to the creditor and are to form the subject-matter of the hire-purchase agreement, then if the agreement is subsequently executed the preliminaries carried out by the dealer are regarded as 'antecedent negotiations' on behalf of the finance company and are binding on both creditor and dealer: this is very important because it means that if there have been misrepresentations, the debtor may sue either the creditor or the dealer or both.

(c)   Any clause in the agreement which purports to regard the dealer as agent for the debtor (bailee), and/or to exclude or limit the liability of the creditor for the dealer's acts or omissions is void.

(d)   Where a dealer is deemed to receive a notice (or a payment) as agent for the creditor, he is regarded as being under a contractual duty to the creditor to notify him (or pay over the moneys received).

8.2.6 Obligations of the bailee (debtor)

Most of the obligations of a debtor under a hire-purchase agreement are now to be governed by the Consumer Credit Act 1974. However, the Act does not (in this respect) cover all hire-purchase agreements, but only those regarded as consumer credit agreements, ie, where the debtor is a private individual, partnership or other unincorporated association, and the total credit given does not exceed £15,000. Therefore, resort may still be needed to common law remedies by the other party (or parties) to the agreement where the agreement is not covered by the Act, or the Act does not contain a satisfactory remedy for breach of a statutory obligation.

The obligations of the bailee are as follows:

(a)   *To take delivery of the goods* - If the debtor defaults in this respect the creditor must not remain passive and sue later for all instalments then due. Instead, he must try to mitigate his loss by trying to dispose of the goods in some other way. Applying the principle in *Hadley v Baxendale (1854)*, the measure of damages claimable would normally be the creditor's loss of profits.

(b)   *To take care of the goods* - While reasonable wear of goods must be expected while they are in a bailee's possession, any excessive wear or damage caused by the bailee's negligence will entitle the creditor to sue the bailee in damages for the loss in value of the relevant assets. It has been held that neither the total agreement price nor the amount obtained when the relevant item is sold may be regarded as a measure of the damages which should be awarded to the creditor. However, if goods are stolen, or destroyed by an act of God, the doctrine of frustration applies; in this case, the debtor's liability is limited to the amount of the instalments (if any) which have accrued to date but are still unpaid.

(c)   *To pay instalments* - At common law, when a debtor elects to terminate a hire-purchase agreement he is liable to pay any instalments accrued to the date of termination which are still outstanding, together with any extra sums which may be due following termination in accordance with the terms of the agreement.

If the 1974 Act applies, S99 thereof provides that if the debtor elects to terminate the agreement, his liability is the amount by which one half of the total price (ie cash price plus interest) exceeds the total sums already paid and those due at the date of termination but not yet paid (these last named forming a separate liability), or such lesser amount as may be specified in the agreement. If the agreement makes no mention of a payment on termination, the debtor will incur no liability (except, of course, for instalments already due but unpaid). If the court considers that a lesser sum than the figure referred to in S99 would provide adequate compensation for the creditor, it has power to substitute the lesser amount. On the other hand if the debtor has not taken the amount of care of the goods that is required by the agreement he may be required to recompense the creditor in addition to what is required by S99.

If the debtor defaults in paying instalments when due, the creditor is usually entitled to terminate the contract forthwith. At common law, no specific guide is given for the measurement of damages claimable, although the case of *Yeoman Credit Ltd v Waragowski (1961)* suggests that the damages should be calculated by the following formula:

damages = total agreement price - (option to purchase money
                                                                    + deposit
                                                                    + proceeds of sale)

In the above case Y (the plaintiff) let out a van to W (the defendant) on hire-purchase. The terms of the agreement provided for an initial payment of £72, followed by 36 monthly instalments of £10.0s.9d; there were finally an amount of £1 to be paid on W's exercising his option to buy the van. The total price was therefore £434.7s.0d. W paid the £72 deposit and obtained possession of the van, but he paid none of the instalments. Six months later, Y repossessed the van (under powers included in the agreement) and sold it for £205; Y then sued W for the balance of the total price. It was held that Y was entitled to the arrears of the instalments due to the date of repossession (ie 6 x £10.0s.9d = £60.4s.6d, and, as damages for breach of contract, the difference between the total price less the £1 'option money' and the sale price obtained and the deposit and instalment arrears. Damages were therefore:

£434.7s.0d (less £1) - (£205 + £72 + £60.4s.6d) = £96.2s.6d.

If the debtor is in arrears with his instalment payments but has not repudiated the agreement, the creditor may do so in exercise of his contractual right. In this case, the creditor's claim will be limited to the amount of the outstanding instalments (plus, where applicable, the estimated damages arising from the debtor's failure to take reasonable care of the goods, and the cost of retaking the goods).

Section 87(1) of the Consumer Credit Act 1974 provides that, before a creditor is, inter alia, entitled to terminate an agreement or to repossess the goods following the debtor's default, the creditor must serve on the debtor the prescribed default notice, which specifies:

(i)   the nature of the alleged breach;

(ii)   (if the breach can be remedied) what action is required to remedy it and the date before which action is to be taken;

(iii)   (if the breach cannot be remedied) the sum (if any) required to be paid as compensation for the breach, and the date before which it is to be paid.

The date by which compensation is to be paid must be not less than seven days after service of the default notice, and no action may be taken by the creditor until the relevant date has passed.

The Act further provides that a creditor is not permitted to enter premises to retake goods subject to a regulated hire-purchase agreement (ie, one coming under the terms of the Act), without a court order. If the creditor contravenes the statute in this respect, he will be unable to claim anything at all from the debtor without a court order and may be liable for an action for breach of statutory duty.

Sections 90 and 91 of the 1974 Act deal with protected goods, ie, goods in respect of a regulated hire-purchase agreement where at least one third of the total price has been paid by the debtor. Section 90(1) provides that the creditor is not entitled to regain possession of such goods without first obtaining a court order (although such order is not required where the debtor has exercised his option to terminate the agreement). Section 91 provides that if the creditor attempts to repossess protected goods in breach of section 90(1), the agreement is terminated, but the debtor is entitled to be released from all outstanding liability and also to recover all sums paid by him in respect of the agreement.

If the debtor falls into arrears with the payment of the instalments, the courts will consider all circumstances concerning the particular regulated agreement (eg, the total sum paid so far by the debtor, the reason for the debtor's non-payment of certain instalments, the nature of the goods covered by the agreement, etc) and the order will be made accordingly. Court orders may take the following forms:

(i)   Time order, which sets out the number of instalments, and the interval between instalments, as the Court considers reasonable.

(ii)   Return order, directing that all the goods in question are to be returned at once to the creditor.

(iii) Transfer order (made when a substantial portion of the total sum of an agreement covering a number of goods has been paid), directing that certain goods be returned to the creditor, while the property in the other goods be transferred to the debtor.

(d) *Not to deal with the goods in an unauthorised manner* - It is obvious that while the hire-purchase agreement is in operation, the debtor has possession and control over the relevant goods. However, he has no power to deal with them in an unauthorised manner. For example, the debtor may be sued in conversion if he attempts to sell the goods or to give them away.

Once the agreement is terminated, the debtor must return the goods to the creditor, and if he fails to do so he may be liable. (This applies whether the debtor is holding on to the goods, or whether they have been lost or destroyed through the debtor's negligence.)

(e) *To give information when required* - The 1974 Act provides that if the debtor in a regulated agreement receives a written request from the creditor as to the present location of the goods, the debtor must, within seven working days of receiving the request, supply the creditor with the appropriate details. If he fails to do so within the following fourteen days, he will have committed an offence.

8.2.7   Formalities of hire-purchase agreements

The method of entering into a hire-purchase agreement which does not fall within the category of a regulated agreement under the 1974 Act is governed by the common law. Therefore, the usual requirements of a valid contract will apply, and the remainder of this section will be devoted to consideration of the provisions of the Consumer Credit Act 1974 in respect of regulated agreements.

Disclosure

Under S55 of the 1974 Act certain information must be given to the debtor before an agreement is made. If not, the agreement, when executed, will be unenforceable by the creditor without a court order (referred to above).

The information required relates to:

(a) the names of the parties to the agreement and their addresses;

(b) the amounts of all payments due under the agreement and when and to whom they are payable;

(c) the total charge for the credit, ie, the cost to the debtor of having the credit;

(d) the true annual rate of the total charge for credit, expressed as a percentage rate per annum;

(e) the debtor's right to pay off his debt earlier than agreed.

Furthermore, the agreement and every copy of it must:

(f) contain all the terms of the agreement; and

(g) contain details of the debtor's right to cancel the agreement.

Form and content of agreement

Section 60 of the 1974 Act provides that the debtor must be made aware of his rights and duties, and must be told the amount and rate of total credit charge, and the protection and remedies available to him under the Act.

A regulated agreement is not properly executed (and hence unenforceable against the debtor except by court order) unless:

(a)   The document is in the prescribed form (setting out all the information required by the Act), and is signed (in the prescribed manner):

      (i)   by the debtor; and
      (ii)   by (or on behalf of) the creditor.

(b)   The document contains all the terms of the agreement (other than those terms implied by statute).

(c)   The document is prepared in such a form that, when sent or given to the debtor, its terms are clearly legible.

Statutory copies

If a document is unexecuted (ie unsigned) by, or on behalf of, the creditor when presented personally to the debtor for signing, the debtor must at the same time be handed a copy for retention after he has signed and returned to the creditor (or his agent) the original copy. Similarly, if the document is sent unexecuted to the debtor, it must be accompanied by a duplicate for his retention (S62 1974 Act). The second copy must be a genuine duplicate, ie, it must include all the details appearing in the copy signed by the debtor.

Under S63(1) of the 1974 Act, where the document is presented personally to the debtor after it has been signed by or on behalf of the creditor, a duplicate copy should at the same time be given to the debtor. The debtor's signing the original copy and returning it to the creditor or his agent makes the agreement complete. Unless the agreement is complete following the debtor's signature, a copy of the executed document (ie, showing the signatures of debtor and creditor) must be sent to the debtor within seven days of the debtor signing the document (S63(2)).

If the requirements concerning statutory copies are not observed, the agreement will not have been properly executed and will not be enforceable without a court order (S65 1974 Act). If the document refers to a cancellable agreement (see below) and these statutory requirements are contravened, the court will refuse to make an order unless a copy of the agreement and other relevant documents are given to the debtor before proceedings are begun by the creditor.

Where the statutory copies regulations apply to a cancellable agreement, the creditor must send to the debtor (by post) a notice of the debtor's right to cancel the agreement, when and how the right may be exercised, and to whom the notice of cancellation should be sent (S64 1974 Act).

Debtor's right to cancel agreement

Where a debtor signs a regulated agreement at a place (usually his own home) other than the place of business of the dealer or creditor, and the dealer or his agent made oral representations before the debtor signed the agreement, the debtor is given a statutory right to cancel the agreement within a certain period following his signing the document (S67 1974 Act). This period is referred to as the 'cooling-off' period, and gives the debtor time to reflect whether he genuinely wishes to acquire possession (and probably eventual ownership) of the goods, or whether he was induced, against his better judgement, by the persuasive powers of the dealer or his agent.

Section 68 of the 1974 Act entitles the debtor in a cancellable agreement to serve notice of cancellation at any time between his signing the unexecuted agreement and the end of the fifth day following the day on which he received a copy of the executed agreement (under S63(2)) or the notice of cancellation rights (under S64).

The notice of cancellation need not be in any particular form, so long as it shows clearly that the debtor wishes to withdraw from the agreement (S69 1974 Act). It must be served on the creditor, or the dealer who carried out the preliminary negotiations, or (when S64 applies) the person named in the notice of cancellation rights sent to the debtor (if the person named is neither the creditor nor the dealer). If it is sent by post, it is deemed to have been served at the time of posting, whether or not it ever reaches the addressee (S69(7)).

The consequences of cancellation are as follows:

(a)   The debtor is entitled to repayment of all sums paid by him under the agreement, and he is relieved of any liability (provided he has not damaged, or lost, or otherwise prejudiced the owner's rights in the goods).

(b)   The creditor or other person who gave the goods to the debtor is entitled to their return (although the debtor has a lien on the goods until sums paid by him are repaid).

(c)   Repayment to the debtor should normally be by the party who received the moneys. However, where the dealer received the deposit and sold the goods to the finance company, the finance company would probably have paid to the dealer the selling price less the deposit, so in this case the finance company (not the dealer) should repay the amount of the deposit to the debtor.

(d)   Where the total sum under the agreement included commission due to the dealer as agent, and the early payments by the debtor were used to pay such commission, the debtor is entitled to recover all the relevant amounts except for £1.

(e)   Although the debtor must restore the goods to the person from whom he received them, he is not obliged to deliver them (except from his own premises) to the person concerned, but he must take reasonable care of them pending collection by the other person.

(f)   If the other person requests delivery within twenty-one days of the cancellation, and the debtor refuses to comply, his duty to take care continues until the goods are delivered by him or sent back, but if the request is not made within the said period of twenty-one days, the debtor's duty of care ceases at the end of that period.

(g)   If the debtor delivers goods to the person named in the notice of cancellation, or sends them to that person at his own expense, his obligation to take care of the goods ceases forthwith.

8.2.8   Other matters relating to hire-purchase

In addition to the principal obligations imposed by the 1974 Act on the creditor and debtor of a regulated agreement, the following methods dealt with in the Act are of some importance.

Creditor's duty to give information to debtor

On receiving a written request, and a fee of 15p from the debtor, the creditor must give the debtor a copy of the executed agreement (and of any document referred to therein), together with a statement (signed by the creditor) giving particulars of:

(a)   the total sum to date paid by the debtor;
(b)   any amounts (in detail) which have become due but are still unpaid;
(c)   the amounts (in detail) which are to become due in future;
(d)   the dates when each of the amounts in (b) and (c) became due or will be due respectively.

If the creditor fails to comply with this provision, he will be unable to enforce the agreement while the default continues. Furthermore, if default lasts for more than one month, the creditor will have committed an offence (S77 1974 Act).

Appropriation of payments

Under S81 of the Act of 1974, where a debtor is liable for payments due under two or more regulated agreements, he may indicate to which agreement(s) a particular payment is to be applied. The creditor has no right to decide to which agreement(s) the particular payment is to be appropriated. If the debtor does not indicate, then payment is appropriated to the agreements pro rata according to the amounts outstanding on each.

Variation of agreements

Under S82 of the 1974 Act, if a regulated agreement gives the creditor power to vary the agreement, the variation (when made) will not be effective until notice of it has been given to the debtor in the prescribed manner. The varied agreement (or agreements where more than one is involved) will be governed by the provisions of the 1974 Act as if the revised form had existed from the outset. (It is interesting to note that this is so even in cases where the variation increases the total credit to an amount over £15,000, the revised agreement will remain a regulated agreement even though this would not have been true had the agreement originally provided for credit in excess of £15,000.)

Early payment by the debtor

The debtor may at any time during the currency of a regulated agreement notify the creditor that he wishes to pay the balance of the total sum still outstanding ahead of the time when it is due under the agreement. The 1974 Act sets out details of rebates which may be due to the debtor where the total indebtedness is prematurely discharged (S95 1974 Act).

Judicial control over extortionate agreements

The 1974 Act repealed the Moneylenders Acts 1900 to 1927, which were introduced to protect debtors where the interest or other credit charges levied by the suppliers of credit were considered to be exorbitant. (Contracts providing for annual interest at a rate over 48% were regarded prima facie as harsh and unconscionable.) However, the Moneylenders Acts did not apply to hire-purchase agreements.

Although most of the 1974 Act applies only to regulated agreements, the provisions relating to extortionate credit bargains apply to **all** credit transactions. If the court considers a particular transaction to be 'extortionate' it may order the agreement to be reopened in order 'to do justice between the parties'. A credit bargain will be treated as being extortionate if it:

(a)   requires the debtor to make payments which are grossly exorbitant; or

(b)   otherwise grossly contravenes ordinary principles of fair dealing.

In determining whether a particular transaction is extortionate, the court will take into consideration:

(a)   the general level of interest rates prevailing at the date of execution of the agreement;

(b)   the age, business experience and state of health of the debtor, and the amount of financial pressure to which he was subjected, at the time of the bargain;

(c)   the degree of risk which the creditor was likely to be taking in granting credit to the particular debtor;

(d)   any other relevant matters.

The court may reopen an agreement on the application of the debtor (and, where relevant, his surety, ie, guarantor), and the rectification may be achieved by means of an order:

(a)   setting aside (in part or in total) any obligation imposed on the debtor or a surety by the credit bargain;

(b)   requiring the creditor to repay the whole or part of any sum paid by the debtor or a surety under the credit bargain;

(c)   directing the return to the surety of any asset provided by him as security for the bargain;

(d)   altering the terms of the security, or any security instrument.

If the debtor alleges that a bargain is extortionate, the onus of proving the contrary is on the creditor.

8.2.9   Advertisements

Another statute repealed by the Consumer Credit Act 1974 is the Advertisements (Hire-Purchase) Act 1967, and the 1974 Act deals, *inter alia*, with advertisements for hire-purchase facilities by persons carrying on a consumer credit business. However, an advertisement is not governed by the 1974 Act if it indicates that:

(a)   the credit afforded must exceed £5,000 and that either no security is required or the security is to consist of property other than land; or

(b)   the credit is available only to a body corporate.

For those advertisements which are covered by the Act, the following rules must be observed. An advertisement must be in an approved form, and the details must convey a fair and reasonably comprehensive indication of the nature of the credit facilities and their true cost. If an advertisement includes information which is misleading or false (eg, that the advertiser intends to do something when, in fact, he has no intention of acting in that way), the advertiser commits an offence.

Where an advertiser is in breach under either of those two cases, the publisher of the faulty advertisement is also deemed to have committed an offence, unless he can prove that he acted innocently (ie, he was unaware of the fault in any part of the advertisement).

The advertiser himself may have a defence under the 1974 Act, S168, if he can satisfy the court that the defect in the details of the advertisement was of a technical nature, for whose accuracy the advertiser had to rely on the opinion of an expert. In order to avail himself of this defence, the advertiser must give the prosecution (at least seven days before the hearing) details of the defence and the identity of the other person on whose skill, etc, the advertiser had relied.

8.3   Other forms of consumer credit agreement

8.3.1   Conditional sale agreement

A conditional sale agreement is defined by the 1974 Act as 'an agreement for the sale of goods, under which the purchase price (or part of it) is payable by instalments, and the property in the goods is to remain in the seller (notwithstanding that the buyer is to be in possession of the goods) until such conditions as to the payment of instalments or otherwise as may be specified in the agreement are fulfilled'.

The principal features of a conditional sale agreement are:

(a)   The agreement is for the sale of goods (not their hire), and so the parties thereto are the seller and the buyer, and the provisions of the Sale of Goods Act 1979 apply (except to the extent of the property in the goods passing to the buyer at the time of the sale).

(b)   Although the agreement consists of a sale, the buyer has the right to terminate the agreement prematurely, or to return the goods to the seller so as to relieve himself of liability for future instalments, by giving the seller the relevant notice of termination - in this case, the provisions of S99 of the 1974 Act apply (see 8.2.6, 'to pay instalments').

(c)   Because the property in the goods does not pass to the buyer until all instalments have been paid, the buyer is unable to transfer a good title to an innocent purchaser during the currency of the agreement.

Most of the provisions relating to regulated hire-purchase agreements also apply to conditional sale agreements. These include:

(a)   the licensing of creditors (vendors) and dealers;

(b)   the obligations of the seller or creditor as to title, description, merchantability and fitness for purpose of the goods;

(c)   the effectiveness of exemption clauses;

(d)   the guidelines for determining whether a conditional sale agreement or a hire-purchase agreement falls within the definition of a 'consumer credit agreement' (namely, credit not exceeding £15,000 and with an 'individual' as the debtor or buyer);

(e)   the method of entering into agreements, the position of the credit broker, the right of cancellation, the obligations of the creditor and debtor (seller and buyer) to give information, the appropriation of payments, the variation of agreements, early payment by the debtor, extortionate agreements and advertisements.

It should be noted that in a conditional sale agreement, the buyer may be able to repudiate the contract for breach of a condition even if he has 'accepted' the goods (by keeping them after he has had reasonable opportunity to examine them without giving notice of rejection). However, the breach of condition will only be treated as a breach of warranty (entitling the buyer to damages but not to rescission) if he does anything which affirms the contract after he becomes aware of the breach.

8.3.2 Credit sale agreement

A credit sale agreement usually results in the property in the goods passing immediately to the purchaser. Therefore, although most of the provisions of the 1974 Act relating to consumer credit sales apply equally to regulated credit sale agreements, the buyer has no right to terminate the agreement. The Act covers credit sale agreements where the buyer is an 'individual' and the maximum credit is £15,000, although 'small agreements' with credit not exceeding £30 are excluded from the 1974 Act provisions (apart from those dealing with extortionate agreements and advertisements).

8.3.3 Consumer hire agreement

A consumer hire agreement differs from the types of agreement so far considered in that there is no intention by either party (ie, owner or hirer) that the property in the goods is eventually to pass to the hirer. Before the 1974 Act, there was no statutory provision covering simple hire agreements, and unscrupulous dealers or creditors sometimes prepared what were really agreements for hire-purchase in the form of hire agreements, with the view to avoiding the restrictions in the Hire-Purchase Acts.

The 1974 Act defines a consumer hire agreement as 'an agreement made by a person with an individual (the 'hirer') for the bailment of goods to the hirer which:

(a)   is not a hire-purchase agreement;
(b)   is capable of subsisting for more than three months; and
(c)   does not require the hirer to make payments exceeding £15,000'.

The hire of such articles as electricity meters by electricity boards and telephones by British Telecom has been exempted from the provisions of the 1974 Act.

The Sale of Goods Act 1979 does not apply to consumer hire agreements. However, the following are covered by common law:

(a)   An implied condition (binding on the owner) that he has a valid title, breach of which entitles the hirer to sue for damages.

(b)   An implied condition that the goods are as fit for their purpose as reasonable care and skill can make them (except where any defect is apparent, or where the hirer is not relying on the owner's skill or judgement).

(c)   An obligation on the hirer to take reasonable care of the hired goods - the hirer will be liable to the owner for damage to, or loss of, the goods (unless the hirer can prove he was not at fault).

                      0070x

(d)   Obligations on the hirer to return the goods at the end of the hiring period, and not to dispose of the goods in the meantime - a breach of these obligations entitles the owner to bring an action.

The 1974 Act gives the hirer in a regulated consumer hire agreement a right to terminate the agreement prematurely. Termination will not be effective until at least eighteen months after the execution of the agreement, and the hirer is liable to pay all amounts due to the date of termination.

The minimum period of notice (unless the agreement provides for a shorter period) is as follows:

(a)   If payments under the agreement are at regular intervals, the period is the length of one interval or three months (whichever is the lesser period).

(b)   If the payments are due at differing intervals, the period is the lesser of the shortest interval and three months.

(c)   In any other case, the period is three months.

The statutory right to terminate prematurely does not apply to certain agreements - for instance, an agreement which requires the hirer to make payments which in total (and without breach of the agreement) exceed £300 in any one year.

Most of the provisions of the 1974 Act covering regulated consumer hire-purchase agreements also apply to regulated consumer hire agreements. These include:

(a)   licensing (in this case, of owners);

(b)   entry into agreements, and the position of the owner;

(c)   the rights of cancellation, variation of agreements, and appropriation of payments;

(d)   the right of the hirer to demand a copy of the agreement, and details of amounts paid, due and payable in future; and

(e)   the requirements in advertisements.

The owner is entitled to repossess the hired goods if the hirer does not pay the hire charges, but the owner may do so only after serving the appropriate default notice. If he recovers possession without taking the correct course of action, the hirer may apply to the court to be relieved of outstanding charges and to be repaid some or all of the amounts already paid. The court will then make an appropriate order, taking into consideration the amount of use of the goods enjoyed by the hirer.

8.3.4   Loan agreement for fixed sum credit

Any loan to an individual not exceeding £15,000 is covered. The 1974 Act brought lenders, such as banks, excluded from previous statutory control (ie, the Moneylenders Acts 1900 to 1927) under the jurisdiction.

Most of the provisions of the 1974 Act apply, eg, default notices, formalities for entry, right of cancellation, right to information, extortionate agreements, and provisions on advertisements.

8.3.5   Loan agreement for running account credit

This is a facility under a personal credit agreement whereby the debtor is entitled to receive from time to time from the creditor or a third party, cash, goods or services up to a credit limit. This includes bank overdrafts, shop budget accounts, credit cards and option accounts.

The following provisions of the Act apply: entry into the agreement, right of cancellation, early repayment, default notices, provision of information.

8.3.6   Debtor-creditor-supplier agreements

This type of agreement occurs when a supplier of goods has a pre-existing arrangement for credit agreements to be made by a finance company to customers, eg, where a garage has an arrangement with a finance company for finance for customers, Access cards, Barclaycards etc. When this type of agreement is made, a claim for misrepresentation or breach of condition by the purchaser may be brought against the supplier or the creditor.

8.3.7   Pledges

Regulations concerning the pawning of goods are contained in s114 to s122 of the Consumer Credit Act 1974.

8.4   Revision exercise

In order to ensure that you have understood this session attempt the following questions. Check your answers against the references given.

(1)   What is the basic nature of a hire-purchase agreement?   **(Solution: 8.1.1)**

(2)   Define a conditional sale.   **(Solution: 8.1.1)**

(3)   What is a credit sale agreement?   **(Solution: 8.1.1)**

(4)   What is the distinction between a hire-purchase, a credit sale and a conditional sale?
    (Solution: 8.1.1)

(5)   What must those intending to operate a consumer credit business obtain from the Director-General of Fair Trading?   **(Solution: 8.2.1)**

(6)   What exceptions are there as regards goods forming the subject-matter of a hire-purchase agreement to the *nemo dat rule*?   **(Solution: 8.2.3)**

(7)   Examine the obligations of the creditor in a hire-purchase agreement.
    (Solution: 8.2.4)

(8)   What are the obligations of the debtor in a hire-purchase agreement?
    (Solution: 8.2.6)

(9)   What formalities are relevant to hire-purchase agreements?   **(Solution: 8.2.7)**

(10)   What are the consequences of the exercise of the debtor's right to cancel a regulated agreement?   **(Solution: 8.2.7)**

(11)   What is, and what are the principal features of, a conditional sale agreement?

(Solution: 8.3.1)

(12)   Does the Sale of Goods Act 1979 apply to consumer hire agreements?

(Solution: 8.3.3)

(13)   Explain what is meant by a debtor-creditor-supplier agreement.   **(Solution: 8.3.6)**

8.5   Conclusion

Having studied this session you should now have a sound knowledge and understanding of the law regarding consumer credit. In particular you should be able to explain the nature of and distinguish between the various forms of consumer credit arrangement; should have a detailed knowledge of the law regarding hire purchase in general and the rights and duties of the parties to such an arrangement specifically; and should appreciate the law regarding the other forms of consumer credit agreement.

8.6   Questions

Objective test questions

(1)   Within how many days of receiving a copy of the executed agreement or notice of cancellation rights has a debtor a right to cancel a regulated consumer credit agreement?

    A   Three days.
    B   Four days.
    C   Five days.
    D   Six days.

(2)   S55 of the Consumer Credit Act 1974 requires that certain information must be given to the debtor before an agreement is made. If not, the agreement when executed will be:

    A   Void.
    B   Voidable.
    C   Unenforceable.
    D   Unenforceable by the creditor without a court order.

(3)   A consumer credit agreement under the terms of the Consumer Credit Act 1974 is a personal credit agreement between an individual and any other person by which the creditor supplies the debtor with credit not exceeding:

    A   £5,000.
    B   £12,500.
    C   £15,000.
    D   £17,500.

(4)   Lawrence enters into a regulated consumer credit agreement to purchase a video recorder. What form must the credit arrangement take if an innocent third party is to acquire good title should Lawrence sell the machine before the credit has been satisfied?

    A   Hire purchase.
    B   Credit sale.
    C   Conditional sale.
    D   Hire purchase, credit sale or conditional sale.

(5)   Which of the following is not an exception to the nemo dat rule where the goods forming the subject-matter of a hire purchase agreement are involved?

    A   A sale in market overt.
    B   Purchase of a motor vehicle by a private person acting in good faith.
    C   Assignment by a bailee of an option to purchase.
    D   Resale by a buyer in possession.

Written test questions

8.1   Charles and Trevor

(a)   What is a hire-purchase contract? How does it differ from:

    (i)   a credit sale contract; and
    (ii)   a conditional sale contract?

(b)   Charles buys a second-hand sports car from Peter after reading Peter's advertisement in the local newspaper. Charles pays Peter in cash the £500 agreed price and takes delivery of the car. Two days later Charles is visited by a representative of the Bunter Finance Company who informs him that the car is the subject of a hire-purchase agreement with Peter who has not paid all the instalments. Charles refuses to surrender the car. Discuss the legal position.

(c)   Trevor took a washing machine on hire-purchase (total hire-purchase price £180) and after £65 had been paid on it, Trevor made a further agreement with the same owner, relating to the washing machine and a dishwasher (total hire-purchase price £330). Trevor paid another £10 and then fell into arrears with his instalments. The owner has written to Trevor threatening to seize the articles if the arrears are not paid by return of post. Advise Trevor.

8.2   James and Joseph

(a)   James, a client of yours, wishes to introduce hire-purchase facilities in his shop. Explain to him what a hire-purchase contract is and what formalities are necessary for the creation of a valid hire-purchase contract under the provisions of the Consumer Credit Act 1974. Also explain to him the legal consequences of the failure to comply with these formalities.

(b)   Joseph bought a car on hire purchase for £1,000 (total hire-purchase price). He paid £350 but then fell into arrears. Bright Motors Limited, the owner, took possession of the car without his consent. Realising the 'irregularity' of their action they took the car back and left it outside Joseph's house. Bright Motors Limited regard the contract as being still in force and wish to sue Joseph for the outstanding instalments and the return of the car. Advise Joseph of his legal position.

Negotiability, bills of exchange, promissory notes and cheques

Careful study of this session will give you:

- an understanding of the concept of negotiability and the characteristics of a negotiable instrument;

- a comprehensive knowledge of the Bills of Exchange Act 1882 and the law regulating bills of exchange;

- a practical knowledge of the law regarding cheques;

- an appreciation of the relationship of banker and customer and the protection afforded to paying and collecting bankers.

9.1 The concept of negotiability

9.1.1 The nature of negotiability

The general rule of English law is that the true owner of an item of property is the only person capable of transferring to anyone else an indisputable legal title to that property. If B acquires an item of property from A but A was not the true owner of it then B is not the true owner either. This rule is embodied in the Latin phrase *nemo dat quod non habet*: no one can give what he does not have.

Currency has always been excepted from this rule. If A gives B coins or Bank of England notes in settlement of some obligation then the money is B's absolutely unless B actually knew when he was given it that the money did not belong to A. It is not necessary to inquire into the previous history of coins or banknotes. If currency could not be handled with freedom from doubt about its ownership then it would cease to be useful as a means of settling debts.

The business community has customarily treated certain types of document evidencing an entitlement to receive money as being as free from doubt as banknotes are. Such documents are said to be negotiable and are termed 'negotiable instruments'. A person who acquires a negotiable instrument for value and in good faith is entitled to ignore all previous claims to the document.

There has to be general agreement about which kinds of document are to be treated as negotiable: if someone is offered a document in settlement of a debt he ought to be able to tell whether it is negotiable or not. Negotiability is established by custom but becomes recognised by the courts when they hear disputes concerning negotiable instruments. The most important type of negotiable instrument is the bill of exchange: a cheque is a kind of bill of exchange. The extensive body of case law and customary rules concerning bills of exchange was codified in the Bills of Exchange Act 1882.

9.1.2 Requirements of negotiability

In order that the holder of a negotiable instrument may have all the rights which such a document can give, the following conditions must be satisfied:

(a) *Value must have been given* - This is the principle of consideration found in the law of contract and which evidences that the agreement of the parties is a bargain. However, in the case of negotiable instruments past consideration is good consideration, for example, a cheque is valid even if issued in settlement of an existing debt. If the present holder of the instrument has not himself given value but some previous holder had done the holder is a holder for value and he is given some measure of protection but is not a holder in due course.

(b) The holder of the instrument must have acted in *good faith* ie, honestly, *without knowledge of any defect in title* of a previous holder.

(c) *The instrument must be complete and regular* - The instrument must appear to be in order on the face of it; it must not be overdue or show signs of unauthorised alterations.

(d) *The instrument must be deliverable* (ie, capable of transfer by being physically handed over) - If the document is payable to any person who holds it, that is to the bearer, it can be negotiated, ie, transferred with good title, merely by delivery. If it is payable to a named person or to his order that is, an order bill, then that person must sign on the reverse side or indorse it in order to make the instrument capable of being negotiated by delivery to the next holder.

A person who receives a transfer complying with all these requirements is known as a 'holder in due course' and acquires full rights to enforce the instrument, even if his transferor had no rights, or only limited rights.

9.1.3 Characteristics of negotiable instruments

The essential characteristics of a negotiable instrument are:

(a) The instrument and the rights which it embodies are capable of being transferred by delivery, either with or without indorsement according as to whether the instrument is in favour of order or bearer.

(b) The person to whom the instrument is negotiated can sue on it in his own name.

(c) The person to whom a current and apparently regular negotiable instrument has been negotiated, who takes it in good faith and for value, obtains a good title to it, even though his transferor had a defective title or no title to it.

Unless an instrument possesses these three characteristics it is not a negotiable instrument.

9.2 Bills of exchange

9.2.1 Nature

Nowadays cheques are the commonest kind of bill of exchange but cheques only became widely used in the twentieth century. The Bills of Exchange Act 1882 is mainly concerned with a different kind of financial document which is nowadays only used in international trade.

Suppose Fromages de France SA sells a consignment of cheese to English Grocers Ltd for £5,000. To get the English company to pay the money the French company can simply write out an order to pay:

> To English Grocers Ltd, Melton Mowbray,
> At sight, pay to ourselves the sum of £5,000.
> Signed, Fromages de France SA.

'At sight' means 'As soon as you see this order'.

If the two companies have agreed a credit period of 90 days the order could be worded:

> To English Grocers Ltd, Melton Mowbray,
> At 90 days after sight, pay to ourselves the sum of £5,000.
> Signed, Fromages de France SA.

Both of these orders are examples of bills of exchange, which are usually called drafts in international trade. The first is a sight bill, otherwise known as demand bill because it is payable 'on demand'. The second is a time bill, also called a term bill.

Fromages de France SA is called the drawer of the bills, which are said to be drawn on English Grocers Ltd, who are called the drawee.

The drawee of a bill is not actually liable to pay it unless he puts his name to it. This is called accepting the bill and it is done by writing 'Accepted' (traditionally across the face of the bill) and signing. When accepting the second of the two bills quoted above, English Grocers would date the acceptance and the bill would be payable 90 days after that date.

In the two bills quoted above Fromages de France asked for payment to themselves. They could just as well have asked for payment to someone else, for example their agent in London. The person to whom the money is to be paid is called the payee.

Once a bill has been accepted it is a document entitling the payee to payment of the amount stated in the bill at the time stated. The payee can sell that entitlement to someone else. For example, if Fromages de France have a bill accepted by English Grocers for payment of £5,000 in 90 days' time they could sell it immediately for, say £4,800. The French company would then have cash to carry on its business; the buyer of the bill would collect £5,000 in 90 days' time in return for an investment of £4,800. However, the buyer of the bill will only buy it if he knows that he will acquire the legal title to the payment of £5,000, and that is why bills of exchange must be negotiable.

The Bills of Exchange Act 1882 defines precisely what constitutes a bill of exchange and under what circumstances a bill is negotiable. All references in the rest of this session are to sections of the 1882 Act, unless otherwise stated.

9.2.2 Statutory definition

By S3(1) of the Bills of Exchange Act 1882, a bill of exchange is an unconditional order in writing, addressed by one person to another, signed by the person giving it, requiring the person to whom it is addressed to pay on demand to or at a fixed or determinable future time a sum certain in money to or to the order of a specified person, or to bearer.

By S3(2), an instrument which does not comply with these conditions, or which orders any act to be done in addition to the payment of money, is not a bill of exchange.

The three parties to a bill of exchange are:

the drawer	-	the person giving the order to pay;
the drawee	-	the person to whom the order to pay is given;
the payee	-	the person to whom payment is to be made.

There are other possible parties to a bill in the terminology of bills of exchange:

(a)   the holder   -   the person to whom a bill is made payable either as original payee or by indorsement and who is in possession of it or, if the bill is payable to bearer, the person who is in possession of it;

(b)   an indorser   -   any person who has written his name on the back of the bill usually to negotiate the bill previously made payable to him;

(c)   an indorsee   -   any person to whom a bill has been made payable by indorsement;

(d)   an accommodation party   -   a person who has accepted liability on a bill by signing it without receiving value. He lends his credit to the bill by way of guarantee.

(e)   the acceptor   -   when the drawee signs the bill to indicate his consent to be bound he becomes known as the acceptor.

The definition of a bill of exchange is worthy of further examination and analysis.

(a)   *An unconditional order* - In order to create a bill, there must be an imperative order to pay. A mere request or authority to pay is insufficient. Further the order to pay must not be made subject to any condition, though by S3(3) of the Act an order to pay out of a particular fund is not unconditional.   However, advice on how the drawee may reimburse himself after making the payment does not constitute a condition. Thus, 'Pay £1,000 to X out of the proceeds of sale of asset A' is not unconditional; but 'Pay £1,000 to X and charge it against the consignment of 50 tonnes of asset Y' is unconditional.   A requirement that a bill must be presented to the drawee for acceptance before payment can be made is not regarded as a condition.

(b)   *In writing* - Most bills are found to be in printed form, but there is no reason why they should not be handwritten.

(c)   *Addressed by one person to another* - As stated above there are three parties to a bill of exchange - drawer, drawee and payee. Both the drawee and the payee must be identified with reasonable certainty. If, however, the payee is fictitious or non-existent, it is provided by S7(3) 1882 Act that the bill may be treated as payable to bearer. For the purposes of the Act a payee may be fictitious even though he is a real or existing person if he was never intended by the drawer to receive payment under the bill.

In *Bank of England v Vagliano Brothers (1891)*, X, an employee of V, forged the signature of one of V's overseas agents to a bill drawn on V in favour of P, one of V's business acquaintances. V accepted the bill and X then forged P's indorsement before presenting it to V's bank for payment in cash. The bank, having paid X, then debited V's account but V, on learning of the fraud, claimed that his account should not have been charged by the bank. It was held that although P was an actual person, the drawer of the bill (ie, X) never intended that he should receive payment under the bill and so P was a fictitious payee. Consequently the bill was payable to bearer. As the bank had paid the bearer of the bill (ie, X), V's claim failed, and the bank was entitled to charge his account with the amount of the bill.

In *Vinden v Hughes (1905)*, X, an employee of V, persuaded V to draw cheques in favour of certain persons who were actual customers of V, by telling V untruthfully that the amounts of the cheques were owing to the persons concerned. X then forged the indorsements of the payees and obtained payment of the cheques by purporting to negotiate them to H. The court held that, as the payees were existing persons and the drawer of the cheques (V) intended payment to be made to those payees, the payees were not fictitious and the cheques were not payable to bearer; the forgeries by X prevented H from obtaining a good title. V was therefore able to recover from H the amounts paid by H by V's banker.

(d)   *Signed by the person giving it* - The person drawing the bill must sign it. The mode of signature is irrelevant provided that it is made with the intention of being the drawer's signature.

(e)   *Requiring the person to whom it is addressed to pay on demand or at a fixed or determinable time* - A bill is payable on demand if it says so or if it says that payment is to be made 'at sight' (by the drawee) or 'on presentation' (to the drawee), or if no time is appointed (S10 1882 Act). Demand for payment must be made within a reasonable time or the bill will be regarded as overdue (S36(3) 1882 Act). By custom banks regard cheques (which are payable on demand) that are more that six months old as having been in circulation for an unreasonable length of time.

A bill is payable at a determinable future time if it is expressed to be payable:

(i)   At a fixed period after the date written on the bill (which is presumed to be the date the bill was drawn, unless the contrary is proved, though a bill is not invalid by reason only that it is ante-dated or post-dated or, incidentally, that its date is a Sunday).

(ii)   At a fixed period 'after sight', ie, after the date of its acceptance.

(iii) On, or at a fixed period after, the occurrence of a specified event that is certain to happen, though the time of the happening may be uncertain.

If a bill that is to be paid a fixed period after the date on which it was drawn is issued without being dated then a holder of the bill may insert the true date of issue and it will be payable accordingly. The same may be done if the date of acceptance is not recorded on a bill that is payable a fixed time after sight. If the wrong date is inserted then a subsequent holder in due course is entitled nevertheless to rely on the date as written and have the bill paid accordingly (S12 1882 Act).

The date of payment may be expressed with reference to an event that is certain to happen but not one that may not happen. Thus:

(i)   An instruction to 'Pay 10 days after the death of A' is a bill of exchange because A is certain to die (*Colehan v Cooke, 1742*).

(ii)   An order to pay 'when I am in good circumstances' is not a bill of exchange (*Ex parte Tootel, 1798*).

(iii) An order to pay two months after the arrival of a certain ship in a named port is not a bill of exchange - the ship might sink or be diverted (*Palmer v Pratt, 1824*).

(f)   *A sum certain in money* - Section 9 of the 1882 Act says that a sum is certain even if required to be paid:

(i)   With interest.

(ii)   By stated instalments.

(iii) By stated instalments, with a provision that upon default in payment of any instalment the whole shall become due.

(iv)   According to an indicated rate of exchange or according to a rate of exchange to be ascertained as directed by the bill.

If the sum payable is expressed in words and also in figures and there is a discrepancy between the two, the sum denoted by the words is the amount payable.

(g)   *To or to the order of a specified person* - The bill may be payable to P in which case, provided that the bill does not contain any words restricting its transfer, it is payable to P of his order. The same result will follow where the bill itself contains the words 'or order' eg, 'to P or order'.

(h)   *Or bearer* - A bill will be payable to bearer where:

(i)   it is expressed to be so payable;
(ii)   where the only or last indorsement is an indorsement in blank;
(iii) if the payee is a fictitious or non-existent person.

9.2.3   Holders and indorsements

The payee of a bill is entitled to the amount of the bill and he may assign this entitlement to someone else. Under the general law of property no special formality would be necessary for the assignment, provided the intention to assign was clear, but if the drawee failed to pay the bill then only the original payee could sue the drawee. The Bills of Exchange Act 1882 relaxes this restriction by providing that any holder of a bill is entitled to sue for payment of it. The Act defines very carefully what is meant by a 'holder of a bill'.

If a bill is drawn payable to a named person then the first holder of the bill is that named person. He becomes the holder when the bill is issued to him: that is, when the drawer gives him possession of it.

A named payee may indorse the bill: that is, sign his name, traditionally on the back of the bill. (Indorse comes from the Latin *in dorsare*, meaning 'on the back'; the word is often spelled 'endorse'.) If, after indorsing the bill, the payee gives possession of it to another person then that other person becomes the holder of the bill.

The new holder may be named in the indorsement. If AB was the named payee of the bill and he wishes to transfer it to CD then he may sign the bill and add 'Pay CD'. This is called a special indorsement. Only the person named in a special indorsement (he is called the indorsee) can be the new holder of the bill and, in effect, he becomes the payee of the bill. However, he may indorse it himself and give possession to yet another person who will thereby become the holder. Indorsements are deemed to have been made in the order in which they appear on the bill until the contrary is proved (S32(5) 1882 Act).

If a bill is drawn payable to bearer then the person in possession of the bill is holder of it.

If an indorsement does not name a new holder then it is called an indorsement in blank and it makes the bill payable to bearer so that anyone in possession of it becomes its holder. Any holder of a bill indorsed in blank is entitled to add his own name to the indorsement, and thereby turn the indorsement in blank into a special indorsement to himself.

A person can become a holder of a bill only if the bill is delivered to him with (unless the bill is payable to bearer) the indorsement of the person entitled to payment. Conversely, S31 defines negotiation of a bill as delivery to a person who thereby becomes a holder.

An indorsement is not effective until the indorser to someone acting under his authority has delivered the bill. Until then the indorsement may be revoked (by cancelling the signature). If the bill is no longer in the possession of the indorser it is presumed to have been validly and unconditionally delivered until the contrary is proved (S21(3) 1882 Act).

If the holder of a bill payable to his order assigns it for valuable consideration without indorsing it then the assignee may insist on it being indorsed (S31(4) 1882 Act).

Liability on a bill

No one can be liable for payment of a bill unless he or his duly authorised agent has signed it (S23 1882 Act). This means that a drawee is not liable for payment of a bill until he has signified his acceptance. On the other hand, in general, everyone who does sign a bill is made individually liable for its payment (Ss54-6 1882 Act), though anyone except the acceptor is permitted to add to his signature an express statement limiting or negativing liability (S16 1882 Act). In order to negative liability completely it is conventional to add to a signature the words *'Sans recours'* (French for 'without recourse').

Note that in order to defeat a suit for payment of a bill a defendant only has to prove that he did not transfer it for value and that no one after him transferred it for value. The position of the acceptor is special: he does not normally make a transfer of the bill after accepting it, he merely returns it to the person who presented it for acceptance. So the acceptor is made liable unless he can prove that the bill has never at any time been transferred for value.

The general rule is that the court is not concerned with whether the value given for a bill is adequate or not.

Note that the onus is on a defendant to show that transfers of the bill were not for value (S30(1) 1882 Act).

Holder in due course

Negotiation, by itself, does not avoid the problem of *nemo dat quod non habet*. Suppose A is the payee of a bill. He indorses it in blank, intending to sell it to B, but leaves it unattended in his office from which C steals it. C then sells it to B and disappears with the money. Under the usual rules of property law, C had no right to the bill and so B would have no right to it, and would have to hand it back to A or pay A the value of it. In the law on bills of exchange, however, B will have no liability towards A, provided that he is holder in due course, which is defined by S29 of the 1882 Act as a holder who has taken a bill, complete and regular on the face of it, under the following conditions:

(a)   that he became the holder of it before it was overdue, and without notice that it had been previously dishonoured, if such was the fact;

(b)   that he took the bill in good faith and for value, and that at the time the bill was negotiated to him he had no notice of any defect in the title of the person who negotiated it.

A holder in due course holds the bill free from any defects in title of prior parties (S38(2) 1882 Act). It is conclusively presumed that every party to the bill prior to him made a valid delivery of it (S21(3) 1882 Act).

A holder of a bill is always presumed to be a holder in due course unless another party can produce evidence that he may not be (S30(2) 1882 Act).

A person will be a holder in due course if all of the following apply:

(a)   *The bill must be complete and regular on the face of it* - A bill is not complete of the name of the payee or the signature of the drawer is absent. A post-dated cheque is regular but an undated bill is, apparently, incomplete.

(b)   *The bill must not be overdue* - When overdue it may be negotiated but only subject to any defects of title which existed at the time it matured (S36(2) 1882 Act).

(c)   *There must be no notice of previous dishonour*, if such was the case.

(d)   *The bill must be taken in good faith* - Under S90 of the 1882 Act an act is deemed to be in good faith where it is in fact done honestly, whether it is done negligently or not.

(e)   *The bill must be taken for value* - In the case of bills of exchange this means any consideration which would be sufficient to support a simple contract or a debt or liability which existed before the bill was negotiated.

(f)   *The bill must be taken without notice of any defect in the title of the person who negotiated it* - Section 29(2) of the 1882 Act lists some circumstances which, it says, render title defective. They are: that the person obtained the bill or its acceptance by fraud, duress, or other unlawful means, or for an illegal consideration; or that the person negotiated the bill in breach of faith or under circumstances that amount to fraud.

However, the initial delivery of a bill to its payee is not a negotiation of the bill and so cannot make the payee a holder in due course. Therefore if as a result of B's fraud A is induced to draw a   bill of exchange in C's favour, A will have a defence to C's action against him on the bill even though C in all other respects satisfies the definition of holder in due course (*R.E. Jones Ltd v Waring & Gillow Ltd, 1926*).

Restricting who can be a holder in due course

By S8(1) of the 1882 Act, a bill that contains words prohibiting transfer, or indicating an intention that it should not be transferable, is not negotiable. Either the drawer or an indorser (S35 1882 Act) may make a bill not negotiable.

The wording of this provision causes some difficulty because it is uncertain whether it is possible to prohibit transfer as such (that is, assignment of the right to receive payment of the bill). In practice, the usual way in which a bill is made not negotiable is to express it to be payable to a named person 'only'. This is sufficient to indicate 'an intention that it should not be transferable'. By S8(4) of the 1882 Act the mere omission of the words 'or order' after the name of a payee or indorsee does not render a bill not negotiable.

After a bill has been made not negotiable, any subsequent transferee of the bill (assuming that transfers are still possible) will not be a holder of the bill (because negotiation is defined as the action which constitutes a transferee the holder of the bill) and therefore cannot be a holder in due course.

It is likely that writing the words 'not negotiable' on a bill will prohibit further negotiation. When the Bills of Exchange Act was drafted there was no custom of writing those words on a bill, they were only written on cheques, and so the Act only mentions them in the context of cheques.

9.2.4   Acceptance

Acceptance means indication by the drawee of a bill that he assents to the order of the drawer. The only valid way of indicating acceptance is by writing it on the bill. The signature of the acceptor (as the drawee is called when he has accepted the bill) is essential and, indeed, an acceptance may consist of the acceptor's signature only. Acceptance may be qualified (see below) but must not express that the drawee will perform his promise by any other means than the payment of money (S17(2) 1882 Act).

Acceptance may often be dispensed with, but it is essential, under the 1882 Act, if:

(a)   a bill is payable after sight (because presentment for acceptance fixes the date of payment);

(b)   a bill expressly stipulates that acceptance is required;

(c)   a bill is payable elsewhere than at:

(i)   the place of business of the drawee; or
(ii)   his place of residence.

9.2.5   Rights and liabilities of parties to bills

Liabilities of acceptor, drawer and indorsers

The drawer of a bill is deemed to have given a promise that it will be accepted on due presentment and if it is not then the drawer is liable to the holder for the amount of the bill (S55(1) 1882 Act) though the holder must give him notice of dishonour in order to render him liable.

A bill imposes no liability on its drawee until he has accepted it, but the acceptor of a bill, by accepting it, engages that he will pay it according to the tenor of his acceptance (S54 1882 Act).

Since the drawer is also deemed to have promised that the bill will be paid on due presentment (S55 1882 Act), non-payment of an accepted bill may render both drawer and acceptor liable. However, the drawer is liable only if the bill is duly presented for payment and notice of dishonour is given to him, whereas an acceptor is liable as soon as the bill becomes due, whether or not it is actually presented to him then, unless he gives a qualified acceptance specifying the time and/or place of payment.

An indorser is deemed to have given the same promises as the drawer (S55(2) 1882 Act). Like the drawer, the indorser is liable only if there is due presentment and notice of dishonour. An indorser's position is rather like a guarantor's. An indorser who has to pay a dishonoured bill has a right to be compensated by the drawer or by an earlier indorser and this right may be enforced against an earlier indorser who did not himself have a good title to the bill (S55 1882 Act).

Capacity and liability

Under the 1882 Act, S22, capacity to incur liability as a party to a bill is co-extensive with capacity to contract. If a bill is drawn or indorsed by a minor then the drawing or indorsement entitles the holder to receive payment of the bill and to enforce it against any other party (S22(2)), but not against the minor (even if the bill was given in return for necessaries).

Signatures

A person is not liable on a bill if he has not signed it, or has not authorised someone else to sign on his behalf (S23 1882 Act). A signature may be of a person's full name, or of his surname and the initials of his Christian or forenames. A facsimile signature may be used if authorised. If a person signs a bill in a trade or assumed name he is liable on it as if he had signed it in his own name. The signature of the name of a partnership is equivalent to signature by all the partners.

A signature by procuration (ie, by someone acting as an agent, usually signified by per pro or 'pp') operates as notice that the agent has but a limited authority to sign, and the principal is only bound by such signature if the agent in so signing was acting within the actual limits of his authority (S25 1882 Act). However, if the agent was not acting within the limits of his authority then either the principal may ratify the signature or the agent may be sued for damages for breach of warranty of authority.

An agent is not personally liable on a bill if he has expressly stated (by words added to his signature) that he signs for and on behalf of a principal, or in a representative capacity (S26(1) 1882 Act). In determining whether a signature on a bill is that of the principal or that of the agent by whose hand it is written, the construction most favourable to the validity of the instrument shall be adopted (S26(2)).

If, in a bill payable to order, the payee or indorsee is wrongly designated, or his name is misspelt, he may indorse the bill as therein described, adding, if he thinks fit, his proper signature (S32(4) 1882 Act).

A forged or unauthorised signature does not convey title in a bill: it is no signature at all. Normally a holder of a bill who has it after a forged or unauthorised signature was put on it, may not sue anyone if it is dishonoured (S24 1882 Act). However, in accordance with the principle that a holder in due course must be able to take a bill at its face value, such a holder may recover the value of the bill from persons who become parties to it after a forged or unauthorised signature was put on it.

However, no one, not even a holder in due course, may recover on a bill from a person whose signature on it was forged or unauthorised or who signed it before a forged or unauthorised signature was put on it. The worthless signature acts as a barrier between people after it and people before it.

Discharge of some parties

Under S16 of the 1882 Act, a drawer or indorser is entitled to negative or limit his liability by inserting an express disclaimer in the bill or his indorsement. Traditionally, the words 'sans recours' (without recourse) are used to avoid liability.

The holder of a bill or his agent may discharge any party liable on it by intentionally cancelling that person's signature. If that is done, any indorser who would have a right of recourse against the party whose signature is cancelled is also discharged (S63(2) 1882 Act).

At or after the maturity of a bill, its holder may renounce the liability of any party to the bill: the renunciation must be in writing but it cannot affect the rights of any holder in due course who does not have notice of the renunciation (S62(2) 1882 Act).

Material alteration

A material alteration to a bill - one which changes the effect of the bill or the liabilities of its parties - discharges any party who did not make it or assent to it but it will bind subsequent indorsers. However, the parties have greater liabilities towards a holder in due course: if he has a bill which has been materially altered but the alteration is not apparent then he may avail himself of the bill as if it had not been altered and may enforce payment of it according to its original form.

Alterations of the following details are specifically listed in the Act as material: the date; the sum payable; the time of payment; the place of payment and, where a bill has been accepted generally, the addition of a place of payment without the acceptor's assent. An alteration is 'apparent' when it is one that would be noticed by an intending holder scrutinising the document with reasonable care.

Qualified acceptance

A drawee or his agent, when presented with a bill for acceptance, may:

(a)   give a general acceptance in which case he will be liable to pay the bill when it becomes due; or

(b)   refuse acceptance; or

(c)   give a qualified acceptance.

By custom, refusal is presumed if acceptance is not given by the business day following that on which the bill was presented and the presenter must then treat it as dishonoured for non-acceptance or he will lose his right of recourse against the drawer and indorsers.

Acceptance may be qualified in one or more of the following ways (S19 1882 Act):

(a)   by including a condition (eg, that the drawer release a security given by the drawee);

(b)   by being partial (eg, on a £100 bill, 'Accepted for £50 only');

(c)   by specifying at one place only (an acceptance to pay at a particular place is a general acceptance unless it expressly states that the bill is to be paid there only and not elsewhere);

(d)   by specifying a time for payment different from that expressed in the bill;

(e)   on a bill addressed to joint drawees, if one or more of them do not accept.

If the holder of a bill with a qualified acceptance wishes to do so, he may agree to that form of acceptance; however, the other parties (ie, the drawer, payee and other indorsers) are discharged from their liability on the bill unless they too have assented to the qualified acceptance. Such assent is presumed if, after having been notified by the presenter of the bill of the qualified acceptance, they do not dissent within a reasonable time. (There is an exception in the case of partial acceptance, where the presenter does not have to get the assent of the other parties in order to keep their liability on the bill alive. However, he must notify the others that the bill was partial accepted.)

9.2.6   Discharge of bills

Methods of discharge

A bill is discharged, ie, all liabilities on the bill are extinguished, by:

(a)   *Payment in due course by or on behalf of the drawee or acceptor.* 'Payment in due course' means payment made at or after the maturity of the bill to the holder thereof in good faith and without notice that his title to the bill is defective.

(b)   *The acceptor becoming the holder of it in his own right*, at or after its maturity (S61 1882 Act).

(c)   *A holder renouncing his rights* against the acceptor absolutely and unconditionally at or after the maturity of the bill and either in writing or by delivery the bill to the acceptor (S62(1) 1882 Act).

(d)   *Intentional cancellation by the holder or his agent*, if the cancellation is apparent (S63(1) 1882 Act). A cancellation made unintentionally, or under a mistake, or without the authority of the holder, is inoperative; but where a bill appears to have been cancelled the burden of proof lies on the party who alleges that the cancellation was made unintentionally or under a mistake or without authority (S63(3)).

Effect of forgery

Section 24 provides that payment to a holder whose title derives from a forged or unauthorised signature on a bill does not discharge the bill. Anyone who pays on such a bill before the worthlessness of the signature is discovered will probably be entitled to recover the money as money paid under a mistake of fact: *National Westminster Bank Ltd v Barclays Bank International Ltd (1975)* and may sue the drawee/acceptor for damages for the tort of conversion, ie, wrongful interference with goods (the piece of paper on which the bill is written) inconsistent with the owner's right of possession.

In the National Westminster Bank case, B, a resident of Nigeria, had a long-standing account with the plaintiffs. One of B's cheques was stolen and his signature forged. The cheque was presented to the plaintiffs. The forgery was undetectable except to an expert, and the bank honoured the cheque. When the forgery was discovered the money was still in the payee's account at Barclays Bank International. The court held that the plaintiffs were entitled to recover the money as they had paid under a mistake of fact and their honouring of a cheque with an undetectable forgery did not amount to an implication that the signature was genuine, ie, they were not estopped from succeeding in their claim.

As will be seen later in the session banks have a very wide protection against actions for conversion.

A cheque on which the drawer's signature is forged is not a valid instruction to the bank to debit the customer's account. If the bank pays the cheque by mistake then it must stand the loss itself, or seek to recover from the party paid. If the bank has not acted negligently, it is likely that an action for recovery will succeed.

A person whose signature has been forged or used without authority must denounce the worthless signature on discovery, otherwise he may be estopped (precluded) from denying that it is his signature.

In *Greenwood v Martins Bank Ltd (1933)*, G opened an account with the M Bank in the names of his wife and himself, and it was agreed that cheques would be signed by both of them. Later, G opened another account with the same bank but this time in his sole name; however, the cheque books and pass books for both accounts were kept by Mrs G. Subsequently, G discovered that there was no money in either account, because cheques had been forged to withdraw the bank balances which G believed to exist. While not admitting that she herself had forged the cheques, Mrs G told her husband she knew who had done so. She led G to believe it had been necessary for her to lend the money to her sister to meet the cost of legal proceedings, but eight months later G discovered that his wife had been lying. He then told his wife that he was going to report the forgeries to the bank, whereupon Mrs G killed herself. G then brought an action against the bank in respect of the forged cheques. It was held that, by not reporting the forgeries as soon as he discovered them, G had prevented the bank from bringing an action against Mrs G in respect of the forgeries. G was therefore now estopped from denying the regularity of the signatures on the cheques, and he accordingly failed in his action.

9.2.7 Accommodation bills

Nature

An accommodation bill is an ordinary bill of exchange, except that one of the parties thereto has signed as drawer, acceptor or indorser without having received any value for the bill. He is called an accommodation party and his purpose in signing is to lend his name and credit to one of the other parties (the party accommodated). If the accommodation party signs as acceptor there is an assumption that the party accommodated (the drawer) will put up the money before the bill is due for payment: if this is not done then the accommodation party may sue him for the amount of the bill.

The point is that an accommodation party is liable on the bill to a holder for value; and it is immaterial whether, when such holder took the bill, he knew that it was an accommodation bill (S28(2) 1882 Act).

If an accommodation bill is paid in due course by the party accommodated then the bill is discharged (S59(3) 1882 Act).

Anyone who signs a bill not as a drawer or acceptor incurs the liabilities of an indorser to a holder in due course (S56 1882 Act).

9.2.8 Rules of presentation for acceptance and payment, notice of dishonour

It has been seen that in order to make a drawer and indorsers liable on a dishonoured bill it is essential that the bill was duly presented and notice of dishonour was given. The Bills of Exchange Act 1882 gives detailed rules about these procedures.

Presentment for acceptance

Section 41 of the 1882 Act sets out the following rules:

(a) Presentment must be made:

(i) by or on behalf of the holder;

     (ii)   to the drawee or to some person authorised to accept or refuse acceptance on his behalf;

     (iii) at a reasonable hour;

     (iv) on a business day;

     (v)   before the bill is overdue.

(b)   If a bill names two or more drawees then presentment must be made to each of them, unless they are partners.

(c)   Presentment may be made to the personal representative of a deceased drawee, or the bill may be treated as dishonoured.

(d)   If the drawee is bankrupt then presentment may be made either to him or to his trustee, or the bill may be treated as dishonoured.

(e)   Presentment may be made through the post if this method is expressly agreed upon, or is supported by commercial usage.

A bill may be presented for acceptance in some other way (eg, when it is overdue) and an acceptance obtained then will be valid, but if acceptance is refused on the ground that the presentment is irregular then there will be no right of recourse against drawer and indorsers.

Dishonour by non-acceptance

A bill is dishonoured by non-acceptance if it is duly presented for acceptance and acceptance is refused or cannot be obtained (S43(1)(a) 1882 Act).

A bill may be treated as dishonoured by non-acceptance if:

(a)   The drawee will give only a qualified acceptance (S44 1882 Act).

(b)   The drawee is dead or bankrupt, or is a fictitious person or a person not having capacity to contract (S43(1)(b) and S41(2)(a) 1882 Act).

(c)   After the exercise of reasonable diligence, due presentment cannot be effected (S43(1)(b) and S41(2)(b) 1882 Act).

(d)   Presentment was irregular but acceptance was refused on some other ground (S43(1)(b) and S41(2)(c) 1882 Act).

When a bill is dishonoured by non-acceptance its holder has an immediate right of recourse against drawer and indorsers. He does not have to wait until the date that the bill is due for payment.

Presentment for payment

A bill payable on demand should be presented for payment as soon as possible, and certainly within a reasonable time (which varies according to the circumstances of each case), otherwise the parties other than the acceptor are discharged from their liability on the bill. (The reasonable time is calculated from the date of issue so far as the liability of the drawer is concerned, and from the date of indorsement so far as the particular indorsers' liability is concerned.) If a bill is not payable on demand, it must be presented for payment on its due date, or else the other parties (ie, drawer and indorsers) will be discharged from liability.

Presentment for payment is dispensed with where:

(a) After the exercise of reasonable diligence, it cannot be effected (eg, the acceptor cannot be found).

(b) The drawee is a fictitious person (in which case the drawer is liable).

(c) The acceptor is an accommodation party: in this case, the holder may still sue the accommodation party and also the party (drawer or indorser) being accommodated.

(d) The need for presentment has been waived, either expressly or by implication.

Notice of dishonour

Notice of the dishonour of a bill (by non-acceptance or non-payment) must be given by the presenting holder to his immediate transferor and to every prior party whom the presenter wishes to hold liable on the bill. The immediate transferor must, in turn, notify all prior parties in order to preserve his rights against them. The notice need not be in any special form (provided that it sufficiently identifies the bill and spells out the fact of and the reason for the bill's dishonour), but it must be given to the relevant parties within a reasonable time.

Notice of dishonour is dispensed with:

(a) By waiver (express or implied).

(b) Where, after reasonable diligence has been exercised, notice is not possible.

(c) As regards the drawer, where:

    (i) the drawer and drawee are the same person (this is unlikely unless an accommodation party has accepted the bill);

    (ii) the drawee is a fictitious person, or has no (or insufficient) capacity;

    (iii) the drawer is the person to whom the bill was presented for payment (eg, where the presenter knows that the acceptor is an accommodation party who will not pay, or where the bill was not accepted);

    (iv) the drawee is under no obligation to the drawer to accept or pay the bill;

    (v) the drawer has countermanded payment.

(d) As regards an indorser, where:

    (i) the drawee was a fictitious person, or of insufficient contractual capacity, and the indorser knew this;

    (ii) the indorser is the person to whom the bill is presented for payment;

    (iii) the bill was made or accepted for the indorser's accommodation.

If a bill has been dishonoured by non-acceptance, and the requisite notices of dishonour have been given, it is not necessary to give notice of non-payment (unless the bill has, in the meantime, been accepted).

Acceptor for honour

If a bill is dishonoured by non-acceptance, the holder usually has recourse to the drawer. But a drawer may anticipate the possible dishonour by including in the bill the name of a person to whom the holder may resort should the drawee fail to accept the bill generally.

That person is called a referee in case of need, and if he is asked to accept the bill in place of the drawee, he becomes an acceptor for honour (ie, the honour of the drawer). (Note, however, that the holder does not have to present it to the referee for acceptance.)

If the referee accepts for honour, he is liable for payment of the bill provided that:

(a)   it is first presented to the drawee for payment; and
(b)   it is not paid by the drawee; and
(c)   it is protested (see below) for non-payment; and
(d)   the acceptor for honour is notified of these facts.

Noting and protesting

It is sometimes obligatory, and often desirable, that a dishonoured bill of exchange should be noted and/or protested. Noting and protesting are both performed on behalf of the holder of the bill by a solicitor carrying out the office of notary public (usually referred to simply as a notary).

(a)   *Noting* - The notary first makes formal demand of the drawee or acceptor for the bill to be accepted or paid (as the case may be). On the drawee's or acceptor's refusing respectively to accept or pay, the notary records this fact on the bill, together with details of:

> (i)   the date of noting;
> (ii)   the notary's charges;
> (iii)   the reference number in his register relating to the noting;
> (iv)   the notary's initials.

The notary's register contains full details of the bill, and a record of the answer received from the drawee or acceptor.

(b)   *Protesting* - In this case, the notary prepares a more formal document (often under seal), incorporating a solemn declaration setting out the loss sustained by the holder of the bill as a result of its not being accepted or paid. The protest contains:

> (i)   a copy of the dishonoured bill;
> (ii)   the person requesting the protest:
> (iii)   the date and place of the protest;
> (iv)   the reason for the protest;
> (v)   the demand made, and the answer (if any) received.

If a notary is not available, the protest may be carried out by a householder (or substantial resident) who will issue a certificate of dishonour which needs to be attested by two witnesses.

It is obligatory to protest foreign bills for non-acceptance or non-payment, but this is not essential for inland bills (except to make an acceptor for honour liable). However, the advantages of noting and protesting, such as the fact that the notary's record of the noting is admissible as evidence in an action on the dishonour of a bill, leads to these procedures being used sometimes even in the case of inland bills.

Inland and foreign bills

A foreign bill is a bill of exchange which is not regarded as an inland bill. An inland bill is one which is both drawn and payable within the British Islands or drawn within the British Islands upon some person resident therein. For this purpose, the British Islands comprise the United Kingdom, the Channel Islands, the Isle of Man and the islands adjacent to them.

Inland bills are usually drawn sola (ie, they consist of one copy only), but foreign bills are usually drawn in 'sets' of three (as is also the case with bills of lading). The drawee and indorser should respectively accept or indorse one copy only, otherwise they will be liable to the holder of each copy bearing their signature. (The reason for 'sets' of bills is historical; in the past, it was more likely that one copy would be lost at sea, but today the practice of issuing bills in sets appears to be archaic.)

Role of banks in collecting payment of bills

In the simplest case the drawer of a time bill presents it to the drawee for acceptance; the drawee accepts it and returns it to the drawer who holds it until maturity and then presents it to the drawee/acceptor for payment. In practice drawer and drawee are usually in different countries and they employ banks as their agents in the collection process.

The drawer of a time bill hands it to his bank and asks it to arrange presentation. His bank will remit the bill to a bank in the drawee's country. The drawer's bank is therefore called the remitting bank. The bank to which the bill is remitted is called a collecting bank and it acts as agent for the remitting bank. The collecting bank passes the bill to a branch near the drawee's place of business to make presentation for acceptance. If it does not have a conveniently situated branch it may employ another bank as a presenting bank.

When the drawee accepts the bill he will usually indicate that, on maturity, it will be paid by his own bank. He writes on the bill, for example: 'Accepted payable at Borchester Bank Ltd, Felversham branch.' He must not suggest that this is the only place at which it is payable for that would be a qualified acceptance. The bill is said to be domiciled with the bank that is to make payment.

Having obtained the acceptance the presenting bank will hold the bill until maturity (unless it has been instructed to return it to the remitting bank) and will then present it to the paying bank for payment. Presentation for payment by one bank to another is usually made through a clearing house, such as the London Bankers' Clearing House.

If the drawer wants to negotiate the bill he will ask for it to be returned to him after acceptance. He then negotiates it. Whoever is holding the bill at maturity will get his own bank to collect the payment.

9.3   Promissory notes

9.3.1   Definition

A promissory note is an unconditional promise in writing made by one person to another, signed by the maker, engaging to pay, on demand or at a fixed or determinable future time, a sum certain in money to, or to the order of, a specified person or to bearer (S83(1) of the 1882 Act).

On comparing the definition of a promissory note with that of an ordinary bill of exchange it will be observed that the requirements for each type of instrument are basically similar.

9.3.2   Distinctions between promissory notes and bills of exchange

(a)   A bill has three principal parties, ie, the drawer (usually the creditor), the drawee (a person usually indebted to the drawer) and the payee (who may be the drawer himself or a person to whom the drawer is indebted. A promissory note has two parties, namely, the maker, or promisor (who is usually the debtor), and the promisee (who is usually the promisor's creditor).

(b)   A bill is complete once it has been prepared (ie, even before it is handed to the payee and/or presented to the drawee for acceptance) but a note is incomplete until it is delivered to the payee (ie, the person to whom it is addressed) or to bearer.

(c)   Unlike a bill, whose drawee is usually called upon to accept liability, a note never requires acceptance because the maker of a note, by preparing and signing it, has already undertaken to pay it.

(d)   A note does not have to be presented for payment to make the promisor liable, but presentment of a bill for payment is usually necessary.

(e)   A dishonoured foreign note does not have to be protested, but this is usually necessary with a dishonoured foreign bill.

A note need not be presented for payment within a reasonable time after its due date in order to keep open the liability of the maker, but an endorser's liability on the note may be discharged if presentation of the note for payment is not made within a reasonable period after it becomes due.

Because the maker of a note is the person primarily liable to pay it, and a note has only two parties, an inland note is one which is made and payable within the British islands. Any other type is a foreign note.

9.4   The nature of a cheque

9.4.1   Definition

Section 73 of the Bills of Exchange Act 1882 gives the following definition: 'A cheque is a bill of exchange drawn on a banker payable on demand'. Dr Hart in *Law of Banking* states:

> A cheque is an unconditional order in writing, drawn on a banker, signed by the drawer requiring the banker to pay on demand a sum certain in money to, or to the order of, a specified person or to bearer, and which does not order any act to be done in addition to the payment of money.

From these definitions it may be seen that a cheque has the following characteristics:

(a)   It is payable on demand.

(b)   It is drawn on a banker.

(c)   The amount payable is a sum certain, so that interest (although rare) may be provided for (but payment may not be by instalments because a cheque is payable on demand).

(d)   If a cheque contains a requirement that a receipt (usually on the reverse side) has to be signed, the document is a conditional order and not a cheque, but if the requirement to sign the receipt is expressed as an instruction to the payee then the cheque is valid because the order (to the banker as drawee) contains no condition.

9.4.2   Differences between cheques and other bills

(a)   No acceptance of a cheque is required; the banker (as drawee) must honour the cheque if it appears to him to be in order and it is received in the ordinary course of business and the drawer has sufficient funds in his account or an authorised overdraft limit.

(b)   If a cheque is dishonoured, the banker, because he had not accepted it, has no obligations as drawee of the cheque. However, a banker may be liable if he wrongfully dishonours a cheque (thereby causing damage to his customer); in this case, the liability will be to the drawer, not the holder.

(c)   Although cheques and bills may be indorsed in various ways, only cheques may be crossed (see below).

(d)   A banker who pays an order cheque bearing a forged or unauthorised indorsement is not liable to the true owner so long as he pays the cheque in good faith and in the ordinary course of business, but if the drawee of a bill pays on a forged indorsement he will still be liable to the true owner.

(e)   Obviously, from the definitions, a cheque must be drawn on a banker and must be payable on demand; a bill may be drawn on anyone and may be payable either on demand or at a fixed or determinable future time.

(f)   If a cheque is not presented for payment within a reasonable time (six months is usually regarded as reasonable) then the drawer is not discharged unless he has suffered damage by the delay (eg, if the banker on whom the cheque was drawn has become insolvent) (Bills of Exchange Act 1882, S74). A drawer of a bill that is not a cheque is discharged if the bill is not duly presented for payment.

9.4.3   Crossings on cheques

Types of crossing

A cheque may be 'open' (ie, uncrossed) or 'crossed'. Crossings take the following forms (Bills of Exchange Act 1882, S76):

(a)   *A general crossing* consists of two parallel transverse lines across the face of the cheque either with or without the words:

(i)   'and company' (or any abbreviation thereof); and/or
(ii)   'not negotiable'.

(b)   *A special crossing* consists of the name (with or without the address) of a banker, written (or stamped) across the face of a cheque, and with or without:

(i)   parallel transverse lines; and/or
(ii)   the words 'not negotiable'; and/or
(iii)   the words 'and company' (or any abbreviation thereof); and or
(iv)   the words 'account payee'

A crossing on a cheque is an instruction, to the bank on which the cheque is drawn, that the cheque should only be paid to a bank. A special crossing is an instruction that the cheque should only be paid to the bank named in the crossing (or another bank that is acting as agent for the named bank).

The words 'and company' (or '& Co') are now simply an embellishment, and have ceased to have any significance whatsoever. The words 'account (or A/C) payee' do not concern the paying banker, but they are a direction to the collecting bank (eg, the bank holding the account of the payee of the cheque): if a collecting banker chooses to ignore these words, and there is no defect in the title of his customer, the banker commits no wrong, but if it transpires that his customer's title was in some way faulty, the banker will have acted negligently and so will lose the protection given to him by the Cheques Act 1957, S4 (see the section on statutory protection of the collecting banker).

The words 'not negotiable' on a cheque destroy the cheque's negotiability but not its transferability. As a result:

(a)   No person may become a holder in due course after the relevant words have been inserted on the cheque.

(b)   A holder may have a good title, but only if there was no defect in the title of any previous holder.

(c)   Any holder may cross, or use words on, a cheque which makes payment more restrictive, without that person's having to disclose his identity; however, any attempt to remove a crossing or restricting words constitutes a material alteration, and if the amendment was not authorised by the drawer he will be discharged from his liability on the cheque.

Crossings on other types of financial document

The following types of financial document may be crossed, though they are not cheques, or even bills of exchange. All the provisions of the Bills of Exchange Act relating to crossed cheques also apply to these documents when crossed (Cheques Act 1957, S5).

(a)   Any document issued by a customer of a banker which, though not a bill of exchange, is intended to enable a person to obtain payment from that banker of the sum mentioned in the document. This includes 'cheques' that are not bills of exchange because they require signature of a receipt.

(b)   Any draft payable on demand drawn by a banker upon himself, whether payable at the head office or some other office of his bank, ie, a banker's draft.

In addition, S95 of the Bills of Exchange Act 1882 applies the crossed cheques provisions to 'a warrant for the payment of dividend'. This section seems to have been necessary because dividend warrants in the nineteenth century were commonly conditional orders (they required a receipt) and so could not be cheques. Company dividend warrants are nowadays always cheques and do not require a receipt.

The Bills of Exchange Act does not provide any procedure for 'opening' a crossing and, probably, it is not legally possible to neutralise the effect of a crossing on a cheque so that it may be paid in cash across the counter. However, most bank customers use cheque forms with crossings printed on them. Therefore a bank will normally pay in cash to the drawer of a crossed payment mandate to 'cash or order' on such a form if it has the words 'Pay cash' and the signature of the drawer written between the parallel lines of the crossing. Payment would also be made to a known agent of the drawer. The theory is that as only the drawer is involved he is unlikely to protest.

9.5 Statutory protection

9.5.1 Statutory protection of the paying banker

A cheque is a mandate of the customer to his bank, which is under a duty, if certain conditions are satisfied, to obey the drawer's instructions and pay the cheque to the holder who presents it or to his bank. If the cheque is payable to bearer, the bank can debit its customer's account with the amount of the cheque if it pays in good faith any person who pays or presents the cheque, whether in fact he is entitled to the payment or not. If such a payment is made in due course it amounts to a valid discharge and the paying bank is protected by the Bills of Exchange Act 1882 Ss60 and 80 and the Cheques Act 1957 S1 if it pays a cheque to someone who has no title to it. Nevertheless, if the bank pays the cheque inconsistently with the drawer's order it is still unable to debit the drawer's account and it may be liable to the true owner of the cheque.

Protection under S60 Bills of Exchange Act 1882

By S60 the paying banker is protected if he pays a cheque in good faith and in the ordinary course of business to a person other than the true owner of it where the defect in the title of the person who receives payment is the forgery of an indorsement on the cheque. The section applies to both crossed and uncrossed cheques and, apparently, even though the paying banker has been negligent in making the payment, provided that he has acted in good faith and in the ordinary course of his business. A banker who pays in obviously suspicious circumstances will lose the protection of S60 if he pays the instrument without a proper inquiry, as payment will not then be in the ordinary course of business.

Protection under S80 Bills of Exchange Act 1882

This provides that, where a banker on whom a crossed cheque is drawn pays it in good faith and without negligence, the banker paying the cheque is placed in the same position and has the same protection as if the payment of the cheque had been made to the true owner.

Protection under S1 Cheques Act 1957

This section provides protection to the paying banker if he pays a cheque in good faith and in the ordinary course of business when the cheque is not indorsed or is irregularly indorsed.

9.5.2 Statutory protection of the collecting banker

S4 Cheques Act 1957

If a bank's customer pays in a cheque and the bank credits it to the customer's account, the bank will then send it to the bank on which it is drawn and collect the money. If the customer did not have a good title to the cheque then the possibility arises that the true owner could sue the bank for damages for conversion. When cheques first came into use on a large scale in the nineteenth century it was believed that banks would be reluctant to handle them because they would have a constant fear that their customers would keep paying in stolen cheques for collection and the banks would be liable for actions in conversion. Banks were therefore given the statutory immunity which is now contained in S4 of the Cheques Act 1957. This states that if the collecting banker has acted in good faith and without negligence then he does not incur any liability to the true owner of a cheque by reason only that he has received payment of the cheque. (Section 4 also applies to all the forms of financial document previously listed.)

Definition of a customer

The protection of S4 is available only if the banker collected the cheque or payment mandate 'for a customer' or credited 'a customer's account' with the value of the instrument. In the *Great Western Railway Co v London & County Banking Co Ltd (1901)*, it was said that a customer is 'a person who has some sort of account, either deposit or current account or similar relation, with a banker'. In that case it was held that a man who did not have an account was not a customer. The common problem, however, is that an account is opened with an unlawfully obtained cheque. There has been a theory that a person could only be a customer is there was an 'established course of dealing', so that collection of a cheque with which an account was opened would not be collection for a customer. However, this view was rejected in *Ladbroke & Co v Todd (1914)* and the judgment in the case is now generally regarded as the best view. The judge said: In my opinion a person becomes a customer of a bank when he goes to the bank with money or a cheque and asks to have an account opened in his name, and the bank accepts the money or cheque and is prepared to open an account in the name of that person.

These were the facts of the case of *Ladbroke & Co v Todd (1914)*. Thieves intercepted all the letters which Ladbrokes, bookmakers, had sent to clients with their winning cheques on one particular day. The thieves took out the cheques and substituted crude forgeries. One of the cheques was for £75. 11s. 3d payable to a Mr Jobson and crossed 'A/c payee only'. One thief took this cheque to the John Bull Bank, which was owned by Mr Todd, and opened an account in Jobson's name (though he gave erroneous Christian names), using the stolen cheque as initial deposit and asked for that cheque to be specially presented. This was done, the cheque was paid and the next day 'Mr Jobson' withdrew the money from his account and disappeared. Mr Todd said that he had not made any enquiries at all about 'Mr Jobson' because he was obviously a University man and told a plausible story about not wishing his usual banker to see a cheque drawn by a bookmaker. The court held that 'Mr Jobson' was a customer of the bank from the moment his account was opened but that the banker had been negligent in not making enquiries, for example, at the college he claimed to attend, which could easily have revealed him as an imposter.

Without negligence

The conditions under which the collecting banker is given protection differ slightly from those under which the paying banker receives protection. It is not required that collection should be in the ordinary course of business; instead, the collection must be 'for a customer'. However, there is a requirement that the banker acts without negligence. A banker is not to be treated, for the purpose of S4 of the Cheques Act 1957, as having been negligent by reason only of his failure to concern himself with the absence of or irregularity in, indorsement of an instrument.

The following have been held to be cases where the banker has been negligent:

(a)   Where an account has been opened for a person without making inquiries as to his identity and circumstances.

(b)   Where the banker has received payment for a customer's account of a cheque payable to the customer's employer, without inquiring as to the customer's title to the cheque. In *A L Underwood Ltd v Bank of Liverpool and Martins (1924)* U was the managing director and sole director of A L Underwood Ltd. He indorsed cheques made out to the company 'A L U Ltd ALU sole director' and paid them into his own bank account. His own bank had no knowledge that the company had a bank account at another bank. Underwood died leaving his company insolvent. In an action brought by the company on behalf of a debenture holder for conversion of the cheques, it was held that the bank was not entitled to the statutory protection because of their negligence in failing to enquire whether a separate account for the company existed.

(c)   Where the banker has received payment for a customer's private account of a cheque made payable to the customer in a representative capacity, without making suitable inquiries.

(d)   Where the banker has received payment for a customer's account of a cheque, drawn by the customer's employer in favour of a third party or to bearer, without inquiring as to the customer's title to the cheque. In *Lloyds Bank Ltd v E B Savory & Co (1933)*, P and S, employees of S & Co, stole bearer cheques from their employers and paid them into branches of Lloyds Bank. The paying-in was made at branches of Lloyds other than those where the employees' accounts were kept, with the result that the branches at which the accounts of P and S were kept were unaware of the nature of the items paid in. Neither branch, when opening accounts for P and S respectively, had made enquiries regarding the identity of P's and S's employers. It was held that the bank had been negligent and was obliged to refund to S & Co the value of the cheques.

In recent years the courts have tended to show a more lenient attitude towards collecting bankers regarding the question of negligence. In *Orbit Mining & Trading Co Ltd v Westminster Bank Ltd (1962)*, W and E, directors of the plaintiff company (O) were authorised to sign cheques jointly on behalf of the company. Before going abroad, W signed some cheques in blank, leaving them in E's custody. E completed the cheques 'pay Cash or order', signed them, added the words 'for and on behalf of O' above the signatures of W and himself, and paid them into his account with the defendant bank. It was held that the bank had not been negligent because:

(i)   there was nothing suspicious in having cheques made payable to 'Cash or order';

(ii)   E's signature was illegible, and there was nothing to indicate to the collecting bank that their customer had had anything to do with the drawing of the cheque.

In *Marfani & Co Ltd v Midland Bank Ltd (1967)*, X, the managing director of the plaintiffs (M & Co) signed a cheque for £3,000 which had been drawn by the plaintiff's office manager, K, and was payable to a Mr Eliaszade. After signing the cheque, X gave it to K, who, claiming to be Eliaszade, used it to open an account with the defendant bank. The bank asked for references and was given the names of two satisfactory customers of the bank. One referee, who believed that K's name was Eliaszade, gave a good reference, but the second referee did not reply. K drew a cheque for £2,950 and absconded with the proceeds. Despite the fact that the bank did not ask to see E's passport, and employees of the bank failed to notice any similarity between the writing of the cheque for £3,000 and its indorsement, it was held that the bank had not been negligent, and was entitled to the protection of S4 of the Cheques Act 1957.

Two judicial comments on the matter are valuable. In *Lloyds Bank v Chartered Bank of India, Australia & China (1929)*, Sankey, LJ, stated:

In my view, a bank cannot be held liable for negligence merely because they have not subjected an account to a microscopic examination. It is not expected that officials of banks should also be amateur detectives.

In *Commissioners of Taxation v English, Scottish & Australian Bank (1920)*, this comment was made:

> The test of negligence is whether the transaction of paying in any given cheque, coupled with the circumstances antecedent and present, was so out of the ordinary course that it ought to have aroused doubts in the bankers' mind and caused them to make inquiry.

(e)   Where the banker has received payment for a customer's account of a cheque drawn by the customer as agent for a third party but made payable to the customer personally, without enquiring as to the customer's title to the cheque.

(f)   Where the banker has received payment for a customer's account of a cheque, drawn in favour of a third party and marked 'account payee', without inquiring as to the customer's title to the cheque.

(g)   Where the banker has failed to examine a customer's account from time to time in order to consider whether or not it appears to be a genuine one.

If the same bank is both paying and collecting a cheque then it must satisfy both sets of conditions in order to claim protection: it must pay in due course and good faith and must collect for a customer in good faith and without negligence (*Carpenters Co v British Mutual Banking Co (1937)*).

Suing for dishonoured cheques

If a customer pays in a cheque in order to reduce an overdraft, or if a customer draws against the value of a paid-in cheque before it has cleared, then problems may arise if the cheque is dishonoured. When the value of the dishonoured cheque is debited to the customer's account it may leave an overdraft that seems to the bank to go beyond the customer's capacity to repay. One course open to the bank (unless the cheque was crossed 'Not negotiable') is to claim to be a holder in due course of the cheque and then sue everyone liable on it for its value.

Even though a customer does not indorse an order cheque before paying it in, if the bank gives value for it then the bank is constituted a holder for value by S2 of the Cheques Act 1957, which provides:

> A banker who gives value for ... a cheque payable to order which the holder delivers to him for collection without indorsing it, has such (if any) rights as he would have had if, upon delivery, the holder had indorsed it in blank.

(Note that this provision does not apply to documents that are not cheques.) Provided the cheque was regular and complete when the bank took it, and providing the bank took it in good faith and without notice that it had previously been dishonoured, if such was the case, then the bank will be a holder in due course of the cheque, and the customer who paid it in will be liable on it as an indorser.

The bank must give notice of dishonour to the drawer of the cheque and to the customer who paid it in and to other indorsers, if there are any. The bank should not part with the cheque. If the cheque was returned with an answer indicating that the drawer had countermanded payment then notice of dishonour need not be given to the drawer (Bills of Exchange 1882, S50(2)(c)).

The problem is to identify when a bank has given value to a customer for a cheque that the customer thinks is being collected for his account. If the cheque was paid in so as to reduce the customer's overdraft and the bank had already made it clear that the customer would not be permitted to draw any further on the account then the bank will have given value for the cheque.

In *Westminster Bank Ltd v Zang (1966)*, Zang lost over £2,000 playing cards one Easter Saturday. Tilley gave him £1,000 in cash (the day's takings from his car-dealing business) in return for Zang's cheque which was made payable to Tilley personally. However, Tilley paid it into the overdrawn account of his company, Tilley's Autos Ltd, at Westminster Bank, without indorsing it. The cheque was dishonoured. The bank sued Zang, saying that it was a holder in due course because the cheque had reduced the overdraft of Tilley's Autos Limited. It was held that the bank had not given value for the cheque. It had continued to charge interest on the full amount of the overdraft without allowing for the amount of the cheque while waiting for it to be cleared. The printed paying-in slip had on it a statement that the bank reserved the right to refuse withdrawals against uncleared cheques (bank paying-in slips no longer state this). There was no evidence of any specific agreement regarding this cheque or any general agreement between Tilley and the bank that the bank would do anything for Tilley in return for being handed the cheque for collection. Therefore, since S2 did not apply, the bank was not a holder of the cheque. It did not have and was not deemed to have Tilley's indorsement and could not sue on the cheque.

A case in which a bank was regarded as a holder in due course is *Barclays Bank Ltd v Astley Industrial Trust Ltd (1970)*. In November 1964 Barclays allowed its customer, Mabons Garage Ltd, a temporary overdraft of £2,000. On 18 November the overdraft was £1,910 and cheques for £2,673 drawn on the account were presented for payment. The branch manager agreed to pay these cheques only after receiving an assurance from the directors of Mabons Garage Ltd that cheques for £2,850 drawn by Astley Industrial Trust would be paid in the next day. Unfortunately, Astley stopped payment of the cheques claiming they had been obtained by fraud. Barclays took this action for the value of the cheques on the ground that it was a holder in due course. The bank succeeded. It was held that the cheques had been taken in consideration for £2,673 paid the previous day: there was a specific agreement to this effect.

Unindorsed cheques as evidence of payment

Section 3 of the 1957 Act provides that:

> An unindorsed cheque which appears to have been paid by the banker on whom it is drawn is evidence of the receipt by the payee of the sum payable by the cheque.

The effect of this provision is that a paid unindorsed cheque, like an indorsed one, is prima facie evidence of the receipt by the payee of the amount of the cheque.

Collecting bills of exchange that are not cheques

A bank's duties when collecting for a customer payment of a bill of exchange that is not a cheque or a banker's draft are more onerous than in relation to the other financial documents considered in this session. A bank has no protection against an action for wrongful interference if it collects such a bill on behalf of someone who is not its true owner.

9.6 Relations of banker and customer

9.6.1 Banker's obligation to pay

The banker's obligation to pay means that, generally, a banker is obliged to honour cheques drawn on him by his customer, provided that:

(a)   The amount of the cheque is fully covered by:

   (i)   a credit balance on the customer's account; or,
   (ii)   an authorised overdraft limit.

(b)   The cheque appears to be regular on the face of it.

(c)   It comes into the banker's hands in the ordinary course of business.

The banker need not pay a cheque if:

(a)   It is only partly covered by the customer's credit balance or agreed overdraft limit.

(b)   It has been drawn against uncleared items (eg cheques paid in for collection), unless the banker has expressly or impliedly agreed to this being done.

(c)   The cheque appears to be irregular in some respect, eg:

   (i)   it is post-dated;
   (ii)   it contains a material alteration not bearing the drawer's signature or initials;
   (iii)   the words and figures differ.

A banker who unjustifiably refuses to pay a cheque is liable primarily to his customer. He is entitled to return the cheque to the presenter, marked 'Refer to drawer', if he is not sure that the cheque is genuine, or if it does not accurately convey his customer's wishes. However, by usage, the simple words 'Refer to drawer (or R/D)' have come to imply that the customer's account has insufficient funds to meet the cheque. A banker should therefore be careful to explain why he is returning the cheque, eg, 'Words and figures differ', or 'Altered figures require drawer's initials'.

If a banker wrongly dishonours his customer's cheque, he may be sued for damages by the customer. An example of this would be returning the cheque 'R/D - insufficient funds' when, in fact, an adequate amount to cover the cheque had been paid in by the customer for the credit of his account although, due to an error of the bank's staff, it had been credited to the wrong account.

The measure of the damages recoverable will vary according to the position of the customer. For private (ie, non-business) customers damages are usually small (in some cases nominal), but if the customer is in business and can satisfy the court that his business reputation has been seriously prejudiced as the result of the cheque's being dishonoured, he may be awarded substantial damages against the banker.

9.6.2 Customer's obligation to take care

A customer should exercise reasonable care when drawing a cheque. If a cheque is drawn so carelessly that it can be altered in a way that is not apparent from a normal examination of the cheque, the banker may be able to debit his customer's account with the altered amount.

In *London Joint Stock Bank Ltd v Macmillan & Arthur (1918)*, K, an employee of Macmillan & Arthur, prepared a cheque for one of his employers to sign. The cheque was made payable to bearer, K asserting that it was intended for petty cash. The cheque showed a figure of £2, but the amount in words did not originally appear. After the cheque had been signed, K fraudulently altered it to show £120 in figures, and added that amount in words. K then cashed the cheque for the altered amount, and Macmillan & Arthur subsequently brought an action for the recovery of £118 from the bank. The action failed, because there was an obligation on a customer of a bank to draw cheques with sufficient care to minimise the risk of their being easily altered.

9.6.3   Revocation of the banker's authority

By S75 of the Bills of Exchange Act 1882, the duty and authority of a banker to pay his customer's cheques are brought to an end (ie, revoked) by the customer specifically countermanding payment or by the customer's death.

Where the customer countermands payment, the countermand must be unambiguous, must be brought to the actual notice of the banker, and the bank must be satisfied that it is made by the customer himself. In *Curtice v London City and Midland Bank Ltd (1908)*, C drew a cheque on the defendant bank (L) but countermanded payment by telegram on the same day. Because of the negligence of some of L's employees the telegram was ignored for two days, during which time the cheque was paid. It was held that the bank was not liable to refund C the amount of the cheque, because C's countermand was not effective. Even if the telegram has been acted upon immediately it was received, it would have merely been authority for the bank to defer payment until it received a proper (formal) countermand from C.

A more complex example occurs in the case of *Burnett v Westminster Bank Ltd (1965)*. B had current accounts with two branches (X and Y) of the defendant bank. The bank had recently converted to computer records, and cheque books contained a notice that customers were not to use cheques for any branch other than that already printed thereon. (This was because details of the bank number, branch number, and customer number were already printed on the cheques in magnetic ink.) However, B did not read the notice, and on a cheque originally drawn on the X branch he altered the details in ordinary ink to refer to the Y branch. Later, he telephoned the Y branch countermanding payment. However, the computer ignored the ink alteration and debited the cheque (for £2,300) to B's account at the X branch. The court held that B was entitled to recover £2,300 from the defendant bank because he had not instructed the bank to debit his X branch account; furthermore, it was shown that he had not agreed to the provision concerning non-alteration of cheque details given in the notice.

9.7   Revision exercise

In order to assess your knowledge of the above session, attempt the following questions. Check your answers against the references given.

(1)   What do you understand by the concept of negotiability?   **(Solution: 9.1.1)**

(2)   In what circumstances does the holder of a negotiable instrument have all the rights that such a document can give?   **(Solution: 9.1.2)**

(3)   What are the essential characteristics of a negotiable instrument?   **(Solution: 9.1.3)**

(4)   What is a bill of exchange?   **(Solution: 9.2.2)**

(5)   Who are the three parties to a bill of exchange?   **(Solution: 9.2.2)**

(6)   When must a bill of exchange be paid?   **(Solution: 9.2.2)**

(7)   What is the meaning of indorsement?   **(Solution: 9.2.3)**

(8)   Who is liable on a bill?   **(Solution: 9.2.3)**

(9)   What are the conditions necessary for a person to become a holder in due course?
                                                                                        (Solution: 9.2.3)

(10)   What is the liability of an indorser of a bill?   **(Solution: 9.2.5)**

(11)   When is an agent liable on a bill?   **(Solution: 9.2.5)**

(12)   Give five ways of qualifying acceptance.   **(Solution: 9.2.5)**

(13)   How may a bill be discharged?   **(Solution: 9.2.6)**

(14)   What is the effect of a forged signature on a bill of exchange?   **(Solution: 9.2.6)**

(15)   What is an accommodation bill?   **(Solution: 9.2.7)**

(16)   By whom, to whom, and at what time must presentment for acceptance be made?
                                                                                        (Solution: 9.2.8)

(17)   In what circumstances may a bill be treated as dishonoured by non-acceptance?
                                                                                        (Solution: 9.2.8)

(18)   In what circumstances is presentment for payment dispensed with?   **(Solution: 9.2.8)**

(19)   To whom must notice of dishonour of a bill be given?   **(Solution: 9.2.8)**

(20)   Explain the terms 'noting' and 'protesting'.   **(Solution: 9.2.8)**

(21)   Differentiate between an 'inland' and a 'foreign' bill.   **(Solution: 9.2.8)**

(22)   Define a promissory note.   **(Solution: 9.3.1)**

(23)   Who is primarily liable to pay on a promissory note?   **(Solution: 9.3.2)**

(24)   What are the distinctions between promissory notes and bills of exchange?
                                                                                        (Solution: 9.3.2)

(25)   What is the definition of a cheque?   **(Solution: 9.4.1)**

(26)   Distinguish between a general and a special crossing.   **(Solution: 9.4.3)**

(27)   Is a paying banker liable on a cheque if he is negligent?   **(Solution: 9.5.1)**

(28)   What protection is given to a collecting banker by S4 Cheques Act 1957?
                                                                                        (Solution: 9.5.2)

(29) How and when is a collecting banker negligent? **(Solution: 9.5.2)**

(30) In what circumstances may a banker refuse to honour a cheque? **(Solution: 9.6.1)**

(31) What obligation does a customer owe his banker? **(Solution: 9.6.2)**

(32) Outline the law regarding revocation of the banker's authority to pay his customers' cheques. **(Solution: 9.6.3)**

9.8 Conclusion

Having completed your study of this session you should now have an understanding of the concept of negotiability in general and the law regarding bills of exchange and cheques in particular. You should feel confident in your ability to:

- determine whether or not any particular instrument constitutes a bill of exchange;

- explain the rights and liabilities of the parties to a bill of exchange;

- deal with problematical questions concerned with payment by cheque;

- apply to factual situations the statutory provisions providing protection to paying and collecting bankers.

9.9 Questions

Objective test questions

(1) A person who has written his name on the back of a bill of exchange to negotiate the bill is termed technically:

A The holder.
B The indorsee.
C The drawer.
D The indorser.

(2) Which of the following is not one of the requisites of being a holder in due course?

A The bill must be complete and regular on the fact of it.
B There must be no notice of previous dishonour if such was the case.
C The holder must not have been negligent.
D The bill must be taken for value.

(3) Which of the following statements regarding the differences between cheques and other bills of exchange is incorrect?

A As a cheque is payable on demand it is never presented for acceptance.
B A cheque can never be negotiated.
C The rules on crossings are generally confined to cheques and do not apply to most other bills of exchange.
D Delay in presenting a cheque does not discharge the drawer unless he suffers actual loss.

(4)   The issue of a bill of exchange constitutes a special kind of contract independent of any prior contract in respect of which the bill is issued. The usual rules for consideration in contracts apply, though there are exceptions. Which of the following is not one of those exceptions:

A   Consideration may be past.

B   Consideration need not move from the promisee.

C   Consideration need not be sufficient.

D   Consideration is presumed in the absence of contrary evidence.

(5)   The indorsement 'Pay X only' is:

A   A general indorsement.

B   A restrictive indorsement.

C   A conditional indorsement.

D   A special indorsement.

Written test questions

9.1   A, B and C

A draws a bill of exchange on B payable to C. The bill is in proper form and falls due three months after date. B accepts the bill and then A sends it to C, who indorses it and hands it to X in settlement of a debt.

Outline the respective promises or engagements of A, B and C as regards the bill.

Can any of them, when signing the bill, add 'Sans recours' and, if so, what effect would these words have?

9.2   Bill of exchange

(a)   A bill of exchange is normally discharged by payment at or after maturity. List four other ways in which a bill can cease to be enforceable.

(b)   On 1 March 19X1, A drew a bill of exchange for £1,000 on B payable to C three months after date. B accepted the bill and returned it to A, who handed it to C. Having indorsed the bill, C sent it to D, but it was lost in the post. D is now pressing C for a duplicate bill. Advise C about the legal position.

9.3   Crossings

Explain the meaning and effect of the phrases 'a/c payee' and 'not negotiable', which often appear on crosed cheques.

SESSION 10

Nature and general concepts of tortious liability

This is the first of four sessions concerned with the law of tort. It examines the nature and general concepts of tortious liability. The session will give you:

- an appreciation of the province of the law of tort;

- an understanding of the basis of tortious liability;

- a detailed knowledge and practical understanding of the concept of vicarious liability as applicable to the law of tort.

10.1   The nature and definition of tortious liability

In modern society it is inevitable that some people will be injured or annoyed by their neighbour's activities. This may take the form of physical injuries (such as in the case of car accidents, defective machinery and the like): or injury to one's reputation or business (from, say, an erroneous newspaper report): or perhaps loss of or damage to property as a result of a reservoir burst; or diminution in the value of one's property due to pursuits of one's neighbour etc.

In all these and many other situations the law of tort governs the question of whether the injured party, the plaintiff, may sue the party responsible for the injury, the defendant, to recover compensation for his loss, and, if so how. It is concerned with the re-adjustment of those losses that are bound to occur in society. In the words of Lord Denning '. . . the province of tort is to allocate responsibility for injurious conduct'.

Professor Winfield defined tortious liability as that which 'arises from the breach of a duty primarily fixed by the law: this duty is towards persons generally and its breach is redressible by an action for unliquidated damages'. Tortious duties exist by virtue of the law itself and are not dependant upon the agreement or consent of the persons subjected to them. It is this lack of agreement or consent which distinguishes tortious from contractual liability. However, it must be appreciated that tortious liability may arise from a contractual relationship.

The primary duty in tortious liability is towards people generally. The breach of such a duty gives rise to a remedial duty owed to a specific person or people. The nature of this primary duty serves to distinguish tort from quasi-contractual duty where no such primary duty exists.

10.1.1   Tortious liability and other branches of the law

(a)   *Tortious liability and crime* - The distinction between tortious and criminal wrongs does not lie in the acts themselves; indeed the same act may give rise to both tortious and criminal liability. Rather the distinction lies in the procedure taken to right the wrong concerned and the reason why such procedure is initiated (be it essentially pumitive, as in criminal law or essentially compensatory, as with actions arising from breaches of tortious liability.

(b)   *Tortious liability and contract* - As already stated, the same incident may give rise to proceedings in tort or contract. However, tortious obligations are fixed primarily by the law rather than by agreement of the parties; tortious obligations are towards people generally, whereas in contract the obligation is towards a specific person or people.

(c)   *Tortious liability and trusts* - No civil injury is to be classed as a tort if it is only a breach of trust or some other merely equitable obligation. Tortious obligations have their origin in the common law, and were unknown to the Court of Chancery.

10.2   The basis of liability in tort

One action for breach of contract has much in common with the next: there will in both cases have been an agreement, an intention to create legal relations, consideration etc. But can this be said of an action in tort? One view is that there is a number of individual torts (one very different from the next) outside which liability does not exist. In particular, one who has suffered damage which does not fit into one of the recognised tort categories (*damnum sine injuria*) has no remedy. Thus, for example, in *Mayor of Bradford v Pickles (1895)* the defendant interfered with the plaintiff's water supply (which reached the plaintiff by undefined channels under the defendant's land), in order to persuade the plaintiff to buy the defendant's land. The court held that the plaintiff had no remedy.

On the other hand there is the view that there is a law of tort, and that there is an underlying theory of tortious liability of which the particular torts are but examples. This view is supported by the simple fact that the courts have continued to develop the law of torts as the needs of society have demanded. However, even though the courts have continued to evolve new heads of tortious liability they do not appear to do so upon any single general principle.

Furthermore, it will appear from an examination of those criteria of liability which most frequently appear in torts that there is no one criterion which is invariably present in tort. The factors to be examined are: damage, fault, wrongful motive, and ability to bear the loss.

10.2.1   Factors present in tort

(a)   *Damage* - *Prima facie* the factor might appear essential to every action in tort. However, there are certain situations *'injuria sine damno'*: torts such as trespass actionable *per se*, that is, without proof of damage. Conversely, it is not for every item of damage suffered that the plaintiff may recover from the defendant. The plaintiff must first show that the defendant's conduct caused the damage and that the damage was not too 'remote' in law.

(b)   *Fault* - It has been said that 'reason demands that a loss should lie where it falls, unless some good purpose is to be served by changing its incidence', and that a sufficient purpose is the punishment of him who caused the loss, provided he is at fault, ie, had acted deliberately or negligently. However, there are very serious objections to the role of fault as a basis of tortious liability.

In the first place as Lord Devlin has pointed out: 'The real wrongdoer hardly every pays for the damage he does. He is usually not worth suing. The payer is either his employer or his insurance company'. Secondly, in certain torts, such as *Rylands v Fletcher*, liability is imposed regardless of any fault on the defendant's part. Thirdly, even where fault is relevant to the question of liability, it is usually judged objectively rather than subjectively. Thus in the tort of negligence, the objective standard of care has been established by the 'reasonable man' principle.

Finally damages in tort are supposed to compensate, rather than to punish.

(c)   *Motive* - The general rule, laid down in *Mayor of Bradford v Pickles (1895)*, is that the defendant's motive is irrelevant: it will not turn a lawful act into a tort; nor will a good motive excuse tortious conduct. There are, however, some exceptions:

     (i)   An improper motive may be relevant as, for example, in cases of nuisance by noise. Thus in *Christie v Davey (1893)* the defendant's whistling, shrieking and banging of tin trays on the party wall seems to have been actionable primarily because it was done, not accidentally, but so as deliberately to annoy the plaintiff whose music lessons had upset the defendant.

     (ii)   The absence of 'malice' in the sense of spite or evil motive may be a defence, as it is when qualified privilege or fair comment are pleaded in an action of defamation.

     (iii)   Damages may be increased in certain circumstances if the defendant acted with an improper motive.

(d)   *Ability to bear the loss* - 'Recent legislative and judicial developments show that the criterion of liability in tort is not so much culpability, but on whom should the risk fall', per Denning LJ in *White v White (1950)*. The argument runs that in most cases losses are actually borne by those best able to hear them, ie, employers, insurance companies (whose function it is to bear them) and the State (through national insurance schemes), and that this is appropriate.

10.3   Parties in the law of tort

(a)   *Minors* - A minor is liable in tort but a claim arising in contract cannot be converted into a claim in tort for the purpose of making the minor liable. Another peculiarity of the law regarding minors is that if the tort alleged requires a mental element, the age of the minor may show an inability to form the necessary intent.

As regards parental liability for the tortious actions of a child, the basic proposition is that this only exists where vicarious liability is established (see 10.4 below). A person is not liable, simply as a parent, unless the injury is caused by his negligent control of the child, and even where he is so liable, it is really for his own tort, ie, negligence in looking after the child: *Bebee v Sales (1916)*. In this case a father allowed his fifteen year old son to retain a shot gun with which he knew he had already caused damage. The father was held liable for an injury to another boy's eye.

(b)   *Husband and wife* - A married woman can sue and be sued in tort like a *feme sole* and since the Law Reform (Husband and Wife) Act 1962, they can sue each other subject to the discretion of the court to stay the action if no substantial benefit would accrue.

(c)   *Mental patients* - If the disease of the mind is such that the person is unable to understand the nature and consequences of his act cannot be liable.

(d)   *Corporations* - A tort affecting the property or business of a corporate body is actionable at its instance; a corporate body is liable for the torts of its servants or agents committed in the course of their employment.

(e)   *Joint tortfeasors* - Persons are joint tortfeasors when one is liable for the tort of another or aids, counsels, or joins the other in committing the tort. Each is liable for the whole loss and if judgement against one is not satisfied, proceedings can be taken against the other till all is recovered. If one has paid the damages he can recover contribution from the other: Law Reform (Married Women and Tortpersons) Act 1935 (as amended).

10.4   Vicarious liability

10.4.1   Definition

The term 'vicarious liability' signifies the liability A may owe to C because of damage suffered by C, as a result of a tortious action committed by B. The commonest instance of this in modern law is the liability of a master for the torts of his servants done in the course of their employment. The relationship required is the specific one of master and servant and the tort must be referable to that relationship in the sense that it must have been committed by the servant in the course of his employment.

10.4.2   The master-servant relationship

A servant may be defined as any person employed by another to do work for him on the terms that he, the servant, is to be subject to the control and direction of his employer in respect of the manner in which his work is to be done. This reflects the traditional test of control used to determine the master-servant relationship and differentiates a servant, for whose acts the employer is responsible, from an independent contractor, for whose torts the employer is not, in general, liable. A servant is one who is employed under a contract for services, an independent contractor on the other hand, is one who undertakes to produce a given result, who in the execution of the work, is not under the order or control of the person for whom he does it, and who may use his own discretion in things not specified beforehand. In recent years, however, the test of control has begun to fall into disrepute and 'professional' employees have been held to be servants notwithstanding the fact that they exercise their own judgement uncontrolled by anybody. Accordingly, it is now recognised that, although the right to control remains an important factor in those cases to which it can be applied, it is not the only factor to be taken into account. All the circumstances must be considered in order to determine whether the contract is one of service and the relationship that of master and servant.

The most significant factors in this regard appear to be the power of selection, payment of wages or remuneration, the right of control and the power of suspension or dismissal, but other factors have been regarded as relevant in deciding difficult cases of relationship. Amongst these may be listed the following - inability of the servant to delegate the task assigned to him; the right of the master to the exclusive services of another; where the work concerned is carried out; the provision of large-scale plant and equipment; the obligation to work; the right to control the hours of work and the taking of holidays. Perhaps the final word on this topic may be left to Denning LJ as he then was, who, in *Stevenson, Jordan and Harrison Limited v MacDonald (1952)* said:

> 'It is often easy to recognise a contract of service when you see it, but difficult to say wherein the distinction lies. A ship's master, a chauffeur and a reporter on the staff of a newspaper are all employed under a contract of service; but a ship's pilot, a taxi-man and a newspaper contributor are employed under a contract for services. One feature which seems to run through the instances is that, under a contract of service a man is employed as part of the business; whereas under a contract for services, his work, although done for the business, is not integrated into it but is only accessory to it.'

10.4.3   The course of employment

In addition to having to show that the relationship between the defendant and the wrongdoer is that of master and servant, the plaintiff must establish that when the servant committed the wrong he was acting in the course of his employment: that the wrong was referable to the relationship.

A wrong falls within the escape of employment if it is expressly or impliedly authorised by the master or is an unauthorised manner of doing something which is authorised, or is necessarily incidental to something which the servant is employed to do. It is sometimes difficult to decide whether a particular act was done during the course of employment. Thus, some acts done by a servant while at work are so personal to him that they cannot be regarded as being within the scope of employment. In *Warren v Henleys Limited (1948)* the employer of a petrol pump attendant was held not liable for the latter's assault on a customer committed as a result of an argument over payment for petrol.

If, however, the tort committed by the servant arises from an improper method of performing an act which is within the scope of his employment, the master will be vicariously liable. Instructive of this point is *Century Insurance Company Limited v Northern Ireland Road Transport Board (1942)*. In this case the driver of a petrol tanker, employed by the defendants, while transferring petrol from the tanker to an underground tank plaintiff's garage, struck a match to light a cigarette and threw it on the floor and thereby caused a conflagration and an explosion which damaged the plaintiff's property. The defendants were held liable: the careless act of their driver was done in the course of his employment.

Two further points worthy of note in this context are:

(a)   that the act done may still be in the course of employment even if it was expressly forbidden by the master. The prohibition by the master of an act or class of acts will only protect him from a liability which he would otherwise incur if it actually restricts what it is the servant is employed to do: the prohibition of a mode of performing the employment is of no avail.

Thus in *Limpus v London General Omnibus Company (1862)* the defendant company was held liable for an accident caused by the act of one of its drivers in drawing across the road so as to obstruct a rural omnibus. It was held to be no defence that the company had issued specific instructions to its drivers not to race with or obstruct other vehicles. In contrast in *Twine v Bean's Express (1946)* the employers had expressly instructed their driver not to allow unauthorised persons to travel on their vehicles and affixed a notice to this effect in the driver's cab. Despite this the driver gave a lift to a person who was killed by reason of the drivers' negligence. The Court of Appeal held that he was acting outside the scope of his employment and accordingly his employers were not liable;

(b)   that it does not necessarily follow that the servant is acting outside the scope of his employment because he intended to benefit himself and not his employer: *Lloyd v Grace, Smith & Co (1912)*. In this case the defendant's clerk fraudulently persuaded the plaintiff to transfer her property to him. It was held that the clerk's acts were within the scope of the apparent or ostensible authority with which he had been clothed by the defendant, and therefore, the defendants were vicariously liable for his acts.

The master's indemnity

The Law Reform (Married Women and Tortfeasors) Act 1935, S6 provides a form of joint liability, and the master may be able to recover from his servant some or all of the damages he has had to pay on account of the tort. In addition, provided the master has not himself, or through some other servant, been guilty of culpable fault, he can recover damages from his servant at common law, and so, in effect, recoup himself for the damages he has had to pay. See *Lister v Romford Ice and Cold Storage Company (1957)*.

10.4.4   Employer and independent contractor

The basic rule is that an employer is not responsible for the torts of his independent contractor. However, there are circumstances in which a person or persons may be liable for the torts of an independent contractor employed by him, viz:

(a)   where the employer authorises or ratifies the torts of the contractor;

(b)   where the employer is negligent himself as where he selects an independent contractor without taking care to see that he is competent to do the work required;

(c)   where the work the employer had instructed the independent contractor to undertake is extra hazardous.

In such cases the liability of the employer is restricted to wrongs necessarily arising in the course of the contractor's employment.

Where an employer is held liable to a third person for the torts of an independent contractor he will, in most cases, be able to claim an indemnity from the contractor.

10.5   Revision exercise

As a means of assessing your knowledge of this session attempt the following questions. Check your answers against the references given.

(1)   What is the province of the law of tort?   **(Solution: 10.1)**

(2)   Define tortious liability.   **(Solution: 10.1)**

(3)   Distinguish between tortious and criminal liability.   **(Solution: 10.1)**

(4)   How do contractual obligations differ from tortious ones?   **(Solution: 10.1)**

(5)   Differentiate between tort and breach of trust.   **(Solution: 10.1)**

(6)   Do we have a law of tort or torts?   **(Solution: 10.2)**

(7)   Examine the relevance of motive in the law of tort.   **(Solution: 10.2.1)**

(8)   To what extent is wrongful intention or culpable negligence a condition of liability in tort?

                                                                                  (Solution: 10.2.1)

(9)   Examine the tortious liability of minors.   **(Solution: 10.3)**

(10)   What is meant by the term 'joint tortfeasors'?   **(Solution: 10.3)**

(11)   Define vicarious liability.   **(Solution: 10.4.1)**

(12)   Define a servant.   **(Solution: 10.4.2)**

(13)   Differentiate between a contract for services and a contract of service.

                                                                                  (Solution: 10.4.2)

(14)   Explain the scope of the course of employment.   **(Solution: 10.4.3)**

(15)   Compare *Limpus General Omnibus Company (1862)* and *Twine v Bean's Express (1946)*.

                                                                                  (Solution: 10.4.3)

(16)   In what circumstances is an employer liable for the tortious acts of an independent contractor?
                                                                                  (Solution: 10.4.4)

10.6   Conclusion

You should now have a sound basic understanding of the nature of tortious liability and how such liability differs from, and relates to, other forms of liability; a knowledge of the basis of tortious liability and the relevance of damage, fault and motive thereto; and a practical understanding of the concept of vicarious liability.

10.7   Questions

Objective test questions

(1)   Which of the following is a true description of the significance of motive in the law of tort?

        A   It is never relevant.
        B   It is only relevant in the tort of negligence.
        C   It is relevant in certain specific torts.
        D   It is always relevant.

(2)   Which of the following is not a true statement as regards tortious liability?

A   The primary duty in tortious liability is towards people generally.
B   The same incident may give rise to proceedings in tort or contract.
C   Tortious obligations have their origin in the Court of Chancery.
D   Certain torts are actionable *per se*.

(3)   The liability A may owe to C because of damage suffered by C, as a result of a tortious action committed by B is known as:

A   Indemnification.
B   Volenti.
C   Vicarious liability.
D   Strict liability.

Written test questions

10.1   **Fault**

Is fault a necessary condition of liability in tort?

10.2   **Motive in tort**

It is generally said that motive is irrelevant in the law of tort. Discuss this statement and examine the exceptional circumstances in which motive is relevant to liability.

10.3   **Tortious liability**

Define tortious liability, taking care to distinguish tort from other legal concepts.

SESSION 11

Tortious liability:
general defences and remedies

This second session concerned with the law of tort falls into two parts. The first part of the session examines the general defences to tortious liability; the second part the various remedies available for breach of tortious liability.

The study of this session will provide you with:

- a thorough knowledge of the defence of *volenti non fit injuria* or consent;

- an appreciation of the other major general defences;

- a knowledge of the remedies for breach of tortious liability and, in particular, the remedy of damages.

11.1 General defences

11.1.1 Exclusion of liability

Position at common law

At common law the defendant may by contract or other agreement or by notice exclude or restrict the duty, if any, which he would otherwise owe to the plaintiff, provided the defendant has taken all reasonable steps to bring the conditions to the plaintiff's notice. Thus, in *Ashdown v Samuel Williams (1957)* the plaintiff, using as a licensee a short-cut across the defendant's shunting-yard, was run over by trucks owing to the defendant's negligence, but was held by the Court of Appeal to be barred from recovering damages by the wording of a widely-worded notice of exclusion whether she had read them all or not.

Limitations: Unfair Contract Terms Act 1977

There are various limitations on the power to exclude liability in tort, but perhaps the most significant are the statutory controls and, in particular, those to be found in the Unfair Contract Terms Act 1977. This Act provides, *inter alia*, that in a business context 'a person cannot by reference to any contract term or to a notice given to persons generally or to particular persons exclude or restrict his liability for death or personal injury resulting from negligence'(S2(1)) and 'in the case of other loss or damage a person cannot so exclude his liability for negligence except insofar as the term or notice satisfies the requirement of reasonableness' (S2(2)).

11.1.2   Volenti non fit injuria (consent)

'No injury is done to one who consents'

There are many occasions on which harm may be inflicted on a person for which he has no remedy in tort because he consented, or at least assented, to the doing of the act which caused this harm. The effect of such consent or assent is commonly expressed in the maxim *volenti non fit injuria*: no injury is done to one who consents.

Form of the consent

Consent may be express or implied, and contractual or non-contractual.

Nature of the consent

A person is *volens* (consenting) only if by his conduct he has agreed to forego his legal remedy. It is not enough, save in rare cases, merely to show that the plaintiff knew of the danger. *Sciens* (knowing) is no substitute for *volens*. The maxim is not *scienti non fit injuria*: the plaintiff's mere knowledge of the danger does not exonerate the defendant from liability. So, in *Smith v Baker (1891)* (quarryman working below crane carrying loads of stone) and *Burnett v British Waterways Board (1973)* (lighterman working on barge with knowledge of a notice purporting to exclude the defendant from liability for injuries) neither plaintiff was barred by *volenti* because in both cases, though the danger was known, the employee was not free to avoid it. However, knowledge may be evidence of consent; may negative the existence of negligence on the part of the defendant; may be proof of contributory negligence on the part of the plaintiff.

A consent obtained by fraud as in *Hegarty v Shine (1878)* where the plaintiff contracted venereal disease from her paramour is not true *volenti*, nor is a consent obtained by withholding full information as in the Canadian case of *Koehler v Cook (1976)*. In that case the defendant, a surgeon operating on the plaintiff to cure the plaintiff's migraine headaches with the result that the plaintiff lost her sense of smell and taste, had not fully made the plaintiff aware of the risk of such as operation.

The 'rescue cases'

If the defendant puts a third party in a situation of danger (whether as regards his person or property) so that the plaintiff is under legal or moral pressure to stage a rescue, then if the plaintiff is injured in the process he is not to be barred from his liability by the defence of *volenti*. So, in *Haynes v Harwood (1935)* a horse and van bolted down a crowded street owing to the defendant's negligence. The plaintiff, a policeman, was injured trying to stop it and was entitled to recover. On the other hand in *Sylvester v Chapman (1935)* a visitor at a circus saw a cigarette smouldering in the cage of a leopard and he crossed the barrier to extinguish some straw that was smouldering. In doing so he was mauled by the leopard. There was no imminent danger and the straw could have been extinguished by other means and as a consequence the defence barred any claim.

Volenti and industrial injuries

As illustrated by *Smith v Baker (1891)* the courts do not favour the application of *volenti* to claims by injured workmen against their employers, except on very clear evidence. This is simply because employees are usually under economic pressure to carry out their ordinary duties despite known dangers. In contrast to the decision in *Smith v Baker* is that in *I.C.I. v Shortwell (1965)*. In that case the House of Lords allowed the defence of *volenti* to defeat a claim by the widow of an injured shot-firer who with his brother (a co-employee of the same status) carried out shot-firing in flagrant breach of safety rules imposed on them.

Limitations

On grounds of public policy the courts are unwilling to recognise *volenti* in cases where the defendant claims the plaintiff agreed to undergo really serious bodily harm, for 'no person can license another to commit a crime'.

11.1.3 Necessity

This defence is put forward when damage has been intentionally caused either to prevent a greater evil or in defence of the realm. For example jettisoning goods: *Mouse's Case (1609)* or discharging oil from a ship in danger of sinking in order to save those on board: *Esso v Southport Corporation (1956)*. Such damage is justifiable if the act was reasonable.

11.1.4 Mistake

The general rule is that mistake, either of law or of fact, is no defence in tort. However, as regards mistakes of fact, the following qualifications must be considered:

(a)   mistake may be evidence that the defendant acted reasonably, and would be relevant, for example, in the determination of liability for negligence;

(b)   mistake is sometimes important in defamation in connection with publication and privilege;

(c)   mistake may negate liability in deceit and certain other forms of tort.

11.1.5 Inevitable accident

An accident by itself cannot afford a defence and accidental damage is not actionable alone. There must be a breach of the duty imposed by law. A person cannot be held liable for the damage caused by an inevitable accident over which he had no control. An example is the bolting of a horse suddenly without obvious cause and despite every effort to control it: *Manzoni v Douglas (1880)*. There must of course be no negligence on the part of the person in charge of the horse, such as leaving it unattended in a busy street. The inevitable accident is one which the reasonable man could not have avoided.

11.1.6 Act of god

A circumstance which no human foresight could provide against. It is something in the course of nature so unexpected in its consequences that the damage caused must be regarded as too remote to form a basis for legal liability: *Nichols v Marsland (1876)*.

11.1.7 Act of State

Sometimes the State finds it necessary to protect persons from actions in court when they have caused damage whilst carrying out their duties. Thus in *Buron v Denman (1848)* the captain of a British warship was held not liable for trespass when he set fire to the barracoon of a Spaniard slave trader on the West Coast of Africa and released the slaves.

11.1.8   Statutory authority

An act otherwise unlawful will involve the defendant in no liability if he has been authorised to do it by statute. Such authorisation is a good defence in respect of all the necessary consequences of the act authorised, provided the defendant has not been guilty of negligence. Thus, in *Fisher v Ruislip U.D.C. (1945)* a local authority had statutory power to erect air raid shelters on the highway; but that did not absolve the Council from negligence in leaving a shelter unlit at night.

The authority given may be either absolute or conditional. Absolute authority is authority to do the act even though it may cause harm to other persons; conditional authority merely authorises conduct provided it causes no harm to others. Whether authority is absolute or conditional is a question of construction; but where it is imperative authority, it is absolute, whereas mere permissive authority is conditional. In *Metropolitan Asylum v Hill (1881)* the defendant having statutory authority to build a smallpox hospital, was held to have gone outside the protection of the statute by erecting it in a residential area so that it constituted a nuisance. The power was permissive rather than imperative and conditional rather than absolute.

11.1.9   Self-defence

This is a defence in respect of person or property provided that the act in defence is reasonable and proportionate to the harm threatened.

11.2   Remedies

Remedies in tort are either:

(a)   *extra judicial* such as the various forms of self-help eg, abatement; or

(b)   *judicial*. The judicial remedies are damages and injunction.

11.2.1   Damages

Nature and form

Damages are awarded to compensate the plaintiff for the loss he has suffered. They may take the following forms:

(a)   *Nominal* - These are awarded in the case of a tort actionable per se and where no actual damage has been committed.

(b)   *Contemptuous* - These are awarded for the commission of any tort but where the court considers that the action should never have been brought.

(c)   *General* - Such are the basic remedy in tort. They represent the damage which is presumed to flow from the defendants, for example, damages for 'pain and suffering' in personal injury cases, and are unliquidated (assessed by the court).

(d)   *Special* - Special damages are not presumed, the plaintiff must prove, as well as specifically claim, them. For example, special damage is loss of earnings.

(e)   *Aggravated* - These are really compensation for hurt feelings. Thus in *Ansell v Thomas (1973)* the plaintiff, the managing director of the defendant company, was ignominiously and forcibly marched out of the defendant's factory by police acting on the instructions of directors of the defendant company who wrongly assumed that the plaintiff had been dismissed.

(f)   *Parasitic* - 'If an actionable wrong has been done to the claimant he is entitled to recover all the damages resulting from that wrong, and nonetheless because he would have had no right of action for some part of the damage if the wrong had not also created a damage which was actionable' per Buckley LJ in *Morton v Colwyn Bay (1908)*.

Thus, in *Huxley v Berg (1815)* the defendant broke into a house to steal and so terrified the wife of the householder therein that she died from fright. Damages for the latter injury were added to those for the trespass.

(g)   *Exemplary* - Exemplary damages are awarded, though rarely, to punish a wrongdoer. They may be awarded in the following situations:

(i)   where the defendant has calculated a profit for himself over and above the likely damages payable for the commission of the tort;

(ii)   where the defendant was a government official guilty of arbitrary, oppressive or unconstitutional conduct; and

(iii)   where a statute allows.

Remoteness

In order to determine the question of remoteness of damage, the first step is to settle the cause of the damage, and evidence must be adduced to show how it happened. The next step is to decide whether what the defendant did is the cause of the tort, and this is a question of fact. If the damage would not have happened but for the fault, the fault is the cause of the damage. If the damage was intended by the defendant then it cannot be said to be too remote. In *Scott v Sheppard (1773)* the defendant threw a lighted squib onto the market stall of one Yates, who threw it away and it landed on the stall of one Royal. He threw it to another part of the market house where it struck Scott, the plaintiff in the face, exploded and put out his eye. It was held that the defendant was liable for the injuries to the plaintiff because he intended the initial act.

In cases of unintended consequences there are two main theories of 'remoteness': the 'directness' test, and the 'reasonable foreseeability' test.

(a)   **The 'directness' test**

In *Re Polemis (1921)* the Court of Appeal made it clear that the defendant was liable for all the direct consequences of his act whether or not he ought reasonably to have foreseen them. In this case a ship was hired under charter and was loaded with petrol. Owing to a leak, the hold became full of petrol vapour and at a port of call an Arab stevedore negligently allowed a plank to fall in the hold. The fall caused a spark which ignited the petrol vapour and there was an explosion which rendered the ship a total loss. All the damage that flowed from the negligence of letting the plank fall was payable by the charterers even though they could not have foreseen those consequences.

(b)   **The 'reasonable foreseeability' test**

The decision in *Re Polemis* was not followed by the Judicial Committee of the Privy Council in *Overseas Tankship v Morts Dock Co (1961)* otherwise known as *The Wagon Mound No 1*, and whilst decisions of the Judicial Committee are not binding on English courts they necessarily have considerable persuasive authority. The facts of the case were that the defendant carelessly discharged oil from a ship, then left. The oil floated towards the plaintiff's wharf where the plaintiff's servants, advised that it was safe to do so, continued their welding operations. Sparks from the welders ignited cotton waste in the oil, then the oil itself. The plaintiff sued for destruction of the wharf by fire. It was held that the defendant was not liable in negligence because it was not reasonably foreseeable that the oil might ignite on water in these circumstances.

It seems that *The Wagon Mound* is becoming the authority on questions of remoteness of damage in tort. In a Scottish case the House of Lords held that even though the actual damage resulting from the negligence was not such as could have been foreseen, some damage must have been foreseen of the same nature as that which did occur although not so serious and the defendant was liable: *Hughes v Lord Advocate (1963)*. On the other hand, where a chemical change took place as the result of the negligence so that the result of the accident was entirely different from the kind of damage that could have been foreseen the element of foreseeability was absent and there was no cause of action: *Doughty v Turner (1964)*. However, it should be noted that 'the unusual plaintiff' rule seems to have survived the decision in *The Wagon Mound*. Thus, in *Smith v Leech Brain and Company Limited (1962)* the plaintiff was struck on the lip by a piece of molten metal. Cancer developed at the seat of the resultant burn and the injured man died three years later. The plaintiffs were negligent and were held liable on the basis that they must take the victim as they found him.

11.2.2   Injunction

Nature

An injunction is an order of the court restraining the commission or continuance of a wrongful act. The remedy, which was developed in the Court of Chancery, is discretionary: it will be awarded if the court thinks it just and equitable to do so, taking into account such matters as the seriousness of the defendant's act, the adequacy of other remedies available, whether it can be enforced etc. An injunction may be either mandatory (commanding something to be done) or prohibitory (forbidding something).

11.3   Revision exercise

Use the following questions to assess your knowledge of this session. Check your answers against the references given.

(1)   In what ways does the Unfair Contract Terms Act 1977 limit the ability to exclude liability in tort?   **(Solution: 11.1.1)**

(2)   What do you understand by *volenti non fit injuria*?   **(Solution: 11.1.2)**

(3)   What form may *volenti* take?   **(Solution: 11.1.2)**

(4)   'Consent must be full, free and unfettered'. Discuss.   **(Solution: 11.1.2)**

(5)   Examine the so-called 'Rescue Cases'.   **(Solution: 11.1.2)**

(6)   Explain the *ratio decidendi* of *Smith v Baker (1891)*.   **(Solution: 11.1.2)**

(7)   What do you understand by the defence of necessity?   **(Solution: 11.1.3)**

(8)   Examine mistake as a defence to tortious liability.   **(Solution: 11.1.4)**

(9)   Is inevitable accident a defence to tortious liability?   **(Solution: 11.1.5)**

(10)   Explain the defence of Act of God.   **(Solution: 11.1.6)**

(11)   In what circumstances does statutory authority amount to a defence in tort?
                                                                                  (Solution: 11.1.8)

(12)   Explain the following adjectives as descriptive of damages:

       (i)   nominal;
       (ii)   special; and
       (iii) aggravated.   **(Solution: 11.2.1)**

(13)   What are exemplary damages?   **(Solution: 11.2.1)**

(14)   Differentiate between the tests of 'directness' and 'foreseeability' as modes of
         determining remoteness of damage.   **(Solution: 11.2.1)**

(15)   What is 'the unusual plaintiff' rule?   **(Solution: 11.2.1)**

(16)   What is a mandatory injunction?   **(Solution: 11.2.2)**

11.4   Conclusion

Careful study of this session will have given you a general knowledge of the various general
defences to tortious liability and, in particular, that of *volenti*. As regards the defence of volenti
you should feel confident to deal with factual situations in which that particular defence plays a
part. You should also have an understanding of the remedies available for breach of tortious
liability.

11.5   Questions

Objective test questions

(1)   Derek and Clive work for a demolition company as warehousemen. In contravention of
         their contracts of employment they secretly remove some fuses and detonators from
         stock to incorporate into the firm's Guy Fawkes Night bonfire, to make it 'go with a
         bang'. Derek is injured when the fire is lit and one of the detonators explodes
         unexpectedly powerfully. He sues his employers as being vicariously liable for Clive,
         who ignited the device. The employers avoid liability by pleading:

    A   *Volenti non fit injuria.*
    B   Inevitable accident.
    C   Act of God.
    D   Lack of intention.

(2)   Which of the following is not a general defence to tortious liability?

   A   The reasonableness of the defendant's action.
   B   *Volenti non fit injuria*.
   C   Statutory authority.
   D   Inevitable accident.

(3)   Remoteness of damage in tort is determined according to the decision in:

   A   *Overseas Tankship v Morts Dock Co (ie, the Wagon Mound (No 1))*.
   B   *Re Polemis*.
   C   *Hadley v Baxendale*.
   D   *Donoghue v Stevenson*.

(4)   The aim of exemplary damages is:

   A   To compensate the plaintiff for hurt feelings.

   B   To compensate the plaintiff for the loss presumed to flow from the defendant's conduct.

   C   To show that the court believes that the action should never have been brought.

   D   To punish the wrongdoer.

Written test questions

11.1   Volenti non fit injuria

The maxim is *volenti non fit injuria*, it is not *scienti non fit injuria*. Discuss.

11.2   Defences to tortious liability

Write **notes** on three of the general defences to tortious liability.

11.3   Reasonable foreseeability

'... some limitation must be imposed upon the consequences for which the negligent actor is to be held responsible - and all are agreed that some limitation there must be - why should that test (reasonable foreseeability) be rejected which, since he is judged by what the reasonable man ought to foresee, corresponds with the common conscience of mankind, and a test (the 'direct' consequences) be substituted which leads to nowhere but the never-ending, and insolvable problems of causation'; per Viscount Simmonds in *The Wagon Mound (1961)*. Discuss.

SESSION 12

General principles of the tort of negligence

This session is concerned with the general principles of the tort of negligence. In particular, it examines the essentials of the tort: those factors that a plaintiff must establish to base a successful action in negligence. The session also looks at the allied concept of contributory negligence. Careful study of this session will give you:

- an understanding of the concept of negligence;

- a knowledge of the essentials of the tort of negligence and an ability to apply that knowledge to factual situations;

- a knowledge of the law regarding contributory negligence.

12.1   The concept of negligence

The word 'negligence' is ambigious in the law of tort. On the one hand, it has an adjectival function in that it may be used to describe a state of mind with which any act may be accompanied; thus one may drive negligently, commit a negligent trespass, or defame someone in a negligent manner. On the other hand, the term negligence is also used as a noun to be the name of a specific tort - the tort of negligence - recognisable as early as 1825 but in its modern form, cast in 1932. In this sense, negligence is the breach of a legal duty to take care which results in damage, undesired by the defendant, to the plaintiff. Thus the tort of negligence has three ingredients, and to succeed in an action the plaintiff must show:

(a)   the existence of a duty to take care which was owed to him by the defendant;
(b)   breach of such duty by the defendant; and
(c)   resultant damage to the plaintiff.

Sometimes judges blur the edges dividing these three theoretical constituents of the tort. In *S C M v Whittall (1971)*, Buckley and Winn LJJ felt that pure economic loss caused by negligent acts was not recoverable because no legal duty was owed in respect of it by the defendant, whereas Lord Denning MR thought there was a duty but that that sort of damage was too remote a consequence of the defendant's breach of duty to be recoverable.

Although it is true that the study of those forms of careless conduct for which the law gives a remedy will involve no clear distinction between these three aspects nevertheless understanding of the three aspects of negligence is vital. In the words of Lord Wright in *Lochgelly Iron and Coal Co v M Mullan (1934)*:

'In strict legal analysis, negligence means more than heedless or careless conduct, whether in omission or commission: it properly connotes the complex concept of duty, breach and damage thereby suffered by the person to whom the duty was owing.'

12.2   The duty of care

No defendant will be liable in the tort of negligence unless the plaintiff proves that a duty of care was owed in law - the notional or legal duty, and in fact, the factual duty - by the defendant to the plaintiff. Whether or not such a duty is owed is a question of law for the judge to decide in all the circumstances of the case.

12.2.1   The notional or legal duty

A notional duty is owed by the defendant if the relationship between the defendant and the plaintiff is one which, at law, is capable of being a 'duty situation'. For example, as between motorist and pedestrian there is a notional duty owed; but as between advocate and client there may not be. It is only in cases where a notional duty is established that it becomes relevant whether or not a duty was also 'in fact' owed (see 12.2.2).

Initially, the law in this regard developed in an empirical manner by decisions that, in some particular circumstances, there was a duty and that in others there was none. However, in 1932 in *Donoghue v Stevenson* Lord Atkin sought to rationalise these decisions and produced the following formula:

> 'In English law there must be, and is, some general conception of relations giving rise to a duty of care, of which particular cases found in the books are instances. The liability for negligence, whether you style it such or treat it, as in other systems, as a species of 'culpa' is no doubt based upon a general public sentiment of wrongdoing for which the offender must pay. But acts or omission which any moral code would censure cannot in a practical world be treated so as to give a right to every person injured by them to demand relief. In this way rules of law arise which limit the range of complainants and the extent of their remedy. The rule that you are to love your neighbour becomes in law, you must not injure your neighbour, and the lawyer's question 'Who is my neighbour?' receives a restricted reply. You must take reasonable care to avoid acts or omission which you can reasonably foresee would be likely to injure your neighbour. Who then, in law, is my neighbour? The answer seems to be persons who are so closely and directly affected by my act that I ought reasonably to have them in contemplation as being so affected when I an directing my mind to the acts or omissions which are called in question.'

In *Donoghue v Stevenson (1932)*, examined in the session concerning specific forms of the tort of negligence, it was held that a manufacturer owed a duty of care to a consumer of its ginger beer from a bottle which, allegedly, contained the decomposed remains of a snail, notwithstanding the absence of any contract between the injured drinker and the manufacturer.

However, in recent times, it has become apparent that the 'neighbour' principle established in *Donoghue v Stevenson (1932)* is inadequate to explain all those situations in which no duty is owed. Increasingly the judges are talking less about 'foreseeability' as a test of duty, and more about 'policy'. In *Anns v London Borough of Merton (1978)* the House of Lords laid down a two-fold test of duty: if the court finds that the neighbour principle of Lord Atkin is satisfied, it must go on to see whether any policy consideration ought to negate or limit the duty of care.

The leading judgement in *Anns v London Borough of Merton (1978)* was that delivered by Lord Wilberforce. It opens with an interesting statement as to how a duty of care is to be established. It is, he said, unnecessary to bring the facts of the problem situation within those of previous situations in which a duty of care has been held to exist. In other words, the duty of care is established by reference to the general 'neighbour' principle and not by a painstaking search through similar factual precedents which may be applied directly or judiciously extended. But the neighbour principle, said Lord Wilberforce, only establishes a *prima facie* duty. One has to proceed in two stages. First, if the plaintiff stands within a sufficient degree of proximity to the defendant, he is a neighbour and a prima facie duty exists. Secondly, if a *prima facie* duty exists, one must seek to discover whether there are 'any considerations, which ought to negative, or to reduce or limit the scope of the duty or the class of person to whom it is owed or the damages to which a breach of it may give rise'.

These latter 'considerations' seem to be matters of 'policy' and, it would seem in truth that determination of whether or not there is a duty of care is a question of policy to be decided by the court in the light of previous judicial decisions and the needs of society. In the words of MacDonald J in the Canadian case of *Nova-Mink v Trans-Canada Airlines (1951)*:

'When . . . a court holds that the defendant was under a duty of care, (it) is stating as a conclusion of law what is really a conclusion of policy as to responsibility for conduct involving unreasonable risk . . . There is always a large element of judicial policy and social expediency involved in the determination of the duty-problem, however, it may be obscured by the traditional formulae.'

These words are reflected in various recent English decisions and judicial dicta. In *Home Office v Dorset Yacht Co (1970)* four out of five Lords based their decision that a duty of care was owed by the Home Office in respect of the conduct of escapee Borstal boys upon the requirements of the public interest, rather than upon the traditional 'foreseeability' criterion which was regarded as a 'principle' as opposed to a 'definition' (per Lord Reid). 'Policy' viewed from another angle was the basis of the judgements of Lord Denning MR in *S C M v Whiltal (1971)* '. . . the risk should be borne by the whole community who suffers the losses rather than rest upon one pair of shoulders' and *Launchbury v Morgans (1971)* '. . . wherever the law imposes vicarious liability, it does so for reasons of social policy'. In *Herrington v British Railways Board (1972)* Lord Reid said that 'how far occupiers are to be required by law to take steps to safeguard children must be a matter of policy'.

It is submitted that only in the light of this thinking can the existence of the 'no-duty' areas such as those of advocate and client referred to above and illustrated by *Rondel v Worsley (1969)* be rationalised. In that case it was held by the House of Lords that a barrister (and perhaps a solicitor per Lord Reid) owes no duty of care to his client if he can show that at the time of his alleged negligence he was acting as an advocate. This immunity was subsequently extended by the House to encompass pre-trial work which is so intimately connected with the conduct of the case in court that it can fairly be said to be a preliminary decision affecting the way that cause is to be conducted: *Saif Ali v Sydney Mitchell (1978)*.

12.2.2 The factual duty

Given that the defendant owed the plaintiff a notional duty, the plaintiff will, nevertheless, have to prove that a duty was, in fact, owed in the particular circumstances of the case. In other words, the plaintiff must have been within the area of risk. He cannot build on a wrong to another. Thus, in *Bourhill v Young (1943)* a motorcyclist negligently got himself killed in an accident. The plaintiff, a pregnant fishwife, had just alighted on the blind side of a tram, so that she was hidden from view, but heard the accident. She suffered a miscarriage as a result of the shock.

The House of Lords held that she had no claim against the motorcyclist's estate, as she had been outside the area of potential danger. In contrast, in *Haley v London Electricity Board (1965)*, it was held that the defendants owed a duty of care to the plaintiff, a blind man, as persons with such a disability should have been in their contemplation and were therefore in the area of foreseeable risk.

12.3 Breach of the duty of care

There must not only be a duty of care owed by the defendant to the plaintiff, in law and in fact; the plaintiff must also show a breach of this duty by the defendant if he is to succeed in the tort of negligence.

12.3.1 The reasonable man

The test for determination of a breach of the duty of care is an objective one and was laid down by Alderson B in *Blyth v Birmingham Waterworks Co (1856)*:

> 'Negligence is the omission to do something which a reasonable man guided upon those considerations which ordinarily regulate the conduct of human affairs would do, or doing something which a provident and reasonable man would not do.'

'The standard of foresight of the reasonable man', said Lord Macmillan in *Glasgow Corporation v Muir (1943)*, 'eliminates the personal equation and is independent of the idiosyncrasies of the particular person whose conduct is in question. Some persons are by nature unduly timorous and imagine every path beset with lions. Others, of more robust temperament, fail to foresee or nonchalantly disregard even the most obvious dangers. The reasonable man is presumed to be free both from over-apprehension and from over-confidence.'

12.3.2 Factors considered

In determining whether or not there has been a breach of the duty of care, the following factors will be considered by the court.

(a) *Imperitia culpae adnumeratur* - The implication of this maxim - 'lack of skill is counted a fault' - is that where anyone is engaged in a transaction in which he holds himself out as having professional skill, the law expects him to show the average amount of competence associated with the proper discharge of the duties of that profession, trade or calling.

  In the *Lady Gwendolen (1965)* a brewery ran its own ship carrying stout from Liverpool to Manchester. The plaintiff suffered damage when the ship's captain relied solely on radar at full speed up the Mersey. It was of no avail to the defendant brewery to claim that, as a firm not primarily concerned with running ships, a lower degree of care should be expected from it. Winn LJ argued that '. . . having become owners of ships, they must behave as reasonable shipowners'.

(b) *General practice of the community* - Commonly, a defendant will support his claim to have shown due care by showing that he conformed to the common practice of those engaged in the activity in question, though such evidence is not conclusive. In *Whiteford v Hunter (1950)* a specialist who failed to diagnose the complaint of the plaintiff was held not to have been negligent when he used the normal methods of British medical specialists, although the use of an instrument usually employed in the United States of America might have resulted in a correct diagnosis.

Conversely, the fact that the defendant has not followed the normal practice is evidence, but not proof, that he was negligent.

(c)   *The likelihood of injury* - The general principle is that before negligence can be established it must be shown, not only that the event was foreseeble, but also that there is a reasonable likelihood of injury. In *Bolton v Stone (1951)*, for example, the House of Lords found that the risk of anyone outside the cricket ground concerned being injured from within was so remote that the defendant was not liable in negligence. In contrast in *Hilder v Associated Portland Cement (1961)*, liability was imposed on a firm which allowed boys to play football on its land adjoining the highway in conditions such that injury to passers-by was reasonably foreseeble.

(d)   *Seriousness of the injury* - In *Paris v Stepney B C (1951)*, the leading case on this factor, a one-eyed workman, engaged on work underneath vehicles, was blinded in his remaining eye by a metal splinter. The House of Lords held that, though his disability, which, was known to the defendants, his employers, did not increase the likelihood of injury, it made such an injury much more serious than in the ordinary employee.

(e)   *Importance of the object to be attained* - If the defendant is under some compulsion, legal or moral, to act, say, in an emergency, he may be expected to be less careful than otherwise. In *Watt v Hertfordshire C C (1954)*, firemen, in a hurry to rescue a woman trapped under a vehicle, failed properly to secure a heavy jack on the back of their lorry (the vehicle properly equipped for such a task being unavailable), so that the jack slipped and injurred the plaintiff, one of the firemen. The court held that in the circumstances the fire authorities had not been negligent.

(f)   *The burden of adequate precautions* - If safety measures are comparatively easy to take, the balance may weigh in favour (though not necessarily conclusively) of the plaintiff. It is relevant to consider how extensive and costly the measures necessary to eliminate the risk would be. Illustrative of this factor are the facts of *Latimer v A E C Limited (1952)*. In that case, an exceptional storm had caused a factory floor to become flooded; when the water receded, the floor was found to be covered with a slimy mixture of oil and water so that its surface was slippery. The issue was the liability of the factory owners to a workman who some hours later, was injured through slipping on the floor. It was held that there was no negligence at common law.

(g)   *The state of scientific knowledge* - In *Roe v Minister of Health (1954)*, for example, a patient was admitted to hospital for treatment including a spinal injection of nupercaine. The drug had to be stored in ampoules kept in sterilising solution. Unknown to medical science generally, phenol could percolate through microscopic cracks in the ampoules. Thus, the patient came to be injected with carbolic acid and became paralysed from the waist down. It was held that the Minister was not liable for the actions of the doctors involved.

12.4   Res ipsa loquitur

12.4.1   The burden of proof

The basic rule is that it is for the plaintiff to prove negligence: it is not for the defendant to have to rebut a presumption of negligence. The plaintiff must prove his cause 'on a balance of probabilities' otherwise he fails. This is known as the 'formal', 'legal' or 'technical' burden of proof.

12.4.2   Res ipsa loquitur

Despite the basic rule outlined above, there are cases where it is difficult for the plaintiff to show how much care the defendant had taken, and it is a common sense rule of evidence to allow the plaintiff to prove any particular act or omission by the defendant. In such cases the court allows the application of the maxim *res ipsa loquitur*: the facts speak for themselves.

However, before the maxim can apply the following criteria must be satisfied:

(a)   *The thing or activity causing the harm must be wholly under the control of the defendant or his servants* - The defendant need only have the right and opportunity to control; actual control is not required. Thus, in *Green v Metropolitan Railway (1873)* a few minutes after a local train had started its journey the plaintiff leaned against the offside door, which flew open. It was held that this was a *res ipsa loquitur* situation, for the defendant railway company was still in control. However, in *Easson v L N E R Co (1944)* where the plaintiff, aged four, fell out of a door in a corridor train seven miles after the last stop, the doctrine did not apply - anyone might have tampered with the door during the journey.

(b)   *The accident must be one which would not have happened if proper care had been exercised* - Thus, one does not normally find stones in buns: *Chaproniere v Mason (1905)*; or expect cranes to collapse: *Swan v Salisbury Construction Co Limited (1966)*; or sacks of sugar to drop from buildings: *Scott v London Docks Co (1865)*. If such things happen, it may be presumed that someone was negligent.

(c)   *The court need not infer the facts if they are known - Res ipsa loquitur* does not apply if an exact explanation is available to the plaintiff. In such circumstances, there is no need to invoke the maxim. In *Barkway v South Wales Transport Co Limited (1949)* the plaintiff was able to succeed in negligence for injuries received in a bus crash without reliance on *res ipsa loquitur*, since there was evidence of the defendant's failure to take reasonable care of the tyres of the bus, one of which had burst.

12.4.3   Effects of the maxim

The applicability of the maxim does not mean that the plaintiff is bound to succeed. The defendant may be able to prove how the accident happened and that he was not negligent; or, even if he cannot prove the cause of the accident, he may be able to prove that it could not have arisen from negligence; or, he may suggest ways in which the accident could have happened without his negligence, and the court may find his explanations convincing.

12.5   Resultant damage

12.5.1   The necessity of resultant damages

The third essential of the tort of negligence is resultant damage. The plaintiff must establish that the breach of the duty of care owed to him gave rise to damage. This requirement involves the plaintiff in establishing first, that he has suffered actual damages to person or property as a result of the branch; second, that there is a legal causal connection between the defendant's breach of duty and the injury or damage he has suffered; and, third, that as a matter of law, the damage he suffered was not too remote.

12.5.2   Causation

The requirement here is that the plaintiff must establish evidence which tends to show how the accident happened and that his injury may have resulted from the conduct of the defendant. This requirement is best illustrated by reference to case law.

Barnett v Chelsea Hospital (1968). A nightwatchman was admitted to a casualty ward complaining of vomitting. The casualty officer sent him home. A few hours later the man died of arsenic poisoning. It was clear that the doctor owed him a duty, had probably been in breach of it, and damage had been suffered. However, there was no liability in negligence for the nightwatchman would have died anyway: the breach had not caused the damage.

Robinson v Post Office (1974). The plaintiff, a Post Office worker, grazed his leg in falling from a ladder which was slippery due to the defendant's negligence. The plaintiff's doctor negligently failed to test properly for anti-tetanus serum reaction and after treatment the plaintiff contracted encephalitis and suffered brain damage. It was held that the doctor's negligence was not a cause of the brain damage. A proper test would not have revealed the plaintiff's susceptibility. The defendant was therefore fully liable, having to take his victim as he found him.

In some cases where some person or event has intervened between the defendant's wrongful act and the plaintiff's damage and is, sufficiently potent to absolve the defendant from liability for that damage, such an act is a *novus actus interveniens* and, as such, breaks the chain of causation. Thus, in *McKew v Holland and Hannen and Cubitts (Scotland) Limited (1969)* the plaintiff suffered an injury during the course of his employment for which his employers were liable. The injury caused him occasionally and unexpectedly to lose the use of his left leg. On one occasion he left a flat and started to descend some stairs which had no handrail. His leg gave way and he sustained further injury. It was held that the plaintiff's conduct broke the chain of causation.

12.5.3   Remoteness

The question of remoteness has already been discussed in a general way. As stated the two leading cases on the principle are *Re Polemis and Furness Withy and Co Limited (1921)* and *Overseas Tankship (UK) Limited v Morts Dock and Engineering Co Limited (1961)*. The latter, though a decision of the Judicial Committee of the Privy Council, and, therefore not strictly binding on the English courts, is being treated by them as a correct statement of the law, subject in *Hughes v Lord Advocate (1963)* to an additional principle that the precise chain of circumstances need not be envisaged if the consequence turns out to be within the general sphere of contemplation and not of an entirely different kind which no one can anticipate. In *Hughes v Lord Advocate* the facts were that workmen opened a manhole in the street and left in unattended, having placed a tent above it and warning parrafin lamps around it. The plaintiff and another boy, who were aged eight and ten years respectively, took one of the lamps and went down the manhole. As they came out the lamp was knocked into the hole and the explosion took place injuring the plaintiff. The explosion was caused in a unique fashion because the paraffin had vapourized (which was unusual) and been ignited by the naked flame of the wick. The defendants argued that although some injury by burning was foreseeable, burning by explosion was not. The defendants were held liable.

12.6 Contributory negligence

12.6.1 Position at common law

At common law it was a complete defence if the defendant proved that the plaintiff was guilty of negligence. Thus, in *Butterfield v Forrester (1809)* the defendant wrongfully put a pole across the road 'just when they were beginning to light candles'. The plaintiff came riding along at full speed and though the pole should have been discernible at a hundred yards, he hit it and was injured.

The plaintiff's action failed.

12.6.2 The Law Reform (Contributory Negligence) Act 1945

The law regarding contributory negligence is now governed by the Law Reform (Contributory Negligence) Act 1945. S1 of the Act provides that:

> 'where any person suffers damage as the result partly of his own fault and partly of the fault of any other person or persons, a claim in respect of that damage shall not be defeated by reason of the fault of the person suffering the damage, but the damages recoverable in respect thereof shall be reduced to such extent as the court thinks just and equitable having regard to the claimant's share in the responsibility for the damage.'

Thus, in cases of contributory negligence, damages are to be apportioned according to fault.

The terms 'damage' and 'fault' used in S1 of the 1945 Act are defined as including loss of life and personal injury, and as 'negligence, breach of statutory duty of other act or omission which gives rise to a liability in tort, or would, apart from this Act, give rise to the defence of contributory negligence' respectively. Illustrative of the operation of the Act and, of the need, if it is to operate, for both parties to be at fault is *Davies v Swan Motors (1949)*. In that case, the plaintiff, employed as a dustman by Swansea Corporation and in breach of orders rode on the steps of the dust cart. Due to negligent driving by the driver of the cart and the driver of an on-coming bus belonging to the defendants, the plaintiff was injured. The plaintiff's damages were reduced by twenty per cent as a result of his contributory negligence.

The fact that the injured party is a child is relevant to determination of whether or not there has been contributory negligence on the child's part, for what may be regarded as contributory negligence in the case of an adult is not necessarily to be so regarded when committed by a child. In *Gough v Thorne (1966)*, for example, a girl aged thirteen years was held not guilty of contributory negligence in crossing a road without looking when signalled to do so by a lorry driver who was unaware that he was being overtaken.

12.7 Revision exercise

In order to assess your assimilation of the above information attempt the following questions. Check your answers against the references given.

(1)   Define the tort of negligence.   **(Solution: 12.1)**

(2)   What are the essentials of the tort of negligence?   **(Solution: 12.1)**

(3)   What do you understand by the notional duty of care?   **(Solution: 12.2.1)**

(4)   What is the 'neighbour' principle?   **(Solution: 12.2.1)**

(5)   What is the significance of policy in determination of the existence of a duty of care?   **(Solution: 12.2.1)**

(6)   Illustrate by reference to case law the 'factual duty' of care.   **(Solution: 12.2.2)**

(7)   Explain the concept of the reasonable man.   **(Solution: 12.3.1)**

(8)   Explain the operation of the maxim *imperitia culpae adnumeratur*.   **(Solution: 12.3.2)**

(9)   What factors have the courts taken into account in determining whether or not there has been a breach of the duty of care?   **(Solution: 12.3.2)**

(10)   What do you understand by the maxim *res ipsa loquitur*?   **(Solution: 12.4.2)**

(11)   What criteria must be satisfied for the maxim *res ipsa loquitur* to apply?   **(Solution: 12.4.2)**

(12)   Examine the signficance of damages in the tort of negligence.   **(Solution: 12.5.1)**

(13)   Illustrate by reference to case law the concept of causation as applicable to damage in the tort of negligence.   **(Solution: 12.5.2)**

12.8   Conclusion

Now that you have completed this session you should have a clear understanding of the concept of negligence in tort; a working knowledge of the essentials of the tort of negligence; and a knowledge of the law regarding contributory negligence.

12.9   Questions

Objective test questions

(1)   The essentials of the tort of negligence are:

A   Duty and breach.
B   Duty, special relationship, breach and damage.
C   Duty, breach and damage.
D   Breach and damage.

(2)   *Imperitia culpae adnumeratur* means:

A   The facts speak for themselves.
B   Lack of skill is counted as a fault.
C   No injury is done to one who consents.
D   Buyer beware.

(3)   X is a pedestrian who negligently walks into the path of a car driven carelessly along the road by Y. X claims damages for injuries sustained to the extent of £6,000 from Y. The court finds that X was one third to blame for the accident. The effect of this is that:

    A   That X's claim will fail.
    B   X will be awarded £2,000 damages.
    C   X will be awarded £6,000 damages.
    D   X will be awarded £4,000 damages.

(4)   Which of the following is not a criterion for the application of the maxim *res ipsa loquitur*?

    A   The thing or activity causing the harm must be wholly under the control of the defendant or his servants.

    B   The court need not infer the facts if they are known.

    C   The plaintiff must be able to prove that the defendant was negligent.

    D   The accident must be one which would not have happened if proper care had been taken.

Written test questions

12.1   Breach of duty of care

What factors will the court bear in mind in determining whether or not there has been a breach of the duty of care?

12.2   Accident

'There are many cases in which the accident speaks for itself, so that it is sufficient for the plaintiff to prove the accident and nothing more.' Discuss.

12.3   Contributory negligence

How has the Law Reform (Contributory Negligence) Act 1945 affected the law regarding contributory negligence?

SESSION 13

Specific forms of the tort of negligence: strict liability: breach of statutory duty

On concluding your study of this session you should have:

- a knowledge of the tort of negligence as it relates to liability for misstatements, dangerous goods, employment and dangerous premises;

- an understanding of the concept of strict liability and, in particular, that form of strict liability known as *Rylands v Fletcher*;

- an appreciation of liability in tort for breach of statutory duty.

13.1 Forms of the tort of negligence

13.1.1 Liability for negligent mis-statement

Liability for negligent mis-statement lies in ordinary negligence: it is not a separate tort. So the usual duty, breach and damage of the tort of negligence have to be proved. However, it was not until 1963 that liability for negligent mis-statement was first recognised.

Hedley Byrne and Company Limited v Heller and Partners Limited (1964)

Where monetary loss results from the defendant's negligent mis-statement rather than his acts, it was originally necessary to prove the existence of a contractual or fiduciary relationship in order to establish a duty of care and the same was true if the plaintiff received physical injuries as a result of the defendant's careless instructions. However, in *Hedley Byrne and Company Limited v Heller and Partners Limited (1964)* the House of Lords ruled that there would be liability in negligence, even if there were no contractual or fiduciary relationship between the parties, provided there was a special relationship between the parties creating a situation occasioning a duty to take care.

The facts in the *Hedley Byrne* case were that the appellants, advertising agents, were anxious to discover the creditworthiness of Easipower Limited, who had instructed the appellants to arrange substantial advertising contracts. Hedley Byrne asked their bank, the National Provincial, to make enquiries. The bank on two separate occasions made these enquiries of Hellers, a firm of merchant bankers, who were financing Easipower as well as being their bankers. The first enquiry was specifically stated by the bank to be 'without responsibility' on the part of Hellers, and the second enquiry, asking whether Easipower was 'trustworthy, in the way of business, to the extent of

13.1

£100,000 per annum' was answered by Hellers stating 'without responsibility on the part of the bank or its officials', that Easipower was a 'respectably constituted company, considered good for its ordinary business engagements. Your figures are larger than we are accustomed to see'. This reference was passed on to Hedley Byrne, who relied upon it, and suffered loss to the extent of £17,000 when, as del credere agents, they had to pay the sums due on advertising contracts when Easipower went into liquidation.

The House of Lords did not decide whether Hellers had been negligent for they held that the disclaimers were sufficient to negative any duty of care which might have existed on the assumption that there was a special relationship between the parties. 'I consider', said Lord Morris, 'that it follows and that it should not be regarded as settled that if someone possessed of a special skill undertakes, quite irrespective of contract, to apply that skill for the assistance of another person who relies on such skill, a duty of care will arise . . . Furthermore, if, in a sphere in which a person is so placed that others could reasonably rely on his judgement or his skill or on his ability to make careful enquiry, a person takes it on himself to give information or advice to, or allows his information or advice to be passed on to, another person who, as he knows of, or should know, will place reliance on it, then a duty of care will arise.'

Subsequent developments

It was initially thought that such liability could be placed only upon those who were in business to advise or had, or claimed, a special skill in a particular area, such as solicitors and accountants. However, this restriction was removed by the decision in *Esso Petroleum v Mardon (1976)*. In that case Mr Mardon was awarded damages for a negligent mis-statement by a senior sales representative of Esso in regard to the amount of petrol he could expect to sell per year from a petrol station which he was leasing from Esso.

Furthermore, in *J E B Fastners v Marks Bloom and Company (1981)* the law moved from a test of knowledge to a test of foresight and thereby increased the scope of potential liability for careless mis-statements. In that case the plaintiff bought the entire share capital of a company called B G Fastners in June 1975. He claimed to have relied on the audited accounts of the company for the year ended 31 October 1974 prepared by the defendants who were the company's auditors and a firm of chartered accountants. The plaintiff alleged that the accounts did not give a true and fair view of the state of the company although they were given an unqualified audit certificate and that in consequence the plaintiff suffered 'loss' because he had purchased a company which was not worth what it appeared from the accounts to be worth. It was held, that the auditors owed a duty of care to the plaintiff but judgement was given for the defendants, it being felt by the court that on the evidence the plaintiff would still have bought the company, even if the true position of the accounts had been known, for the real object of the purpose was to acquire the services of two directors of B G Fastners.

Another line of development evidenced by subsequent cases has been that the plaintiff need no longer have relied on the statement in order to ground an action. Thus, in *Ross v Caunters (1979)* a solicitor who had drafted a will for a testator failed to warn him that it should not be witnessed by the spouse of the beneficiary. The will was attested by the husband of the plaintiff who was a beneficiary and she lost her gift. It was held that the solicitor was liable in negligence to the plaintiff for economic loss. The solicitor's duty was not merely to the testator.

13.1.2   Liability in negligence for dangerous goods

The essential point to grasp about this head of liability is that the ordinary rules of negligence apply in the usual way. Indeed, we are concerned here with *Donoghue v Stevenson (1932)* in its 'purest' form.

The facts of the case were that the appellant's friend purchased a bottle of ginger beer from a retailer in Paisley and gave it to her. The respondents were the manufacturers of the ginger beer. The appellant consumed some of the ginger beer and her friend was replenishing the glass, when, according to the appellant, the decomposed remains of a snail came out of the bottle. The bottle was made of dark glass so that the snail could not be seen until most of the contents had been consumed. The appellant became ill and served a writ on the manufacturers claiming damages. The question before the House of Lords was whether the facts constituted a cause of action in negligence. It was held by a majority of three to two that they did. 'A manufacturer of products', said Lord Atkin, 'which he sells in such a form as to show that he intends them to reach the ultimate consumer in the form in which they left him with no reasonable possibility of intermediate examination and with knowledge that the absence of reasonable care in the preparation or putting up of the products will result in an injury to the consumer's life or property, owes a duty to the consumer to take reasonable care.'

Subsequent developments

The subsequent history of the *ratio decidendi* of *Donoghue v Stevenson* has been one of its gradual extension. It has been extended as follows:

(a)   *'A manufacturer'* - The defendant, who invariably in these cases seems to find himself in a res ipsa loquitur situation, includes not only the maker of the offending chattel, but also a fitter: *Malfroot v Noxal (1935)*; an erector: *Brown v Cotterill (1934)*; a cargo-loader: *Denny v Supplies and Transport Company (1950)*; and even a water board supplying unwholesome water: *Read v Croydon Corporation (1938)*.

(b)   *'Of products'* - This seems to embrace every article including underwear, gas, food and drink, hair-dye and lifts.

(c)   *'Ultimate consumer'* - This is construed very widely so as to include any user of the product, like the sweet-shop keeper injured by a metal chip protruding from a sweet in *Barnett v Packer (1940)*, and anyone else within the foreseeable 'area of risk', like a bystander hit by a defective lorry wheel: *Stennett v Hancock (1939)* or the girl hit by the gravestone in *Brown v Cotterill (1934)*.

(d)   *'Which he (the defendant) sells'* - Almost any type of transfer may suffice.

(e)   *'With no reasonable possibility of examination'* - It should be noted that:

(i)   the plaintiff's full appreciation of the danger may exclude the defendant's liability. Thus, in *Farr v Butters Brothers and Company (1932)* the defendant crane makers sent out a crane in parts to be assembled by the buyers. An experienced foreman realised it was defective, but assembled and worked it and was killed. The defendant was held not liable;

(ii)   a warning, provided adequate in the circumstances, may absolve the defendant: *Kubach v Hollands (1937)*;

(iii)   there must now be a probability (not a mere possibility) of intermediate examination, and of a type likely to reveal the defect, if the defendant is to be absolved.

(f)   *'The preparation or putting up of the products'* - The duty to exercise reasonable care extends to packaging, labelling, any necessary instructions, etc.

(g)   *'Injury to the consumer's life or property'* - Injuries covered are the usual ones of person, property and consequential financial loss within the normal remoteness rules.

(h)   *'Duty to take that reasonable care'* - As always, the legal burden of proof is on the plaintiff, even though the defendant frequently finds himself in a res ipsa loquitur situation and thus having to discharge an evidential burden. Naturally, the defendant is liable only for failing to take reasonable care: he does not have to ensure that the goods are perfect.

Consumer Protection Act 1987

The Consumer Protection Act 1987 introduced into English law strict liability for damage caused by defective products. The Act supplements rather than replaces existing liability rules. It covers cases of personal injury and death, as well as some areas of property damage. However, damage to the item of which it forms a component is excluded. In this case the Sale of Goods Act remedy has to be used.

Strict liability can be imposed on a number of parties to the production process: the manufacturer, the person who won or abstracted the item or who processed it, a person who by his presentation of the item holds himself out as the producer, the person who imported it into the EEC and a supplier who fails to identify the producer when requested to do so. An item is defined as defective if its safety 'is not such as persons generally are entitled to expect'. The safety of the item is judged at the time that the item is placed on the market. The definition of safety recognises the fact that many everyday products are unsafe if abused. It takes into account the marketing and packaging of the item, the use reasonably to be expected of it, and the time at which it was supplied. It is specifically stated that the fact that products marketed at a later date were safer, does not raise an inference that earlier examples were unsafe.

The Act provides a number of defences to this liability: in particular, contributory negligence and the so-called 'state of the art' defence. Under this latter there will be no strict liability if the state of scientific and technical knowledge at the time when the item was put into circulation, was not such as to enable the existence of the defect to be discerned. Other defences are non-supply, compliance with statutory requirements and, in the case of component suppliers, the fact that the defect was due to the person who incorporated the component in another one. It is impossible to remove the statutory liability by use of an exclusion clause.

13.1.3   Liability in negligence of a master to his servants

Apart from contract, liability in ordinary torts and under various statutes, masters owe their servants a common law duty of care, in the *Donoghue v Stevenson* sense.

The duty

The leading case is the House of Lords decision in *Wilsons and Clyde Coal Company v English (1938)* in which it was held that the master must use reasonable care and skill for the safety of the servant. For convenience the duty may be divided into three aspects:

(a)   The duty to provide reasonably competent supervision and workmates.
(b)   The duty to provide proper premises, plant and materials.
(c)   The duty to furnish a safe system of work.

The duty is personal and non-delegable by the master. If the master does delegate the duty, he himself remains responsible.

(a)   *Competent staff* - This facet of the duty is no longer so important since the abolition in 1948 of the doctrine of 'common employment' by which a servant was understood to have agreed to bear the risks arising from the negligence of fellow servants for the purpose of vicarious actions. An example of the obligation is to be found in *Hudson v Ridge Manufacturing (1957)* where the servant had a four-year record of tomfoolery at work. The plaintiff, a cripple, was injured by one of the servant's antics and was held entitled to succeed against the master.

(b)   *Safe premises and equipment* - The employer must take reasonable care to provide safe plant, machinery and premises. Thus, an employer was held liable for sending an employee on a long journey in an unheated van in cold weather whereby the employee suffered frostbite: *Bradford v Robinson Rentals Limited (1967)*. In another case, an employee slipped on a 'duck-board' which was in a slippery condition, and was injured. Although at the time she was seeking to wash a cup for her own purposes her employer was held liable. The obligation to provide safe plant, etc, extends to cover all acts which are normally and reasonably incidental to a day's work: *Davidson v Handley Page Limited (1945)*.

Where an employee suffers an injury in the course of his employment because of a defect in equipment provided by his employer for the purposes of the business, and the defect is attributable wholly or in part to the fault of a third party, the injury is also deemed to be attributable to the employer's negligence: Employer's Liability (Defective Equipment) Act 1969. Thus, the employee may sue his employer rather than pursuing the manufacturer or supplier; the employer may then seek a contribution from the third party.

(c)   *Safe system* - In *Wilson's Case (1948)* it was held to be an unsafe system to place dangerous cutting machinery in a narrow mine passage through which men had frequently to pass. Likewise in *Bux v Slough (1973)* the defendant was liable for breach of duty to provide a 'safe system' in that goggles had been supplied to the plaintiff, a Pakistani with limited English, working with molten metal (some of which splashed into his eye), but steps had not been taken to persuade him to wear them. However, the plaintiff's damages were reduced by 40% owing to his contributory negligence.

13.1.4   Liability in negligence for dangerous premises

The liability of occupiers of premises to persons suffering injury thereon may be regarded as a further aspect of negligence.

The Occupiers' Liability Act 1957

Before 1957 the law on the liability of an occupier to a person coming on to his premises depended on the category in which the entrant fell and, in particular, whether he was an invitee or a licensee. The common law rules attaching to each type were complicated, and as a consequence the Occupiers' Liability Act 1957 was passed. The Act abolished the distinctions between the categories and the varied duties of care applicable to each. The Act now establishes one category of persons, namely, that of visitor, and provides that the occupier of premises owes a common duty of care to all his visitors.

(a)   *'Occupier'* - The term occupier includes anyone with physical control of the premises. There may be more than one occupier of the same premises at the same time.

(b)   *'Premises'* - They include land and buildings and any fixed or moveable structure, including any vessel, vehicle or aircraft.

(c)   *'Common duty of care'* - This is the duty to take such care as in all the circumstances of the case is reasonable to see that the visitor will be reasonably safe in using the premises for the purposes for which he is invited or permitted by the occupier to be there. The circumstances relevant for the present purpose include the degree of care and want of care, which would ordinarily be looked for in such a visitor. For example:

    (i)   an occupier must be prepared for children to be less careful than adults; and

    (ii)   an occupier may expect that a person, in the exercise of his calling, will appreciate and guard against any special risks ordinarily incident to it, so far as the occupier leaves him free to do so.

(d)   *'Visitors'* - Visitors are those who at common law would have been entrants under a contract, invitees or licensees; and those such as policemen, postmen, etc, who enter 'as of right' whether they are given permission by the occupier or not. In determining whether the occupier of premises has discharged the common duty of care to a visitor, regard is to be had to all the circumstances. For example:

    (i)   where damage is caused to a visitor by a danger of which he had been warned by the occupier, the warning is not to be treated as absolving the occupier from liability, unless in all the circumstances it was enough to enable the visitor to be reasonably safe; and

    (ii)   where damage is caused to a visitor by a danger due to the faulty execution of any work of construction, maintenance, or repair by an independent contractor employed by the occupier, the occupier is not to be treated as answerable for the danger if in all the circumstances he has acted reasonably in entrusting the work to an independent contractor and has taken such steps (if any) as he reasonably ought in order to satisfy himself that the contractor was competent and that the work had been properly done.

The Occupiers' Liability Act 1984

The liability of occupiers to trespassers is now governed by the Occupiers' Liability Act 1984, S1 of which replaces the rules of the common law governing the duty of an occupier of premises to 'persons other than visitors'. Such persons include not only trespassers but also those who enter under rights of way and were not visitors within the meaning of the Act of 1957. An occupier owes a duty to such persons if:

(a)   he is aware of the danger or has reasonable grounds to believe that it exists;

(b)   he knows or has reasonable grounds to believe that the other is in the vicinity of the danger concerned or that he may come into the vicinity of the danger (in either case, whether the other has lawful authority for being in that vicinity or not); and

(c)   the risk is one against which, in all the circumstances of the case, he may reasonably be expected to offer the other some protection.

Where the duty arises the occupier must take such care as is reasonable in all the circumstances of the case to see that the person to whom the duty is owed does not suffer injury on the premises by reason of the danger concerned. The risk in respect of which the duty is owed is the risk of the non-visitor suffering injury on the premises '. . . by reason of any danger due to the state of the premises or to things done or omitted to be done on them'. The occupier incurs no liability under the Act in respect of any loss of or damage to property. The duty may be discharged by giving a warning of the danger; and the defence of *volenti* is available in respect of any action.

13.2   Strict liability

13.2.1   Nature

As stated in the session on tortious liability there are certain forms of tortious liability in which the liability is strict, that is, in which a person may be liable even though he has been in no way at fault. However, even where liability is strict the defendant has certain defences open to him.

13.2.2   The rule in Rylands v Fletcher

The celebrated case of *Rylands v Fletcher (1868)* is the leading authority for the liability for breach of duty to prevent damage from dangerous things and animals. It is one of the most important cases of strict liability recognised by English law, and is examined here as an example of that concept.

The rule may be formulated thus:

> The occupier of land who brings and keeps on it anything likely to do damage if it escapes is bound at his peril to prevent its escape, and is liable for all the direct consequences of its escape, even if he has been guilty of no negligence.

The facts of the case were that the defendants constructed a reservoir upon their land, in order to supply water to their mill, and upon the site chosen for this purpose there was a disused and filled-up shaft of an old coal mine, the passages of which communicated with the plaintiff's adjoining mine. Through the negligence of the contractors by whom the work was done this fact was not discovered, and the danger caused by it was not guarded against. When the reservoir was filled the water escaped down the shaft and thence into the plaintiff's mine, which it flooded. It was not immediately obvious what cause of action was available, but in the judgement of the Exchequer Chamber delivered by Blackburn J the defendants were held liable and the House of Lords dismissed their appeal. Blackburn J said:

> 'We think that the true rule of law is that the person who for his own purposes brings on his lands and collects and keeps there anything likely to do mischief if it escapes, must keep it in at his peril, and if he does not do so is prima facie answerable for all the damage which is the natural consequence of its escape. He can excuse himself by showing that the escape was owing to the plaintiff's default; or, perhaps, that the escape was the consequence of vis major or the act of God; but as nothing of the sort exists here, it is unnecessary to enquire what excuse would be sufficient'.

This was approved by Lord Cairns LC who added that in his opinion liability under the rule should be limited to a non-natural user of the land. Non-natural user is a vague expression as will appear from a consideration of the cases mentioned below.

Scope of the rule in Rylands v Fletcher

(a)   *Things within the rule* - Instances of things within the rule are: electricity: *National Telephone Company v Baker (1893)*; yew trees: *Crowhurst v Amersham Burial Board (1878)*; wire fencing: *Firth v Bowling Iron Company (1878)*; explosives: *Rainham Chemical Works v Belvedere Fish Guano Company (1921)*.

(b)   *Escape* - In order for the rule to apply, there must be an escape of the thing which inflicts the injury from a place over which the defendant has occupation or control to a place which is outside his occupation or control: *Read v J Lyons and Company Limited (1947)*.

(c)   *Brought on the land* - This means for the purposes of the defendant and not necessarily financial purposes.

(d)   *Land or plaintiff must be interfered with* - It is by no means clear that the rule is limited to interference with the use of land though if the plaintiff has no interest in any land he cannot recover for financial loss due to an escape: *Weller v Foot and Mouth Disease Research Institute (1965)*.

(e)   *Non-natural user* - The rule does not apply to the land itself, or to things which are the product of natural forces operating in geological time: *Pontardawe R D Company v Moore-Gwynn (1929)*. It applies only to things which are brought and kept upon the defendant's land and does not apply to things which are naturally there, however dangerous they may be: *Giles v Walker (1890)*.

(f)   *Damage must be proved* - Damaged must be proved as the tort is not actionable *per se*.

Exceptions to the rule in Rylands v Fletcher

(a)   *Statutory authority* - Statutory authority may exempt a public utility corporation but the terms of the statute must be clear: *Green v Chelsea Waterworks Company (1894)*.

(b)   *Act of God* - Extraordinary rainfall that could not reasonably have been anticipated caused artificial pools to overflow: *Nichols v Marsland (1876)*, but meritable accident would be no defence, as the liability is strict.

(c)   *Consent of the plaintiff* - In *Attorney-General v Cory Bros (1921)* the consent of the plaintiff constituted a defence in respect of the soil dumped by the defendant.

(d)   *Default of the plaintiff* - The rule is not applicable where the escape arose as a result of the plaintiff's conduct.

(e)   *The act of a stranger* - The defendant will not be liable if the escape occurred as a result of the act of a stranger, unless the act of the stranger was due to the defendant's negligence. Thus, in *Box v Jubb (1878)* the defence succeeded as the overflow of the reservoir concerned was caused by a third party, but in *Shiffman's Case (1936)* it failed as the action of the mischievous boys who cut the guy ropes of the flag-pole was foreseeable.

13.3 Breach of statutory duty

13.3.1 Nature

A plaintiff may have a right of action in tort as the result of a breach of duty imposed by a statute. Whether or not such a right exists depends upon the construction of the particular statute. Such liability if it exists is strict; for if the statute grants to the plaintiff a remedy, the plaintiff is entitled to it irrespective of whether the defendant's breach was intentional or negligent, notwithstanding that many statutes allow a remedy only if the defendant has been careless.

13.3.2 Factors to be established by the plaintiff

In order to establish an action for breach of statutory duty the plaintiff must prove:

(a)   *that he was owed a duty under the statute.* Essentially the plaintiff must establish that he is within the class of person protected by the statute and that a civil action for damages will lie under the statute in the event of a breach of its provisions;

(b)   *that the defendant was in breach of his statutory duty.* This clearly depends on the circumstances of each case. Thus, for example, in *Longhurst v Guildford Water Board (1963)* there was no liability under the Factories Act 1961 because the defendant's premises where the plaintiff was injured were not within the definition in the Act of a 'factory';

(c)   *the breach of duty must have caused the damage suffered.* The plaintiff must prove legal casual connection between the breach and his injury;

(d)   *that the injury was of a type which the statute was intended to guard against.* Thus, in *Gorris v Scott (1874)* statute required pens for cattle on a ship, to prevent spread of a sheep disease called murrain. The plaintiff's sheep were swept overboard due to the absence of pens, and he failed to recover.

13.4 Revision exercise

To assess your knowledge of the above, attempt the following questions. Check your answers against the references given.

(1)   What was the significance of the decision in Hedley Byrne?   **(Solution: 13.1.1)**

(b)   Explain the term 'special relationship'.   **(Solution: 13.1.1)**

(3)   How has the liability recognised in Hedley Byrne been extended by subsequent decisions?

(Solution: 13.1.1)

(4)   What was the *ratio decidendi* of *Donoghue v Stevenson (1932)*?   **(Solution: 13.1.2)**

(5)   Who constitutes 'a manufacturer' for the purposes of liability under *Donoghue v Stevenson (1932)*?   **(Solution: 13.1.2)**

(6)   Outline the main provisions of the Consumer Protection Act 1987.   **(Solution: 13.1.2)**

(7)   In what sense is an employer's liability under *Wilson's Case (1938)* personal?   **(Solution: 13.1.3)**

(8)   Examine the employer's obligation to provide safe premises and equipment.   **(Solution: 13.1.3)**

(9)   What do you understand by a 'safe system of work'?   **(Solution: 13.1.3)**

(10)   What is the nature of 'the common duty of care' owed under the Occupiers' Liability Act 1957?   **(Solution: 13.1.4)**

(11)   How may the obligation under the 1957 Act be discharged?   **(Solution: 13.1.4)**

(12)   Define the term 'visitor' for the purposes of the 1957 Occupiers' Liability Act.   **(Solution: 13.1.4)**

(13)   Outline the provisions of the Occupiers' Liability Act 1984.   **(Solution: 13.1.4)**

(14)   What is strict liability?   **(Solution: 13.2.1)**

(15)   Explain the rule in *Rylands v Fletcher*.   **(Solution: 13.2.2)**

(16)   What exceptions are there to the rule?   **(Solution: 13.2.2)**

(17)   What do you understand by breach of statutory duty?   **(Solution: 13.3.1)**

(18)   What must the plaintiff prove in order to establish liability for breach of statutory duty?   **(Solution: 13.3.1)**

13.5   Conclusion

Conscientious study of this session will have given you:

●   a thorough understanding of the law regarding liability for negligent mis-statement;

●   an appreciation of the liability in negligence of an employer to his employees;

●   a knowledge of the liability in tort for dangerous goods;

●   a practical knowledge of the statutory obligations of an occupier of premises;

●   an appreciation of the concept of strict liability especially as evidenced in the rule in *Rylands v Fletcher*;

●   a knowledge of the factors that must be established to claim damages in tort for breach of statutory duty.

13.6 Questions

Objective test questions

(1) The decision in *Wilsons and Clyde Coal Company v English* established:

    A   Liability in negligence for misstatements.
    B   Liability in negligence of an occupier of premises.
    C   Liability in negligence of a master to his servants.
    D   The concept of contributory negligence.

(2) The common duty of care owed under the Occupiers' Liability Act 1957 is owed to:

    A   Invitees only.
    B   Invitees and licensees.
    C   Visitors.
    D   Trespassers.

(3) Jane buys a box of chocolates for a friend. Due to the manufacturer's negligence the friend becomes ill after eating the sweets. Whom may she claim against in tort?

    A   Jane.
    B   The shopkeeper who supplied the sweets.
    C   The manufacturer.
    D   All three.

(4) Which of the following is not a defence to liability in *Rylands v Fletcher*?

    A   Act of God.
    B   Default of the plaintiff.
    C   Reasonable care.
    D   Consent of the plaintiff.

Written test questions

13.1 Occupier liability

Explain the liability of the occupier of premises to persons who, whilst lawfully on such premises, suffer injury from defects therein.

13.2 Blunder

Blunder, a director of Rock Company, is leaving a company meeting with Madcap, the company's accountant. Making it clear to Madcap that he is seeking advice in his private capacity, Blunder asks Madcap his opinion of Bubble plc from the viewpoint of an investor. Madcap, without reasonable grounds for saying so, replies that investment in Bubble plc would be bound to bring a profit of at least 100% per annum to any investor. Relying on this advice, Blunder invests, and, almost immediately, upon the liquidation of Bubble plc, loses £10,000. News of this spreads so that Blunder's overdraft facilities are withdrawn and his resultant cash shortage compels him to sell other shares in a buyer's market, at a further loss of £1,000.

Advise Blunder whether he may sue Madcap. Would it make any difference if Madcap had known that his advice was spurious?

13.3   An operation

P enters D's hospital for an operation, to be performed by a surgeon S, at a fee previously arranged by P and S. S instructs a nurse, N, employed by D, to inject P with an anaesthetic manufactured by M Company and purchased from a retail chemist, R, which proves to have been contaminated.

P who, as a result of the injection, is now partially paralysed, wishes to know whom he may sue and for what torts. Advise him.

SESSION 14

The contract of employment 1

The subject matter of this and the next session is the contract of employment. This particular session is concerned with the contract itself. Careful study of the session will provide you with:

- a practical knowledge of the law regarding the formation of the contract of employment;

- an understanding of the duties, express and implied, imposed upon the parties to such a contract and, in particular, their obligations relating to health and safety at work;

- an appreciation of employment protection rights.

14.1 Nature and formation of the contract of employment

14.1.1 Nature

It is necessary to understand at the outset that a contract of employment is only one of several types of working relationship. It is important to differentiate the contract of employment (sometimes referred to as a **contract of service**) from other contracts under which one person agrees to perform work for another. Many new statutory rights are conferred only on persons employed under contracts of employment. In addition, the doctrine of vicarious liability generally attaches liability to the employer of the negligent workman only if a contract of employment exists between them. Where a person agrees to perform work for another but does not agree to become the employee or servant of that other person his legal relationship is often described as a **contract for services**, the person who does the work being referred to as an independent contractor.

There are other categories of worker with special attributes. Examples are policemen, public office holders, civil servants (but not local authority employees), and company directors. The rules of employment law may not always be applied without modification in these cases. One example is seen in *Yates v Lancashire County Council (1975)*, in which a policeman claimed a redundancy payment under the Redundancy Payments Act 1965 (now part 6 of the Employment Protection (Consolidation) Act 1978). His claim failed on the ground that, as he was not an employee of the Council, the Act did not apply to him, the Tribunal finding that he was the holder of public office. Regarding civil servants, the accepted view is that their relationship with the Crown as their employer is basically contractual. The Crown retains the right to dismiss them at will, and while civil servants may now present claims for unfair dismissal, industrial tribunals are required to reject an application if the dismissal was for the purpose of national security.

From what has been said, clearly it is important to be able to identify a contract of service. Over the years the courts have indicated how this should be done. At different times the courts have attached special significance to certain factors. It was at one time believed that a person could only be held to have a contract of employment if the employer could control not only what was done but also how it was done. Thus in *Performing Rights Society v Mitchell & Booker (Palais de Danse) Limited (1924)*, it was held that the musicians in a dance band were employees of the dance hall owners because of the degree of control the owners could exercise over the band. The contract between the owners and the musicians provided that: the band would appear at other dance halls in London if required to do so by owners; the band was not to operate elsewhere; if one member became ill the owners reserved the right to choose a deputy; and the bandleader was to control the band subject to the directions of the owners. Also the band agreed to comply with the rules of the management. However, where the job involved great skill or natural ability it was difficult to apply the 'control' test. Accordingly the courts have been forced to adopt different criteria and the element of control is now merely one of several factors which the courts will consider in deciding whether a contract of employment exists. Recently, in *Ferguson v John Dawson & Partners (Contractors) Limited (1976)*, Lord Justice Lawton stated that there is no single test for deciding whether a man is a servant of another (ie, has a contract of employment). Control of working is one factor; the intention of the parties must also be considered. Other factors include:

(a)   method of payment;

(b)   whether income tax and social security contributions are deducted from wages;

(c)   whether the person and the work he does are integrated into the other's organisation or merely ancillary to it;

(d)   whether the person doing the job benefits from his own management;

(e)   which party provides tools and equipment.

This is not an exhaustive list; new factors which might be of vital importance are continually arising. Thus in *Massey v Crown Life Insurance Co (1977)*, the Court of Appeal stated that in a case of doubt the 'label' given to a particular relationship might be the deciding factor.

The solution is to be found by weighing up the factors of each case. No one factor is decisive, although in one set of circumstances one factor may receive more weight than it would in others.

14.1.2   Sources

The contract of employment normally derives from several different sources, some express, some implied. Examples of these sources are:

(a)   an agreement between the parties;

(b)   an agreement between unions and employers which the parties agree to operate;

(c)   a term being implied from common law;

(d)   the custom of a trade;

(e)   a statutory provision which requires the parties to the contract to observe a certain term. (For example, the Employment Protection (Consolidation) Act 1978 provides for employees who are laid off to get guarantee payments.)

14.1.3   Formation

Generally, a contract of employment may come into existence without any legal formalities. It follows that a contract of employment may be created by written agreement, by oral agreement, or by actual service. However, there are exceptions to this general rule. The Merchant Shipping Act 1970 requires that the crew of British merchant vessels enter into a written agreement with employers. The practical effect of the Companies Acts 1985-1989 is that a company director's service agreement must be in writing, and that a copy of each such agreement must be kept at the company's registered office.

The present trend is for contracts of employment to be in writing, as a result of the provisions of the Contracts of Employment Act 1963, which are now contained in the Employment Protection (Consolidation) Act 1978.

14.1.4   Provisions of the Employment Protection (Consolidation) Act 1978

By S1 of the Employment Protection (Consolidation) Act 1978 an employer must give employees covered by the Act, within **thirteen weeks of the beginning of the period of employment**, a written statement which:

(a)   Identifies the parties.

(b)   Gives the date when the period of continuous employment began, and where employment with a previous employer counts as part of the employee's period of continuous employment the date when the previous employment began. If the contract is for a fixed term the statement has to give the date of expiry.

(c)   Gives particulars of the following terms of employment:

    (i)   the scale or rate of pay and payment intervals;
    (ii)   hours of work;
    (iii)   holidays, holiday pay and entitlement to accrued holiday pay;
    (iv)   sick pay/leave provisions;
    (v)   pensions and pension schemes;
    (vi)   notice required for termination by employer and employee;
    (vii) job title (**not** job description).

If no particulars exist regarding one or more of these matters that fact shall be stated.

The statement must also include a note of any disciplinary rules and specify the person who will deal with the employee's grievances generally and disciplinary grievances in particular, together with the details of the procedure and subsequent steps in reviewing any grievances.

The employer is entitled to refer the employee to any reasonably accessible document, such as a national collective agreement or a company handbook, for information as to disciplinary rules, grievance procedures and the terms of employment. Employees must be informed of any changes in the terms set out in the written statement or the document referred to, within one month of the change becoming effective.

The written statement is a unilateral declaration by the employer. Of itself it is not a contract, but it is usually accepted as a true reflection of the terms of the contract and is frequently issued in the form of an offer of employment on the terms stated. If the employee signifies his agreement by signing the statement this may convert it into a binding contract.

If the employer fails to provide a written statement the employee may complain to an industrial tribunal. The tribunal may issue a determination of the terms which ought to have been included in the written statement. This is the only remedy available where an employer has failed to provide a written statement. Frequently a complaint of this nature is joined with, for example, a complaint of unfair dismissal or redundancy, in which case the powers of the tribunal will include an award of compensation.

Under the Act, written statements must be provided for all employees who normally work at least sixteen hours per week for thirteen weeks. However, if:

(a)   an existing employee changes from working 16 hours or more a week to working eight hours or more, or

(b)   an employee has been working eight hours or more for five years,

he is to be treated as one who normally works for sixteen hours per week.

14.2   The employer's duties

14.2.1   Payment of wages

The payment of wages is sometimes described as the employer's primary duty - in that a failure to pay on the part of the employer will be regarded as breach of a fundamental term of the contract, entitling the employee to leave immediately. In *Duckworth v Farnish Limited* (1969), D was loaned to another employer by Farnish Limited. When, a short time later, D was informed by Farnish Limited that he would have to look to his new employer for his wages the Court held that this was a fundamental breach of contract by them.

The Wages Act 1986

This Act provides that deductions from an employee's pay are unlawful unless:

(a)   authorised by statute, eg, income tax, national insurance contributions, or under the Attachment of Earnings Act 1977;

(b)   agreed in the contract of employment; or

(c)   agreed in advance by the employee in writing.

Further, employers of workers in retail employment must not deduct or demand more than one-tenth of the gross pay due to them on any given pay day to make up for stock or cash shortages.

Complaints of unauthorised deductions can be made only to an industrial tribunal, and must if reasonably practicable be made within three months of the last deduction by or payment to the employer. Contract terms limiting employees' rights under the Act are void.

Provision of an itemised pay statement

By the Employment Protection (Consolidation) Act 1978 every employee is entitled to an itemised pay statement containing the following details:

(a)   gross pay;

(b)   variable and fixed deductions and their purposes;

(c)   net pay;

(d)   where different parts of net wages are paid in different ways, the amount and method of payment of each part.

By S9 of the Act an employer may reduce the detail given for fixed deductions, if he has previously given the employee written details of such deductions. If any employer fails to observe these provisions an industrial tribunal may require him to pay an employee the aggregate of unnotified deductions over thirteen weeks prior to the application to tribunal.

Payment during sickness

Where a contract of employment is silent regarding wages during the employee's absence through sickness, the employer remains liable to continue paying wages so long as the contract is not ended by giving proper notice.

Other duties regarding wages

(a)   *Wages Councils Act 1979* (as amended by the Wages Act 1986) - Wages councils have been set up in many industries where unionisation is weak. Where a wages council has been set up for an industry, employers in that industry are required to observe the wage rates and other conditions promulgated by the council.

(b)   *The Equal Pay Act 1970, as amended by the Sex Discrimination Act 1975* - This Act implies a term into women's contracts of employment which requires equal treatment in terms of pay, holidays, sick pay and hours of work.

14.2.2   Employer's duty to indemnify employee

It is implied in every contract of employment (unless the contrary is expressly stated) that the employee who incurs expense on his employer's behalf is entitled to be indemnified. The expense or payment must have been made in the course of the employee's duties.

14.2.3   Employer's duty to provide work

It is sometimes said that an employer is under a duty not just to pay wages but also to provide work. The accepted view is that an employer will not be failing in his contractual duties by not providing work, provided he continues paying wages except:

(a)   in the case of piece-worker who requires to be given work to earn wages;

(b)   in the case of public performers who require the opportunity of work to maintain and enhance their reputation;

(c)   where failure to provide work extends over such a length of time as to indicate a deliberate intention not to carry out the contract.

Also an employer who agrees to employ an employee for '40 hours per week' is required to pay the employee for 40 hours whether work is available or not. The employer has no right unilaterally to reduce the working week.

14.2.4   Safety

It is the duty of every employer at common law to take reasonable care for the safety of his employees, and failure to do so will render the employer liable in damages to an injured employee or his dependants. Other duties regarding the health and safety of employees and others (non-employees) are laid down by statutes, eg, Factories Act 1961, Health & Safety at Work Act 1974. Some of these statutes or regulations made under them create specific duties for particular types of work. Health and safety at work as regulated by statute is examined in detail below.

Additionally, the employer must provide a safe system of work. This may involve the selection of competent staff and proper supervision, the provision of safe premises, plant and materials, and the merger of all these factors into a system which ensures that the work may, with reasonable care, be executed in safety. The standard is one of reasonable care. In assessing reasonableness the following factors may be relevant:

(a)   foreseeability of risk of injury;

(b)   the nature of the risk and the probable consequences of a breach of this duty by the employer;

(c)   the known characteristics of the employee;

(d)   the cost of prevention; this must be weighed according to what is practicable in the circumstances.

Where the work is simple and straightforward the employer need not promulgate a system; he may rely on the employee's skill and discretion in approaching the job. The employer's duty to provide safe working conditions extends to employees working on premises belonging to a third party.

In addition to a civil action for damages brought by an employee, an employer may lay himself open to criminal proceedings if he fails to take reasonable care. The Health and Safety Executive set up under the Health and Safety at Work Act etc 1974 may initiate such a prosecution.

In *Davie v New Merton Board Mills (1959)*, the court decided that an employer properly performs this aspect of his duty of care owed to employees if he obtains his supplies from reputable suppliers because the employees could not be expected to carry out tests which might show up latent defects. This had the effect of requiring the employee injured by unsafe plant, etc, to sue its manufacturer or supplier or lose his remedy completely. To combat this problem for employees the Employer's Liability (Defective Equipment) Act 1969 provides that where an employee sustains a personal injury while acting in the course of his employment as a result of a defect in equipment provided by his employer and the defect is due to the fault or negligence of a third party (usually the manufacturer) the injury should be deemed to be also due to the fault of the employer. This statutory provision allows the employee to sue his employer, who may in turn sue the third party if he wishes.

In *Latimer v AEC Limited (1953)*, the factory in which L worked was flooded by unusually heavy rainfall. The flood water mixed with greasy substances in ducts running along the passageways, and when it subsided left a slippery film of grease over the floors and passageways. The employers dealt with the problem by detailing a squad of forty men to spread several tons of sawdust over the areas affected. L slipped on a part of the floor which had not been covered because the supply of sawdust ran out. The court held that AEC had not failed in their duty to provide safe premises. They had taken reasonable steps to protect their employees but they could not be expected to close down the factory pending cleaning of the floors.

The case of *Paris v Stepney Borough Council (1951)* illustrates the factor of the known characteristics of the employee. P was almost completely blind in one eye and this fact was known to the employers. A piece of metal entered P's good eye leaving him completely blind. The Court held that the employers had failed to take reasonable care for P's safety by providing goggles even though goggles were not usually provided for P's type of work.

In *Hudson v Ridge Manufacturing Limited (1957)*, H was tripped and injured by a fellow employee, who was known for his practical jokes and for which he had received numerous warnings from his employers. The court held that the employer had failed in his duty of reasonable care by not removing the source of danger: the practical joker, who was unable to respond to warnings.

The employer's right to rely on the skill and discretion of the employee is shown by the case of *Qualcast Limited v Haynes (1959)*. H, an experienced moulder, spilt molten metal on his foot. Protective footwear was available for those employees who wished to wear it. It was held that the employers had performed their duty of reasonable care, since H was an experienced moulder dealing with an obvious risk.

14.3 The employee's duties

There is an underlying duty of faithful service implied into every contract of service. This is frequently subdivided into separate duties. It is better to remember that there is an underlying duty of fidelity or loyalty but that it is sometimes manifested in different ways. Often, of course, contracts of employment will contain express provisions regarding the employee's duties and these may provide additional or supplementary obligations.

14.3.1 Duty of care

There is implied into every contract of employment a duty that the employee performs his contract with proper care. In *Lister v Romford Ice & Cold Storage Co Ltd (1957)*, the employee drove his employer's vehicle negligently and injured another. The employer's insurance company, which had to meet the claim brought by the injured employee, required the employers to exercise their right to sue the careless employee for his negligent driving. The court held that an employee owes a contractual duty of care to his employer and breach of that duty founds an action for damages.

14.3.2 Duty of cooperation

Even where the employer promulgates a rulebook containing instructions for the execution of the work the employee is under an obligation not to construe the rules in a way designed to defeat the efficiency of the employer's business. In *Secretary of State for Employment v ASLEF (No 2) (1972)*, railway workers worked strictly in accordance with British Rail's rulebook and caused considerable delays in the operation of trains. The court held that while the employees were free to withdraw their goodwill they must not wilfully obstruct the employer's business.

14.3.3   Duty of obedience

In the absence of express provisions an employee is required to carry out all reasonable and lawful orders of the employer. Some orders clearly do not require obedience:

(a)   An employee is not required to do anything illegal or immoral. Therefore an employee is entitled to refuse to:

       (i)   falsify sales records on employer's instructions;

       (ii)   drive an unroadworthy vehicle which may lead to his prosecution under the Road Traffic Acts.

(b)   An employee may not be ordered to work outside the scope of his contract except perhaps in an emergency.

(c)   An employee is not required to obey an order which requires acceptance of unforeseeable and unreasonable risk. In *Ottoman Bank v Chakarian (1930)*, the Court held that an employee who was under a death sentence imposed by the Turkish authorities was entitled to refuse to obey the employer's order to work in Turkey.

14.3.4   Mutual respect

It was at one time thought that an employee owed to his employer a duty of respect. The modern approach is that employers and employees owe each other mutual respect in their dealings. Thus it is a breach of contract for the employer to insult the employee by using foul and offensive language while addressing him. The employer's conduct may be so gross and insulting as to amount to a fundamental breach of the contract, entitling the employee to leave without notice.

14.3.5   Loyal service

This duty may be expressed, in general, as follows:

(a)   To use all reasonable steps to advance his employer's business within the sphere of his employment.

(b)   Not to do anything which might injure the employer's business. This may prevent a skilled employee from giving his assistance to a competitor despite the fact that such assistance is given by the employee in his own time and despite the fact that no confidential information has been disclosed. This duty of fidelity to a lesser extent continues even after the contract has been lawfully terminated. The ex-employee should not make use of or disclose any information imparted to him in confidence by his former employer.

14.4   Health and safety at work

14.4.1   Sources of health and safety law

An employer's duties regarding the health and safety of his workforce have the following sources:

(a)   Common law.

(b)   Particular statutes and regulations for particular industries or types of work (eg, Factories Act 1961, Woodworking Machines Regulations 1974).

(c)   The Health and Safety at Work, etc, Act 1974 which imposes on employers, employees and the self-employed certain general statutory duties regarding safety without the limits of, for example, the Factories Act 1961.

(d)   Codes of practice issued or approved by the Health and Safety Commission. These codes contain practical guidance for dealing with:

   (i)   the general duties imposed by the Health and Safety at Work Act;

   (ii)   the implementation of particular regulations made by the Secretary of State for Employment.

A failure to observe the provisions of a Code of Practice will not of itself render a person liable to legal proceedings but the failure may be taken into account by a court.

Many statutes and regulations have been passed to cope with particular risks. Perhaps the most well known is the Factories Act 1961 and the regulations made under it. Part 2 of the 1961 Act deals with safety and prescribes rules dealing with a variety of matters - from the fencing of machinery to means of escape in cases of fire. A failure to observe the provisions of the 1961 Act may lead to civil action for damages by an employee, or criminal prosecution by the Factory Inspectorate (now part of the Health and Safety Executive) of the offending employer, or to both.

14.4.2   The Health and Safety at Work, etc, Act 1974

The 1974 Health and Safety at Work, etc, Act does not deal with civil liability. That area of law is already dealt with by the common law duty of care and the creation of specific statutory duties. In many cases, the 1974 Act does little more than enshrine the common law duty in statutory form. For example, S2 of the Act declares that it shall be the 'duty of every employer to ensure, so far as is reasonably practicable, the health, safety and welfare of all his employees'. A failure to perform the statutory duties imposed by the 1974 Act may result in a prosecution which could lead to a fine or, in the case of a serious breach, imprisonment. The 1974 Act imposes certain general duties on employers either expressly or by virtue of the employer also being in control of premises.

Section 2 imposes on every employer the duty to ensure so far as is reasonably practicable, the health, safety and welfare of his employees and others. Detailed requirements are:

(a)   The provision of safe premises, plant and systems of work.

(b)   Arrangements for safety and absence of risks regarding handling or storage.

(c)   The provision of information, instruction and training to ensure the health and safety of employees.

(d)   The maintenance of the place of employment in a safe condition including safe access and egress.

(e)   The provision of a working environment for employees without risk to health and adequate facilities for welfare at work.

(f)   The preparation and revision of written safety policy and organisation for carrying out that policy.

(g)   Consultation with safety representatives to promote cooperation between employer and employees for developing and checking safety measures.

(h)   A duty on the employer to conduct his operation in such a way as to ensure so far as is reasonably practicable, that non-employees are not exposed to risks.

(i)   A duty on persons in control of non-domestic premises in respect of non-employees to whom the premises are made available that the premises and plant are, so far as is reasonably practicable, safe and without risk to health.

(j)   A duty on persons in control of premises emitting noxious substances to use the best practical means of preventing or rendering harmless the emission.

(k)   A duty on persons who design, import or supply articles for use at work to ensure so far as is reasonably practicable that:

   (i)   they are safe when used;
   (ii)   they are examined to ensure their safety;
   (iii)   information about use and conditions for safe use are supplied.

(l)   A duty on every employee while at work to:

   (i)   take reasonable care for others who might be affected by his actions;

   (ii)   cooperate with his employer and with others in the performance of statutory duties (of safety).

(m)   A duty on every person not to interfere with anything provided in the interests of safety.

(n)   A duty on an employer not to charge employees for anything provided in compliance with safety requirements.

Machinery of health and safety law

The main purpose of the Health and Safety at Work, etc, Act 1974 is to bring within the umbrella of the one organisation almost all the inspection and enforcement machinery for health and safety at work instead of having different bodies managed under different legislation dealing with the matter in a piecemeal fashion. While much of the previous legislation will remain, it is intended that it will be phased out after detailed and up-to-date regulations have been promulgated by the Health and Safety Commission. Eventually, health and safety at work will be the responsibility of the Health and Safety Commission, Executive and Inspectors.

The Health and Safety Commission

Generally the Commission is required to oversee the operation and implementation of the Act. This includes:

(a)   assistance and encouragement of the achievement of general health and safety objectives;
(b)   research and publication of information to help achieve those objectives;
(c)   provision of advice to employers, trade unions and government departments;
(d)   preparation of regulations for health and safety.

The Health and Safety Executive

The Executive is required to give effect to policy and directions of the Commission. The Executive is also specifically charged with the enforcement of the statutory provisions; for this the Executive will appoint inspectors.

Health and safety inspectors

Inspectors have the following powers:

(a)   To enter premises and require that they are left undisturbed to:

      (i)   examine and investigate as necessary;
      (ii)   take measurements and photographs;
      (iii)   take away samples;
      (iv)   remove or dismantle any dangerous substance or article.

(b)   To receive truthful answers to questions.

(c)   To take copies of books or documents.

(d)   To issue Improvement Notices and Prohibition Notices where any person (eg, an employer) is breaking the health and safety law in some way. The Notices may require an improvement in the safety arrangements, usually within a period of time or, in the event of a serious risk, may require that the articles, plant, process, etc, be prohibited in its use immediately. Appeals against Notices lie to industrial tribunals.

Health and safety representatives and committees

While the Health and Safety at Work Act contains criminal penalties and allows dangerous practices to be prohibited by inspectors, it is also a firm hope of the Act that the question of health and safety at work may become the subject of employer/trade union discussion and solution. In implementation of this, regulations (effective from October 1978) provide that a recognised trade union may appoint health and safety representatives from among the workforce. Their functions are:

(a)   to represent employees in consultations with the employer to promote health and safety;
(b)   to investigate potential hazards;
(c)   to investigate complaints by employees;
(d)   to make representations to the employer;
(e)   to carry out inspections of the workplace.

To facilitate the performance of these functions and training for them, the representative is entitled to paid time off. Employers are required to make available to these representatives information necessary to fulfil their functions. Where an employer is requested to do so by two representatives he must set up a safety committee within three months.

14.5   Employment protection rights

The Employment Protection (Consolidation) Act 1978 (as amended) gives protection for employees in connection with a wide variety of matters. Each of these matters is briefly examined in turn in the paragraphs which follow.

14.5.1 Maternity pay and leave

By the provisions of the Employment Protection (Consolidation) Act 1978 (as amended), women who qualify are given the following statutory rights:

(a)   the right not to be dismissed on grounds of pregnancy;
(b)   the right to maternity pay;
(c)   the right to return to work.

Right not to be dismissed on grounds of pregnancy

The Act declares that the dismissal of a woman because of pregnancy or a reason connected with pregnancy shall be unfair except where:

(a)   she has not been employed for a period of two years immediately prior to her dismissal; or

(b)   she is incapable of adequately doing her job; or

(c)   either she or her employer would be breaking the law by continuing her employment while pregnant.

However, even if one of the exceptions can be proved by the employer it will nevertheless be an unfair dismissal if the employer fails to offer a suitable available vacancy before terminating her original contract. It is a requirement that this new work should be available immediately on the ending of the original contract, suitable for the woman and not substantially less favourable to her.

In *George v Beecham Group (1976)*, G had a history of poor attendance. When allowed time off for a gynaecological operation G was warned that she would be dismissed if she was absent during the six months following her operation. Shortly after return to work G was absent due to a miscarriage and was dismissed. It was held that the dismissal was unfair since a miscarriage was a reason connected with pregnancy.

In *Brear v Wright Hudson Limited (1977)*, B was dismissed from her job in a small pharmacy when it was learned that she was pregnant. It was held to be fair because she was incapable of adequately doing her job which involved a considerable amount of carrying and lifting stock. There was no other vacancy.

The dismissal in *Martin v BSC Footwear (Supplies) Limited (1977)*, was held to be unfair because the employer could have offered employment in a less demanding job, which was usually done by another who was in hospital for an unknown length of time.

Right to maternity pay

Part V of the Social Security Act 1986 made major alterations to the maternity payment scheme. Prior to that Act a woman who qualified received maternity pay under the Employment Protection (Consolidation) Act 1978, Ss33-44 from which the State maternity allowance was deducted. Maternity pay was then recouped by the employer from the Maternity Pay Fund. The Social Security Act 1986 repeals Ss33-44 and the Maternity Pay Fund is wound up.

Under the Social Security Act of 1986 the old provisions are replaced by statutory maternity pay (SMP) payable through the employer who will recoup it from National Insurance contributions (on the model of the statutory sick pay scheme). To qualify the woman must have worked for her present employer for at least six months. If so, she will be entitled to a payment at the lowest rate of statutory sick pay for 18 weeks. Women who have been with the employer for two years or more will receive SMP of 90% of earnings for the first six weeks of the maternity leave.

However, women will be able to choose when to take their paid maternity leave. Thirteen weeks of the leave must be taken to cover the period of six weeks before the baby is due and the seven weeks after it is born, but women will be free to choose when to take the other five weeks.

Right to return to work

This is the right to return to the job done for her employer at the time when she stopped work due to pregnancy. The right normally has to be exercised within 29 weeks of the birth. The employee is entitled to return to work without any alteration in:

(a)   the capacity in which she had been employed;
(b)   the place employed;
(c)   seniority, pension and similar rights.

Only if the job previously done has become redundant is the employer permitted to offer 'alternative employment'. Both the employer and employee may postpone the resumption of work by up to four weeks, even if that extends the period of absence to more than 29 weeks after the birth. Where an employee is entitled to return to work but is refused by her employer, the period of absence will not interrupt the continuity of employment and she will be treated as having been dismissed by her employer.

In some cases the employer will have to take on someone to do the work of the employee on maternity leave. In this case it is provided that the dismissal of a temporary employee who receives on engagement, a written statement that his or her employment will be terminated to accommodate the return of the woman on maternity leave, will be for a substantial reason such as to justify his dismissal.

In order to qualify for the right to return to work the woman must have informed her employer in writing of her intention to return at the time she notified him that she was going to be absent to have a baby. Under the Employment Act 1980, where an employer requests in writing, not less than 49 days after the notified expected week of confinement, that written confirmation be given that she still intends to return to work and he accompanies the request with a written statement of the effect of this new requirement, she will lose her right to return if she does not reply within 14 days or as soon as reasonably practicable. It is irrelevant whether employer and employee regard her contract of employment as continuing to subsist during her period of absence.

In *McFadden v Greater Glasgow Passenger Executive (1977)*, after her maternity leave, Mrs M was placed in a different department from the one in which she was originally employed, and as a supernumerary whereas previously she was on permanent staff. It was held that she had not been allowed to return to the job she was originally employed to do on not less favourable terms. An employee who is not permitted to return to her job is deemed to have been dismissed. In this case the reason for not permitting her to return to her job was that a permanent replacement had been appointed. The dismissal was therefore unfair.

It should be noted that a woman's right is to return to the job previously held. Accordingly it does not entitle her to return to part-time employment on the same grading, etc, as when previously employed in a full-time capacity.

The Employment Act 1980 provides two cases where the right to return to work may be excluded:

(a)   where there are five or fewer employees and it is not reasonably practicable to reinstate or offer a suitable alternative;

(b)   if reinstatement would mean a redundancy and the employer does offer a suitable alternative.

The onus is on the employer to show that the exclusion of the right is justified.

Time off for ante-natal care

The 1980 Act provides that a woman is entitled to time off for ante-natal care and to receive the appropriate remuneration for such time off.

14.5.2   Medical suspension pay

Sections 19 to 22 and Schedule 1 of the Employment Protection (Consolidation) Act 1978 give an employee who is suspended from work by his employer on medical grounds the right to be paid for a maximum period of 26 weeks. However, the entitlement only arises if the continued employment of the employee is contrary to law or a provision of a code of practice issued under the Health and Safety at Work, etc, Act 1974. Further, the entitlement does not operate during any period for which:

(a)   the employer has offered to provide the employee with available alternative work and the employee has unreasonably refused to perform the work; or

(b)   the employee does not comply with reasonable requirements imposed by his employer with a view to ensuring that his services are available.

14.5.3   Guarantee payments

Sections 12 to 18 of the Employment Protection (Consolidation) Act 1978 give employees who are not provided with work for the whole of a day on which they would normally work for some time, a right to receive a guarantee payment. However, the non-provision of work must be due to: either a decrease in the employer's demand for the kind of work the employee does; or something which affects the part of the employer's business in which the employee works.

The qualifications for guarantee payments are:

(a)   four weeks' continuous employment before the week in which lay-off occurs;

(b)   the day of lay-off must be one on which the employee is normally required to work according to his contract of employment;

(c)   no work was provided for the whole of the day;

(d)   if the lay-off was caused by a trade dispute the employee loses the right to a guarantee payment **only** if the trade dispute involves an employee of the laying-off employer or an associated employer;

(e)   the employee must not unreasonably refuse suitable alternative employment;

(f)   the employee makes his services available to his employer.

The maximum daily rate for a guarantee payment is established and reviewed from time to time by statutory instrument. An employee may receive a guarantee payment only in respect of five days in any period of three months. The previous rule stipulating fixed three-month periods was amended by the Employment Act 1980.

In *Mailway (Southern) Limited v Willsher (1978)*, a casual worker was not entitled to a guarantee payment because she was not **required** to work under a contract of employment. She could take or leave the work when it was available.

In *Thompson v Priest (Lindley) Limited (1977)*, the following rule was laid down. Where various factors including a trade dispute cause a lay-off, it must be determined whether there would have been a lay-off but for the trade dispute. If the answer is no, the employee is not entitled to a guarantee payment.

In *Meadows v Faithful Overalls Limited (1977)*, an employee who walked out because the factory was too cold was not entitled to a guarantee payment because she had not ensured her services were available to the employer.

14.5.4   Time off

Section 29 of the Employment Protection (Consolidation) Act 1978 requires employers to permit employees reasonable unpaid time off for performing the duties of the following:

(a)   Justice of the Peace;

(b)   member of local authority;

(c)   member of statutory tribunal;

(d)   member of Health Board or Authority;

(e)   member of managing or governing body of educational establishment of local authority or (Scotland), a school or college council or governing body of a central institution or college of education;

(f)   member of water authority or river purification board.

For trade union duties

Section 27 of the Employment Protection (Consolidation) Act 1978 requires an employer to give to an official of an independent trade union recognised for collective bargaining reasonable paid time off for carrying out his duties concerned with industrial relations or training in aspects of industrial relations approved by the TUC. Duties connected with industrial action are not necessarily excluded.

For activities of trade union

Employers are required to permit employees reasonable time off without pay for activities of an independent trade union recognised by the employer. No time off need be given for activities which are themselves a form of industrial action.

To look for work

An employee dismissed on grounds of redundancy is entitled to time off with pay to look for work provided that he has at least two years' continuous employment.

For safety representatives

Safety representatives must be allowed such paid time off as is reasonable for performing safety functions or receiving training.

14.5.5 Employee's remedies

If an employer fails to recognise the rights given by the Employment Protection (Consolidation) Act 1978, the employee's remedy is through an application to an industrial tribunal. Depending on the nature of the complaint the tribunal may:

(a)   order the employer to make the payment (eg, in the case of non-payment of guarantee pay);

(b)   declare the rights of the parties (eg, in the case of failure to permit time off);

(c)   award compensation (eg, in the case of failure to allow time off). In the case of time off to find new work the maximum award is two fifths of a week's pay.

14.6   Revision exercise

In order to assess your knowledge of the above, attempt the following questions. Check your answers against the references given.

(1)   What is the difference between a contract of service and a contract for services?
(Solution: 14.1.1)

(2)   What factors determine whether a contract of employment exists?   **(Solution: 14.1.1)**

(3)   Give three sources of a contract of employment.   **(Solution: 14.1.2)**

(4)   What remedies are available to an employee who does not receive a written contract of employment?   **(Solution: 14.1.4)**

(5)   In what sense may the obligation of an employer to pay wages be described as his primary duty?   **(Solution: 14.2.1)**

(6)   What are the main provisions of the Wages Act 1986?   **(Solution: 14.2.1)**

(7)   In what circumstances may a manual worker be paid other than in coin of the realm?   **(Solution: 14.2.1)**

(8)   What is a wages council?   **(Solution: 14.2.1)**

(9)   Has an employer an obligation to provide his employees with work?   **(Solution: 14.2.3)**

(10)   Outline the common law obligations of an employer in respect of safety.
(Solution: 14.2.4)

(11)   What is the underlying duty of the employee in a contract of service?   **(Solution: 14.3)**

(12)   Give three exceptions to the duty of obedience owed by an employee.
(Solution: 14.3.3)

(13)   Can an employee work for a competitor in his spare time?   **(Solution: 14.3.5)**

(14)   What are the sources of health and safety law?   **(Solution: 14.4.1)**

(15)   Outline the general duties established by the Health and Safety at Work, etc, Act 1974.   **(Solution: 14.4.2)**

(16)   What machinery has been established to enforce the Health and Safety at Work, etc, Act 1974?   **(Solution: 14.4.2)**

(17)   Outline the statutory rights of a female employee regarding maternity pay and leave.   **(Solution: 14.5.1)**

(18)   Examine the law regarding guarantee payments.   **(Solution: 14.5.2)**

(19)   In what circumstances does statute provide employees with a right to time off?   **(Solution: 14.5.4)**

14.7   Conclusion

Careful study of this session should have given you:

●   a practical knowledge of the law regarding the formation of the contract of employment;

●   an understanding of the obligations of the parties to such a contract;

●   an appreciation of employment protection rights.

14.8   Questions

Objective test questions

(1)   Within how many weeks of the beginning of the period of employment must an employer provide his employee with written particulars of his employment?

    A   Three weeks.
    B   Fifteen weeks.
    C   Twelve weeks.
    D   Thirteen weeks.

(2)   Which of the following is not an obligation of an employer?

    A   To pay wages.
    B   To indemnify the employee.
    C   To provide a reference.
    D   To take reasonable care for the safety of his employees.

(3)   Which of the following statements regarding the obligations of an employee is incorrect?

    A   An employee must perform his contract with proper care.

    B   An employee must take all reasonable steps to advance his employer's business within the sphere of his employment.

    C   An employee must obey the instructions of his employer.

    D   An employee must not wilfully obstruct his employer's business.

(4)   The Employment Protection (Consolidation) Act 1978 provides that the dismissal of a woman because of pregnancy or a reason connected with pregnancy shall be unfair except, *inter alia*, she has not been employed for a period of:

    A   One year.
    B   Six months.
    C   Two years.
    D   Eighteen months.

(5)   Which of the following is not one of the qualifications for guarantee payments?

    A   Four weeks' continuous employment before the week in which the lay-off occurs.

    B   No work was provided for the whole of the day.

    C   The employee may not refuse alternative employment.

    D   The employee makes his services available to his employer.

Written test questions

14.1   **Martin**

What legal provisions exist to protect workers from injuries arising from the use of dangerous machinery?

Martin is employed by DS Mills Limited. One day during working hours he went to see his friend, Norman, who worked in another department of the company, about a private matter. Martin dropped a packet of cigarettes and, as he bent over to pick it up, his clothing became caught in the machinery. Martin was seriously injured as also was Norman who tried to pull him clear.

Advise DS Mills Limited.

14.2   **Employer's common law duties**

Outline the common law duties owed by an employer to his employee in the absence of any specific provisions in the contract of service.

14.3   **Hairdresser**

Your employer owns and operates a chain of hairdressing salons. Advise him of the legal position with regard to the actions of the following employees:

(a)   Michael, a hair stylist, is carrying out hairdressing in his spare time.

(b)   Marion, a hair stylist, asks for a reference for a new job for which she is applying.

(c)   Robert, the manager of one of the salons, has accepted a commission from a commercial salesman in return for recommending the use of a particular brand of shampoo to clients.

SESSION 15

The contract of employment 2

This session examines the ways in which the contract of employment may be terminated and the implications of its termination.

Careful study of this session will provide you with:

- a practical understanding of the law regarding termination of the contract of employment with particular reference to the statutory concept of unfair dismissal;

- an understanding of the law governing entitlement to statutory redundancy payments.

15.1 Termination of employment

15.1.1 Termination by notice

At common law the contract of employment may be terminated by either party for any reason or for no reason upon giving notice of a reasonable length, unless the contract is one for a fixed term or unless it specifically restricts the reason for which it may be terminated.

Proper notice may be either:

(a) what the contract provides;

(b) what is reasonable if there is no contractual term regarding notice;

(c) what is provided by the Employment Protection (Consolidation) Act 1978. A contractual term providing for notice shorter than is specified in the 1978 Act is void and therefore unenforceable.

The Employment Protection (Consolidation) Act 1978 lays down minimum periods of notice for both employer and employee. A contract of employment may not permit either side to give less than the minimum period of notice. However, either party may waive his right to notice or take a payment in lieu, and the Act does not affect the right to terminate a contract without notice in the event of gross misconduct.

The Act relates the employee's entitlement to notice to length of service according to the following table:

Periods of continuous service	Length of notice
More than four weeks but less than two years	One week
Between two years and twelve years	One week for each year of continuous service
Not less than twelve years	Not less than twelve weeks

Thus an employee with eighteen months of continuous service is entitled to one week's notice; an employee with ten years of continuous service should receive ten weeks' notice. The Act requires an employee who has four weeks' continuous service to give at least one week's notice. The employee's obligations are not related to length of service.

15.1.2   Summary termination

At common law either party may lawfully terminate the contract summarily, ie, without giving any notice, if the other party has committed a serious breach of the contract. Whether the breach is sufficiently serious to justify summary termination has to be answered in the context of each particular contract. Thus, in *Pepper v Webb (1969)* the plaintiff's offensive remark and conduct, taken against the background of his previous disobedience and insolence, was held to indicate clearly an intention to repudiate his contract of employment; though in contrast in *Wilson v Racher (1974)* an isolated instance of obscene language arising from the provocation of the employer was held not to justify the plaintiff's summary dismissal.

15.1.3   Remedies at common law

If an employer terminates a contract of employment contrary to, or in breach of contract, ie, without giving the appropriate period of notice or summarily but without justification such amounts to what is technically termed a wrongful dismissal. Only in very rare circumstances will the common law require the employer to reinstate a wrongly dismissed employee because the contract of employment is regarded as one of a very personal nature. The damages remedy at common law is also very limited, for even in the case of wrongful summary dismissal damages in respect of loss of earnings are limited to earnings during the period of notice required to terminate the contract, on the assumption that the employer would have given the employee proper notice to terminate the contract if he had not dismissed him summarily. Further, the common law has developed no general requirement that the employee be given a hearing before dismissal or the reason for his dismissal, whether the termination is by notice or otherwise. Finally, as already noted, a dismissal on due notice is generally lawful. To mitigate these defects in the common law Parliament has created the quite separate statutory concept of unfair dismissal with its own statutory remedies.

15.2   Unfair dismissal

By the Employment Protection (Consolidation) Act 1978, every employee who qualifies is given the right not to be unfairly dismissed by his employer.

15.2.1   Onus of proof

Three aspects of a case must be proved:

(a)   The **employee** must prove that he has been dismissed. (The employer could, in defence, try to show that the employee left of his own accord.)

(b)   If dismissal is proved (or admitted) then the **employer** must show what reason he had for dismissing. (The employee, at this stage, could try to show that the employer's real motive was not the one he has claimed.)

(c)   There are then four possibilities:

     (i)   If the reason is an inadmissible reason then the dismissal is automatically unfair.

     (ii)   If the reason is one which, on the face of it, is a substantial reason then the tribunal must decide whether the dismissal was fair or unfair in the circumstances (including the size and administrative resources of the employer's undertaking) and this must be determined in accordance with equity and the substantial merits of the case.

     (iii)   If the reason does not fall within the foregoing two categories (or if the employer cannot prove what his reason was) then the dismissal is unfair.

     (iv)   If, in some circumstances, an employee is dismissed for not being a member of an appropriate union where a closed shop operates then the dismissal is automatically fair.

Proof of dismissal

Dismissal is defined as including:

(a)   termination of the contract by the employer with or without notice;

(b)   expiry of a fixed term contract without renewal;

(c)   termination of the contract by the employee with or without notice in circumstances such that he is entitled to terminate it without notice by reason of the employer's conduct.

This last form of dismissal is called 'constructive dismissal'. Conduct which will entitle the employee to leave without notice is that which is a significant breach of contract going to the root of the contract of employment, or which shows that the employer no longer intends to be bound by one of the more essential terms of the contract. The decision by the Court of Appeal in *Western Excavating (ECC) Limited v Sharp (1978)*, is important in defining what conduct of the employer amounts to constructive dismissal. S, because of a period of suspension without pay, was in financial difficulties and asked his employer for an advance of accrued holiday pay. His request was refused. S left his employment to perfect his right to accrued holiday pay and claimed he had been constructively dismissed. The Court held unanimously that although the employer's refusal of his request for an advance of holiday pay might have been unreasonable it did not amount to a significant breach of contract going to the root of the employment relationship and this was necessary for constructive dismissal.

15.2.2   Reasons for dismissal

Substantial

The following are reasons for which a dismissal **may** be fair:

(a)   *The capability or qualification of the employee* for the job he is employed to do (see *Woods v Olympic Aluminium Company (1975)*, below).

(b)   *The conduct of the employee.* Whilst the misconduct need not take place in the course of employment it has to affect the employee when doing his work, or, at least, could be thought to do so (see *Grace v Harehills Club (1974)* and *Whitlow v Alkanet Construction Limited (1975),* below).

(c)   *Redundancy of the employee.* However, an employee unfairly **selected** for redundancy will be unfairly dismissed (see below).

(d)   *The employee could not continue in his job without either employee or employer breaking the law.* (For example, employee employed exclusively as driver being disqualified from driving by court.)

(e)   *Some other substantial reason* of a kind to justify the dismissal of the employee from the position held (see *Creffield v BBC (1974),* below).

(f)   *The fact that there is a closed shop and the employee has resigned from the relevant union* or, having been taken on for employment at a place where a closed shop operated has nevertheless refused to join the relevant union, unless he genuinely objects on grounds of conscience or other deeply held personal conviction to being a member of any trade union whatsoever or of a particular trade union.

However, by S60 of the 1978 Act, the dismissal of a woman for the reason that she is pregnant, or for any reason connected with her pregnancy, must be unfair unless:

(a)   at the effective date of termination of employment she is, or will have become, because of her pregnancy, incapable of adequately doing the work which she is employed to do; or

(b)   because of her pregnancy she cannot, or will not, be able to continue after that date to do that work without contravention (either by her or her employer) of a statutory duty or restriction.

But an employer can rely on these exceptions only if he has tried but failed to provide alternative work for the woman. He must prove either that there was no suitable vacancy or that he offered a suitable alternative but it was refused.

The question of the suitability of the employee's qualifications for the job he is employed to do is considered in the case of *Woods v Olympic Aluminium Company (1975).* An accountant who was dismissed for lack of management ability was held to have been unfairly dismissed because he was not employed as a manager but as an accountant.

The following two cases illustrate what may or may not be regarded as misconduct. In *Grace v Harehills Club (1974),* it was held unfair to dismiss a 40 year old divorced club steward who was living with a 17 year old girl in the club premises because the tribunal has not the right to judge the morality of the situation but to judge fairness in the industrial sense. The conduct of the steward had not had an adverse effect on the club at the time of dismissal.

However, in *Whitlow v Alkanet Construction Limited (1975),* Mr Whitlow, a carpenter, engaged in love-play and sexual intercourse with the wife of the chief executive of the company that employed him, having been asked to go to the chief executive's house to do some work. It was held that Mr Whitlow's dismissal without notice was fair: it was for a reason relating to his conduct as an employee and was reasonably treated as being a sufficient reason for dismissal.

An example of 'some other substantial reason of a kind such as to justify the dismissal of an employee holding the position which that employee held' is provided by the case of *Creffield v British Broadcasting Corporation (1974)*. The applicant was employed as a film cameraman. He was convicted of indecently assaulting a 13 year old girl and was dismissed because of this conviction. It was held that the conviction was a substantial reason justifying dismissal of an employee in his position because the BBC were apprehensive about him working on assignments which might involve working with young people.

Not only must the reason be one recognised by the Act, but the employer must also have acted fairly in treating it as sufficient to justify dismissal. In *Parkers Bakeries Limited v Palmer (1976)*, P was dismissed from his job as van salesman for discrepancies in deliveries to customers. Accordingly there was no doubt that the reason was related to his conduct. In deciding whether it justified dismissal the industrial tribunal must ask, what would reasonable employers have done on the facts which they knew or ought to have known in the circumstances of the case? While there was no positive admission of guilt in this case the employee had made something approaching a tacit one by offering to reimburse the company.

The fairness of the dismissal may depend on the procedures adopted and warnings given prior to dismissal. The Code of Practice on Disciplinary Practice and Procedures provides that:

(a)   employees should be informed of complaints and given the opportunity of stating their case;

(b)   employees have a right to be accompanied by a trade union representative or a fellow employee;

(c)   except for gross breach of discipline employees should not be dismissed for a first offence;

(d)   no action should be taken until the case has been fully investigated.

While warnings are usually necessary in the pre-dismissal procedure it may also be said that:

(a)   it is a question which depends on facts of each case;

(b)   in the case of incompetence the same need for prior warnings as in the case of misconduct does not always exist;

(c)   a case may show such irremediable incapacity that a warning would not be necessary;

(d)   even a gross failure to follow proper procedure may not, in certain circumstances, render the dismissal unfair.

Inadmissible

If dismissal is shown to be for any of the following reasons then it will automatically be deemed to be unfair:

(a)   that the employee was, or proposed to be, a member of an independent trade union;

(b)   that the employee had taken, or proposed to take part at any appropriate time in the activities of an independent trade union;

(c)   that the employee was not a member of any trade union, or (unless it is fair to enforce a closed shop, see below) was not a member of a particular trade union (or of one of a number of particular trades' unions), or had refused or proposed to refuse to become or remain a member;

(d)   that the employee had been convicted of an offence if the rehabilitation period for that conviction has expired (Rehabilitation of Offenders Act 1974, S4(3)(b)).

An 'independent' trade union is one that is not dominated or financed by the employer or by an association of employers.

15.2.3   Qualifications

Any employee may make a claim that a dismissal was unfair on the ground that it was for an inadmissible reason.

If an employee is dismissed for a reason other than an inadmissible reason then he may make a claim that the dismissal was unfair only if he satisfies the following conditions:

(a)   He must have been continuously employed for two years. (Though if a worker in certain dangerous trades is dismissed instead of suspended because of medical grounds on which suspension is required by health regulations then he may make a claim if the dismissal occurred after four weeks of continuous employment.)

(b)   He must not have reached the normal retiring age for the employment, or be over 65 if male or over 60 if female.

(c)   If an employee is employed under a contract for a fixed term of one year or more then the employee may agree (though the agreement must be in writing) that he will not make a claim for unfair dismissal if the contract is not renewed at the end of its term.

The provisions relating to unfair dismissal do not apply to the police or to registered dock workers.

Dismissal of strikers

By S62 of the 1978 Act an industrial tribunal may not entertain a complaint from an employee dismissed during a strike, other industrial action, or lock-out, unless:

(a)   one striking employee has not been dismissed but the complainant has; or

(b)   all striking employees were dismissed but one was, within three months of his dismissal, offered re-engagement whereas the complainant was not.

This provision is intended to permit an employer to dismiss an entire striking workforce and replace it with a new one, but not to dismiss selected strikers. If all strikes are dismissed but selected strikers are re-engaged then those not re-engaged may complain to an industrial tribunal, but instead of examining the reasons for their dismissal the tribunal will examine the reasons for not re-engaging them.

It should be noted that the duration - and particularly the end - of the strike or lock-out is critical. If the strike has ended by the time the dismissal takes place the dismissal complaint will be heard by the tribunal in the usual way. It is sufficient that at least one striking employee has been offered re-engagement. Acceptance is not essential.

Redundancy and unfair dismissal

As previously briefly mentioned the dismissal of an employee for redundancy may be an unfair dismissal. Section 59 of the 1978 Act provides that the dismissal is unfair if redundancy affected other employees in a similar position, and the complainer was either selected for dismissal for an inadmissible reason, or selected in contravention of an agreed procedure or customary arrangement for dealing with redundancy and there was no special reason for departing from that procedure or arrangement.

Written reasons for dismissal

By S53 of the 1978 Act an employee is entitled, within two weeks of making a request, to receive from his employer a written statement giving particulars of the reason for his dismissal. The statement is admissible in any subsequent industrial tribunal hearing and must contain 'particulars'. Accordingly a brief statement like 'dismissed for misconduct' will not suffice. Failure to provide a written statement may lead to compensation of two weeks' pay being awarded to the employee.

Instant dismissal

It is worth noting that in spite of the legal protection against unfair dismissal an employer still retains the right to dismiss an employee instantly, without notice or money in lieu of notice. However, it is a severe action and justified only in the most exceptional circumstances. Furthermore, whether the employer is justified in an instant dismissal is always to be judged according to the facts of each case.

15.2.4   Remedies for unfair dismissal

If an industrial tribunal upholds a claim for unfair dismissal it has the following remedies at its disposal: reinstatement; re-engagement; and compensation. In the event of an employer not complying with a tribunal's order of reinstatement or re-engagement an additional award of compensation can be made. The tribunal should award reinstatement/re-engagement whenever practicable.

A tribunal may award such amount of compensation as it considers just and equitable having regard to the loss sustained in consequence of the dismissal which is attributable to the action of the employer. The basic award may be reduced if the employee refused an offer of alternative employment or because of his conduct.

The Act contains detailed rules on the maximum amount which may be awarded in any particular case, depending on the employee's length of service, age, and earnings.

15.3   Redundancy

15.3.1   Definition of redundancy

Since 1965, by the Redundancy Payments Act, employees who have two years' continuous employment are entitled to compensation in the form of a redundancy payment if their employer makes them redundant. Before there is a right to a redundancy payment there must be a dismissal by reason of redundancy.

Dismissal is defined in the same way as for unfair dismissal. The law regarding redundancy is now contained in the Employment Protection (Consolidation) Act 1978 and Part 4 of the Employment Protection Act 1975.

The 1978 Act provides that a dismissal is for redundancy if it is attributable wholly or mainly to either of the following two situations:

(a)   The fact that the employer has ceased, or intends to cease, carrying on the business for the purposes of which the employee was employed by him, or has ceased, or intends to cease, carrying on that business in the place where the employee was so employed.

(b)   The fact that the requirement of that business, for employees to carry out work of a particular kind, or for the employee to carry out work of a particular kind in the place where he was so employed, has ceased or diminished or is expected to cease or diminish.

Where the employer disputes redundancy it is for him to provide the dismissal is not for redundancy.

The following two cases give examples of redundancy. In *O'Brien v Associated Fire Alarms Limited (1968)*, O was employed at the employer's Liverpool office, the regional office for the North and West of England. When work in the Liverpool area decreased, O, who had previously worked in the Liverpool area, was ordered to work at Barrow-in-Furness. He refused because he would be unable to return home each night. The Court of Appeal held the place where O was employed was not the North and West of England but within the Liverpool area. The dismissal of O was for redundancy therefore.

In *Bromby & Hoare Limited v Evans (1972)*, E was one of several employees dismissed when the employing company decided to have the work, previously done by E and others, done by outside contractors. It was held E was redundant because the business no longer had a requirement or need for employees to do that kind of work; it would be done more cheaply by self-employed contractors.

The next case shows a situation which did not give rise to redundancy. In *Vaux & Associated Breweries Limited v Ward (No 2) (1969)*, the employers dismissed Mrs W who worked in their pub as a barmaid. The pub was modernised and younger ladies were engaged to serve drinks. The question to be answered was whether the work that the barmaid in the altered premises was going to do, was any different from the work a barmaid in the unaltered premises had been doing? The industrial tribunal held it was not. Therefore Mrs W was not dismissed on grounds of redundancy.

A change in the hours or time of work may lead to the conclusion that the needs of the business for the purposes for which the employee was employed have ceased or diminished. But whereas the 1978 Act specifically mentions a change in the place of work, a change in the hours or time of work receives no mention. Accordingly where the same number of employees are required to do the work but are now required to work at different times, employees who are dismissed because they refuse to work at the new times will not be dismissed for redundancy.

15.3.2   Offer of alternative employment

If an employer makes an employee an offer, before his original contract ends, to renew his contract or to re-engage him under a new contract with an interval of no more than four weeks between the contracts, then, provided the main terms of contract are the same or, if different, constitute an offer of suitable alternative employment, the employee will lose his right to a redundancy payment if he unreasonably refuses such an offer.

An employee who receives an offer is allowed a trial period of four weeks in which to decide on the suitability of the employment offered. Provided the employee does not remain after the end of the trial period, he may when he leaves, still claim he has been dismissed for redundancy.

15.3.3 Lay-off and short-time

In certain circumstances where periods of lay-off and short-time last over a number of weeks and where there is little prospect of a resumption of full working, an employee laid off or on short-time will be entitled to claim a redundancy payment. (He may be entitled to a guarantee payment if the lay-off is not sufficiently protracted to entitle him to a redundancy payment.)

15.3.4 Calculation of redundancy payment

The amount of payment an employee is entitled to is arrived at by the application of a formula based on the employee's age, his weekly earnings (subject to a specified maximum established by statutory instrument) and his length of service (maximum 20 years). (The monetary limit is reviewed annually.)

For each year of service:

(a)	below age 21	½ week's pay
(b)	between age 22 and 40	1 week's pay
(c)	between age 41 and 64 (59 for women)	1½ week's pay

Males who have reached 64 and females who have reached 59 lose one twelfth of the total payment for every month worked thereafter. The maximum payment is:

Weekly earnings (subject to specified limit) x 20 (length of service limit) x 1½

15.3.5 Qualifications for redundancy payment

The minimum service qualification for a redundancy payment is:

(a)   two years' continuous service;

(b)   sixteen hours' employment for each week of continuous service; those with between eight and sixteen hours per week may, however, qualify if they have been employed for five years.

Certain groups of employees are excluded. Examples are Crown servants, domestic servants employed by a relative, share fishermen and registered dock workers.

15.3.6 Redundancy claims

An employee who is refused a redundancy payment by his employer may submit a claim to an industrial tribunal within six months of the dismissal. If the tribunal upholds the claim the employer must make payment.

15.3.7 Redundancy procedure

The Employment Protection Act 1975 (Ss99-107) provides for consultation with recognised trades' unions and for notification to the Secretary of State of certain redundancies.

Where an employer anticipates even a single redundancy he must consult with the recognised trade union(s) at the earliest opportunity. Where groups of employees are affected the following times must be allowed for consultation:

Number being dismissed	Time to be allowed
Not fewer than 100 employees at one establishment within a period of 90 days	90 days before first dismissal effective
Not fewer than 10 at one establishment within a period of 30 days	60 days before first dismissal effective

To facilitate proper consultation the following information has to be supplied to the recognised union or its representatives:

(a)   reasons for redundancy proposals;
(b)   numbers and types of employees affected;
(c)   total number of such types of employee;
(d)   selection criteria;
(e)   procedure for carrying out dismissals.

There is no obligation to notify the Secretary of State for Employment where fewer than 10 employees are to be made redundant. Otherwise the following times must be allowed:

Number being dismissed	Amount of notification
100 or more at one establishment in 90 days	90 days before first dismissal effective
10 or more at one establishment in a period of 30 days	60 days before first dismissal effective

Failure to consult or notify

If an employer fails to consult as required, the recognised trade union (not an employee) may apply to an industrial tribunal for a protective award. If a protective award is made, the employer must continue to pay the employees concerned for the period of the award. Only if the employer fails to do this, may an employee affected submit a claim to an industrial tribunal.

15.3.8   Employment Protection (Consolidation) Act 1978: Compensation limits

As at April 1989 the compensation limits, etc, under the provisions of the Employment Protection (Consolidation) Act 1978 are as follows:

Statutory maternity pay

Basic rate: £36.25 (lower earnings limit, £43 per week).
Higher rate: 90% of earnings.

Statutory sick pay

For those earning less than £43 per week: nothing.
For those earning between £43 and £83.99 per week: £36.25.
For those earning more than £84 per week: £52.10.

A week's pay

The figure to be used in computing compensation for unfair dismissal, redundancy, and so forth, is increased to £172 per week maximum. (Those paid less have their entitlement calculated on their actual weekly earnings.)

15.4 Revision exercise

In order to ensure that you have assimilated the information given above regarding termination of employment and its implications attempt the following questions. Check your answers against the references given.

(1)   Outline the minimum periods of notice for employer and employee laid down by the Employment Protection (Consolidation) Act 1978.   **(Solution: 15.1.1)**

(2)   Explain the concept of summary dismissal.   **(Solution: 15.1.2)**

(3)   Differentiate between wrongful and unfair dismissal.   **(Solution: 15.1.3 and 15.2.1)**

(4)   Define the term 'dismissal' as used for the purposes of unfair dismissal.

(Solution: 15.2.1)

(5)   Dismissal of an employee can only be fair if. . . if what?   **(Solution: 15.2.1 and 15.2.2)**

(6)   Who can complain of unfair dismissal?   **(Solution: 15.2.3)**

(7)   What are the remedies for unfair dismissal?   **(Solution: 15.2.4)**

(8)   Define redundancy.   **(Solution: 15.3.1)**

(9)   How are redundancy payments calculated?   **(Solution: 15.3.4)**

(10) What are the minimum service qualifications for a redundancy payment?

(Solution: 15.3.5)

15.5 Conclusion

You should now have an understanding of the law regarding termination of the contract of employment and especially the concepts of wrongful dismissal, unfair dismissal and statutory redundancy payments.

15.6 Questions

Objective test questions

(1)   A has been employed on a full-time basis by B for a period of five years. How many weeks notice is he entitled to by statute?

A   Four.
B   Five.
C   Ten.
D   Two.

(2)   A claim for unfair dismissal would be heard in:

      A   The County Court.
      B   An Industrial Tribunal.
      C   The High Court.
      D   An administrative tribunal.

(3)   Which of the following is not as such a recognised ground for dismissal under the unfair dismissal provisions of the Employment Protection (Consolidation) Act 1978?

      A   The conduct of the employee.
      B   Redundancy.
      C   Qualification of the employee.
      D   Age of the employee.

(4)   What period of service is required of an employee to come within the unfair dismissal provisions of the Employment Protection (Consolidation) Act 1978?

      A   Six months.
      B   One year.
      C   Eighteen months.
      D   Two years.

(5)   Which of the following cannot be awarded by an industrial tribunal as a remedy for unfair dismissal?

      A   Re-engagement.
      B   Compensation.
      C   Specific performance.
      D   Reinstatement.

Written test questions

15.1   Dismissed employees

The employees in the following circumstances are all dismissed. Explain whether or not a claim for unfair dismissal is likely to succeed.

(a)   Brenda has become pregnant.

(b)   Charles, a van driver, has been disqualified from driving for three months.

(c)   David promised when he was engaged that he would make no claim in the future for unfair dismissal.

15.2   John

(a)   Compare and contrast compensation for unfair dismissal and redundancy payment.

(b)   John is the chief accountant of an engineering company. His company is taken over by another company and John is offered the post of deputy accountant with the new organisation at a lower salary. He writes a letter of protest to the managing director but takes up the new post and works for three weeks whilst looking for another appointment. Upon finding this, he leaves. Discuss the legal position.

15.3   **Arnold**

Arnold is employed as an office manager. His employer gradually installs a number of new office machines, the operation of which Arnold does not understand, nor does he make any attempt to do so. Eventually he is dismissed.

Advise Arnold on his possible right to redundancy payment.

How, if at all, would your advice differ, if, before dismissal, the employer had offered him the managership of another office which had not been so mechanised?

Answers

Session 1: Sources of law and forms of liability

Objective test answers

(1)	D	(2)	B	(3)	C	(4)	B	(5)	B
(6)	A	(7)	B	(8)	D	(9)	B	(10)	B

Written test answers

1.1   Common law and equity

The difference between common law and equity is historical. The common law is that part of the law of England which was formulated, developed and administered by the common law courts. It was originally based on the common customs of the country. It is a judge made system of law, originating in ancient customs, which were clarified, extended and made universal by the judges. Common law is that part of the law which was developed and formerly administered by the 'common law courts'. It was a unification of the customs of the English, welded together by the practice of the royal courts.

Equity, on the other hand, is that part of the law which was developed and formerly administered by the Court of Chancery to supplement the rules and procedure of common law. The Court of Chancery worked on the principles of conscience and fairness, and the early Chancellors (being ecclesiastics) probably borrowed some rules from canon law. Equity may be defined as the body of rules applied by the Court of Chancery. In this sense equity has no longer any connection with fairness as an ideal of justice. As the Court of Chancery dealt only with cases for which common law either provided no remedy or only insufficient remedies, equity was never a complete legal system in the way that common law was. Professor Maitland referred to equity as a 'gloss on common law'.

In its earlier days equity merely consisted of principles of fairness, equality and good conscience, but by the nineteenth century it had become a rigid set of rules standing side by side with the rules of common law, but administered in different courts.

The main differences between common law rights and equitable rights are:

(a)   common law remedies can be claimed as of right, while equitable remedies are discretionary;

(b)   equity acts *in personam* while common law acts *in rem*. This means that equitable rights were (and are) valid only against persons who are in conscience bound to recognise them, while legal rights are valid against the whole world;

(c)   common law rights must be claimed within the strict time limits laid down by the rules of limitation, but equity is not so rigid about the application of rules of limitation: equitable remedies are granted if claimed promptly.

Since the passing of the Judicature Acts 1873-1875, the administration of common law and equity has been merged. The Acts also provide that where there is a conflict between the rules of equity and the rules of common law, the rules of equity shall prevail.

1.2   Judicial precedent

The most outstanding characteristic of English law is that it is largely 'judge-made'. The bulk of common law and equity has not been enacted by Parliament but has been developed over the centuries by the judges applying established or customary rules of law to new situations and cases as they arose.

A precedent is a previous decision of a court which may, in certain circumstances, be binding on another court in deciding a similar case. The practice of following the previous decisions (stare decisis) of a superior court originated in the medieval judges' desire to create a system of law common to the whole country. The system also introduced consistency and certainty into the law.

Where a judge decides a case involving a new point of law, he not only disposes of the immediate problem before him, but he also lays down a legal principle which other judges will have to follow, subject to certain exceptions.

The legal principles and reasons on which the judgement is based are called the *ratio decidendi*. This is the only part of the judgement that can be binding on future judges.

The parts of the judgement that are not essential to the judgement are known as *obiter dicta*. In this part the judge discusses hypothetical situations and matters which are not directly relevant to the problem before him. *Obiter dicta* do not create binding precedents, though they may be strongly persuasive in certain circumstances.

A judge may refuse to follow a previous decision if the decision was given *per incuriam* or if there exists come material difference between the facts in the earlier case and those applying in the case before the court now.

The **advantages** of the doctrine are:

(a)   it makes the law more certain, precise and predictable;

(b)   the law grows and develops according to the changing needs of society: it is more flexible and provides more detail than is possible in a purely enacted system of law, and it can also provide for exceptions;

(c)   it can be altered comparatively easily without requiring lengthy parliamentary proceedings;

(d)   it is more practical in that there exists no legal rule for which there cannot be found practical illustration.

The main **disadvantages** of this system are its bulk and complexity.

1.3   Delegated legislation

In recent times legislation has become the chief means by which the law is developed to cope with the problems of rapidly changing society.

All legislative power is vested in Parliament and Parliament may therefore (and often does) by Act delegate legislative powers to other bodies or individuals. This is because Parliament cannot cope with the task of making the detailed rules necessary to translate these changes in society into practice.

The main reasons for delegated legislation are:

(a)   Parliament is short of time and can do no more than lay down the general principles, leaving the task of filling in the details to subordinate bodies;

(b)   the subject matter may be so technical that it is beyond the competence of most members of Parliament;

(c)   Parliament may delegate its powers to another body if the rules have to be changed quickly: Parliamentary procedure is not known for its speed and is too slow and cumbersome to permit a quick change.

The main forms of delegated legislation include:

(a)   orders in Council (ie, orders made under powers delegated to the Privy Council);

(b)   ministerial regulations (ie, made by individual ministers relating to their departmental responsibilities);

(c)   by-laws of local authorities, which have the force of law within the area of the authorities concerned;

(d)   rules made by certain professional bodies (under power granted by Parliament) governing the conduct of the members of the bodies concerned, for example, the Law Society has such powers under the Solicitors Act 1974.

Advantages

(a)   Parliament can concentrate on questions of principle and need not waste its time on relatively trivial matters of detail.

(b)   Rules can be changed quickly, and in emergencies the government can act at short notice.

(c)   Local and specialist knowledge may be drawn upon when local authority by-laws are passed.

Delegated legislation has been criticised as giving too much power to civil servants, who are not elected representatives. They are not, it is argued, subject to the control of the electorate. It is submitted that such criticism is not well-founded because Parliament exercises control over the use of these powers through the ministers responsible, while there also exists a significant element of judicial control.

Parliamentary control means that:

(a)   Parliament can withdraw the powers delegated;

(b)   ministers are answerable to Parliament for the rules and regulations made by their departments;

(c)   under the Statutory Instruments Act 1946, ministerial orders and regulations must be submitted to Parliament when made and will either cease to be operative if either House of Parliament resolves so within 40 days or, in the case of the more important of these instruments, will not be operative at all unless they have been approved by both Houses of Parliament.

Judicial control means that the courts control delegated legislation by declaring void any regulation that is not authorised by the statute under which it purports to be made; ie, if it is ultra vires or beyond the scope of the powers given. The courts can also declare rules to be void if they are unreasonable.

The courts can never challenge the validity or reasonableness of a statute.

Session 2: Administration of the law and the settlement of disputes

Objective test answers

(1)   B   (2)   C   (3)   B   (4)   C   (5)   C

(6)   D   (7)   C   (8)   C   (9)   C   (10)   D

Written test answers

2.1   Judicature acts

One of the main objects of the Judicature Acts was to remodel the entire judicial system. The Courts of Common Law, Chancery, Admiralty, Divorce and Probate, each administered different systems of law by means of different procedures, and this state of affairs led to inevitable abuse and delay. The Courts of Common Law were the King's Bench, Common Pleas and Exchequer with appeal to the Exchequer Chamber and thence to the House of Lords; Chancery was presided over by the Lord Chancellor and Master of the Rolls, with appeal to the House of Lords; and the Courts of Probate and Divorce dealt with probate and matrimonial business; whilst the Admiralty Court tried admiralty cases, with appeal to the Judicial Committee of the Privy Council.

In the place of all these courts, the Judicature Act 1873 set up the Supreme Court of Judicature (now known as the Supreme Court) composed of the High Court and the Court of Appeal. The Supreme Court is a court of complete jurisdiction but for administrative purposes the High Court is in divisions reflective of the original distinct jurisdictions of the previous courts. There were originally five such divisions though subsequent changes have reduced that number to three and have seen a redistribution of work between them. The present divisions are Queen's Bench, Chancery and Family.

The Court of Appeal has also undergone subsequent restructuring and by the Criminal Appeal Act 1966 the Court of Criminal Appeal, established in 1907, was brought within the Court of Appeal. This now consists of two Divisions: Civil and Criminal.

2.2   Criminal appeal

An appeal to the Criminal Division of the Court of Appeal may be made by a person who has been convicted on indictment by the Crown Court. The appeal may be against sentence or against conviction. A person convicted by a Magistrates' Court but sentenced by the Crown Court may appeal to the Court of Appeal against sentence. An appeal to the Criminal Division may be made in any case on a point of law, but only with the leave of the Court of Appeal on a question of fact or a question of mixed law and fact.

If a prosecutor is dissatisfied with the legal grounds for an acquittal in the Crown Court then the Attorney-General may refer the legal point to the Criminal Division of the Court of Appeal for a ruling. Such a reference is not really an appeal because the Court of Appeal cannot alter the verdict of acquittal, though its ruling will provide a precedent for the future.

The Criminal Division of the Court of Appeal may disregard one of its previous decisions if given *per incuriam*; and if it finds that two of its earlier decisions conflict then it may choose which to follow. The Court must reject one of its earlier decisions if, in its opinion, the decision is in conflict with, though not expressly overruled by, a House of Lords decision. The Criminal Division will overrule one of its earlier decisions if:

(a) the appellant is in prison and, in opinion of a full court of five or more judges, wrongly so;

(b) the Court thinks the law was misunderstood or misapplied; or

(c) the Court is giving directions on sentencing.

2.3 Prerogative orders

The purpose of prerogative orders is to safeguard the private rights of individuals who appear to have been adversely affected by decisions of administrative bodies. These decisions can be brought before the ordinary courts, for consideration, by whichever of the following orders is considered to be the most suitable for the particular case in issue:

(a) *Mandamus*, which lies in the absolute discretion of the court, is an order to an administrative organ or other public authority to do its duty. It may, for example, direct a tribunal to hear and determine a certain appeal or compel a local authority to produce its accounts for inspection by a ratepayer. However, the order is **not** available for a purely private or domestic duty required of an individual, nor can it be used against the Crown, as such.

(b) *Prohibition*. This order may be made against public (or semi-public) bodies in order to prevent those bodies exceeding their authority in the exercise of judicial or quasi-judicial functions. For example, it may control the activities of quasi-tribunals such as the Commissioners of Inland Revenue or of HM Customs and Excise.

(c) *Certiorari* is an order which may be used to review the acts and/or orders of an authority having power to impose a liability or to make a decision affecting the rights of certain individuals. For example, it may be used to make a decision taken by the Ministry of Housing regarding a development scheme (or, more recently, a direction of the Minister of Education to a district of Manchester ordering all schools within the district to go comprehensive).

Session 3: Law of contract 1

Objective test answers

(1)	D	(2)	C	(3)	C	(4)	C	(5)	D
(6)	C	(7)	C	(8)	B	(9)	B	(10)	C

Written test answers

3.1 White and Black

(a) An offer is a statement of willingness to be bound on certain specified terms. If such an offer is accepted by the offeree a contract will come into existence and the offeror will be bound. Thus, the most important feature of an offer is that the offeror must intend to be bound without further negotiation by a simple acceptance by the offeree of the terms offered.

(i) An invitation to treat is a statement made by a person which is intended to elicit offers. It may be described as an invitation to others to begin negotiations. An invitation to treat, unlike an offer, has no legal force because any offer it elicits can be accepted or rejected without obligation. Invitations to treat take many forms, eg, the display of goods in a shop window with the prices marked on them: *Fisher v Bell*; the display of priced goods in a self-service store: *Pharmaceutical Society v Boots*.

(ii) A statement of intention. A declaration of intention to make an offer is not an offer. There is no intention that such a declaration should be accepted and therefore it cannot form the basis of a contract. Such a declaration only means that an offer is to be made or invited at some future time: *Harris v Nickerson*.

It may be difficult in some cases to determine whether a statement constitutes on offer, an invitation to treat or a declaration of intention; but clearly the legal distinction between them is vital, since an offer, if accepted, brings into being a contract which imposes obligations on the parties to it which can be enforced against them. This does not apply in respect of an invitation to treat or a statement of intention.

(b) The death of an offeror does not affect an offer which is impersonal to the offeror. The offer by White to sell his house is one which is impersonal to White. His death will not prevent the performance of the contract if the offeree accepts the offer without knowledge of the death.

Use of the post as the means of communicating an acceptance is evidently contemplated by the parties and, therefore, Black's acceptance is effectively communicated at the moment when he posts his letter: *Household Fire Insurance v Grant*.

Black is not aware of White's death at the time of acceptance, that is, on 23 June. There is a valid and binding contract to sell his house. White's executor will execute a transfer or conveyance in favour of Black, the purchaser. The consideration of £50,000 will be paid to the executor who will apply the purchase money in accordance with the terms of the deceased's will.

3.2 Tim

(a) A minor (that is a person under the age of eighteen years) is obliged to pay for necessaries that have been supplied to him. Necessaries in this sense means goods suitable to the condition in life of the minor and to his actual requirements at the time of sale and delivery: S3 Sale of Goods Act 1979.

Thus, Arthur will have to establish first, that the goods are suitable to the condition in life of the minor; second, that they are necessary to the minor's requirements at the time of the sale; third, that they are necessary to the minor's requirements at the time of delivery; and fourth, that the minor was not sufficiently supplied with such goods at the time of sale and delivery.

Even if Arthur can establish these facts, Tim will only be liable to pay a reasonable, and not the contractual, price for the goods.

(b)   There is nothing to prevent a minor from entering into a partnership agreement but this constitutes one of the class of voidable contracts which minors can repudiate either during minority or within a reasonable time of attaining majority. But the minor who effectively repudiates liability cannot recover money unless he can demonstrate a total failure of consideration: *Steinberg v Scala Leeds Limited*. If the minor does not repudiate he will become equally liable with the other parties, but not for the debts contracted during his minority: *Goode v Harrison*.

A minor who is a partner cannot incur contractual liability for partnership debts, so that a judgment against the 'firm' in respect of such debt cannot be enforced against the 'firm' as a whole but only against partners other than the minor: *Lovell and Christmas v Beauchamp*. Nor can a minor be made bankrupt except for legally enforceable debts. The adult partners - in this case Peter and Paul - can require the partnership assets to be applied in payment of the liabilities of the firm before any part is allocated to the minor shareholder. To this extent, therefore, third parties may recover their debts out of the minor's property.

3.3   Jack, Derek and Christopher

(a)   Contractual terms differ in importance and may be classified as conditions and warranties. A condition is an important term which is vital to the contract and goes to its very root. It is so essential that its non-performance changes the nature of the contract. A warranty, on the other hand, is subsidiary to the main purpose of the contract; it is an obligation that should be performed and its non-performance causes financial loss to the innocent party.

The practical importance of the distinction lies in the legal consequences that follow the breach. Breach of a condition gives the injured party a right to rescind or repudiate the contract **in addition** to claiming damages. Breach of a warranty only gives the innocent party the right to sue for damages, **not** to repudiate the contract.

Whether a stipulation is a condition or a warranty is a question of the intention of the parties, and the intention is deduced from the circumstances of the case. It is the parties who ultimately determine whether a term is a condition or a warranty, by indicating the importance they attach to a particular stipulation. If there is no such indication, the Court may address itself to the commercial importance of the term.

The distinction between conditions and warranties may be illustrated by reference to the following two cases:

In *Bettini v Gye*, where a singer was four days late for rehearsals, it was ruled that the rehearsal clause was only subsidiary to the main purpose of the engagement. The singer's late arrival was held to be only a breach of warranty which entitled the management to recover damages but not to terminate the contract.

On the other hand, in *Poussard v Spiers & Pond* a singer failed to turn up for the first few performances of a new production. The producers, who had been forced to engage a substitute, then refused her services. It was held that her failure to perform was a breach of a condition, which entitled the management to terminate her contract.

(b)   Although it is clear in this case that a valid contract has been made, it is still necessary to determine the extent of the obligations that it creates. At common law, the purchaser of goods is expected to determine carefully the precise nature of the goods he intends to buy. If he does not get precisely what he thought he was bargaining for, then generally speaking he cannot avoid the contract; the court will not repair a bad bargain at the instance of the disappointed buyer. In addition, a party to a contract is not usually under an obligation to disclose any facts concerning the contract and may remain silent provided there is no fraud of misrepresentation.

Derek was under a misapprehension about a material fact when he telephoned Christopher and agreed to buy 'the Range Rover'. Christopher wanted to sell a 1973 Range Rover while Derek wanted to buy one made in 1974. The contract is not void by mistake, since the court will try to ascertain 'the sense of the promise'; ie, the sort of bargain which a reasonable person looking at the facts would have thought had been made by the parties. In *Tamplin v James*, in which the facts were similar, it was held that there had been no misrepresentation and no ambiguity in the terms of the contract. The contract was held to be binding and enforceable.

It is submitted that Christopher may sue Derek for damages for his breach of contract. Even though there was no agreement on the age of the vehicle, there was a definite agreement as regards the sale of the vehicle. Derek had agreed to buy the vehicle and no stipulation regarding its age was made at the time of sale. The fundamental rule in contracts for sale of goods is *caveat emptor*. As Jack is not an agent of Christopher his statement about the age of the car does not entitle Derek to repudiate the contract.

Session 4: Law of contract 2

Objective test answers

(1)	B	(2)	A	(3)	D	(4)	C	(5)	D
(6)	D	(7)	B	(8)	B	(9)	A	(10)	C

Written test answers

4.1   James and Robert

(a)   Money paid under a contract which is illegal is not usually recoverable. However, there are certain exceptions to this rule; namely:

(i)   where the parties are not equally at fault the innocent party can recover money paid under the contract (*Hughes v Liverpool Victoria Friendly Society*);

(ii)   if the illegal purpose has not been substantially performed, a party who has paid money under a contract may recover it if he has repented;

(iii)   where one party has an illegal intent unknown to the other and the contract is lawful in its inception;

(iv)   where the action for recovery of property does not require the illegal contract to be disclosed (eg, where the plaintiffs claim possession of goods which were let under hire-purchase agreements which are admitted to be illegal (*Bowmakers Limited v Barnet Instruments Limited*)).

(b)   The agreement between James and Robert is illegal because it is injurious to the public service. It will only be possible for James to recover the money if he can claim the money without having to disclose the illegal agreement, but this is clearly impossible (*Parkinson v College of Ambulance Limited*).

Alternatively, James might be able to recover the £1,000 if he could show that the illegal purpose had not been substantially carried out and that he had genuinely repented. It seems that James could not succeed because the only reason why the illegal contract has not been completed is because Robert has been dismissed, **not** because James has had a change of heart.

4.2   Bernard's Garage Limited

(a)   A contract in restraint of trade is one whereby a person who has entered into a contract agrees to suffer some restriction as to carrying on his trade, profession or calling. A contract in restraint of trade (partial or general) is *prima facie* void and cannot be enforced unless the restraint is considered reasonable in the circumstances.

Contracts in restraint of trade are of three main categories:

(i)   agreements where an employee undertakes that he will not, after leaving his present employment, complete with his employer either by setting up a business of his own or by entering the service of another employer;

(ii)   agreements where merchants or manufacturers combine for the purpose of regulating their trade relations;

(iii) agreements between the vendor and buyer of the goodwill of a business whereby the vendor promises that he will not carry on similar business in competition with the purchaser.

The courts will enforce a contract in restraint of trade in the following circumstances:

(i)   it must not be a restraint 'in gross', for example, and must be imposed to protect some proprietary interest: an employer may impose a restraint to protect his trade secrets and his business connections, because he is deemed to have a proprietary interest in both of them (*Forster & Sons Limited v Suggett*);

(ii)   the restraint must be reasonable in the interests of both of the contracting parties and must not be against the public interest;

(iii) the restraint must not be wider than is reasonably necessary to protect the covenantee's interest: reasonableness will depend upon the area and the duration of the restraint;

(iv)   where a contract contains a void restraint, only the restraint is ineffective: the validity of the rest of the contract is not affected.

An employee will be released from the obligations imposed upon him, even if it was a reasonable restraint, if an employer commits a breach of the contract.

(b) In the present case, the agreement in restraint of trade, in order to be enforceable, must satisfy the test of reasonableness. In this case the crucial consideration must be the length of time the agreement was to last. It is considered that the period of 25 years is too long to be regarded as reasonable.

It is submitted that the restraint is invalid and that Bernard's Garage Limited is entitled to redeem the mortgage and to buy petrol elsewhere.

It must be pointed out that if the restraint had been for a shorter period (eg, four years) the courts might regard the restraint as reasonable and enforce the contract.

In a recent case (*Esso Petroleum Co Limited v Harper's Garage (Stourport) Limited*), the facts of which were similar to those of the problem, it was held that the restraint was unreasonable and invalid. The House of Lords held that the rule of public policy against unreasonable restraints of trade applied to solus agreements and to the mortgage. In another case (*Cleveland Petroleum Co Limited v Dartstone Limited*) it was held that if a man, who is out of possession, is let into possession by the oil company on the terms that he is to 'tie' himself to that company, such a tie is valid. It is submitted that where a lessee is let into land on the express understanding that he will observe the covenants in the lease, he cannot then challenge the validity of the covenant.

4.3 Sykes

(a) (i) The general rule on mistake was stated in the case of *Smith v Hughes*:

'If, whatever a man's real intention may be, he so conducts himself that a reasonable man would believe that he was assenting to the terms proposed by the other party, and that other party upon that belief enters into a contract with him, the man thus conducting himself would be equally bound as if he had agreed to the other party's terms.'

It follows, therefore, that if one party to a contract is mistaken about the quality (or some other term) of the contract, but that mistake has not been induced by some wrongful representation by the other party, the first party cannot avoid his liability merely because he had made a mistake.

However, there are certain exceptions to the general rule, and these are known as cases of operative mistake. If an operative mistake is held to exist in a particular case, the contract in question is **void**; consequently, neither party acquires rights or liabilities under such a 'contract'.

(ii) Operative mistakes can be classified as follows:

- mistake about the nature of the contract itself;
- unilateral mistake (ie, a mistake made by one party only);
- bilateral mistake, where both parties are mistaken.

Unilateral mistake arises where one party is mistaken about some material fact concerning the contract, and the other party knows, or ought to know, that the mistake exists. Knowledge by the other party of the mistake's existence is essential, otherwise (as stated in Smith v Hughes) the first party is liable under the contract. The principal cases of unilateral mistake are mistakes about the identity of one of the parties. Recent decisions would appear to be conflicting, but it seems that the acid test is whether or not the party making the mistake intended to contract **only** with the person whom he believed the other party to be; if so, the contract will be declared void. However, if it is shown that he intended to contract with the person before him **irrespective of that person's true identity**, the contract may be upheld. Even if it is shown that the person representing himself to be someone else had committed a fraud on the first party, the contract is voidable at the option of that first party, and not void.

(b)   The facts in this case involve unilateral mistake, because only the shopkeeper was mistaken; namely, about the true identity of the rogue. The courts will have to decide whether the shopkeeper intended to deal with the person before him only because he claimed to be Lord Rich, or whether he would have sold the tape recorder to the purchaser irrespective of the latter's identity. In *Phillips v Brooks Limited*, where the facts were similar to those in the present case, it was held that the identity of the customer merely influenced the vendor's decision on whether or not to allow credit. If the same decision applies to the present case, the rogue received title to the tape recorder (albeit a voidable title because he never intended to pay for it), so that he was able to convey a good title to the dealer. This would mean that the original vendor would not be able to recover the item from the dealer (assuming that the latter bought it in good faith from the rogue).

However, if it were decided that the shopkeeper sold the tape recorder to the rogue **because** he believed him to be Lord Rich, there would be no contract, and the rogue could not transfer a good title to the relevant item. Here, as in *Ingram v Little*, the innocent third party (namely the person who 'bought' the item from the rogue) would have to return it to the original owner (ie, the shopkeeper).

Session 5: Law of contract 3

Objective test answers

(1)	C	(2)	C	(3)	D	(4)	C	(5)	B
(6)	B	(7)	C	(8)	C	(9)	C	(10)	C

Written test answers

5.1   Barber and Foot

(a)   (i)   A contract is discharged by frustration when it is rendered impossible of performance by external causes beyond the contemplation of the parties. After the parties have made their agreement, unforeseen contingencies may occur which prevent the attainment of the purpose they had in mind. It may also be said that a contract is frustrated (and therefore terminated) if, between the time when a contract is made and when it is completed, an event occurs which destroys the basis of the contract, but which is not the fault of either party. Under the doctrine of frustration the parties may be discharged from their obligations, the performance of which has become impossible or sterile. The basic common law rule is that the contract is not discharged merely because its performance has become more onerous or expensive due to unforeseen happenings.

The general rule laid down in *Paradine v Jane* is that, when the law casts a duty up]on a man which, through no fault of his own, he is unable to perform he is excused for non-performance, but if he binds himself by contract absolutely to do a thing he cannot escape liability for damages by proving that, as events turned out, performance is futile or even impossible. The party to a contract can, of course, guard against such unforeseen contingencies by express stipulation. The doctrine of frustration is an exception to the rule on absolute contracts enunciated in *Paradine v Jane*. It mitigates the harshness of the rule by introducing a number of exceptions to it.

(ii)   A contract may be discharged by frustration in the following circumstances:

(a)   *Supervening incapacity.* A contract for personal services may be discharged by supervening incapacity; therefore, in the case of a contract of employment, it will be discharged by the death or physical disability of one of the parties.

(b)   *Supervening illegality.* A contract may be frustrated if subsequent legislation has rendered it unlawful. If the illegality affects some major object of the contract the whole contract will be deemed to have been discharged. If the main purpose is not frustrated, the illegality will not discharge the contract.

(c)   *Physical impossibility.* A contract may be discharged where the subject-matter has been destroyed (*Taylor v Caldwell*). In this case the parties were held to have been discharged from their obligations when the hall to be hired was destroyed by fire before any of the concerts had taken place. The contract would also be discharged if the subject or the party ceases to be available (*Jackson v Union Marine Insurance Co Limited*). If a particular method of performance was contemplated by the parties and it has become impossible, the contract will be frustrated.

(d)   *Frustration of the common venture.* A contract will be frustrated where the common venture that the parties had in mind is no longer possible.

(iii) The occurrence of the frustrating event brings the contract to an end forthwith, without further action and automatically. The contract is not void *ab initio* but is terminated as to the future only. These contracts are perfectly valid when they are entered into but are abruptly terminated by the happening of the frustrating event. This rule on automatic termination formerly led to unhappy consequences because it was held that the loss stayed where it fell on the happening of the frustrating event. So any money paid could not be recovered event though the consideration had failed completely.

The harshness of this rule was slightly mitigated by the decision in the *Fibrosa* case, but now the position is regulated by the Law Reform (Frustrated Contracts) Act 1943. The Act provides that the money paid before the happening of the frustrating event can be recovered subject to deduction of expenses incurred by the payee. Firstly, if one party has conferred a benefit upon the other he may claim the value of this benefit from the other or may set off the value against any claims which the other may have against him.

Contracts for the sale of specific are excluded from the operation of the Act, because they are governed by the provisions of the Sale of Goods Act 1979. The 1943 Act also does not apply to charterparties, contracts of insurance and contracts for the sale of specific goods which have perished.

(b)   (i)   As the factory in which the machinery was to be installed has been burnt down, the contract for the installation of the machinery is frustrated by subsequent impossibility of performance; the parties are accordingly discharged from further performance of their obligations under it (*Appleby v Myers*). Now, under the Law Reform (Frustrated Contracts) Act 1943, where a contract has been frustrated (as in this case), any money paid under the contract is to be refunded subject to a deduction for any expense incurred by the payee towards performing his contractual obligation. Hence Foot & Co Limited will be entitled to a refund of the £500 they paid Barber & Co Limited, less a deduction of £200 for the expenses Barber & Co Limited incurred in building the platform.

    (ii)   Under the 1943 Act, a distinction is drawn between the case where money has been paid under a contract which subsequently becomes frustrated and the case where no money was so paid. If no money has been paid, then the party who has incurred expenses cannot recover them from the other party to the contract, unless he shows that his expenditure has conferred some valuable benefit on that other party.

        In this problem, even though Barber & Co Limited incurred expenses in raising the platform, it is clear that now the factory has been burnt down, no valuable benefit has been acquired therefrom by Foot & Co Limited and so Barber & Co Limited cannot recover the expense of £200 from them.

5.2   Contractual remedies

(a)   A **penalty** is a sum named in a contract to be forfeited on breach of contract. It differs from **liquidated damages** in that the latter are an attempt to value the financial damage likely to be suffered as the result of a breach whereas a penalty is a security for the performance of the contract.

A court will not be influenced by the fact that a sum payable on breach is called liquidated damages if it is, in fact, a penalty and not a genuine pre-estimate of the damage. This could be the case where:

    (i)   the prescribed sum is extravagant in comparison with the maximum loss that could follow from a breach; or

    (ii)   the contract provides for payment of a certain sum but a larger sum is stipulated to be payable on a breach; or

    (iii)   the same sum is fixed as being payable for several breaches which would be likely to cause varying amounts of damage.

The court will not enforce a penalty clause, and if the contract is broken only he actual loss suffered can be recovered. However, a sum fixed as liquidated damages will be payable, whether this is greater or less than the actual damage incurred.

(b)   A claim on a *quantum meruit* is a claim for the value of work done by a party to a contract whereas a claim for damages is for compensation in respect of loss suffered consequent on a breach of contract.

The general rule is that if a contract provides for services to be rendered in return for payment of a lump sum, nothing can be claimed unless the work has been completely performed (*Cutter v Powell*). Exceptionally, however a claim can be made under a *quantum meruit* if:

(i)   the innocent party has elected to accept the benefit of the work done (eg, where a lessor quantity has been delivered under a contract for the sale of goods than is stipulated in the contract); or

(ii)   the contract is divisible (eg, where goods are to be delivered by instalments but the contract has not been completed); or

(iii)   complete performance has been prevented by the wrongful act of the other party (*Planche v Colburn*).

A *quantum meruit* claim is also appropriate if the plaintiff has rendered services under a contract which is later found to be void. An example is where the managing director of a company was employed under a service agreement made on behalf of the company. The agreement was found to be void since none of the directors had taken up their qualifications shares within the necessary time but the managing director sued the company on a *quantum meruit* for reasonable remuneration in respect of the services which he had rendered to the company. He succeeded in quasi-contract (*Craven-Ellis v Canons Limited*).

5.3   Exceptions to privity of contract

In general, third parties cannot sue for the carrying out of promises made by the parties to a contract. Thus, if a contract between A and B requires B to benefit C, the privity rule prevents C from suing B.

However, there are cases in which a person is allowed to sue upon a contract to which he is not a party.

(a)   A principal, even if undisclosed, may sue on a contract made by an agent.

(b)   If the third party can establish that a party to the contract was a trustee of the promise for the third party. Thus, in *Tomlinson v Gill* the defendant promised a widow to pay her late husband's debts. It was held that the widow was a trustee of the promise for the husband's creditors, who could thus enforce the promise against the defendant.

(c)   The assignee of a debt or chose in action may, if the assignment is a legal assignment, sue the original debtor.

(d)   The holder for value of a bill of exchange can sue prior parties and the acceptor.

(e)   Under the Resale Prices Act, 1976, S26, the supplier of goods is given a statutory cause of action, so he may enforce against a person not a party to a contract of sale a condition as to re-sale. However, the re-sale price agreement must have been approved under the provisions of the Resale Prices Act, 1976, otherwise there can be no enforcement of it.

(f)   If a man insures his life for the benefit of his wife and/or children, or a woman insures her life for her husband and/or children, a trust is created in favour of the objects of the policy, who, although they are not parties to the contract within the insurance company, can sue upon it: S11 Married Women's Property Act, 1882.

(g)   The position in land law is that benefits and liabilities attached to or imposed on land may, in certain circumstances, follow the land into the hands of other owners.

Session 6: Agency

Objective test answers

(1)   D   (2)   C   (3)   C   (4)   B   (5)   D

Written test answers

6.1   A, P and T

(a)   An agency will arise by implication where the principal places the agent in a situation where it would be normal (either by reason or trade custom or otherwise) for the agent to contract on behalf of the principal, although no express authority to do so has been conferred to him. Thus, a person appointed to act as a land agent may have implied authority to sign tenancy agreements on behalf of his employer, although the latter has not specifically authorised him to do so.

Agency by implication could also arise where the principal is estopped from denying the agency. An example would be where a wife has been accustomed to order goods on her husband's account and he has met the bills. By so doing he has held her out as his agent and if he wishes to cease being liable he must notify the tradesmen who have been supplying her; it is not sufficient for him to tell his wife not to pledge his credit.

A third example would be where the principal has permitted X to act as if he were his agent although no principal-agent relationship was intended. But the principal will only be liable if he has acted in some way to support the appearance of authority. If there is no holding out by the alleged principal it is the agent alone who is liable to the third party.

In all three examples given above it can be seen that it is the **apparent** authority of the agent, and not his actual authority, which is decisive.

(b)   The facts given in this problem show that A acted as the authorised agent of P for some years, that P terminated the agency but failed to notify the third party T, and that A continued to contract but in his own name and on his own behalf.

This is similar to the second example given above, where the principal has terminated the agency but without notifying the third party. The principal P will be estopped from denying the agency and will be liable unless he can show that T should have realised, from the facts, that the agency had come to an end.

6.2   Thomas, Andy and Peter

(a)   If an agent acts for an undisclosed principal, it is the agent himself who is primarily liable under the contract negotiated, and is entitled to enforce it by taking legal action against the other party (third party to the agreement).

However, the undisclosed principal can reveal his identity and enforce the contract in his own name, an anomalous right allowed by law so that the needs of the business community resorting to this device may be met.   This right is subject to some limitations. The undisclosed principal has no right of action if the terms of the contract expressly excluded an agency of this type. In *Humble v Hunter* the plaintiff's son entered into a charter-party with the defendant, the son describing himself as owner of the vessel. It was held that evidence was not admissible to allow the son to show that he was only an agent of the plaintiff. Such evidence would contradict the express term of the contract in which he stated that he was the owner. Nor can the undisclosed principal sue if it is evident that the personality of the agent was vitally important to the third party. For example, a trader may have been willing to contract only with selected clients and may have given credit terms to the agent personally because he could be trusted to settle his indebtedness. The trader is unwilling to extend credit to a principal of whom he knows nothing.

The undisclosed principal cannot acquire better rights under the contract than those possessed by the agent. The third party may have a right to set off his indebtedness under the contract against the agent's indebtedness to him in respect of a previous transaction. The undisclosed principal is bound by such third party rights unless, when dealing with the agent, the third party realised that the agent might be contracting for an undisclosed principal but did not enquire further into this matter.

When the principal has been disclosed, the third party may sue the principal or the agent, but not both. He is not bound by his choice unless he was unaware of the true situation. If he has already begun proceedings against the agent, he may continue to sue him or may sue the principal instead (on first learning of the latter's existence). Once judgment has been given against the agent, he cannot sue the principal, every thought the judgment is not fully satisfied by payment of the debt.

(b)   Thomas should be advised that he is entitled to succeed against Andy. The institution of proceedings against either Andy or Peter did not amount, as a matter of law, to a binding election so as to bar proceedings against the other party. The institution of proceedings was normally strong evidence of such election, but as Thomas had never withdrawn the threat to sue Andy, Thomas has not by suing Peter unequivocally elected to hold Peter liable for the price. In *Clarkson Booker Ltd v Andjel*, the facts of which were similar, the Court of Appeal upheld the judgment against the agent.

6.3   X, Y and Z

(a)   Where the agent, without the authority of his principal, enters into a contract with a third party on behalf of his principal, the principal can do one of two things:

(i)   refuse to ratify the contract, thereby incurring no personal liability: in this case, the third party would be entitled to sue the agent for breach of warranty of

(ii) authority, ratify the contract, thereby creating a contractual relationship between himself and the third party.

Ratification is the express adoption by the principal of the contract, or conduct showing unequivocally that the principal adopts the contract made by the agent.

Before a principal can effectively ratify his agent's contracts the following conditions must be fulfilled:

(i) the contract must have been entered into specifically on behalf of the principal: if the agent purports to act on his own behalf, the principal cannot ratify;

(ii) the principal must have been in existence and must have had contractual capacity to enter into the contract when the contact was made;

(iii) a void contract cannot be ratified;

(iv) the principal must ratify the contract within any period of time fixed for ratification, or if none has been fixed then within a reasonable time;

(v) the principal, before ratification, must have been aware of all the material facts;

(vi) the principal must ratify the whole contract: partial ratification of only those parts of the contract that are beneficial to the principal is ineffective.

The legal effect of ratification is to make the contract as binding on the principal as if the agent had had the authority of the principal right at the start before the contact was made. It related back to the making of the contract by the agent.

(b) In this case the ratification relates back to acceptance; ie, to the moment when there was a finally concluded contract between X and Y. It therefore follows that X's attempted revocation is inoperative as being too late, and Z is entitled to sue X for breach of contract: *Bolton Partners v Lambert*. It must be appreciated that the ratification would be effective only if the offer had been accepted unconditionally. So if Y's acceptance on 2 June was qualified, or was subject to ratification by Z, there would be no contract until Z ratified, and a revocation by X before that date would be effective. So X should be advised that he is bound by the contract.

The rule that ratification relates back does not apply where the agent and the third party have by mutual consent cancelled the unauthorised transaction before the principal ratifies: *Walter v James*. X should be advised that since the contract was cancelled by mutual consent before ratification, X is not bound by the contract.

Session 7: Sale of goods

Objective test answers

(1)	B	(2)	C	(3)	B	(4)	D	(5)	B
(6)	B	(7)	C	(8)	B	(9)	B	(10)	C

Written test answers

7.1   **Sale of goods contract**

(a)   A contract for the sale of goods is defined in the Sale of Goods Act 1979 as a contract by which the seller transfers or agrees to transfer the property in goods to the buyer for a money consideration, called the price (S2). Goods are also defined in the Act to include all personal chattels but not things in action (ie, legal rights) or money (S61).

(b)   A yacht is a personal chattel and so the sale of Goods Act will apply here. Under the Act the price may be fixed by the contract, or left to be fixed as agreed therein, or determined by the course of dealing between the parties. If it is not so fixed the buyer must pay a reasonable price (which depends on the circumstances of the case) (S8).

     (i)   There is a judicial dictum that the provision in the Act that the buyer should pay a reasonable price will apply only if the contract is silent on the subject of price (*May and Butcher Ltd v R*).

           The Court will try to uphold an agreement as valid if this is at all possible and will look at the previous course of dealings between the parties and the usages of a particular trade to find some indication of the price intended (*Hillas & Co v Arcos Ltd*). However, if this is unsuccessful, the provision that the price shall be mutually agreed later would make the agreement void for uncertainty as being an agreement to agree in the future.

     (ii)   If the contract states that the price shall be fixed by C, this would come under the provision in the Act for the price to be fixed 'as agreed therein'. Provided that a price is decided by C this will be the price to be paid.

     (iii)   If the contract is silent as to price, it may be determined under the Act by the course of dealing between the parties. If this is no guide as to the price, B must pay a reasonable price which will, in the last resort, be determined by the court.

7.2   **Smith**

In a case where the plaintiff seller is a dealer, what follows from the breach in the usual course of things is that the plaintiff loses the profit that he would have made had the sale to that particular buyer been completed, and he is entitled to be recompensed for the loss. It is no defence to say that the dealer has sold, or may readily sell, the goods to another person, for even if he has been successful the fact remains that he has profited from one sale instead of two.

In *W L Thompson Ltd v Robinson (Gunmakers) Ltd*, where the facts were very similar to those in the problem, the judge rejected the contention of the defendants that they were liable only for nominal damages (given that the plaintiffs could have sold the car to another customer), or could (as they had in fact done) return it to their supplier. What the plaintiffs had lost was the profit of that particular bargain. They had sold one car less than they would otherwise have sold. The dealers should be advised that Smith is not correct in his assertion that they are entitled to recover the loss of their profit from him. If demand exceeds supply then *Charter v Sullivan* applies and nominal damages only will be awarded.

7.3   Unpaid seller

(a)   An unpaid seller acquires a lien over goods he has sold where:

 (i)   the goods have been sold without any stipulation as to credit; or
 (ii)   if credit has been given, the term has expired; or
 (iii)   the buyer becomes insolvent.

The lien can be enforced by the resale of the goods. This right arises where the goods are perishable or where the buyer does not, after notice from the vendor of his intention to resell, tender the price within a reasonable time.

The lien may be lost if the unpaid vendor gives the goods to a carrier for transmission to the buyer without reserving the right of disposal, or where the buyer or his agent lawfully obtains possession of them, or if the right is waived. It is not lost merely because the vendor obtains judgement for the price.

(b)   An unpaid seller has the right to stop goods in transit if the buyer becomes insolvent (Sale of Goods Act 1979, section 44). For this purpose a buyer is deemed to be insolvent if he has ceased to pay his debts in the ordinary course of business (ibid, section 61). The goods are in transit until they come into the actual or constructive possession of the buyer (ibid, section 45).

If B is in fact insolvent, A is entitled to stop delivery of the diamonds and to claim damages for any loss he has suffered as a result of the breach of contract on the part of the buyer.

If, however, the information given to C was not correct and B was solvent, he can sue A for damages for non-delivery of the diamonds. He could also sue C, but is unlikely to succeed against him unless he can show that C was acting as B's agent.

Session 8: Consumer credit agreements

Objective test answers

(1)   C   (2)   D   (3)   C   (4)   B   (5)   D

Written test answers

8.1   Charles and Trevor

(a)   The owner of a chattel may transfer possession of it to some other person by way of hire in return for payment of rent; if the person paying the rent has an option either to return the goods or to acquire ownership of them provided a certain sum has been paid then it is a hire-purchase agreement. The hirer, if he wishes, may decide not to buy. Ownership passes to the buyer only after he has paid the agreed sum. The hirer may terminate the agreement if he so wishes. If there were no option to return the goods the agreement would be a contract for the sale of goods.

A conditional sale is very similar to a hire-purchase agreement. It is an agreement for the sale of goods, whereby the purchase price is payable by instalments and ownership remains with the seller until fulfilment of all conditions governing payment of instalments and other matters specified in the agreement. The buyer may be given possession of the goods until ownership is acquired.

A credit sale agreement is one for the sale of goods (the purchase price being payable by instalments) which is not a conditional sale agreement. Under such an agreement the ownership in the goods passes to the buyer immediately the agreement comes into effect, and on general priciples the buyer may pass a good title to another person.

(b)   The unrepealed provisions of the Hire Purchase Act 1964 (reproduced in the Consumer Credit 1974 Act) give special protection to the 'private purchaser' of a motor vehicle which is subject to a hire-purchase agreement. The provisions of this Act apply even if the value of the goods is more than £15,000 and the private purchaser is a company. A 'private purchaser' is someone who is not carrying on a business as a dealer in motor vehicles or of providing finance for hire-purchase transactions in motor vehicles. Where the hirer (bailee) of a motor vehicle disposes of it to a private purchaser who takes it in good faith and without notice of the hire-purchase agreement, such disposition has effect as if the title of the owner to the vehicle had been vested in the bailee immediately before that disposition. 'Disposition' means any contract of sale or hire-purchase agreement. In other words, the title of the purchaser is protected against a claim by the original owner or seller.

The provisions are intended for the protection of the private purchaser of a motor vehicle and do not affect the civil or criminal liability of a bailee or buyer who sells the vehicle contrary to his contractual undertaking to the original owner or seller.

In the light of this, it would appear that Charles is protected and can retain the car provided that he bought it in good faith and without notice of the hire-purchase agreement.

(c)   If goods have been let under a hire-purchase agreement and if, at any time after one-third of the hire-purchase price has been paid or tendered, the owner makes a further agreement with the bailee relating to the whole or any part of these goods (with or without other goods), the provisions of S82 of the Consumer Credit Act 1974 apply to the second agreement, irrespective of whether one-third of the hire-purchase price mentioned in the second agreement has been paid or not.

So, in the present problem, Trevor should be advised that the owner is not entitled to seize either of the articles but must obtain a court order. In such a case all the goods in the new agreement immediately become 'protected goods' even though one-third has not been paid.

8.2   James and Joseph

(a)   A hire-purchase contract is a contract whereby an owner of goods contracts to hire them out on the understanding that the hirer will make periodical payments to the owner and that the hirer will have the option of becoming the owner of the goods on his completing the necessary payments for the goods and on complying with the other terms of the contract. The ownership does not pass until the final payment has been made. It is a bailment of goods to the hirer coupled with the grant of an option to purchase the goods. It must be distinguished from a credit sale agreement.

Formalities under the Consumer Credit Act 1974

(i)   The agreement must be in writing.

(ii) It must be signed by the hirer (referred to as bailee in the Act) and by or on behalf of all the other parties to the agreement.

(iii) The contract must contain a statement of the total cash price, the total hire-purchase price, the amount of each instalment and the dates on which instalments are due. It must also contain a list of the articles sufficient to identify them.

(iv) If the agreement was signed at a place other than the trade premises of the seller, two statutory copies must be delivered to the bailee. The bailee must be given the first statutory copy at once, or if the document is sent to him the first statutory copy must be enclosed. The second statutory copy has to be sent to him by post within seven days of the making of the agreement. On the other hand, if the agreement is signed by both parties at the trade premises of the seller, only one copy has to be given to the bailee. The copies should comply with regulations made by the Director-General of Fair Trading concerning legibility and layout.

(v)   If the total price exceeds £30, the Director-General may make regulations about where the signature of the hirer must appear and what words should accompany it. The provisions of the Act do not apply if the total hire-purchase price exceeds £15,000.

(vi) There must be a statement relating to the hirer's right of cancellation if the hirer has signed at a place other than 'appropriate trade premises'.

(vii) There must be a notice that the Act restricts the owner's right to recover possession of the goods when one-third of the hire-purchase price has been paid.

(vii) The court may grant dispensation with most of the above requirements, where it is satisfied that a failure to comply has not prejudiced the hirer and it considers it just and equitable to dispense with them.

Failure to comply with these formalities makes the contract unenforceable by the owner or the seller. In addition, the owner is not entitled to enforce:

(i)   any contract of guarantee or indemnity made at the request of the bailee; or

(ii) any security given by the bailee or guarantor; or

(iii) any right to recover the goods from the bailee, so the bailee may keep the goods without having to pay for them.

(b)   The facts of this problem are similar to those of *Capital Finance Co Ltd v Bray* where it was held that the hire-purchase agreement had been terminated by the owners taking possession without a court order and without the consent of the hirer, and that the hirer was released from his liability. He was held to be entitled to the return of the money paid by him under the agreement. He was not liable to the owners in detinue for not returning the car. (Actions for detinue have now been abolished but it would seem that the alternative action for conversion would also have failed.)

So Joseph is not liable on the contract and is entitled to recover £350 from the owners. He would not be liable in conversion.

Session 9: Negotiability, bills of exchange, promissory notes and cheques

Objective test answers

(1)   D   (2)   C   (3)   B   (4)   C   (5)   B

Written test answers

9.1   A, B and C

A is the drawer. The drawer of a bill, by drawing it, engages that on due presentment it shall be accepted and paid according to its tenor, and that if it be dishonoured he will compensate the holder or any indorser who is compelled to pay it, provided that the requisite proceedings on dishonour be duly taken (Bills of Exchange Act 1882, S55(1)).

B is the acceptor. The acceptor of a bill, by accepting it, engages that he will pay it according to the tenor of his acceptance (S54(1)).

C is an indorser. An indorser of a bill, by indorsing it, engages that on due presentment it shall be accepted and paid according to its tenor, and that if it be dishonoured he will compensate the holder or a subsequent indorser who is compelled to pay it, provided that the requisite proceedings on dishonour are duly taken (S55(2)).

By S16, a drawer or an indorser may add to his signature an express stipulation negativing or limiting his liability. The words *sans recours* would entirely negative liability. An acceptor cannot add *sans recours* to his name because this would nullify the whole acceptance: he may give a qualified acceptance but then the person asking for the acceptance may treat the bill as dishonoured.

9.2   Bill of exchange

(a)   (i)   When the acceptor of a bill is or becomes the holder of it at or after its maturity, in his own right, the bill is discharged (Bills of Exchange Act 1882, S61).

(ii)   When the holder of a bill at or after its maturity absolutely and unconditionally renounces his rights against the acceptor the bill is discharged. The renunciation must be in writing unless the bill is delivered up to the acceptor (Bills of Exchange Act 1882, S62(1)).

(iii)   Where a bill is intentionally cancelled by the holder or his agent, and the cancellation is apparent thereon, the bill is discharged (Bills of Exchange Act 1882, S63(1)).

(iv)   Where a bill or acceptance is materially altered without the assent of all parties liable on the bill, the bill is avoided except as against a party who has himself made, authorised, or assented to the alteration, and subsequent indorsers (Bills of Exchange Act 1882, S64(1)).

(b)   Where a bill has been lost before it is overdue, S69 enables a person who was the holder (in this case C) to get a duplicate from the drawer (A), subject to giving him an indemnity if required, but there is no provision for obtaining a second time the acceptance (of B) and any indorsements. C should immediately advise A and B of the loss and get payment stopped . A, the drawer will normally insist on a full indemnity before giving a duplicate bill because in the absence of forgery he would have to pay the lost bill if it got into the hands of a holder in due course and was dishonoured by the acceptor B.

9.3   Crossings

'A/c payee' is an instruction to a collecting bank that it must collect the cheque only for the credit of the payee named on the cheque. The banks have never seriously disputed that a bank would be negligent if it ignored the instruction. Cases such as *Bevan v National Bank Limited* indicate that a court would hold a bank that ignored the instruction to be negligent.

'Not negotiable' on a crossed cheque means that the cheque cannot be negotiated. If the words are put on befoe the cheque leaves the payee's possession then no one can become a holder in due course of the cheque. If the words are put on by a holder in due course then no one else can becone a holder in due course.

Session 10: Nature and general concepts of tortious liability

Objective test answers

(1)   C   (2)   C   (3)   C

Written test answers

10.1   Fault

'The ultimate purpose of the law in imposing liability on those who do harm to others', said Salmond, 'is to prevent such harm by punishing the doer of it. He is punished by being compelled to make pecuniary compensation to the person injured. It is clear, however, that it is useless to punish any person, either civilly or criminally, unless he acted with a guilty mind. No one can be deterred by a threat of punishment from doing harm which he did not intend and which he did his best to avoid. All that the law can hope to effect by way of penal discipline is to make sure that men will not either wilfully or carelessly break the law and inflict injuries upon others. pecuniary compensation is not in itself the ultimate object or a sufficient justification of legal liability. It is simply the instrument by which the law fulfills its purpose of penal coercion. When one man does harm to another without any intent to do so and without any negligence, there is in general no reason why he should be compelled to make compensation. The damage done is not thereby in any degree diminished. It has been done and cannot be undone. By compelling compensation the loss is merely shifted from the shoulders of one man to those of another, but it remains equally heavy. Reason demands that a loss shall lie where it falls, unless some good purpose is to be served by changing its incidence; and in general the only purpose so served is that of punishment for wrongful intent or negligence. There is no more reason why I should insure other persons against the harmful results of my own activities, in the absence of any *mens rea* on my part, than why I should insure them against the inevitable accidents which result to them from the forces of nature independent of human actions altogether.'

This view, however, is subject to serious objections. In the first place, as Lord Devlin has said, in England today 'the real wrongdoer hardly ever pays for the damage he does. He is usually not worth suing. The payer is either his employer or his insurance company'. Indeed, the tendency in the modern law of tort - both statutory and judicial - is to shift the liability for loss upon those who have a greater capacity to bear it, and in particular on to those who are in a position to spread the loss by passing it on to the public by way of increased prices or insurance premiums.

Secondly, in some forms of tortious liability, liability is imposed regardless of fault. Thus, in *Rylands v Fletcher* it was held that the occupier of land who brings and keeps on it anything likely to do damage if it escapes is bound at his peril to prevent its escape, and is liable for all the direct consequences of its escape, even if he has been guilty of no negligence.

Thirdly, even where fault is relevant to the question of liability, it is usually judged objectively rather than subjectively. Thus, in the tort of negligence determination whether or not there has been a breach of duty is determined objectively by the standards of the 'reasonable man'.

10.2   Motive in tort

In tort, the intention or motive for an action is generally irrelevant. The leading case is *Bradford (Mayor of) v Pickles* in which the defendant was held not liable for intentionally intercepting, by means of excavations on his own land the underground water than would otherwise have flowed into the adjoining reservoir of the plaintiffs, although his sole motive in so doing was to coerce the plaintiffs to buy his land at his own price. It was already settled law that the abstraction of underground water not flowing in defined channels is not an actionable wrong, even though done intentionally, but in the present case an attempt was made to establish an exception to this rule when the damage was caused not merely intentionally but maliciously. The House of Lords rejected this contention, Lord Macnaghten saying 'In such a case motives are immaterial. It is the act not the motive for the act, that must be regarded. If the act apart from the motive gives rise merely to damage without legal injury, the motive, however reprehensible it may be, will not supply that element.'

There are, however, some exceptions:

(a)   *malicious prosecution* - no action will lie for the institution of legal proceedings, however destitute of reasonable and probable cause, unless they are instituted maliciously - that is to say, from some wrongful motive;

(b)   *malicious falsehood* - this tort consists of causing damage to another by making false and injurious imputations. Such false statements must be motivated by malice - a desire to injure, or some other improper motive;

(c)   *defamation* - the presence of malice will destroy the defence of 'qualified privilege' and is also relevant to the defence of 'fair comment';

(d)   *conspiracy* - where two or more persons act without lawful justification for the purpose of wilfully causing damage to the plaintiff and actual damage results, they commit the tort of conspiracy. The combination will be justified if the predominant motive is self interest or protection of one's trade rather than injury of the plaintiff;

(e)   *nuisance* - motive is relevant in the tort of nuisance in determination of whether or not the defendant's act is reasonable.

Thus, in *Hollywood Silver Fox Farm v Emmelt* the defendant, a developer, felt that a notice board inscribed 'Hollywood Silver Fox Farm' was detrimental to his neighbouring development.

When the plaintiff refused to remove the notice the defendant caused his son to discharge guns on his land to interfere with the breeding of the foxes. It was held that his action constituted a nuisance.

10.3 Tortious liability

There is no precise definition of tortious liability. Indeed some authorities argue that there cannot be a specific definition because there is no such thing as tortious liability, merely a list of specific torts. This view was championed by Sir John Salmond who defined a tort as 'a civil wrong for which the remedy is a common law action for unliquidated damages and which is not exclusively the breach of a contract or the breach of a trust, or other merely equitable obligation'. According to Salmond's view liability in tort may only be established if the damage suffered can be brought under a known or recognised head of liability.

On the other hand we have the view that submits that there is a law of tort, all harm being actionable in the absence of just cause or excuse. This view, which was expounded by the late Professor Winfield, is supported by the fact that if there was merely a law of specific torts, then no new torts could be created by the courts and the categories of tortious liability would be closed. Professor Winfield defined tortious liability as that which arises from the breach of a duty primarily fixed by the law; this duty is towards ersons 'generally and its breach is redressible by an action for unliquidated damages'.

According to Winfield tortious duties exist by virtue of the law itself and are not dependent upon the agreement or consent of the persons subjected to them. It is this lack of agreement or consent which distinguishes tortious from contractual liability. Although, of course, the statement that agreement is the basis of contract needs considerable qualification; and the fact that tortious liability may arise from a contractual relationship cannot be ignored.

The primary duty envisaged in the definition (that is the duty not to slander, not to libel etc), is towards persons generally. The breach of such a duty giving rise to a remedial duty owed to a specific person or persons. The nature of this primary duty serves to distinguish tort from quasi-contractual duty where no such primary duty exists.

Finally, as regards Winfield's definition the basic remedy for a breach of tortious liability is an action for unliquidated damages.

Whilst it is possible to distinguish a tort from a crime chiefly because a crime is a breach or violation of a public right and affects the community, whereas a tort affects the civil rights of the person injured, many torts are also crimes. Indeed the distinction between tortious and criminal wrongs lies not in the acts themselves, for the same act may give rise to both forms of liability, but rather in the procedure taken to right the wrong concerned and the aim with which such procedure is initiated. The aim of criminal law is essentially punitive and the aim of tort is essentially compensatory.

In conclusion, it should be noted that no civil injury is to be classed as a tort if it is only a breach of trust or some other merely equitable obligation.

Session 11: Tortious liability: general defences and remedies

Objective test answers

(1)   A   (2)   A   (3)   A   (4)   D

Answers

Written test answers

11.1   Volenti non fit injuria

The expression *volenti fit injuria* means in tort that 'to him who consents no legal injury is done'. Whether the consent is contractual or non-contractual, express or implied, relates to deliberate harms (eg, surgical operations) or accidental ones (like the result of careless driving), it must always amount to full, free and unfettered consent to forego the otherwise available legal remedy. The expression *scienti non fit injuria* is not appropriate in torts since, apart from special cases like the gratuitous bailment of a manifestly defective chattel, mere knowledge of, rather than consent to, the risk or danger will afford no defence to the defendant.

The leading authority is the House of Lords decision in *Smith v Baker* in which the plaintiff, an employee working beneath a crane which he knew conveyed loads of stone overhead, was granted a remedy following his injuries from falling stones for, although he was well aware of the danger, he had not voluntarily undertaken the risk of injury. The same sort of economic pressure to carry out his job despite known dangers negated the application of *volenti* in a case where a bargeman was injured when the rope by which his barge was being towed parted and injured him: *Burnett v British Waterways Board*. By contrast, shotfirers, injured by their own wilful failure, in breach of statutory and other regulations imposed on them, to take safety precautions, were held by the House of Lords to have consented to have run the risks of their own folly: *I.C.I. v Shatwell*.

Further support can be adduced from the 'rescue cases'. A rescuer, by his very nature, is presumably well aware of the danger, yet out of moral or legal obligation, acts in spite of it. But he is not barred by *volenti* from suing him who created the dangerous state of affairs which caused his injuries. So, in *Baker v Hopkins* the doctor who attempted to aid men trapped at the bottom of a shaft due to the defendant's negligence well knew the danger from gas. Yet his estate was able to recover damages from the defendant in respect of his death.

Mere knowledge of the risk is not, however, devoid of importance. Proof that the plaintiff knew of the danger is evidence that he consented to it: indeed it would be difficult for the defendant to prove 'volenti' in the plaintiff who was not aware of the hazard. Further, knowledge of the danger is a factor in contributory negligence.

11.2   Defences to tortious liability

(a)   **Statutory Authority**

    (i)   Acts done in pursuance of an express command of Parliament are not torts, and harm caused thereby is not actionable unless it is caused by negligence: *Fisher v Ruislip U.D.C.*.

    (ii)   When the legislature gives mere permission to do something, it must be done in as harmless a manner as possible: *Metropolitan Asylum District v Hill*.

(b)   **Consent**

    (i)   A person who has voluntarily consented to the commission of a tort may not sue on it - *volenti non fit injuria*.

    (ii)   The consent of the plaintiff whether it be express or implied, must be a true consent to both the physical and legal risks.

(iii)   Rescue Cases - the defence of consent does not apply where a dangerous situation has been created by a defendant's negligent action and a person is placed in an emergency situation and has to decide to act to save or protect the lives of others: *Haynes v Harwood*.

In these 'rescue' cases the tests to be applied are:

-    Did the rescuer intervene to rescue someone who was put in peril by the negligence of another? and

-    Was the act such as could be expected of a man of ordinary courage and ability situated in similar circumstances?

(c)   **Necessity**

(i)   In some cases even damage done intentionally may be excused where the defendant was acting under the compulsion of necessity to prevent a greater evil.

(ii)   The defence is rare although it was successfully raised in *Cope v Sharp*.

11.3   Reasonable foreseeability

The consequences of a defendant's wrongful act or omission may be endless. Even so a plaintiff who has established that the defendant's wrong caused his loss may be unable to recover damages because his loss is not sufficiently connected with the defendant's wrong to make the latter liable. In other words, the loss is too remote a consequence to be recoverable.

As regards determination of remoteness in *Re Polemis* the Court of Appeal made it clear that the defendant was liable for all the direct consequences of his act whether or not he ought reasonably to have foreseen them. In this case a ship was hired under a charter and was loaded with petrol. Owing to a leak, the hold became full of petrol vapour and at a port of call an Arab stevedore negligently allowed a plank to fall into the hold. The fall caused a spark which ignited the petrol vapour and there was an explosion which rendered the ship a total loss. All the damage that flowed from the negligence of letting the plank fall was payable by the charterers even though they could not have foreseen the consequences.

The decision in this case was not followed by the Privy Council in *Overseas Tankship v Morts Dock Co*, otherwise known as *The Wagon Mound* and whilst decisions of the Privy Council are not binding on English Courts they necessarily have considerable persuasive authority. The facts in the case were simple. Furnace oil escaped from the defendant's ship into Sydney Harbour. A piece of debris was floating in the oil beneath M's wharf and on the floating debris was a piece of smouldering cotton waste. The oil burst into flames and M's wharf was destroyed. The Privy Council reversing the Supreme Court of New South Wales held that it is a principle of civil liability that a person is responsible for the probable consequences of his acts and then only if the resulting damage could have been foreseen, by a reasonable man. Foreseeability was the effective test and it is not enough that the damage was a direct consequence of the negligent act.

This decision, with its basis in reasonable foreseeability, seems to accord more with common sense than the principle established in *Re Polemis* and its basis of direct liability (according to which a defendant was often made liable for damage which he could not possibly have foreseen). However, the exact status of the *'The Wagon Mound'* is not quite clear, for although it appears to be becoming the authority on questions of remoteness in tort - see *Hughes v Lord Advocate* - *Re Polemis* has never been directly overruled.

Session 12: General principles of the tort of negligence

Objective test answers

(1)　　C　　(2)　　B　　(3)　　D　　(4)　　C

Written test answers

12.1　　Breach of duty of care

Negligence may be regarded as an omission to do something which a reasonable man guided upon those considerations which ordinarily regulate the conduct of human affairs would do, or doing something which a prudent and reasonable man would not do.

In determining whether or not there has been a breach of duty of care and whether or not the defendant has acted negligently the court will consider, *inter alia*, the magnitude of the risk involved, the importance of the object to be attained, and the practicability of the precautions taken.

As regards the magnitude of the risk to which others are exposed, two factors must be considered - the seriousness of the injury risked, and the likelihood of the injury being in fact caused. Thus in *Paris v Stepney Borough Council* the plaintiff, who had only one good eye, was blinded in the course of his employment. He contended that his employers, by omitting to provide him with goggles, were in breach of their duty to take reasonable care of his safety because, though it was not the practice to provide goggles for that class of work, they must have known that the consequences of an accident to his good eye would be peculiarly disastrous. The Court accepted the plaintiff's contention. With respect to the likelihood of injury it must be shown not only that the event was foreseeable but also that there is a reasonable likelihood of injury: *Bolton v Stone; Hilder v Associated Portland Cement Manufacturers Limited*.

The court will also have to consider the importance of the object which the defendant was seeking to achieve. Thus the saving of life and limb justifies taking risks which would not be permissible in the case of an ordinary commercial enterprise: *Daborn v Bath Tramways Motor Co.*

The risk must be balanced against the practicability of the measures necessary to eliminate it. The remoter the risk, the less that can be expected in the way of precautions, though, if the risk is great, the measures to be taken by the defendant must reflect this fact. If the risk to life or property is really substantial, and no precautions would avail against it, it may be the duty of the defendants to cease to carry on the particular activity in question: *Latimer v A E C.*

Finally, it should be remembered that where anyone is engaged in a transaction in which he holds himself out as having professional skill, the law expects him to show the average amount of competence associated with the proper discharge of the duties of that profession, trade or calling -imperitia culpae adnumeratur.

12.2   Accident

'In some circumstances, the mere fact that an accident has occurred raises an inference of neglience against the defendant' (Fleming). *Res ipsa loquitur* is an exotic though convenient label to describe a rule of evidence by which the court assists the plaintiff to prove negligence against the defendant who was in control of the situation which, despite the absence of exact explanation, caused the plaintiff's injury in circumstances in which one would not expect injury without negligence.

One does not normally find stones in buns: *Chaproniere v Mason*; or expect cranes to collapse: *Swan v Salisbury Construction Co Limited*; or sacks of sugar to drop from buildings: *Scott v London Docks Co*. If such things happen, it may be presumed that someone was negligent.

That negligent person may be presumed to be the defendant if the defendant, by virtue of his exclusive knowledge or control of the events, may be thus linked with the incident. The negligence may be pinned on the defendant more readily if the plaintiff falls through the door of an empty compartment in the defendant's train soon after departure: *Gee v Metropolitan Ry Co*, than if he falls from the corridor of the defendant's express train after a seven-mile run: *Easson v L N E R*. If the defendant is the only person, apart from the plaintiff himself, with access to a shed containing the defendant's gas meter and pipes: *Lloyde v West Midlands Gas Board*, it will be easier to infer that the defendant was responsible than where a building collapses: *Carruthers v MacGregor*, or a drain tube left in the plaintiff's bladder: *Morris v Winsbury-White*, and any one of two or more independent persons might be responsible.

Res ipsa loquitur does not apply if an exact explanation is available to the plaintiff. Not only can he not invoke the maxim: he does not need to. Thus, in *Barkway v South Wales Transport Co Limited* the plaintiff was able to succeed in negligence for injuries received in a bus crash without reliance on *res ipsa loquitur* since there was evidence of the defendant's failure to take reasonable car of the tyres of the bus, one of which had burst.

Once the ingredients of *res ipsa loquitur* are present, the plaintiff has raised a presumption of negligence by the defendant, which it is the defendant's 'evidential' burden to rebut (per Lord Pearson in *Henderson v Jenkins (Henry E) and Sons and Evans*. If the defendant does produce some rebutting evidence, such as by showing how the accident happened and that there was to breach of duty by the defendant (as in *Colvilles v Devine*), or by showing no lack of care by the defendant, as in *Pearson v North Western Gas Board*, then the ball may be back in the plaintiff's court, and he may have to add greater weight to his cause; for the legal burden of proof is always on the plaintiff and 'at the end of the trial the judge has to decide whether he is satisfied on a balance of probabilities that the accident was caused by negligence on the part of the defendant and, if he is not so satisfied, the plaintiff's action fails', per Lord Pearson.

Thus, to say that the plaintiff has 'to prove the accident and nothing more' requires some qualification.

12.3   Contributory negligence

Sometimes, when an accident occurs, both parties have been negligent and this raises the doctrine of contributory negligence. At one time a plaintiff guilty of contributory negligence could not recover any damages unless the defendant could, with reasonable care, have avoided the consequences of the plaintiff's contributory negligence. Thus, the courts were often concerned to find out who had the last chance of avoiding the accident, and this led to some unsatisfactory decisions.

Now, however, under the Law Reform (Contributory Negligence) Act 1945, liability is apportionable between plaintiff and defendant. The claim is not defeated but damages may be reduced according to the degree of fault of the plaintiff. S1(1) of the Act reads:

> 'Where any person suffers damage as the result partly of his own fault and partly of the fault of any other person or persons, a claim in respect of that damage shall not be defeated by reason of the fault of the person suffering the damage; but the damages recoverable in respect thereof shall be reduced to such extent as the court thinks just and equitable having regard to the claimant's share in the responsibility for the damage.'

'Damage' is defined in S4 of the Act to include loss of life and personal injury, and probably it covers any loss for which damages can at common law be awarded. 'Fault' on the part of the plaintiff means negligence, breach of statutory duty or other act or omission which would, apart from the Act, give rise to the defence of contributory negligence - S4.

In reducing the damages, the court is required by S1(1) to have regard to 'the claimant's share in the responsibility for the damage'. This requires consideration of the causative potency of the act and the extent to which the plaintiff deviates from the standard of the reasonable man in looking after his own safety.

Session 13: Specific forms of the tort of negligence: strict liability, breach of statutory duty

Objective test answers

(1)   C   (2)   C   (3)   C   (4)   C

Written test answers

13.1   Occupier liability

The liability of the occupier of premises to persons who, whilst on such premises, suffer injuries from defects thereon, depends on the character in which such persons come upon his premises.

Before the Occupiers' Liability Act 1957 such persons would be regarded in law as entering either (a) in persuance of a contract with the occupier, or (b) not in persuance of a contract, but as (i) invitees, (ii) licensees or (iii) trespassers, and the duty towards them was measured according to the particular character they answered, it being governed by the express or implied terms of the contract under (a) and being of descending scope in the case of (b) (i), (ii) and (iii).

The effect of the 1957 Occupiers' Liability Act has been to render the liability of an occupier to a person on his premises dependent upon whether or not that person is a visitor. It has achieved this by abolition of the common law distinction between invitees and licensees, and substitution for it of a single common duty of care owed by the occupier to his visitors. Visitors are defined by S1(2) of the Act as those persons who would at common law be treated as either invitees or licensees. However, it retains the separate category of contractual entrants, though in the absence of any express provision in the particular contract, the Act provides that there shall be implied into the contract a term that the occupier owes the entrant the common duty of care (S5). Thus, it may be generally stated that the common duty of care is owed by the occupier to all his lawful visitors and, as the Act has not affected the law governing the occupiers' liability to trespassers, the dichotomy under the Act is that of lawful and unlawful visitors.

The common duty of care owed by an occupier to his lawful visitors is defined in the Act as 'a duty to take such care as in all the circumstances of the case, is reasonable to see that the visitor will be reasonably safe in using the premises for the purpose for which he is invited or permitted by the occupier to be there' (S2(2)). However, the occupier, insofar as he is free to do so, may extend, restrict or exclude that duty to any visitor or visitors by agreement or otherwise.

As regards the duty of care the following points are worthy of note:

(a)   the circumstances relevant include the degree of care and of want of care which would ordinarily be looked for in the visitor, so that an occupier must be prepared for children to be less careful than adults and may expect that a person, in the exercise of his calling, will appreciate and guard against any special risks ordinarily incident to it, so far as the occupier leaves him free to do so;

(b)   warning of danger will be enough to enable the visitor to be reasonably safe;

(c)   the occupier is not liable for the faulty work of his independent contractor where he had taken reasonable steps to satisfy himself that the contractor was competent and had properly done the work.

13.2   Blunder

The House of Lords in *Hedley-Byrne v Heller* held that 'if in a sphere in which a person is so placed that others could reasonably rely upon his judgement or his skill or upon his ability to make careful enquiry, a person takes it upon himself to give information or advice to, or allows his information or advice to be passed on to, another person who, as he knows or should know, will place reliance upon it, then a duty of care will arise . . .' (per Lord Morris).

The difficulties which have arisen in connection with liability for causing financial loss through reliance on careless statements have been not so much in connection with the rules of 'breach of duty' and 'resultant damage' (which are the same as in any other form of the tort of negligence), as in terms of the 'duty' question.

The law lords seemed satisfied that the duty arises only when there is a 'special relationship', though they did not all agree on a definition of it. Lord Devlin considered 'the idea of a relationship equivalent to contract all that is necessary to cover the situation'; Lords Morris (above) and Hodson felt that it depended on the defendant's assumption of responsibility for his advice; and general favour was bestowed on the dissenting judgement of Denning LJ in *Candler v Crane Christmas* who said that the duty was 'limited to cases where the information or advice is given in response to an enquiry for the guidance of the very person in the very transaction in question'.

Apart from the requirement of 'special relationship', it appears that an accountant is now regarded as the sort of person who may assume responsibility for his statements, that the defendant must be someone on whose advice the plaintiff may reasonably expect to rely; and that it matters not at all that there is no consideration for the advice.

It is clear that their lordships in the principal case did not envisage liability on 'social occasions' (eg, solicitor giving casual advice on a train) and of course it will have to be shown by Blunder, if he is to succeed, that his meeting with Madcap did not fall into that category. Otherwise, the facts of the problem fall neatly into the formula supplied by Denning LJ (above).

However, Blunder may have a greater burden if the English courts follow the approach of the Privy Council in the Australian case of *Mutual Life v Evatt*. There, 'special relationship' was confined to cases where the defendant was either in the business of supplying information or advice, or had claimed to possess the necessary skill to give it and the preparedness to take care in giving it. The test is applied to the role or capacity of the defendant at the time he makes the representation (here, after the company meeting) rather than at any other time: so Blunder's best hope may be that the English courts refuse to follow Evatt and adopt instead a much wider interpretation of 'special relationship'.

If Madcap made the representation knowing it to be false, then Blunder may sue in the tort of deceit which has the advantage that it does not require proof of a duty of care at all. It consists 'in the act of making a wilfully false statement with intent that the plaintiff shall act in reliance upon it, and with the result that he does so act and suffers harm in consequence' (Salmond). Another advantage of this action is that any contributory negligence on the part of Blunder may be ignored; in the negligence action it would be 'reasonable foreseeability'. In the negligence action it is doubtful whether there would be a remedy at all in respect of the further loss of £1,000 because this loss seems to be attributable to the impecuniosity of Blunder which resembles that of the plaintiff in *The Liesbosch*. But if deceit lay the £1,000 might be recoverable because in *Doyle v Olby*, in which damages were awarded for the loss caused to the plaintiff by the sale of an ironmongers' business of which the financial position had been fraudulently misrepresented to him by the defendant, the Court of Appeal awarded damages, inter alia, for that loss caused by the fact that the plaintiff 'could not afford to employ a traveller' (per Lord Denning MR).

13.3   An operation

P may be able to sue all or any combination of D, N, S, M and R in the tort of negligence. In each case he must prove the normal ingredients of a duty of care owed to P, in law and in fact; a breach of that duty by the person or persons sued; and that his injury was both caused by the breach and of a kind which was reasonably foreseeable.

In particular, the following issues are raised by the problem:

If D is to be liable, presumably this must be vicarious liability for the negligence, if any, of N provided N was a servant acting in the course of her employment at the time of the injection. On other other hand, the indications are that D would not be liable for any tort committed by S who appears to be an independent contractor. In *Roe v Ministry of Health* Denning LJ held that hospital authorities 'are responsible for the whole of their staff ... permanent or temporary, resident or visiting, whole-time or part-time . . . The only exception is the case of consultants or anaesthetists . . . employed by the patient himself'. Of course, the same might apply in the case of N if she were 'hired' from a nursing agency.

In *Roe* medical staff were held not liable, in circumstances similar to those in the problem, because the events by which the anaesthetic came to be contaminated were not reasonably foreseeable at the time in the light of contemporary medical knowledge. Thus the defendants here (D, N and S) will be liable only if, in all the circumstances, N and S failed to take reasonable care to avoid reasonably foreseeable risks. If the risks are reasonably avoidable but not avoided, then liability will be incurred notwithstanding absence of exact knowledge of precisely how the contamination causes the paralysis: *McGhee v NCB*.

The liability, if any, of R and M, depends upon the 'narrow rule' in *Donoghue v Stevenson*, ie, upon proof of failure of R or M to take reasonable care in the supply or 'preparation or putting up' of products likely to affect a 'consumer' thereof. A defendant can escape liability by showing that he took reasonable care; but frequently the fact that he was in control of the chattel either during its manufacture (*Grant v Australian Knitting Mills*, underpants containing excess of sulphites), or whilst it is stored in his shop, will invite the maxim 'res ipsa loquitur', at least where the customer is expected to 'use the article exactly as it left the maker . . . and use it as it was intended to be used', per Privy Council in *Grant*.

In *Kubach v Hollands*, a schoolgirl was injured by an explosion in a chemistry laboratory. Manufacturers who had carelessly supplied the wrong chemical to a chemist who had been held liable for re-selling it to the school, were themselves not liable to pay indemnity to the chemist, since they might have supplied it to him for a number of purposes and, though he had been warned to test the substance, he had neither done so nor passed on the warning.

In general, the liability of all the defendants will depend upon whether in all the circumstances (apart from those specifically noted) each has broken his duty. Thus, the usual factors such as practicability of safety precautions (*Latimer v AEC*); magnitude of the risk (*Bolton v Stone*); vulnerability of P (*Paris v Stephen BC*); the question of whether normal procedure was followed (*Roe*), etc, will all be matters for consideration.

Session 14: The contract of employment 1

Objective test answers

| (1) | D | (2) | C | (3) | C | (4) | C | (5) | C |

Written test answers

14.1 Martin

The main legal protection comes from statutory rules, breach of which is a criminal offence. By the Health and Safety at Work, etc, Act 1974, S2, every employer must ensure so far as reasonably practicable the health, safety and welfare at work of his employees. In particular, he must provide plant which, so far as reasonably practicable, is safe. By S6, manufacturers, designers, suppliers and importers of machinery for use at work must ensure, so far as reasonably practicable, that it is so designed and constructed as to be safe when used. By S7, employees too must take reasonable care for themselves and others, and cooperate in ensuring that safety requirements are observed.

The 1974 Act applies to almost all places of work. Other Acts have more limited application. The Factories Act 1961, for example, imposes strict duties on the occupiers of factories. S12 requires that flywheels directly connected to any prime mover be securely fenced. By S13, transmission machinery must be securely fenced unless its position or construction render it as safe as if it were fenced. By S14, every **dangerous** part of any machinery must be securely fenced unless its position or construction render it as safe as if it were fenced. By S16, fencing and other safeguards must be substantial, and constantly maintained and kept in position while the dangerous parts are in motion or use. It must be sufficient to keep workers from contact with dangerous parts, although need not prevent broken parts from flying out. Unlike the 1974 Act, which generally only applies 'so far as reasonably practicable', the Factories Act imposes strict liability. If the machine can only be used unfenced, it must generally not be used. In *John Summers Limited v Frost*, F hurt his thumb on a grinding wheel which could not be used while fenced. The factory occupier was still held to have broken his statutory duty. Special regulations make some exceptions to this strict rule.

The 1961 Act applies to factories. Other Acts, such as the Mines and Quarries Acts and the Offices, Shops and Railways Premises Act 1963 have similar limited application. Like the Factories Act, these Acts are backed by criminal penalties, and enforced by inspectors responsible to the Health and Safety Executive. Breach of these special Acts, although not the 1974 Act, is also civilly actionable by anyone injured.

DS Mills appears to be a factory, and the 1961 Act will apply as well as the Health and Safety at Work Act. The fact that clothing became caught indicates that dangerous machinery is not securely fenced. DS Mills will therefore be liable to prosecution, and may be fined. If the danger is serious, the magistrates' court can forbid use of the machine until it is made safe. Alternatively, an inspector can issue a prohibition notice under the 1974 Act.

Martin can also sue DS Mills for damages for breach of statutory duty under the 1961 Act. The fact that Martin was in a place where he should not have been is not a complete defence. In *Uddin v Associated Portland Cement Manufacturers Limited*, the plaintiff was injured by dangerous machinery while trying to catch a pigeon. APC was still held liable but, as probably in Martin's case here, the damages were substantially reduced for contributory negligence.

Norman will also recover damages for breach of statutory duty. The fact that he came 'voluntarily' to the danger in trying to pull Martin clear is no defence for DS Mills because Norman was acting to save Martin from risk of personal injury caused by the fault of DS Mills; see *Haynes v Harwood*. If DS Mills is their employer, it must be insured against liability to Martin and Norman under the Employers' Liability (Compulsory Insurance) Act 1969.

14.2   Employer's common law duties

The common law duties owed by an employer to his employee in the absence of any specific provisions in the contract of service are as follows:

(a)   A duty to pay the agreed remuneration.

(b)   A duty to indemnify the employee in respect of all losses, liabilities and expenses incurred by the latter in carrying out orders, unless the employee knew that the act was unlawful.

(c)   A duty to provide for the reasonable safety of his employees. This consists of provision of safe premises and equipment and a reasonably safe system of work.

(d)   The employer is under no implied duty to provide work, except:

(i)   where the employee would lose the opportunity to increase his reputation by publicity if no work were provided; and

(ii)   where the remuneration depends upon the amount of work performed.

14.3 Hairdresser

(a) Unless there is a stipulation in an employee's contract of employment forbidding the performance of work in his spare time an employee may perform such work provided it does not harm his employer's interest. In this case it would appear that Michael's spare-time activities may be to his employer's detriment, ie in the loss of work. In common law an employee has a duty of loyalty and good faith and therefore Michael's employers may possibly obtain an injunction preventing his spare-time activity or, if he persists, there may be grounds for dismissal.

In *Hivac v Park Royal Scientific Instruments Limited*, employees of the plaintiff worked for the defendant (a rival firm) in their spare time. The plaintiff was granted an injunction preventing such activity.

(b) An employer is under no obligation to give an employee a reference: *Gallear v J F Watson and Son Limited*. However, if an employer does give a reference he may be liable for defamation of character if any statements tends to lower the employee in the eyes of right-thinking people! The employer may be liable for damages in tort on the grounds of either slander if the statement is made verbally, or libel, if made in a more permanent form. The employer may use the defences of justification (truth) or qualified privilege. If the employer knowingly recommends an employee in terms which he knows to be false, the subsequent misconduct of the employee will render his former employer liable for damages in the tort of deceit. If the misstatement is negligent the employer may be liable for negligent misstatement: *Hedley Byrn and Co Limited v Heller and Partners*.

(c) An employee owes a duty of loyalty and good faith to his employer and thus may not accept bribes or make secret profits. Accordingly the employer is able to recover the bribe from Robert, dismiss him without notice and repudiate the contract with the salesman's employer: *Reading v Attorney-General*.

Session 15: The contract of employment 2

Objective test answers

(1) B (2) B (3) D (4) D (5) C

Written test answers

15.1 Dismissed employees

(a) Brenda's dismissal will certainly be unfair unless the employer can show that her pregnancy made her incapable of adequately performing the work she was employed to do or would have made it illegal for her to continue in that work. If he relies on these exceptions he must also show either that he could not offer her suitable alternative work or that he did make an offer of suitable alternative work but it was refused. In order to make a claim Brenda must have been continuously employed for the appropriate qualifying period.

(b) Possession of a valid driving licence is clearly a qualification required in Charles' job. It would also be illegal for Charles to perform his work while disqualified. Either of these is a substantial reason for dismissing Charles, and he would succeed in a claim for unfair dismissal only if he could show that the employer acted unreasonably in treating his disqualification as a reason for dismissal. On the face of it, this would be very difficult to show.

(c)   In general any agreement to exclude the provisions of the Employment Protection (Consolidation) Act 1978 is void. The only circumstances in which David could have made an enforceable agreement not to pursue an unfair dismissal claim is if he was employed under a contract for a fixed term of one year or more, and his agreement was in writing. If David is not within that exception then he may go to an industrial tribunal if he considers his dismissal was unfair and he has been continuously employed for the relevant qualifying period.

15.2   John

(a)   The rights to redundancy payments was introduced by the Redundancy Payments Act 1965 and amended by the Employment Protection Act 1975. The governing legislation is now the Employment Protection (Consolidation) Act 1978. A redundancy payment is a compensatory payment made to employees who lose their jobs in certain circumstances. The amount of the payment is calculated according to age, length of service and average weekly earnings: subject to various maxima. The purpose of a redundancy payment is to compensate for the loss of security and to encourage employees to accept redundancy without damaging industrial relations.

A redundancy payment is compensation for the loss of a right which a long-term employee has in his job. The concept of unfair dismissal and compensation for unfair dismissal is incorporated within the Employment Protection Consolidation Act 1978. Compensation may be awarded under three different headings.

(i)   *The basic award* - This is calculated in a similar way to a redundancy payment. An award may be reduced where a tribunal finds that an employee has caused or contributed to his dismissal. The basic award may be reduced, or further reduced, where any redundancy payment is made to an employee unfairly dismissed.

(ii)   *The compensatory award* - This is an amount which the tribunal considers just and equitable in all the circumstances, subject to a statutory maximum. In assessing an award the tribunal will take into account immediate and future losses in earnings, loss of benefits in kind such as a company car etc.

(iii)   *The additional award* - The additional award is made where an employer refuses to reinstate or re-engage an unfairly dismissed employee.

The Employment Act 1982 provides special rules for assessing compensation where unfair dismissal is connected with trade union membership or activities.

(b)   The circumstances present John with two possible of claims: first, he may claim that he is redundant; secondly, he may claim unfair dismissal. As far as redundancy is concerned, the new company cannot unilaterally vary the terms of the contract of employment without John's agreement unless there is a provision in the contract for such variation.

In *Marriot v Oxford Co-operative Society* an employer who sought to reduce an employee's wages by £1 per week was held to have constructively dismissed the employee who was entitled to a redundancy payment. John may claim that he has been down-graded by a change in salary and status and that the alternative work offered is completely unsuitable. Unfair dismissal has been judicially held to include the down-grading of an employee thereby making resignation inevitable: *Cox v Phillips Industries Limited*. Where an employer behaves unreasonably John is entitled to terminate his own employment and thereby give rise to a claim based on constructive dismissal.

Providing that John has been employed for 2 years or more he may make the claims outlined above.

15.3   Arnold

Arnold may claim to be redundant if the work he is required to do is fundamentally differed and his original job has effectively ceased. In *Sartin v Co-operative Retail Services* a grocery shop was converted into a supermarked which resulted in a great increase in floor space and turnover. Sartin was manager of the grocery shop but could not cope with the requirements of the new type of business. He was therefore redundant as a new type of manager was required. In contrast in *North Riding Garages v Butterwick* a garage came under new ownership. Butterwick was the workshop manager and was mainly involved in mechanics work. Under the new ownership Butterwick was expected to deal with the administration, but could not cope. It was held that he was not redundant as the requirement was still for a workshop manager. It would appear that Arnold's position is similar to the Butterwick case and he would therefore not receive a redundancy payment.

If Arnold was offered suitable new employment on the same terms, and unreasonably refused; or on different terms, or in a seperate place, and after a reasonable trial period of not less than four weeks, also unreasonably refused, then he would not be entitled to a redundancy payment.

The agreement under the new contract must be in writing stating the date the trial period ends and terms of employment at the end of the trial period. If the employee terminates the contract at the end of the trial period, or before because the work was unsuitable he would be entitled to a redundancy payment. The same situation applies if the employer terminates on the ground that the employee cannot cope with the new type of work.

Glossary

Expression	Meaning
Acceptance	An unconditional assent to all the terms of an offer.
Accord and satisfaction	The purchase of a release from an obligation, whether arising under contract or tort, by means of any valuable consideration, not being the actual performance of the obligation itself. The accord is the agreement by which the obligation is discharged. The satisfaction is the consideration which makes the agreement operative.
Actus reus	A guilty act.
Administrative tribunal	An independent statutory body exercising a judicial function.
Affidavit	A written statement which the maker has solemnly promised to be true.
Agency	The relationship that exists between two persons when one, called the agent, is considered in law to represent the other, called the principal, in such a way as to be able to affect the principal's legal position in respect of strangers to the relationship by the making of contracts or the disposition of property.
Apparent authority	The authority of an agent as it appears to others.
Arbitration	Settlement of a dispute by a person(s) acting as arbitrator(s)
Bill	A draft of an Act of Parliament submitted to Parliament for discussion.
Bill of exchange	An unconditional order in writing, addressed by one person to another signed by the person giving it, requiring the person to whom it is addressed to pay on demand or at a fixed or determinable future time a sum certain in money to or to the order of a specified person, or to bearer.
Case law	Law derived from decisions in specific cases.
Caveat emptor	Buyer beware.
Certiorari	An order requiring proceedings in an inferior court to be transferred to the High Court.
Cheque	A bill of exchange drawn on a banker payable on demand.

Expression	Meaning
CIF	Trade terms under which the seller is responsible for bringing the goods to a named port of destination and must insure the goods against loss during the journey.
Common law	System of law applicable to all persons in England and based on rules established by professional lawyers as shown in respected textbooks and in the judgments of courts from about the 11th century onwards.
Condition	An obligation, that one party has under a contract, that is such an essential feature of the contract that failure to perform it entitles the other party to regard the contract as terminated.
Conditional sale agreement	An agreement for the sale of goods or land under which the purchase price or part of it is payable by instalments and the property in the goods or land is to stay with the seller until conditions specified in the agreement are satisfied.
Consideration	Price paid for the promise of the other party.
Consumer credit agreement	An agreement between an individual and other person by which that other person provides the individual with credit not exceeding £15,000.
Consumer hire agreement	An agreement made by a person with an individual for the bailment of goods to the individual which is not a hire-purchase agreement and is capable of subsisting for more than three months and does not require the individual to make payment exceeding £15,000.
Contract	An agreement enforceable in law.
Contract for services	A contrast establishing the relationship of employer and independent contractor.
Contract in restraint of trade	A contract by which a party restricts his future liberty to carry on his trade, business or profession in such manner and with such persons as he chooses.
Contract of service	A contract establishing the relationship of master and servant.
County courts	Local courts dealing with minor civil cases.
Credit-sale agreement	An agreement for the sale of goods under which the purchase price or part of it is payable by instalments, but which is not a conditional sale agreement.

Expression	Meaning
Crime	An act prohibited with penal consequences.
Crown Court	The principal English court for the trial of criminal cases.
Customer	A person who has an account at a bank.
Damnum sine injuria	Damage without legal injury.
Deed	Writing on paper, parchment or vellum, made by or on behalf of a person whose seal and (unless the person is a corporation) signature have been put on the document and who has shown an intention to be bound by the written statement.
Deposition	A statement of oath of a witness in legal proceedings; especially one made at some stage before the trial (eg, at committal proceedings in a magistrates' court).
Discovery	The process of obtaining, from another party to legal proceedings, documents which may contain evidence relating to those proceedings.
Divisional Court	A tribunal consisting of at least two High Court judges, which is convened to hear, eg, appeals from magistrates' courts.
Duress	Constraint by injury or imprisonment or by threats.
Ejusdem generis rule	The rule that general words which follow two or more particular words in an Act of Parliament must be confined to a meaning of the same kind as the particular words.
Employment appeal tribunal	Court that hears appeals from decisions of industrial tribunals.
Equity	The law administered in the Court of Chancery prior to 1875.
Estoppel	A rule of evidence whereby a party is precluded by some previous act to which he was party or privy from asserting or denying a fact.
Exclusion clause	A term inserted into a contract whereby one party to a contract seeks to exclude or limit his liability to the other in the event of certain contingencies.
Execution	Putting into effect. Execution of a judgment means giving effect to the judgment.

Expression	Meaning
Ex parte	On behalf of. Used to describe: (1) an application made by one party to proceedings without giving the other party a chance to appear; (2) an application made by a person who has an interest in the matter but is not a party to the proceedings (eg, in bankruptcy).
FAS	Trade terms under which the seller is responsible for getting the goods to the quay at which a named ship will berth (or on to lighters if the ship will lie offshore).
FOB	Trade terms under which the seller is responsible for getting the goods placed on board a named ship at a port of shipment named in the sales contract.
Garnishee order	An order requiring a person who owes money to a judgment debtor to pay it instead to the creditor of that debtor.
Habeas corpus	A writ commanding a person who has detained an individual to appear before a court to justify the detention.
High court	Principal English court for the trial of civil cases.
Hire-purchase	A system for buying goods on credit in which the goods are hired to the buyer with an option to purchase them for a nominal sum after a certain amount has been paid in hire charges.
Imperitia culpae adnumeratur	Lack of skill is considered a fault.
Indictment	A written accusation of a crime prosecuted by the Crown in the Crown Court.
Industrial tribunal	Tribunal which hears cases concerning employment law.
Injunction	A order of the court restraining the commission or continuance of a wrongful act.
Injuria sine damno	Legal injury without damage.
Interlocutory injunction	An injunction granted while legal proceedings are in progress and having effect only until final judgment is given in the case.
Invitation to treat	An invitation (to a particular person or the world at large) to offer to make a contract.
Laissez-faire	The policy of non-interference.

Expression	*Meaning*
Legislation	The formulation of law by the appropriate organ or organs of the State, in such a manner that the actual words used are themselves part of the law.
Lien	A right to retain possession of some other person's property until that person has fulfilled an obligation.
Magistrates' court	A tribunal consisting of between three and seven justices of the peace or one stipendiary magistrate which may try minor criminal cases and some matters concerning family law.
Mens rea	A guilty mind.
Merchantable quality	Goods are of merchantable quality if they are fit for the purposes for which goods of that kind are commonly bought.
Minor	A person under the age of eighteen years.
Negligence	The breach of a legal duty to take care which results in damage undesired by the defendant to the plaintiff.
Nominee	A person who is in some legal relationship in name only, having undertaken to exercise all rights and duties attached to the relationship in accordance with another person's directions.
Novation	An arrangement by which a contract between A and B is rescinded and replaced by a contract between A and C.
Obiter dictum	Something said in passing. A remark made by a judge which is not one of the grounds for his decision but which is a comment on the law which may be very influential if the judge is eminent.
Per incuriam	With lack of care. Used to describe a judgment given without realising that it would contradict a precedent.
Pleadings	Documents given by one party to another in the course of legal proceedings stating the claims and defences that it is proposed to argue when the proceedings are tried in court.
Privilege	The right to withhold information during legal proceedings and prevent the information being given in evidence.
Promissory note	An unconditional promise in writing made by one person to another, signed by the maker, engaging to pay, on demand or at a fixed or determinable future time, a sum certain in money to, or to the order of, a specified person or to bearer.

Expression	Meaning
Puisne judge	A High Court judge who does not hold a higher judicial office.
Quantum meruit	An amount claimed under a contract for services in which the consideration was not specified.
Ratio decidendi	The reason for a decision. The grounds on which a court based its decision in a case and which may be used as a precedent in later cases.
Representation	A statement of fact made before a contract is executed with a view to persuading a party to enter into the contract.
Res ipsa loquitur	The facts speak for themselves.
Reservation of title	Arrangement under which a seller of goods retains the legal title to the goods until they are paid for.
Res gestae	Things done. The events accompanying or surrounding an event that is the subject of legal proceedings and which are essential for an understanding of that event.
Sale in market overt	A sale made in accordance with the customs of a lawfully constituted market (or in a shop in the City of London) and which confers a good title on the buyer.
Simple contract	A contract providing for consideration.
Sola	Used to describe a bill of exchange or bill of lading that was issued without any copies.
Specific performance	An order of the court requiring the carrying out of an obligation.
Stare decisis	To stand by decided matters. The doctrine that the rules or principles stated in judicial decisions are of general application.
Statement of claim	A statement made by a plantiff in civil legal proceedings of the claims he is making against the defendant.
Statutory instrument	A document containing orders, rules, regulations or other legislation made under powers delegated by Parliament and which must be published according to set procedures.
Strict liability	Liability without fault.

Expression	*Meaning*
Subrogation	A right, on paying a person compensation for damage he has suffered, to take any legal proceedings that person could have taken in respect of the damage.
Summary trial	Trial of a criminal offence by a magistrates' court.
Supreme Court of England and Wales	Principal court administering English Law. It consists of the Crown Court, the High Court and the Court of Appeal.
Tort	A civil wrong other than a breach of contract or a breach of trust.
Uberrimae fidei	Of the fullest trust. Requiring full disclosure of all relevant facts in order to be a valid contract.
Undue influence	The unconscientious use of power or authority, by one person over another, in such a way that the stronger party acquires a benefit, either for himself or for some person or object indicated by him.
Vicarious liability	The liability A may owe to C because of damage suffered by C as a result of a tortious action committed by B.
Void contract	A contract that the law will not enforce and which gives no rights to either party.
Voidable contract	A contract that one party may declare to be void but which is valid and enforceable unless he does so declare.
Volenti non fit injuria	No injury is done to one who consents.
Warranty	In the law on contracts: an obligation, that one party has under a contract, that is not an essential feature of the contract so that failure to meet the obligation does not entitle the other party to regard the contract as terminated. Insurance law: a condition that must be fulfilled in order to make a claim under a policy.
Writ of summons	A document issued by a court to inform a person that legal proceedings have been started against him and instructing him to defend those proceedings or lose them by default.

Index

The numbers refer to the session and section

0080x

0080x

ABOUT FT COURSES

Financial Training Courses provide the ideal way to study – whatever the student's situation. We provide a flexible, efficient service – designed to adapt to individual needs and to give the best possible chance of success.

- **Study Packs** – At the heart of our courses and programmes are the Financial Training Study Packs; clear, up–to–date texts which are adopted by colleges as set course texts.

- **Revision Packs** – Doing the vital job of supporting the Study Packs, each Revision Pack contains a complete revision programme. Question banks of carefully selected questions ensure familiarity with all parts of the syllabus.

- **Home tuition courses** – Complete learning programmes designed around information you provide. The home tuition course incorporates a unique individual Study Programme, Study Packs, Revision Packs, tutors' assistance and practice examinations.

- **Intensive revision courses** – An invaluable back–up to our other material. Personal contact with tutors in intensive classroom situations gives a much greater chance of success. Each course lasts 3 to 5 days, with convenient locations throughout England and Wales from which to choose.

- **Link courses** – We give our comprehensive Link Course five stars for good reasons. It incorporates all the above elements in addition to providing extra oral tuition. The combination of home study and oral tuition is perfect, as it keeps the student motivated and directly in touch with tutors. Link Courses are our way of making the most of a student's time and chances.

For further information, write or phone us at Financial Training Courses, Parkway House, Sheen Lane, London SW14 8LS. Telephone: 081 876 0499 Fax: 081 878 1749

STOCKISTS AND DISTRIBUTORS

UK

London

Barbican Business Books, 9 Moorfields, London EC2   Telephone: 071 628 7479

Dillons University Bookshop, 1 Malet Street, London WC1E 7JE   Telephone: 071 636 1577

W & G Foyle, 119 Charing Cross Road, London WC2   Telephone: 071 437 5660

Parks Bookshop, 244 High Holborn, London WC1V 7DZ   Telephone: 071 831 9501

Parks Bookshop, 18 London Road, London SE1 6JX   Telephone: 071 928 5378

Cambridge

Heffers Booksellers, 20 Trinity Street, Cambridge CR2 1NG

Birmingham

Parks Bookshops, 3 Windsor Arcade, Birmingham B2 5LJ   Telephone: 021 233 4969

Hudsons Bookshops, 116 New Street, Birmingham B2

Glasgow

Parks Bookshop, 83 St Vincent Street, Glasgow G2 5TF   Telephone: 041 221 1369

Manchester

Parks Bookshops, 19 Brown Street, Manchester M2 1DA   Telephone: 061 834 4019

Financial Training Courses' Study Packs and Revision Packs can also be ordered from any local Financial Training Centre. Ring 081 876 0499 for details.

OVERSEAS

Eire

O'Mahoney & Co, 120 O'Connell Street, Limerick

Hong Kong

Federal Publications Ltd, Unit 903–906 Tower O O/F, Hung Hom, Hong Kong
Commercial Centre, 37 Mo Tau Wai Road, Hung Hom, Kowloon, Hong Kong
The Swindon Book Co Ltd, 13–15 Lock Road, Kowloon, Hong Kong

Malaysia

PAAC, First Floor, Wisma ALMA, 2–4 Jalan Manau, 50460, Kuala Lumpur, PO Box 11201

Mauritius

Editions Le Printemps, 4 Avenue Du Club, Vacoas
Editions De L'Ocean, Stanley, Rose Hill

India

Media International Associates Private Ltd, Gurukrupa Mans, 44 Nagappa Street, Swastik Circle, Bangalore

Sri Lanka

MD Gunesena & Co Ltd, PO Box 246, 217 Olcott, Mawatha Colombo 11

West Indies

Book Traders Ltd, 175–179 Mountain View Avenue, Kingston 6, Jamaica
Sangsters Bookstores Ltd, 101 Water Lane, Kingston, Jamaica
Metropolitan Book Suppliers, Colsort Mall – 1st Floor, 11–13 Frederick Street, Port of Spain, Trinidad
School of Accounting and Management, Corner Eastern Main Road, 1–3 McCarthy Street, St Augustine, Trinidad